Organizations and the Sustainability Mosaic

NEW PERSPECTIVES IN RESEARCH ON CORPORATE SUSTAINABILITY

Series Editors: Sanjay Sharma, *Canada Research Chair in Organizational Sustainability and Professor, Wilfrid Laurier University, Canada* and Mark Starik, *Professor of Strategic Management and Public Policy, School of Business and Public Management, George Washington University, USA*

The complex interaction between organizations and their stakeholders within the context of corporate sustainability is the central theme of this unique series. Each volume will focus on a particular issue and will consist of original contributions from leading scholars on the three sectors of interest (business, governments, and non-profits). Topics will include corporate sustainability and performance; stakeholders; organizational change; strategy; small businesses and sustainability; government policy; alliances, networks and partnerships; and multi-level sustainability interactions.

Titles in the series include:

Research in Corporate Sustainability
The Evolving Theory and Practice of Organizations in the Natural Environment
Edited by Sanjay Sharma and Mark Starik

Stakeholders, the Environment and Society
Edited by Sanjay Sharma and Mark Starik

Corporate Environmental Strategy and Competitive Advantage
Edited by Sanjay Sharma and J. Alberto Aragón-Correa

Organizations and the Sustainability Mosaic
Crafting Long-Term Ecological and Societal Solutions
Edited by Sanjay Sharma, Mark Starik and Bryan Husted

Organizations and the Sustainability Mosaic

Crafting Long-Term Ecological and Societal Solutions

Edited by

Sanjay Sharma

Wilfrid Laurier University, Canada

Mark Starik

The George Washington University, USA

Bryan Husted

Instituto Tecnológico y de Estudios Superiores de Monterrey, Mexico and Instituto de Empresa, Madrid, Spain

NEW PERSPECTIVES IN RESEARCH ON CORPORATE SUSTAINABILITY

Edward Elgar

Cheltenham, UK • Northampton, MA, USA

Published by
Edward Elgar Publishing Limited
Glensanda House
Montpellier Parade
Cheltenham
Glos GL50 1UA
UK

Edward Elgar Publishing, Inc.
William Pratt House
9 Dewey Court
Northampton
Massachusetts 01060
USA

A catalogue record for this book
is available from the British Library

Library of Congress Cataloging in Publication Data

Organizations and the sustainability mosaic : crafting long-term ecological and societal solutions / edited by Sanjay Sharma, Mark Starik, Bryan Husted.
p. cm.—(New perspectives in research on corporate sustainability)
Includes bibliographical references and index.
1. Sustainable development. 2. Industries–Social aspects. 3. Environmental economics. 4. Economic development—Moral and ethical aspects. 5. Social justice. I. Sharma, Sanjay. II. Starik, Mark, 1951– III. Husted, Bryan, 1957–
HC79.E5O745 2007
338.9′27—dc22 2006102955

ISBN 978 1 84542 642 2

Printed and bound in Great Britain by MPG Books Ltd, Bodmin, Cornwall.

DEDICATIONS

To my life partner, Pramodita, and my daughter, Smita, for their constant love and support
Sanjay Sharma

To Margery Moore, loving wife and sustainability partner
Mark Starik

To my mother, Jane
Bryan Husted

Contents

Figures

Tables

Boxes

Contributors

Celio Andrade received his doctorate in administration from the Federal University of Bahia in Brazil. He is a researcher for the Center for Policy and Administration in Science and Technology and for the Bahia Network for Clean Technologies at the Federal University of Bahia. He teaches environmental management and social responsibility at the same university. He is also the coordinator of the professional master's program in business. He is a consultant for several Brazilian governmental agencies. He has published articles in both Brazilian and international journals as well as in the proceedings of scientific conferences. His areas of research interest are in competitiveness, environmental innovation, clean production, socio-environmental strategy, socio-environmental conflict management and corporate social responsibility.

Max H. Bazerman is the Jesse Isidor Straus Professor of Business Administration, and is formally affiliated with the Kennedy School of Government, the Psychology Department, the Institute for Quantitative Social Sciences, the Harvard University Center on the Environment and the Program on Negotiation. In his prior position at Kellogg, Max was the founder and director of the Kellogg Environmental Research Center. Max's research focuses on decision-making in negotiation, and improving decision-making in organizations, nations and society. He is the author or co-author of over 170 research articles and chapters, and the author, co-author or co-editor of 15 books, including the following recently published books: *Judgment in Managerial Decision Making* (2005, Wiley, now in its sixth edition), *Negotiation, Decision Making and Conflict Management* (2005, Edward Elgar Publishers, available in three volumes), *Predictable Surprises* (2004, Harvard Business School Press, with Michael Watkins), and *You Can't Enlarge the Pie: The Psychology of Ineffective Government* (2001, Basic Books, with J. Baron and K. Shonk).

C.B. Bhattacharya received his PhD in marketing from the Wharton School of the University of Pennsylvania in 1993 and his MBA from the Indian Institute of Management in 1984. Prior to joining Boston University, he was on the faculty at the Goizueta Business School, Emory University. His specific expertise is in the areas of customer retention, and the roles of corporate social responsibility and organizational identification in designing marketing strategy. He served on the Editorial Review Board of the *Journal of Marketing* from 2002 to 2005 and has published in journals such as the *Journal of Marketing Research*, *Journal of Marketing*, *Journal of Applied Psychology*, *Organization Science*, and many other journals. He speaks frequently at academic and business forums and won the William Novelli best paper award at the Social Marketing Conference in 1997. C.B. received the 2001 Broderick Prize for Research Excellence at Boston University and the Emory Williams Distinguished Teaching Award in 1995, the highest teaching award at Emory University. He is also part of the select group of faculty on *Business Week*'s Outstanding Faculty list. Prior to his PhD, he worked for three years as a product manager at Reckitt Benkiser plc. He has consulted for organizations such as the Hitachi Corporation, Procter & Gamble Company, Bell South, the Prudential Bank, Information Resources Incorporated, Airwick Industries, Silo Incorporated and the High Museum of Art.

David Casagrande received a master's degree in ecology and biodiversity conservation from the Yale School of Forestry and Environmental Studies and a PhD in ecological anthropology from the University of Georgia. He is currently an assistant professor of environmental anthropology at Western Illinois University. He has published numerous articles, book chapters and encyclopedia entries on topics such as human ecosystems, cultural transmission of indigenous ecological knowledge, ecological restoration that explicitly includes humans, urban ecology, environmental policy and medicinal plants. He has conducted extensive research in Venezuela, Chiapas (Mexico), and various post-industrial cities in the USA. He was editor-in-chief of the *Journal of Ecological Anthropology* from 1998 to 2003, and is currently an associate editor for the *Journal of Ethnobiology and Ethnomedicine* and anthropology topic editor for the *Encyclopedia of the Earth*.

Deborah Rigling Gallagher is Visiting Assistant Professor of Resource and Environmental Policy at the Nicholas School of the Environment and Earth Sciences, Duke University. Previously she served as a policy advisor in the Massachusetts Department of Environmental Protection and as an environmental health and safety manager at Kraft Foods. She holds a PhD in public policy analysis from the University of North Carolina at Chapel Hill.

Andrew J. Hoffman is the Holcim (US) Professor of Sustainable Enterprise at the University of Michigan; a position that holds joint appointments at the Stephen M. Ross School of Business and the School of Natural Resources and Environment. Within this role, Andrew also serves as co-director of the Frederick A. and Barbara M. Erb Institute for Global Sustainable Enterprise. He has published over 50 articles and book chapters, and four books. His books include: *Organizations, Policy and the Natural Environment* (2002, Stanford University Press with Marc Ventresca), *From Heresy to Dogma* (2001, Stanford University Press), *Competitive Environmental Strategy* (2000, Island Press) and *Global Climate Change: A Senior-Level Dialogue* (1998, New Lexington Press). Andrew was awarded the 2003 Faculty Pioneer Rising Star award from the World Resources Institute and Aspen Institute. His book, *From Heresy to Dogma*, was awarded the 2001 Rachel Carson Prize from the Society for Social Studies of Science. Prior to academia, he worked for the US Environmental Protection Agency (Region 1), Metcalf & Eddy Environmental Consultants, T&T Construction & Design and the Amoco Corporation. He holds a bachelors degree in chemical engineering from the University of Massachusetts at Amherst and a masters and joint doctorate degree in management and civil and environmental engineering from the Massachusetts Institute of Technology.

Jennifer A. Howard-Grenville is an assistant professor of organizational behavior at the Boston University School of Management. She studies how cultural and institutional processes constrain or advance organizational change, with a focus on changes in corporate environmental practice. She is particularly interested in the microprocesses of organizational and institutional change. Jennifer's work has been published in *Organization Science*, *Organization & Environment*, *Academy of Management Executive*, *Law and Social Inquiry*, *California Management Review*, *Business Strategy and Environment*, and several edited volumes. She is the co-author of one book, *Greening the Industrial Facility*, with Thomas Graedel. Jennifer received her PhD in technology, management and policy at MIT, her MA at Oxford University, and her BSc at Queen's University, Canada.

Bryan Husted received a PhD in business and public policy from the University of California at Berkeley. He currently holds a joint appointment as Professor of Management at the Instituto Tecnológico y de Estudios Superiores de Monterrey (Mexico) and Alumni Association Chair of Business Ethics at the Instituto de Empresa (Spain). His research focuses on corruption and corporate social and environmental performance. His work has appeared in such journals as *Organization Science*, *Journal of International Business Studies*, *Business Ethics Quarterly*, *Journal of Management Studies*, *Human Ecology Review*, *Management International Review*, *Long Range Planning*, *Business and Society*, *Journal of Business Ethics*, *Growth and Change* and the *Journal of Environment and Development*.

Heather McIlvaine-Newsad is an associate professor of anthropology and Research Fellow at the Illinois Institute for Rural Affairs, at Western Illinois University. She received her PhD from the University of Florida in applied cultural anthropology in August 2000 with a focus on gender, agriculture and natural resource management strategies in Ecuador. She earned an MA in international development from Ohio University, and a BA in German from Denison University. She served as a Peace Corps volunteer in the Dominican Republic. Heather's current research focuses on the influences of gender, ethnicity and socio-economic status on family farms in southern Ohio. She is also conducting longitudinal research with NOAA Marine Fisheries to determine the socio-cultural impact of fishing management plans on fishing communities in the Gulf Coast of the United States.

Francesco Perrini is an associate professor of management and corporate social responsibility (CSR) at the 'G. Pivato' Management Department, Bocconi University, Milan, Italy. He is also Senior Professor of Corporate Finance at the SDA Bocconi School of Management. During 2004–2005 he was Visiting Professor at the Legal Studies and Business Ethics Department, Wharton School, University of Pennsylvania. His primary research interests are management of corporate development processes, corporate responsibility and social entrepreneurship.

Gordon Rands is an associate professor of management at Western Illinois University, where he is also the co-director of the Program for the Study of Ethics. He received a bachelor's degree in natural resources from the University of Michigan, a master's degree in organizational behavior from Brigham Young University, and a PhD in business administration with an emphasis in management from the University of Minnesota. He primarily teaches courses on business and society, and his research focus is on issues relating to organizations and ecological sustainability. He is a co-founder and past chairperson of the Organizations and the Natural Environment Interest Group of the Academy of Management.

Barbara Ribbens is an associate professor of management at Western Illinois University. Barbara has published in the *Academy of Management Journal*, *Asia Pacific Journal of Management* and other venues. She has presented her work at regional, national and international conferences and recently was honored for her work internationalizing the campus at Western Illinois University. She earned her PhD at the University of Connecticut and focuses her research on organizational and individual interactions, particularly in terms of careers, organizational learning and environmental issues.

David Saiia came to the study of business through a series of life experiences and educational opportunities. He observed the operation and eventual loss of a small family business and the effect of external and internal forces on its function. After completing his university training, he was awarded the Watson Fellowship through which he visited Nepal, India, Peru, Brazil and Kenya. While studying the political economy in these countries, David noticed that the establishment and operation of business was a critical and vibrant way to build and stimulate developing economies. Upon his return to the US, he became involved in several small businesses before he returned to research on the island of Guam. He worked through a program at the University of Guam in conjunction with the Guam Economic Development Authority to investigate the impact of the growth in tourism on vital infrastructure including power, water, sewage and labor supply. At this time, he started teaching in the Business School at the University of Guam. During this period, David became increasingly interested in Asian development issues and made several trips to Thailand, Malaysia, Singapore, Indonesia and Papua New Guinea. He eventually moved to Singapore and worked with the Singapore National Council on the Environment and continued research at the National University of Singapore. He returned to the US in 1996 to complete his doctoral degree in strategic management at the University of Georgia. He moved to the University of Northern Iowa upon completion of his PhD in 1999 and has continued his research in business and development in Ecuador where he conducted research and consulting in the coordination of micro-enterprise development and rainforest conservation efforts. David now teaches management at Ithaca College. He has published articles in the *Corporate Reputation Review* (CRR), the *Journal of Corporate Citizenship* and *Business and Society*. He has presented his research in numerous conferences throughout North America and Europe.

Sanjay Sharma is the Canada Research Chair in Organizational Sustainability, director of the CMA Centre for Responsible Organizations and Professor of Strategic Management and Sustainability at Wilfrid Laurier University. His doctoral dissertation from the University of Calgary won the Best Dissertation Award from the Social Issues in Management Division of the Academy of Management in 1996. He has received several research awards including the Jossey Bass/New Lexington Press Award for the Best Academy of Management Paper on Organizations and the Natural Environment (1997), Best Strategy Paper at the Administrative Sciences Association of Canada (2003), and the Barrett-Koehler Best Academy of Management Paper in Organizations and the Natural Environment (2005). He was awarded a Fulbright Fellowship in 2001–2002 and has received several research grants from the Social Sciences and Humanities Research council of Canada (SSHRC). He has served on the council's Research Funding Adjudication Committee. His research has been published in the *Academy of Management Review*, *Academy of Management Journal*,

Academy of Management Executive, *Strategic Management Journal*, *Journal of Applied Behavioral Science*, *Business Strategy and the Environment*, *Journal of Asian Business*, *Journal of Strategic Marketing* and *Revue Francaise de Gestion*, among others. Before pursuing an academic career, he worked for 16 years as a senior manager with multinational corporations. Sanjay is the past chair, program chair, and PDW chair of the ONE Interest Group at the Academy of Management.

Mark Starik is the department chair and a professor of strategic management and public policy in the George Washington University School of Business. He researches, teaches and advises organizations and individuals in the areas of strategic environmental management, environmental and energy policy, environmental entrepreneurship, and sustainable communities and organizations. He is also interested in the connections among the fields of strategic management, business and public policy (including civil society), and sustainability, both domestically and internationally. Mark's research includes publications in a wide variety of both academic and practitioner outlets, including the *Academy of Management Review*, *Academy of Management Journal*, *Journal of Business Ethics* and *Business Strategy and the Environment*, and in the proceedings of several international organization conferences. He is the founder and director of the GW Environmental and Social Sustainability Initiative, which coordinates the research, teaching and service within GWSB on the topic of sustainability, is a co-founder of several organizations, including the Institute for Sustainability Education & Action, Sustainability Now!, and the Academy of Management Organizations and the Natural Environment Interest Group. He has been the faculty advisor for the Students for Responsible Business and GW Net Impact, since each of those organizations was founded. Mark received his doctorate in strategic management in 1991 from the University of Georgia, his masters in natural resources policy and administration in 1978, and his undergraduate degree in economics in 1976, both from the University of Wisconsin-Madison.

Antonio Tencati is an assistant professor of management and corporate social responsibility (CSR) at the 'G. Pivato' Management Department, Bocconi University, Milan, Italy. Since 2000 he has been a member of the Business Ethics Inter-faculty Group of the Master CEMS-MIM (Community of European Management Schools – Master in International Management). His primary research interests include environmental management, management of sustainability and corporate social responsibility.

Peter Utting has a PhD in sociology from the University of Essex. He is deputy director, United Nations Research Institute for Social Development

(UNRISD), where he also coordinates research in the field of corporate responsibility, business regulation and development. His publications include the edited volume *The Greening of Business in Developing Countries: Rhetoric, Reality and Prospects* (Zed Books, 2002).

Christa Walck is the Dean and Professor of Organizational Behavior in the School of Business and Economics at Michigan Technological University and a member of MTU's Sustainable Futures Institute. Her current research investigates organizational impacts on the natural environment from a land use and place-based perspective. She is currently working on historical studies of land use in the Gila National Forest in New Mexico and on Cape Cod, and applying Aldo Leopold's concept of land health to environmental management.

Frank Wijen is an assistant professor of strategic management at RSM Erasmus University Rotterdam and a fellow at research institute Globus, Tilburg University. He holds a PhD in management from Tilburg University, where he also worked as a senior researcher. Frank acquired business experience as marketing manager of a globally operating company and as manager-owner of an international trading firm. His research interests include organizational learning, influence and power, social networks, globalization, institutionalization, and corporate and national environmental management.

1. Organizations and the sustainability mosaic: crafting long-term ecological and societal solutions

Bryan Husted, Sanjay Sharma and Mark Starik

The influential 1987 publication of the World Commission on Environment and Development (WCED) titled *Our Common Future* stated that critical global environmental problems were primarily the result of the enormous poverty in the South and the non-sustainable patterns of consumption and production in the North. It called for a strategy of sustainable development by uniting social and economic development and the environment: 'Sustainable development is development that meets the needs of the present without compromising the ability of future generations to meet their own needs.' While this definition of sustainable development is often criticized (for example, Starik and Rands, 1995), it is at the same time the one most widely accepted by organizations and governments.

As we reiterated in our call for Chapters for this volume, this idea is not new. Many cultures over the course of human history have recognized the need for harmony among the environment, society and the economy. Indeed, there are aboriginal peoples and indigenous tribes across the world that still adhere to principles of environmental stewardship and harmony between human development and nature. However, recent human history is defined in a major way by the industrial revolution and its systems of mass organization and production that have been constantly at odds with the concept of sustainability. Therefore, the articulation of sustainable principles in the context of such global and capital-intensive systems of mass production is a recent phenomenon (Sharma, 2002).

In the organizational and management literature, perhaps some of the earliest theoretical discussions of sustainability are embodied in the articles published in the October 1995 issue of the *Academy of Management Review*. Most articles in this special forum focus on the interface between natural ecosystems and organizations and one of these especially focuses on the inseparable integration of social and ecological sustainability. Gladwin et al. (1995) argue that improving ecological health and integrity without alleviation of poverty, population stability, redistribution of economic opportunity, achievement of social sufficiency (that is, a community's capacity for self-renewal, self-maintenance and self-transformation), security, self-organization and human freedom, across different segments of society and across generations, would only lead to trivial results. Thus they offer a definition of sustainable development as:

> . . . *human development* (widening or enlarging the range of people's choices) . . . in an *inclusive*, *connected*, *equitable*, *prudent*, and *secure* manner. *Inclusiveness* implies human development over time and space. *Connectivity* entails an embrace of ecological, social, and economic interdependence. *Equity* suggests intergenerational, intragenerational, and interspecies fairness. *Prudence* connotes duties of care and prevention: technologically, scientifically, and politically. *Security* demands safety from chronic threats and protection from harmful disruption. (Gladwin et al., 1995, p. 875)

They go on to argue (1995, pp. 896–7) that 'By disassociating human organization from the biosphere and the full human community, it is possible that our theories have tacitly encouraged organizations to behave in ways that ultimately destroy their natural and social life-support systems', and that organizations both partially cause and are affected by 'biodiversity loss, climate change, freshwater scarcity, food insecurity, population growth, persistent poverty, gender bias, and explosion of megacities'.

The inseparability of social and ecological impacts of organizations has been magnified by the trends of globalization and trade liberalization over the last five decades. Increasing globalization of economic activity and liberalization of international trade has had both a rapid and a multiplicative effect on the level of total global economic activity during the last few decades. However, the distribution of economic benefits of globalization amongst various segments of society (for example, indigenous communities, minorities, and women) is uneven with some segments of society actually experiencing a reduction in quality of life, loss of tradition, culture and heritage, reduced social welfare and erosion of economic security. Moreover, the impacts of this increase in economic activity on traditional cultures and heritage, and on the environment, have often been negative or harmful. Therefore, as corporations search for avenues of profitable growth in the developing world markets or seek to source inputs cheaply by taking advantage of cheap labour in such countries, a growing anti-globalization movement requires that these multinationals begin to look at globalization strategies through a new lens of inclusive capitalism (Hart, 2005).

The spread of the internet and other information technologies has enabled thousands, perhaps millions, of groups and individuals concerned about individual and different environmental and social impacts of organizations to communicate with each other and find common cause to generate integrated perspectives on social, environmental and economic impacts of firms (Hart and Sharma, 2004). Since the mid-1990s, groups and individuals have materialized in large numbers at gatherings such as meetings of the World Trade Organization (WTO), the G7 and the World Economic Forum, all dominated by rich countries and their corporations. These coalitions of non-governmental organizations (NGOs) and individuals – smart mobs – are now making it increasingly difficult for governments, corporations or other large institutions to deal separately with each social, ecological or economic issue to the exclusion of other related issues.

Therefore, the lack of consideration of the integrated nature of economic, social and ecological impacts of organizational operations may lead to enhancements in their negative impacts, while the adoption of a holistic sustainability perspective may lead to organizational contributions to ecosystem protection and social justice.

NEGATIVE IMPACTS

Corporations very rarely seek to support internal wars or conflicts in the countries that they operate in, or to condone human rights abuses and genocide. However, when companies operate in zones of internal conflict, they tacitly support the ruling elite, whether a government or warlords, by paying them royalties and revenues and obtaining their protection. When the ruling elite commit genocide or human rights abuses against minorities or a segment of society, then corporations are complicit in such injustice and abuse. The cases of Royal Dutch/Shell in Nigeria and Talisman Energy in Sudan are examples where NGOs and governments in many countries (and the United Nations, in the case of Nigeria) considered these firms as complicit in genocide and human rights abuses even though the companies insisted that they were operating within the law. In such contexts, the negative environmental impacts of the mostly extractive industries such as petroleum, forestry and mining, are tied up with social justice in the form of traditional uses of land, quality of life of local communities and traditional heritage and culture, and economic justice in the form of distribution of benefits for segments of societies or indigenous people.

Related to the above issue is how operations of organizations affect the sovereignty of indigenous people over their lands, their ways of life and their traditional livelihoods and food security. Industrialized agriculture that involves the application of chemicals, hormones and genetic engineering poses unknown health and environmental hazards for indigenous people never before exposed to these substances. Moreover, large-scale modern agriculture and industrial practices and operations lead to pollution such as chemical run-off, topsoil depletion, falling water tables, and overfishing. Industrial-scale aquaculture operations result in chemical run-offs and spread of disease amongst ocean populations of fish. All these result in constrained natural resources and food insecurity for poor and marginal farmers, fishermen and others who have traditionally harvested these resources sustainably for their livelihoods. At the same time, subsidized imports from industrialized countries make it difficult for small farmers to survive and often drive them to seek low-paying jobs with poor working conditions in the city, negatively affecting their quality of life. Similarly, mass manufacture of products destroys the livelihood of small village craftspeople and small family-run businesses, destroying communities, families and often traditional and sustainable ways of life.

Some argue that these people displaced from their villages are better off because their incomes increase as they are absorbed into global manufacturing supply chains (Friedman, 2005). It is not necessarily true that higher income in big expensive cities translates into quality of life or a livelihood that is superior to traditional ways of life in villages. Moreover, this rural-to-urban movement contributes to the destruction of the social fabric of village communities, the separation of families and increasing urbanization with strains on ecosystems. More often than not, contractors for supply chains of global corporations run low-cost sweatshops with poor working conditions and disregard for basic human rights. Occasionally, consumers in the developed world have been exposed to the dark underbelly of global supply chains as NGOs have provided them with information about conditions at contracted factories for companies such as Nike, Wal-Mart and Old Navy.

POSITIVE IMPACTS

Companies in extractive industries such as mining, petroleum, forestry and fishing have increasingly had to consider social justice aspects of their operations as they operate in the developing world and on land on which indigenous groups have traditionally relied for a sustainable livelihood. More recently, companies that are not in extractive sectors but rather in manufacturing or technology sectors have also begun to consider an integrated view of the social and ecological impacts of their operations. There is increasing corporate realization that the rates of economic growth expected by investors are only possible by engaging the poor who have been excluded from the economic benefits of globalization, via business models that build economic capacity at the grassroots rather than relying on trickle-down economic systems that have not been effective over the last five decades (Sachs, 2005). Corporate investments at the base of the economic pyramid that are based on business models which integrate ecosystem protection with social justice and economic capacity-building can result in lifting billions of people out of poverty and desperation, thereby averting social decay, political chaos, terrorism, and environmental damage, and reversing the widening economic gap between rich and poor continues. While this is an emerging area of interest and operation for corporations, academic documentation of case-studies indicates that a wide variety of business models and business sectors are engaged in this experiment. Some examples of case-studies include Grameen Bank in Bangladesh, Cemex in Mexico and Hindustan Lever Ltd in India (Hart and Sharma, 2004), Hewlett Packard in India (Dunn and Yamashita, 2003) and ICICI Bank, ITC and Citicorp – all in the Indian context (Prahalad, 2005). These are attempts by organizations to learn how to integrate economic, social and ecological issues in contexts where such connections may be easier to identify before they attempt such holistic integration in the developed world context.

THE CHAPTERS IN THIS VOLUME

The call for this volume invited research that recognizes the complex interactions amongst social, environmental and development impacts of organizations at the community, regional, national and global levels. The chapters presented in this volume hope to shed light on the way forward amidst such complexity, which we refer to as the sustainability mosaic. By grappling with the sustainability mosaic, we hope to learn lessons that will be vital to crafting long-term solutions to ecological and societal problems.

One of the characteristics of the sustainability mosaic is that efforts are carried out at different levels of analysis. Organizations and individuals cannot be sustainable in isolation, but only as parts of an overall system. Yet for analytical purposes, it is usually necessary to focus on a subset of the system. Rands, Ribbens, Casagrande and McIlvaine-Newsad (Chapter 2) identify the ecological, individual, organizational, political-economic and socio-cultural levels as vital to developing solutions for sustainability. Collectively, the chapters of this volume span each of these levels. Christa Walck in her essay on land use in the American Southwest (Chapter 3) deals extensively with the ecological level. Hoffman and Bazerman (Chapter 4) deal with both the individual and organizational levels as they examine barriers to sustainability. The bulk of the chapters, including Howard-Grenville, Hoffman and Bhattacharya (Chapter 8), Saiia (Chapter 6), Wijen (Chapter 5), and Perrini and Tencati (Chapter 7) all focus on the organizational level. Utting (Chapter 10) analyzes the political-economic level, while Gallagher (Chapter 11) and Howard-Grenville et al. (Chapter 8) also treat the socio-cultural level.

In Chapter 2, Rands et al. provide an appropriate overarching framework as they identify the different levels required for understanding sustainability and examine the multiple, interconnecting and embedded systems that exist amongst these levels. Even though they expressly focus only on ecological sustainability, their chapter embraces the complexity for achieving sustainability from a holistic perspective. By applying their framework to the Republic of the Marshall Islands, they weave the multiple levels together from a systems perspective – examining inputs, throughputs, outputs, feedback loops, as well as values and possible strategies. Their chapter suggests the many routes that need to be followed in order to be developed. The ensuing chapters begin to follow some of these paths.

In examining the ecological level, Chapter 3 by Christa Walck stands out. Her focus on land use demands that the fragile ecosystems of the American Southwest take center stage as she follows the history of social impacts in the form of changing land use as a response to changes in the land, caused largely by environmental degradation through poor range management. She describes how myopic organizations undercut their own viability because of their voracious appetites for public resources and their inability to take the environment 'as is' without imposing preconceived notions of range management based on prior farming experiences. Organizations need to transcend their short-term focus by exploiting the best science, expertise and most appropriate technologies available in order to take the environmental context seriously. In this case, public institutions, imperfect though they may be, play an important role in structuring incentives for private organizations to look beyond the short-term.

In Chapter 4, Hoffman and Bazerman span the individual and organizational levels in their study of the barriers to change for sustainability. They start by looking at decision biases such as the mythical fixed pie (the belief that negotiators are fighting over a finite pool of resources). 'Win–lose' proponents say environmental protection and social responsibility reduce economic competitiveness. The authors argue that decision-makers need to move to the 'recognition that sustainable development is sometimes profit-compatible and sometimes not'. Thus managers and scholars need to focus attention on how sustainable development can be undertaken in profitable ways.

Hoffman and Bazerman briefly mention other cognitive biases such as positive illusions (the tendency of people to see themselves, their future and the world in a better light than what is reality), self-serving interpretations of fairness (the tendency of people to make egocentric judgments of what is fair), overconfidence (the tendency of people to be overconfident in their estimation abilities and not acknowledge the true uncertainties in those assessments), and overly discounting the future (the tendency of individuals to forego upfront capital expenditures that would offer huge annual returns). Organizational barriers are also relevant, such as an over-reliance on regulatory standards where regulation is defined as any form of coercive influence. The problem is that standards focus attention on compliance rather than on overall societal goals, and can restrict optimal solutions. In addition, capital budgets keep managers from making wise long-term decisions regarding total lifespan costing of plant equipment. Financial markets as well as reward and incentive systems foster short-term objectives. Unquestioned assumptions implanted in business school education can deter efforts toward sustainability: habitual routines, fear of the unknown, resource limitations and threats to established power bases. Sensitivity to these obstacles to change is vital if organizations desire to contribute to sustainability.

Related to the concern about organizational barriers to change for sustainability, in Chapter 5 Wijen examines the forces that both promote and undermine the implementation of sustainable business practices. He traces the rise and fall of sustainable management in Greenheart, a pseudonym for a Dutch multinational food company. Although the original owner was thoroughly committed to sustainability, a takeover led to a change in management priorities and policy. Wijen concludes that institutionalized sustainability requires both deeply held and widely shared environmental values as well as thoroughly embedded environmental practices. Based on these two dimensions, Wijen proposes a typology of four kinds of sustainability behaviors: institutionalized, idealistic, realistic and unsustainable. Wijen draws upon both the stakeholder influence and organizational learning literatures in order to understand which of these behaviors is likely over time.

Two chapters examine the nuts and bolts of sustainability management at the organizational level by developing management technologies. First, in Chapter 6, Saiia proposes stakeholder salience mapping as a way for firms to grapple with their complex social environments. This kind of mapping integrates insights from stakeholder theory and issues management by proposing that the stakeholder map is dynamic and changes with respect to specific social issues. He applies this technique to the case of Fundación Maquipucuna, an Ecuadorian NGO focused on sustainable development among rural communities near the ecological reserve of the same name. At stake were questions of land use, which served as the focal issue for the stakeholder salience mapping. By visually representing stakeholder information, managers can more effectively engage stakeholders in order jointly to craft long-term solutions to ecological and societal problems.

Also at the organizational level, in Chapter 7, Perrini and Tencati deal with the very practical aspects of measuring and accounting for sustainability, and recommend integrative performance measures that link social, environmental and financial aspects of sustainability. They propose the Sustainability Evaluation and Reporting System (SERS) as an integrated system for evaluating corporate performance from a stakeholder perspective. It combines the overall reporting system (including the financial, social and environmental reports), with an integrated information system capable of generating key performance indicators for corporate sustainability. This chapter provides a sorely needed dose of reality to some of the other chapters that are more focused on the softer managerial aspects of the sustainability mosaic and less on the accounting aspects.

In Chapter 8, Howard-Grenville, Hoffman and Bhattacharya begin to bridge the organizational and socio-cultural levels using institutional theory and notions of social and cultural capital. The authors determine the kinds of resources and capabilities that companies need in order to become more socially and environmentally sustainable. Capital provides a clear way of understanding the sources of influence that constrain firm decision-making within an organizational field. Cultural capital refers to 'competence or authority to define and defend expertise in a particular arena of social life', while social capital is based on relationships that the firm develops with its many stakeholders. They analyze the kinds of capital or resources needed for four different kinds of change: (1) capturing an issue within a mature field; (2) bridging between fields; (3) creating a new field and/or exiting a mature field; and (4) defending a mature field in crisis (possible for firms with economic capital, but little cultural or social capital). By examining the dynamics of changing field conditions, the authors provide managers with insights into how to marshal resources to create change for sustainability more effectively.

Celio Andrade's Chapter 9 dealing with the Aracruz Celulose S.A. case specifically looks at the formulation of the firm's socio-environmental strategies. Clearly, the chapter is focused on the firm, but takes very seriously the broader institutional, political and stakeholder environments. Rather than seeing strategy as the outcome of a strictly rational planning process by firm management, Andrade takes into account the nature of stakeholder power and resources in the context of an institutional framework. He views the socio-environmental strategies as a way to create legitimacy for the firm rather than contribute to profit maximization through the creation of competitive advantage.

The qualitative game-theoretic approach that Andrade employs provides a way to operationalize the stakeholder framework through an explicit analysis of the problems, rules, rationales, objectives, strategies and agreements of the actors. He is able to integrate both the ecological and the social components of strategy by treating them as two aspects of a single firm environment. In the case of the Tupiniquim and Guarani Indians, their social problems are intimately tied to the context of the natural environment in which they live and work. By examining the strategic interactions between Aracruz and its stakeholders, Andrade provides us with important clues into how firms of all types need to navigate the political-institutional space in which they operate in order to achieve integrative bargaining solutions for firms and their stakeholders.

At the political-economic level, in Chapter 10, Utting examines both 'soft' and 'hard' approaches to private regulation of corporate social responsibility (CSR). Soft approaches focus on self-regulation. Multi-stakeholder initiatives are considered hard approaches because they involve accountability to third parties. Corporate accountability represents a ratcheting-up of the hardness of voluntary initiatives because it involves monitoring, reporting and certification systems. Over time, Utting observes a hardening of voluntary regulatory approaches despite an initial experimentation with soft approaches. In some cases, recourse is made to public policy and the law in order to foster greater accountability. He identifies several dimensions of non-governmental systems of regulation: (1) complementarities among different forms of non-governmental regulation; (2) confrontational and collaborative forms of civil society activism; (3) voluntary versus legalistic approaches to non-governmental regulation; (4) and policy coherence. His examination of soft and hard forms of private regulation in a historical context leads to the conclusion that the softer approaches, like CSR, contradict current forces for deregulation that often lower standards, while harder approaches, like corporate accountability, face considerable political challenges and require firms to develop alliances with such unlikely bedfellows as trade unions and non-governmental organizations.

Finally, in Chapter 11, Gallagher addresses the socio-cultural level by studying the development of professional norms and values among sustainability workers. Specifically, she examines 'how multidisciplinary teams of brownfield professionals develop common language, professional norms, values and identities in the context of sustainability'. Brownfield redevelopment includes both clean-up of land and the 'revitalization of poor urban neighborhoods and the creation of jobs for their inhabitants'. These projects must be financially sustainable in order to attract investors. Brownfield redevelopment requires the participation of such professionals as engineers, financial analysts, lawyers, government agents, architects and land planners. Professionals usually share a specialized knowledge base, a set of transferable skills, a career focus and a code of ethics. In the specific context of sustainable development, professionals face a number of challenges given that they have to envision a new career path, adapt knowledge from varied disciplines and learn to share an evolving ethic.

In order to study the process of professionalization, Gallagher examines the case of a brownfield redevelopment firm, Cherokee Investment Partners. She sent a questionnaire to 92 Cherokee associates, of whom 41 completed the survey. Interestingly, many respondents indicated multiple professional identities. Standard professional identification patterns were absent. They shared to greater and lesser degrees a professional ethic of sustainability. They needed to integrate professional norms, such as transparency, trust and honesty, with personal values about social justice and environmental stewardship. Such integration occurred by working together, sharing ideas, multi-party collaboration and participation in activities like training seminars by the Urban Land Institute, brainstorming sessions and 'happenstance' conversations. Resolving conflicts was a major challenge because of differences among the professional groups in their willingness to advance sustainability concepts. Resolution of such conflicts depended on developing a shared professional norm based on sustainability.

Although each of these chapters can be read separately, collectively they teach important lessons about the sustainability mosaic and the requirements for crafting long-term solutions to environmental and social problems. Among other issues, these chapters provide insights into the place of theory in sustainability studies, the complexity of sustainability – especially in the developing world, the role of networks of organizations, the role of government policy, the professionalization of sustainability, the use of technology, the capabilities and resources needed for sustainability and for change to a more sustainable world, and the forces that foster and limit such change. Let us examine more closely some of these potential lessons.

Rather than constructing unique theories of sustainable organizations, the chapters argue that the organization provides a unique context for acquiring greater understanding of existing theories. None of the chapters advances new theory. For example, Howard-Grenville et al. apply institutional theory to the organization. Wijen applies theories of stakeholder power and organizational learning in his analysis of the Greenheart case. Gallagher applies theory from the sociology of the professions in order to understand the development of shared norms, values and career identities for sustainability professionals. Hoffman and Bazerman use different insights from psychology in order to provide insight into individual and organizational barriers to the implementation of sustainable management practices. Rands et al. rely on systems theory to elucidate the different levels of analysis required to understand sustainability and the many interconnections among them. Rather than developing unique theories of sustainability, we see the authors opting to use existing theories in unique organizational contexts. Instead of continuing the perpetual search for a new paradigm for the 'business and society' field (Clarkson et al., 1994), the authors have taken a much more pragmatic approach by using existing knowledge and engaging in normal science.

Undoubtedly, the pragmatic approach taken in this volume stems from the large number of authors writing about social issues from the base of environmental management, which has had an intellectual history more closely identified with the mainstream management disciplines. This line of inquiry is probably more fruitful given that paradigmatic revolutions do not occur on demand, but as a response to the failure of normal science. As a field, we cannot get to that point until we have exhausted all that current theory and normal science have to offer. The chapters of this volume are a testament to the continued utility of current theories of the organization.

The sustainability mosaic implies that social, ecological and economic issues are intertwined and difficult to separate. This situation is especially true in the developing world. Organizations can help in alleviating global ecological and social problems such as hunger, poverty, human rights, and illiteracy, at the same time as preserving ecological integrity and achieving their core objectives. Certainly, Rands et al. discuss the role for organizations in the case of the Republic of the Marshall Islands. Saiia's study of Fundación Maquipucuna in Ecuador also centers on the role of organizations in sustainable development. Yet their collective message is that the function of organizations is clearly limited and must be embedded within a larger institutional context. Part of this context involves governmental regulation. In this respect, the case of the American Southwest is informative. Although technically part of the developed world, much of the Southwest in the period covered by Walck's study was, in a sense, in a process of development. The failure of individual organizations to take into account broader interests is part of the inherent nature of such organizations. Clearly, government action needs to structure incentives so that private organizations will be directed toward goals that promote societal sustainability, while permitting coordination of an autonomous nature.

Several of the chapters highlight the importance of networks or groups of organizations in sustainable development. Sustainable development may only be possible among groupings or networks of organizations. These networks are not necessarily bounded geographically – locally or regionally – but can be connected globally and are still able to assimilate wastes and ensure social justice. Governance in such networks is a critical issue for sustainability. Networks can be governed by voluntary regulatory systems such as multi-party collaborations (Utting), access to resources and other forms of capital (Howard-Grenville et al.) and shared professional norms (Gallagher). The discussion of organizational fields gives us some idea of how network interfaces will be managed – through dependence on specific kinds of capital. Especially relevant is Gallagher's discussion of conflict resolution. She argues that internal firm conflicts regarding the priority of different aspects of the triple bottom line can be resolved through administrative fiat. However, contractual provisions can resolve such conflicts along the supply chain. Walck's chapter suggests that public policy and regulations play an important role in facilitating the coordination of such networks of professionals.

CONTRIBUTIONS

Some of the issues identified in our call have been addressed by these chapters, while many remain yet to be addressed. The functioning of sustainable networks needs to be probed more deeply. The performance of networks needs to be measured and monitored. How will the inter-organizational interfaces be managed and how will the designs and structures of individual organizations change to facilitate network objectives? Will such networks emerge as planned entities such as eco-parks or industrial ecology networks, or will they be fluid, flexible and constantly evolving? Although contracts may help to resolve conflicts, we still do not understand how such conflicts would be resolved for relationships that fall outside the bounds of contractual obligations.

The concept of local or community self-sufficiency may facilitate the monitoring of the impacts of organizations on the carrying capacity of an eco-system, on the stock of natural capital, the welfare of human capital and the health of natural systems in a bounded geographic region. What will sustainable communities look like? How will they interact and exchange resources with other sustainable communities globally? How will such communities achieve their objectives of smart growth involving better quality of life and the accrual of natural capital?

The chapters provide some clues to the answers of these questions. Saiia hints that relevant members of sustainable communities may vary according to the issue at hand. For example, Gallagher's discussion of brownfield development describes a specific community of professionals that is called into being to deal with a very specific problem. Howard-Grenville suggests that resources will be exchanged within organizational fields according to the influence each organization possesses as represented by its stocks of cultural, social and economic capital. Rands et al. deal with the concept of sustainable societies in which communities are embedded within more global social, environmental and economic systems.

Government policy, at multiple levels and in the multiple functions of the public sector, can both support and undermine efforts by private sector organizations to plan, implement and evaluate sustainability efforts more effectively. Utting deals with the fascinating issue of regulation, especially private regulation involving both soft and hard forms. He specifically examines how governments can encourage the private sector to 'plan, implement and evaluate sustainability efforts'. Walck also looks longitudinally at the evolution of public policy with respect to land use in the American Southwest. In the first phase, government ignored the ranches 'which illegally laid claims to large amounts of public land'. In the second phase, range management became public policy. Congress placed 40 million acres into forest reserves and the Forest Service developed principles for conserving and restoring the resource for grazing. Now public policy 'favored large, efficient cattle ranches which obeyed regulations'. The third and current phase focuses on multiple use and high technology. Over time, there has been a proliferation of regulation. Still, we must be cognizant of the limits of public policy. As Hoffman and Bazerman argue, regulation can undermine private sector efforts to plan, implement and evaluate sustainability efforts more effectively by narrowing concerns of firms to focus on a much more limited range of concerns and their corresponding indicators. They discuss how regulation and standards can create negative organizational biases. Based on these chapters, we can conclude that regulation needs to facilitate the coordination of organizations, which tend to be myopic in nature, without stifling the innovation unleashed by exploiting local knowledge.

Social and environmental professionals and non-profit organizations have played and can still play a very important role in the advancement of sustainable development. Gallagher describes the professionalization of sustainability as involving the integration of shared values of sustainability that cuts across professions. Cross-cutting disciplinary bases also were relevant for land use issues in the Southwest. Conservation biologists, human and physical geographers, animal scientists, and experts in human conflict management and systems all take part in the sustainability efforts examined by Walck. Both chapters emphasize the special challenge to problem-solving and conflict management faced by these professionals. Despite these contributions, additional work needs to be done, for example on the entrepreneurship function within the sustainability profession – an issue largely ignored in this volume.

New technologies play an essential role in creating socially and ecologically sustainable business models in emerging economies. Once again, Walck's case of the US Southwest is instructive. New technologies such as 'computer simulation modeling, global positioning systems, geographic information systems and remote sensing data' all contributed to land use management (Walck). 'Range science at universities began to emphasize specification of ecological conditions to determine optimal grazing systems, and the new science of ecology began to ask hard questions about the impacts of grazing on the ecosystem, using detailed scientific studies and new technologies to develop answers' (Walck). New technology enables a measurement and monitoring of progress that was otherwise impossible. However, different cognitive and emotive (attitudinal) skills and capacities need to be developed among potential professionals in order to incorporate such technologies in sustainable enterprises.

Numerous types of organizational capabilities and change processes enable the integration of social justice and ecological preservation objectives with competitive advantage. Good managerial capacity is vital. Several chapters offer insights into developing such a capacity. Stakeholder salience mapping provides the ability to detect and monitor stakeholders (Saiia). Evaluation and measurement of the economic, social and environmental aspects of sustainability is a particularly important challenge as these evaluation systems permit the transformation of data into key sustainability indicators that guide managerial decision-making (Perrini and Tencati). Beyond these basic managerial capacities, firms need to acquire the ability to create 'ambition' or deeply held and widely shared values for sustainability and to embed sustainability practices into firm routines (Wijen). These shared values are especially important within firms, which usually gather professionals with different attitudes and values regarding sustainability (Gallagher). The case of the American Southwest as well as that of Cherokee Investment Partners illustrates the importance of shared values in order to facilitate collaboration; or, in their absence, a well-developed capacity for conflict resolution would be very helpful. Social, cultural and economic capital is essential to the sustainable operation of the firm (Howard-Grenville et al.). These different forms of capital allow the firm to obtain the resources it needs to pursue sustainability goals in the context of dynamic organizational fields, requiring cross-professional collaboration (Gallagher; Walck). Finally, the work of Hoffman and Bazerman suggests that the capacity for organizational learning, especially the capacity for self-criticism, is essential to overcoming organizational biases, which create obstacles to change.

The creation of the conditions for organizational change is a key factor for the development of long-term solutions for sustainability. Change requires developing financial, social and cultural capital (Howard-Grenville et al.) as well as the capability of overcoming both individual and organizational barriers (Hoffman and Bazerman). In addition, the Greenheart case suggests that resources and capital may be lost if they are not properly institutionalized.

Planned organizational change needs to take into account the changing ecological and cultural context within which organizations are embedded. The experience of the Republic of the Marshall Islands is particularly instructive. Given increases in population and population density, traditional agricultural practices are no longer sustainable. In addition, the Westernization of the Marshallese people implies significant changes in their values and food preferences. As a result, there is an ongoing evolution of both ecology and culture, which makes returning to the past impossible.

Change is also limited by isomorphic pressures that encourage the replication and application of understood and well-accepted models. For example, animal husbandry practices were observed by Walck based on 'Eastern' models where water was much more abundant, rather than on the reality of the US Southwest. Poor practices like overgrazing led to replacement of perennial grasses with juniper, thistle and cheat grass. No longer could the grassland support large numbers of cattle. Large ranches were sold off and broken up into small ranches that supported only a few hundred head of cattle. The lesson is that we must learn from nature, rather than try to dictate to nature. Unfortunately, the very same organization routines that Wijen recognizes as important for institutionalizing sustainability can also limit the organization's capacity for responding to changing ecological and cultural contexts.

These chapters illustrate some of the challenges in integrating the social and environmental pieces of the sustainability mosaic. The first difficulty lies with the conceptualization of this integration. Integration usually requires bringing all parts together in order to make a whole. The chapters approach the idea of integration in very different ways. First, some authors, like Hoffman and Bazerman, and Howard-Grenville et al., treat the environmental and social aspects of sustainability indistinguishably. They simply use the term 'sustainability' and thus allow the reader to pour into that label whatever mix of social and environmental content he or she desires. Second, other authors seem to make one kind of sustainability contingent upon its counterpart. Walck's discussion of the American Southwest is focused on the land as a natural resource, and the impacts of this resource for human well-being are then discussed. But the social impacts are contingent upon the more fundamental problem of environmental degradation. A third approach to integration involves simply mixing environmental and social concepts, measures and systems (Perrini and Tencati). It is a kind of 'tossed salad' approach to integration. Unfortunately, in none of these approaches does integration really occur. Integration requires taking seriously the differences in the nature of social and environmental problems. To treat the concepts indistinguishably prevents us from grappling with the difficulties inherent in integration. To treat one form of sustainability as contingent upon another, gives priority to one. It may create a whole, but an imbalanced whole. Finally, simply including environmental measures and social measures in a reporting system does not create a whole, but only a collection of parts.

One can easily imagine a number of reasons for this incomplete integration. First, the natural environment is material and society is not. This difference has a significant impact on the ability to measure performance as well as to use technology. In terms of the environment, the firm's objective can be crystal clear – for example, zero emissions or no externalities. As a result of the clarity of these objectives, firms like Greenheart are able to develop barometers and dashboards and other types of measures to monitor their progress in achieving these goals. What is the objective of the firm in the social realm? In part, the nature of the firm's social externalities are more difficult to determine. The social problems of the firm are often due to the systemic nature of capitalism, rather than to the concrete action of a single firm. Social inequity in the distribution of income creates all sorts of problems, such as illiteracy. What should the firm's goal be? It could fight to reduce illiteracy. By how much? Among whom? Its employees? Its neighbors? Its community? How much illiteracy can be attributed to the firm's participation in the capitalistic system? As these questions indicate, it is very difficult to establish concrete social objectives for the firm.

Given that goals are clearer with respect to the natural environment, it is much easier to determine the causal links between firm behavior and its environmental impacts. The analysis of causal links between firm behavior and social impacts is hampered both by the lack of clarity of the desirable goals to be achieved, as well as by the lack of well-defined technologies in dealing with social problems. A significant improvement of environmental quality can be achieved through the application of the natural sciences – biology, chemistry, geology and physics – without appeal to the inherently more intractable social sciences. The reduction of social inequities is tied inextricably to socially constructed realities. The introduction of educational or financial technologies may help to change cultures or create incentives, but by their nature are subject to a great deal of 'noise' because of the ambiguity inherent in causal connections between variables involving social relationships. These social technologies are also subject to Selznick's (1957) concern about the 'unanticipated consequences of purposive social action'. Consequently, due to the difficulty in defining social objectives and developing useful social technologies, the social side of the sustainability mosaic continues to be neglected.

Clearly, the challenges of sustainability are immense and time is at a premium. The climate change crisis is already upon us and the problem is now one of minimizing its impacts, rather than of avoiding the crisis. At the same time, social conflicts and the uneven distribution of the benefits of globalization continue to widen the economic and social welfare gap between segments of society. Too often researchers have focused on only pieces of the puzzle of the sustainability mosaic. In addition, the central role of organizations as vehicles for mediating processes of sustainability has too often been neglected. By examining the many facets of the sustainability mosaic, this volume continues the work of understanding the challenges and defining the parameters within which feasible solutions might occur. By learning from the many errors of the past, this volume provides guidelines to help us find a way forward for the future.

POTENTIAL RESEARCH DIRECTIONS FOR INTEGRATING SOCIAL AND ENVIRONMENTAL SUSTAINABILITY

Conceptually, connections between social and environmental sustainability should be vast in number. This is not only because the survival and thriving of human societies is based on the continuation and health of natural environments, but also because human societies are composed of, are embedded within, and are constituent parts of natural environments. However, many human societies over the last several centuries have developed patterns of thinking and acting as if human societies can separate themselves from the rest of their natural environments. Given the self-inflicted challenges such alienation has caused, such as regional, national and international armed conflict, urban sprawl, overconsumption and climate crises, reuniting social and environmental sustainability seems like a prudent idea that was erroneously discarded in the distant past but has been rediscovered in recent times. The hope of sustainability supporters, of course, is that this rediscovery has occurred within a time-frame and with adequate force so that both human societies and natural environments can not only survive but also flourish. Researchers (and their stakeholders) can play key roles in exploring, analyzing and advancing the social and environmental sustainability connection. Linkages between the social sustainability aspects of human rights, gender equity, racial justice and poverty-reducing education, on the one hand, and the environmental sustainability aspects of air and water quality, prudent land use, biodiversity preservation and resource conservation, on the other hand, are virtually ubiquitous.

This volume's authors have explored a number of these connections, including Walck's linkage of Southwestern US rangeland mismanagement and subsequent deterioration, Gallagher's identification of multiple professions involved in environmental and social sustainability activities, and the inclusion of the socio-cultural and political-economic levels in the Rands et al. chapter on environmental sustainability in the Marshall Islands. In addition to considering other geographic locations and timeframes of this volume's studies to explore wider applications of their findings and lessons, social and environmental integration researchers have a cornucopia of opportunities to advance their integration aims. These possibilities can likely be categorized into at least three groupings varying by degree of integration: moderate integration, significant integration and near-total integration.

In the first category of 'moderate integration' are those potential approaches which at least identify a few environmental aspects of social sustainability phenomena, and those environmental sustainability studies which include a few elements of social sustainability. Respectively, these could include diversity, democratic governance or internal equity studies within environmental organizations (whether in the business, government or non-profit sectors) and those which assess the environmental policies, practices and performance of indigenous or minority organizations in any of the three societal sectors (Riley et al., 2006), social service organizations (such as hospitals, nursing homes, schools and self-help groups), and military, defense and local protection-related organizations. Similar to the Wijen chapter highlighting the variability of managerial commitment to sustainability, researchers are advised that attention to social and environmental integration can also change over time, as in the case of the Global Reporting Initiative (GRI). In its 2002 *Sustainability Reporting Guidelines*, the organization suggested that integration of economic, social and environmental indicators be reviewed by organizations and their stakeholders to develop those that are integrative from systemic or cross-cutting perspectives, but in its proposed G3 2006 guidelines, integration is apparently de-emphasized (GRI, 2006).

One potentially obvious result of this moderate level of integration research is that if this research identifies how social sustainability organizations can become 'greener' and how environmental organizations can become more socially sustainable, and if these respective organizations effectively and significantly implemented those lessons learned on a meaningful scale, human activities on the planet would most likely become at least somewhat more sustainable (Starik, 2004). Of course, research on how such effective and significant implementation can be 'scaled up' and/or replicated geographically would be key to this macro result, and the longer human societies delay in actually making this transition, the more complicated such implementation may become. This may especially be the case for rapidly developing large countries, such as China (Ho, 2006) and India.

The second category of integration, one which might be described as 'significant integration', moves beyond the surface-level of connecting social and environmental sustainability to a more substantive set of research possibilities. At this level, human society and natural environments are more than just context variables, but rather are focused on the content of the integration to a greater degree. Along these lines, potential significant integration research topics can include how organizations can be co-designed to advance the full set of both social sustainability and environmental sustainability values. So, for example, questions regarding the extent to which new green businesses have been designed to address social sustainability issues, such as poverty, beyond traditional (and usually marginal) philanthropy, and the extent to which they could do so more effectively in the future, can be salient in such research. Considering philanthropy more directly, questions regarding how organizations can be assessed as to the adequacy of their liquid assets, volunteer time and other resources in the support of both social and environmental goals could be addressed. These questions could include how one set (say, supporting local developing country organizations) could be synergized with another (such as advancing ecological restoration, as in the case of a number of sustainable tourism developments). And, beyond philanthropy, studies on how organizational and value network norms can be developed to advance both social and environmental purposes would be relevant. Returning to the topic of poverty, an area ripe for additional research is the set of environmental and social impacts related to resource extraction industries in developing countries (Kumah, 2006). Finally, research on whether and how integrated sustainability indicators can be developed, promoted and assessed which allow for thinking and acting on both sets of goals simultaneously could be very useful (Hart, 1999).

The last category, 'near-total sustainability integration', sets out research in which there is a very close connection, or near-absence of separation, between social and environmental sustainability phenomena, one which recognizes the linkages between their related processes, as well as context and content. For example, the topic of distributed energy has both social and environmental implications that are very closely linked, with the general observation that the more distributed a renewable energy system, the lower the negative social and environmental impacts (Alanne and Saari, 2006).

Here the opportunities include, among many others, the co-development of business and community sustainability goals, projects and indicators; the integration of both sets of sustainability stakeholders' perspectives into an organization's policies, plans and programs; a deep commitment and immersion of organizations to both social and environmental sustainability norms; and full participation in helping to develop organizational and societal cultures dedicated to advancing both environmental and social sustainability goals (Fraser et al., 2006). One more obvious approach for identifying near-total integrated sustainability research topics is to focus first on those organizations and programs which include both environmental and social sustainability in their respective names, such as the World Bank's Environmental and Social Sustainability network, and those which include both social and environmental goals, such as the Millenium Development Goals and Agenda 21.

For this last 'near-total integration' category, less description and more prescription may be necessary, perhaps requiring researchers to relax some of their assumptions about appropriate research topics and approaches, change a few of their research habits for increasing breadth, and explore fields and theories well beyond those with which they are comfortable. On a more macro level, researchers might begin to question research which does not automatically integrate both social and environmental sustainability phenomenon, and give more value to that which does. One irony of publications is that, in a truly sustainable world in which no distinction is made between social and environmental sustainability, a volume such as the present one would not be necessary. Until that time, however, we offer a series of studies here which begin to address this need for returning to the prudent idea of social and environmental sustainability integration, and we hope we have provided our reader stakeholders with at least a few additional relevant suggestions on how this integration idea could be even further advanced.

REFERENCES

Alanne, K. and A. Saari (2006), 'Distributed energy generation and sustainable development', *Renewable and Sustainable Energy Reviews*, **10** (6), 539–50.

Clarkson, M., M. Starik, P. Cochran and T. Jones (1994), 'The Toronto conference: reflections on stakeholder theory', *Business and Society*, **33** (1), 82–131.

Dunn, D. and K. Yamashita (2003), 'Microcapitalism and the megacorporation', *Harvard Business Review*, **81** (8), 46–54.

Fraser, E.D.G., A.J. Dougill, W.E. Mabee, M. Reed and P. McAlpine (2006), 'Bottom up and top down: analysis of participatory processes for sustainability indicator identification as a pathway to community empowerment and

sustainable environmental management', *Journal of Environmental Management*, **78** (2), 114–27.
Gladwin, T.N., J.J. Kennelly and T.S. Krause (1995), 'Shifting paradigms for sustainable development: implications for management theory and research', *Academy of Management Review*, **20**, 874–907.
GRI (Global Reporting Initiative) (2002), *Sustainability Reporting Guidelines*, Boston, MA: GRI.
GRI (Global Reporting Initiative) (2006), *G3 Release Guidelines, Part 2 Standard Disclosures*, Amsterdam: GRI.
Hart, M. (1999), *Sustainable Development Indicators*, 2nd edn, North Andover, MA: Hart Environmental Data.
Hart, S.L. (2005), *Capitalism at the Crossroads: The Unlimited Business Opportunities in Solving the World's Most Difficult Problems*, Upper Saddle River, NJ: Wharton School Publishing.
Hart, S.L. and S. Sharma (2004), 'Engaging fringe stakeholder for competitive imagination', *Academy of Management Executive*, **18** (1), 7–18.
Ho, P. (ed.) (2006), 'Trajectories for greening in China: theory and practice', *Development and Change*, **37** (1), 3–28.
Kumah, A. (2006), 'Sustainability and gold mining in the developing world', *Journal of Cleaner Production*, **14** (3/4), 315–23.
Prahalad, C.K. (2005), *The Fortune at the Bottom of the Pyramid: Eradicating Poverty Through Profits*, Upper Saddle River, NJ: Wharton School Publishing.
Riley, D.R., C.E. Thatcher and E.A. Workman (2006), 'Developing and applying green building technology in an indigenous community', *International Journal of Sustainability in Higher Education*, **7** (2), 142–58.
Sachs, J.D. (2005), *The End of Poverty: Economic Possibilities for Our Time*, New York: The Penguin Press.
Selznick, P. (1957), *Leadership in Administration: A Sociological Perspective*, Berkeley, CA: University of California Press.
Sharma, S. (2002), 'What really matters: research on corporate sustainability', in S. Sharma and M. Starik (eds), *Research in Corporate Sustainability: The Evolving Theory and Practice of Organizations in the Natural Environment*, Cheltenham, UK and Northampton, MA, USA: Edward Elgar, pp. 1–29.
Starik, M. (2004), 'Holistic environmental leadership: living sustainably beyond 9-to-5', *Human Ecology Review*, **11** (3), 280–84.
Starik, M. and G.P. Rands (1995), 'Weaving an integrated web: multilevel and multisystem perspective of ecologically sustainable organizations', *Academy of Management Review*, **20**, 908–35.
Time (2006), 'Global Warming: Be Worried. Be Very Worried', 3 April, cover article.

2. Envisioning an ecologically sustainable society: an ideal type and an application

Gordon Rands, Barbara Ribbens, David Casagrande and Heather McIlvaine-Newsad

Sustainable development is a concept that is becoming increasingly accepted as a desirable goal for societies. The concept of what a sustainable society might be like, or how it might be created, however, still requires a great deal of attention. It is generally accepted that such a society must be based on widespread adoption of activities that are sustainable in economic, environmental and social terms. Organizational attention to the concept of sustainability has tended to focus on the environmental aspect. For example, a multi-level, multi-systems based model of ecological sustainability applying to organizations was developed by Starik and Rands (1995). This basic framework can be modified and applied to the level of societies. Doing so of necessity requires attention to social aspects of sustainability.

In this chapter we begin by reviewing the concept of sustainable development, and suggest that sustainability requires reconciling not only economic, environmental and social considerations, but cultural and 'managerial' ones as well. We then re-examine the Starik and Rands model, attempt more fully to develop basic assumptions upon which it is built, and develop an analogue of it at the societal level. We further discuss how this model might be used to guide efforts to develop an ecologically sustainable society in a particular nation, the Republic of the Marshall Islands. We examine the Marshall Islands in terms of its potential for sustainable development, and suggest how the characteristics of an ecologically sustainable society might be applied by Marshallese society to move the Marshall Islands closer to sustainability.

THE CONCEPT OF SUSTAINABLE DEVELOPMENT

The concept of sustainable development, while originating in at least the 1970s (Pirages, 1977), entered the public consciousness in the wake of the

1987 report of the World Commission on Environment and Development, *Our Common Future*. The Commission's work laid the groundwork for the 1992 United Nations Conference on Environment and Development, commonly referred to as the 'Earth Summit', held in Rio de Janeiro, Brazil in 1992. The Commission articulated what is still the most widely used definition of sustainable development: 'development that meets the needs of the present without compromising the ability of future generations to meet their own needs' (World Commission on Environment and Development, 1987, p. 43).

The precise meaning of this definition is open to question and dispute (see, for example, Farrell and Hart, 1998; Gladwin et al., 1995). Among the areas of discussion and dispute are the nature and level of 'needs'; whether equitable differences in needs exist across nations, cultures and generations; the time-frames under which future generations are relevant; and whether the holders of needs are solely human or should include other species as well. Farrell and Hart (1998) described two fundamentally different interpretations of sustainable development. First, some interpret sustainable development to mean that there are critical limits on natural resources which people cannot exceed. Thus, society needs to restrain resource consumption or critical elements upon which our society depends will be depleted. Second, others interpret sustainable development to mean that society needs to learn to balance competing economic, social and ecological goals. While there are conflicts between specific applications of these two alternatives, both support maintaining the quality of human life without destroying or irreparably damaging the underlying ecological systems.

While different observers may place greater emphasis on either the social or environmental aspects of sustainability, most observers seem to agree that the concept involves multigenerational time horizons, maintenance or improvement of environmental quality at scales ranging from global to local, increased social welfare via meeting the basic needs of all persons (thus likely requiring greater social equity through at least some adjustments in consumption and redistribution of resources), all done through methods that harness the profit motive. Many scholars have pointed out that sustainable development involves three or four different components: ecological, economic and social, and for some authors, cultural (Brown, Hanson, Liverman and Merideth, 1987; Dixon and Fallon, 1989; Mayer et al., 2004; Redclift, 1992; Agrawal, 1997; Hawkes, 2005). Thus, for an action to be sustainable, it must be sustainable on three different dimensions: environment, equity (social welfare) and economics – the '3 Es' of the 'triple bottom line' (Elkington, 1998).

While the '3 Es' define the sustainability of an activity, they do not address the motivation for attempting such activities. This is influenced by two limiting factors: culture and self-efficacy. That actions also need to be integrated into cultural institutions in order to be sustainable is particularly obvious when attempting to identify activities that can be maintained over time on a societal basis. The literature on traditional societies and community-based sustainable development highlights the importance of integrating sustainable actions into daily routine and ritual behavior (Kaus, 1993), power-based social organization (Natcher and Hickey, 2002), gender roles (Sen and Grown, 1987; Browder, 2002; Shiva, 2005) and widely shared belief systems (Atran et al., 2002). Belief systems are particularly important because they bridge the individual, organizational and socio-cultural scales of analysis we discuss below (Stepp et al., 2003).

An additional crucial component of a sustainable belief system is the notion of self-efficacy (Taylor, 1989) – only if individuals and collectivities believe that they have the capability of successfully engaging in particular sustainable actions will such actions be attempted. As the expectancy theory of motivation (Vroom, 1964) suggests, an individual is unlikely to attempt a behavior unless they believe their effort is likely to result in successful performance. Neither individuals, organizations nor societies are likely to attempt to undertake the hard choices that sustainability requires unless they believe that those difficult actions can be successfully managed. Thus, it appears that there are five components of sustainability: economic, ecological, social, cultural and 'managerial'.

Gladwin et al. (1995) defined sustainable development as 'the process of achieving human development in an inclusive, connected, equitable, prudent and secure manner' (p. 878). This definition shifts the focus of sustainable development from outcome to process. These social processes do not seek 'grand structural transformations' (Escobar, 1992a, p. 31) through revolution, 'rather they empower themselves through the politicization of everyday individual and social spheres, the expansion of the realm of the political in general, and the recovery of the social away from the control by the state' (Escobar, 1992b, p. 427). These definitions emphasize that by improving the process society can move the outcomes closer to achieving the goal of sustainability. We would assert that such movement in itself, even if ultimately unsuccessful in achieving sustainable outcomes, is a worthy goal. Many conceptualizations of sustainability assume that social organization provides the functionality required to achieve sustainability, and that only the goals must change. An emphasis on process suggests that systemic reorganization is also required to renegotiate goals successfully.

Viewing sustainability both as a process but particularly as an outcome, Starik and Rands (1995) defined ecological sustainability as:

> [T]he ability of one or more entities, either individually or collectively, to exist and flourish (either unchanged or in evolved forms) for lengthy time-frames, in

> such a manner that the existence and flourishing of other collectivities of entities is permitted at related levels and in related systems. (p. 909)

Accordingly, if an entity (species, organization, society, and so on) is robust enough to maintain itself in its bio-physical environment, if free of unnatural interference, it is sustainable. If a second entity unnaturally interferes with and causes the cessation of flourishing of the first entity, that second entity is not ecologically sustainable.

ECOLOGICALLY SUSTAINABLE ENTITIES: A MULTI-LEVEL, MULTI-SYSTEM APPROACH

In order to provide some guidance on how ecological sustainability could be attained, Starik and Rands (1995) attempted to create an 'ideal type' (Doty and Glick, 1994) of an ecologically sustainable organization (ESO). Such an organization would itself be able to flourish, and would not negatively affect the flourishing of other entities. Their ideal type is derived by examining the relationships of organizations with natural, human and organizational entities at multiple levels of analysis: ecological, individual, organizational, political-economic and social-cultural. The framework attempts to describe what an ESO would be like by identifying elements of these dyadic relationships based on six system-based characteristics: inputs, throughput processes, outputs, feedback, values and strategies. The last two are derived from the need that the open system characteristic of differentiation creates for integration mechanisms (such as values) and coordination devices (such as strategies) (Katz and Kahn, 1978). In the process Starik and Rands develop a web-like framework for identifying characteristics that contribute to sustainable development.

A fundamental assumption underlying Starik and Rands's work is that no entity can be sustainable through its own actions alone: other systems in which the entity is embedded must facilitate rather than impede its sustainability. This implies that humans and human-created entities may need to act to affect entities at other levels so that these in turn act in ways that facilitate rather than impede sustainable behavior. For example, an erstwhile ESO may need to encourage governments to develop regulations that require other organizations to adopt actions approximating those that the ESO is willing to adopt voluntarily. Otherwise, if the ecologically desirable activities imposed significant economic costs on the organization that it must pass on to customers in the form of higher prices, its competitors could refuse to adopt them and take market share from the first organization, even though it was more ecologically sustainable.

We attempt to build upon the work of Starik and Rands by using their approach to develop an ideal type of an ecologically sustainable society (ESS). To do so, however, it is necessary to address a weakness in their paper. Starik and Rands indicate that their ideal ESO is derived by examining dyadic relationships between organizations with entities at five different levels, along the six system-based dimensions noted above. This implies the existence of an ideal type consisting of 30 different attributes. Their description of an ESO lists only 27 attributes, and upon examination it becomes clear that these attributes are not evenly distributed; many of the 30 'cells' are empty, while others have several specific attributes listed for them.

Accordingly, we begin with a step that Starik and Rands did not take. We identify the essential scope, for each of the six characteristics,[1] of entities at each of the five levels. The resulting list is shown in Table 2.1. This list is neutral in nature; it can be used as the basis for describing attributes under any conditions, not just under sustainable conditions. That Starik and Rands did not explicitly engage in this step helps explain why their explication of an ESO incompletely covers the dimensions they identify.

The characteristics in Table 2.1 are then used as the basis for articulating the essential attributes of an ESS, as shown in Table 2.2. In this, we attempt to follow the approach used by Starik and Rands by articulating characteristics by examining the relationship between entities at the socio-cultural level (a national society as a whole) with entities at each of the five levels. In doing this, we constantly grappled with the amorphous nature of the concept of a society as an entity. While tempted to retreat to the political-economic level and focus on a national government as the focal entity, we decided to keep our focus on society as a whole. Just as Starik and Rands argued that an organization cannot become and remain sustainable through its actions alone, we maintain that a society must engage in activities in its relationships with entities at every level to create conditions that foster sustainability. Below we briefly examine some of the characteristics and attributes listed in Tables 2.1 and 2.2.

ESSENTIAL SYSTEMIC CHARACTERISTICS OF ENTITIES AT DIFFERENT LEVELS

At each of the five levels identified, entities exist and interact. Obviously, human beings act at each of these levels, but the nature and context of their activities are somewhat different. While many mammalian species clearly exhibit thought and have complex social interactions, for the purposes of this chapter, we will take an anthropocentric perspective and limit our discussion beyond the ecological level to human beings (individually or collectively).

Table 2.1 Essential systemic characteristics of entities at each level

	Inputs	Throughputs	Outputs	Feedback	Values	Strategies
Ecological*	Natural resources: sunlight, air, organisms, water, minerals	Ecological processes: photosynthesis, nutrient cycling. Biomass conversion	Transformed biomass, nutrients stored or released, soil built or eroded, water filtered, waste, etc.	Continuity or change in outputs or conditions (soil pH, precipitation, microclimates, population, etc.)	Dynamic stability, Interdependence. Resilience and successional predictability. Diversity	Symbiosis, adaptation to fill niches, recycling. Increased resilience. Evolution. Redundancy. Appropriate scale
Individual	Experiences as: 1. roles: a. citizen b. community member c. consumer d. family member e. employee 2. as shaped by identity: a. gender b. age c. ethnicity d. power e. status f. health	Decision-making the conscious and unconscious reconsolidation of rote daily routines versus abstract beliefs	a. Input to officials, votes b. neighborhood and community involvement c. purchases, wastes and wishes d. children and relationships e. labor/ideas	Changes in knowledge, skills, and attitudes	a. Citizenship, voting, voice b. cooperation, neighborliness c. lifestyle preferences d. value of family and relatives e. work motivation to employer	a. Increase information b. reduce time expended acquiring resources c. maximize caloric intake d. enhance predictability

Table 2.1 (continued)

	Inputs	Throughputs	Outputs	Feedback	Values	Strategies
Organizational	Past experience with operations, societal issues, and institutions. Perceived client and customer demands. Resources	Transformative activities and current operating practices	Products and services. By-products. Socialization of employees and other stakeholders	Requests for legal changes, for resource allocation, for policy changes, for new products and services, for higher quality	Allocation of responsibility. Ethical standards. Conflict resolution. Organizational survival	Coordination for resource acquisition and goal accomplishment (coalitions, mediation, competition)
Political-Economic	Macroeconomic conditions. Social problems Laws, policies. Treaties. Governance structures. Concerns of actors (e.g. consumers, NGOs, foreign governments, competitors)	Political process. Trade, market processes, Administration of laws, treaties, etc. Currency exchange	Changes in legal and political system. Government programs. Products and services. Employment and increase interest rates	Performance indicators and reaction of stakeholders (e.g. election and poll results, media coverage, consumer confidence)	Values that create legitimacy of political/economic system and actors (e.g. patriotism, freedom, concern for others, security, tradition, growth progress)	Use of forums to discuss issues, procedures and agendas. Stabilize conditions. Impression management (e.g. political spin). Elections
Socio-Cultural	Collective history Norms, values and beliefs: a. breadth	Daily interaction within networks. Socialization and enculturation of	Revised knowledge, norms and social networks	Disorder. Ethnic tension. Uncertainty. Doubt. Changes	Individual initiative. Stability/ adaptability.	Debate and exhortation. News dissemination.

	b. depth Practices. Social conditions. Social institutions (e.g. religion, gender, ethnicity)	children. Social construction of narrative, including ecological narrative		in social conditions	Cooperation. Consensus. Reciprocity	Education. Marketing. Quest for supernatural

Note:
* We express appreciation to Eric Ribbens for insights and suggestions regarding the ecological level.

Table 2.2 Attributes of an ESS

	Inputs	Throughputs	Outputs	Feedback	Values	Strategies
Ecological	Sustainable extraction of primarily renewable natural resources; non-renewables used are high in recycled content	Sustainable resource conversion (production, energy generation); renewable energy, zero emissions, 3Rs	Products and by-products are non-toxic, biodegradable, assimilable, recyclable, reuseable, and are consumed sustainably	Changes in ecological conditions are noticed quickly, interpreted accurately, and responded to promptly and effectively	Pro-ecological values are held and practiced: recycling, respect for earth, simplicity, interdependence in nature, etc.	Extensive data collection and analysis, use of EIA for all proposed actions, apply '7th generation' criterion, etc.
Individual	Promote sustainability norms to generate role and identity relevant KSAs	Environmental education combined with community-based planning and enhanced self-efficacy	Pro-ecological: a. input to officials, votes b. neighborhood and community involvement c. purchases, wastes and wishes d. children and relationships e. labor/ideas	Rapid provision of ecological feedback to and from individuals: sensing feedback on pro-e processes. Pro-e KSA used as selection criteria for rewards; anti-e KSA prompt role-based education	Promotion and acceptance of individual responsibility for nature and societal problems, as well as the intrinsic value of nature and other people	Include ecological issues in: increased education, increased lifelong learning, empowerment, relevance, bidirectional forums for feedback
Organizational	Use past environmental operating practices as a basis for reward and further education	Promotion of sustainable transformative activities; transparent practices; accurate assessment of	Demand for sustainable products and services; strong infrastructure for recycling and remanufacture; harmless	Request frequent and prompt dissemination of information re: environmental practices, impacts and system needs	Promotion of sustainability, social and environmental responsibility, transparency, cooperation, involvement, wholism	Requests for sustainability reporting, sustainability as a standing agenda item, use of Community.

		environmental performance	by-products; sensitive/aware employees and stakeholders	requirements; accurate assessment of E performance		Advisory Panels and Sustainability Coordinating Councils, use of other ESO tools
Political-Economic	Past environmental outcomes of laws, policies, economic activity, treaties, and governance structures serve as basis for governmental review; involvement by businesses, NGOs, individuals, etc.	Promote government actions to make processes (electoral, legislative, trade, market administrative, etc.) increasingly sustainable	Promote a sustainable legal, economic and political system; tough standards, market-based incentives, only sustainable subsidies, full-cost accounting, green systems of national accounts	Demand utilization of sustainability performance indicators; promote integration of stakeholders' reactions	Promote democracy, participation, responsiveness, honesty, service, diligence, societal rather than personal benefit	Support and facilitate sustainability-oriented associations, civic education, civic forums, diverse advisory commissions
Socio-Cultural	Traditional norms. Religion. Ethnic groups. Collective history. External ideologies	Environmental and cultural education. Multicultural. Interaction with various natural environments. Construct and disseminate ecological narratives that emphasize sustainability	Internally and externally promote ecological knowledge, skills, attitudes and networks	Advocate recognition of society's threats to sustainability of others, of need for internal social stability, and need to adapt to change	Promote consensus on the need for sustainability, societal responsibility, stability/adaptation, peace/cooperation, multicultural tolerance	Utilize diverse means of inter-societal contact (do not restrict to governmental policy) to focus on external threats to sustainability. Provide and promote environmental education

Ecological Level

Acting at the ecological level entails utilizing natural inputs, converting these inputs into outputs though bio-geo-chemical processes, releasing these outputs into the environment, and adjusting subsequent activities (if possible) based on changes in relevant ecosystems. While natural systems and non-human species can not be truly stated to have values and strategies,[2] their activities can be associated with human values and strategies. In addition, human-based entities clearly can adopt values and strategies such as interdependence and recycling, respectively, to guide their interactions with natural entities.

Individual Level

At the level of individuals, knowledge, skills and past experiences in various roles and settings, as influenced by aspects of an individual's identity, are the primary inputs that individuals use to make decisions (throughput) about what actions to take (outputs). Individuals can engage in daily ritual behaviors that may be in conflict with more abstract beliefs that they share with other individuals in their society. Sources of feedback such as conversations, meetings, interviews and media reports provide individuals with new or revised knowledge, which subsequently serve as new inputs. Individuals rely upon different values in their different roles, such as voice, cooperation, lifestyle preferences, family values and motivation. Depending upon the values held and goals adopted, various strategies may be used, focusing on gaining and utilizing resources to enhance predictability and security.

It is crucial at this point to acknowledge the amount of heterogeneity and identity found among individuals, using gender as an example. The integration of gender as an analytical variable provides an additional window through which to identify and analyze the heterogeneity at the individual level, which will lead to heterogeneity at other levels of analysis. Gender is understood as the social construction that shapes the interactions between men and women (Poats et al., 1987; Feldstein and Poats, 1990).

The specific social construction of gender shapes the roles, identities, experiences, knowledge and power relations between men and women. These social constructions take place on various levels, beginning at the family and household level and extending to the community level and the larger political, economic and cultural tiers. The social construction of gender will vary according to other variables like age, class, religion and ethnicity (McIlvaine-Newsad, 2003, p. 161).

Gender is also shaped and may be recreated several times over the course of an individual's lifetime as an individual depending on such variables as access to education, income and personal characteristics and choices (Espinosa, 1998). Gender therefore shapes the nature of individuals' experience in each of the roles listed in Table 2.1, as do each of the other components of identity.

Organizational Level

At the level of organizations, development, maintenance and enhancement of organizations for the purposes of accomplishing various goals are the primary goals. Various tangible and intangible resources and past organizational experiences with both the internal and external environments are key sources of inputs. Operating practices are used to transform these inputs into products and services; various physical and intangible by-products result as well. Common organizational values relate to allocation of responsibility, ethical standards, conflict resolution, effort and stakeholder satisfaction. Strategies tend to focus on resource acquisition and goal accomplishment. Organizations may behave to self-perpetuate, sometimes at the expense of shared values and goals (Holling, 2003).

Political-Economic Level

The political-economic level focuses on political governance and economic exchange. The strong reciprocal relationship between political and economic processes and conditions necessitates treatment of these at a single level. Laws, policies, macroeconomic factors, treaties and other market and governance structures are primary inputs to interactions at this level. Administrative, political and market processes are the throughputs by which government and market operations occur. New or modified laws, regulations and treaties may result from these processes, as well as changes in production, consumption, employment and other macroeconomic conditions. Changes in these and other indicators (for example, environmental, educational, health) provide feedback to entities in their interactions at this level. Key values tend to focus on affecting the perceived legitimacy of the political and economic systems, and key strategies tend to focus on shaping the nature and operation of the forums in which political and economic decision-making occurs.

Socio-Cultural Level

The socio-cultural level deals with the creation, modification and expression of values. Key inputs at this level are the norms, beliefs, practices, historical experiences and cultural artifacts of social institutions such as religion, media, education, advocacy and social service. Education, entertainment, art and daily social interaction are throughputs by which socialization and enculturation of children occur. Another primary throughput includes the political and ideological struggle to produce the stories we tell ourselves about why things are and how they came to be (that is, socially constructed narratives). Such narratives are created in social networks ranging in scope from kin and community to global media. These throughput processes create new knowledge, norms, beliefs and social networks as outputs. The nature of and the rate of change in these outputs provide complex feedback that can weaken and/or strengthen the throughputs and inputs. The primary focus of the socio-cultural level in this chapter is the interaction of values and shared beliefs with external systems. Consensus, stability, social order, cooperation, spirituality, reciprocity and initiative tend to be highly valued across societies and promote internal cohesion. Information feedback at the socio-cultural level might include perceptions of social disorder and ethnic tension, economic uncertainty or doubt in leadership. Strategies for affecting processes and outputs at this level focus on the universal quest for the supernatural, on the creation, dissemination and acceptance of information, and on the use of that information by entities at all other levels. Often the most effective forms of change result from small, but concrete modifications of shared 'core cultural values'.

MULTI-LEVEL, MULTI-SYSTEM CHARACTERISTICS OF AN ECOLOGICALLY SUSTAINABLE SOCIETY

With these essential systemic characteristics in mind, we can attempt to identify the attributes of an ecologically sustainable society. In keeping with notions of the multifaceted nature of sustainability as discussed earlier, we believe that a society is most likely to become ecologically sustainable if it is also socially, culturally, economically and managerially sustainable. To the degree that all of these conditions are achieved, a society will be truly and fully sustainable. However, our aim in this chapter is not to describe all the attributes of a fully sustainable society, but those of an ecologically sustainable society.

Conditions at the ecological level are the fundamental indicators of whether a society is ecologically sustainable or not. However, whether sustainable interactions at this level can be brought about largely depend upon interactions at other levels. For example, information flow between levels is not perfect, which emphasizes the need for external environmental information feedback to occur at multiple levels (Stepp et al., 2003). Consistent with the approach taken by Starik and Rands (1995), the characteristics listed in Table 2.2 therefore reflect the purposeful interaction of a society with entities at each of the five levels.

Ecological Level

An ecologically sustainable society will rely primarily upon renewable material and energy inputs; those non-renewable inputs used will be high in recycled content, and will eventually be replaced by renewable substitutes (Brown et al., 1993). Throughput processes used will be chosen and designed so as to generate outputs (both products and by-products) that will be non-toxic, and will be of such materials and design that they can be recycled, reused or, if otherwise disposed of, generated in quantities and at locations such that they can be biodegraded or assimilated by ecological processes without negatively impacting ecological systems (Henn and Fava, 1994). An ESS will notice and respond to feedback from ecological systems quickly and effectively (Meadows et al., 1992). Socio-economic values that facilitate ecologically sustainable activities will be widely held, including respect for the earth, simplicity, interdependence with nature, appreciation for beauty and for nature, and so on. Key strategies will include the development and application of procedures and technologies that permit accurate assessment of ecological conditions and of the ecological impacts of proposed activities across the entire life cycle of activities (Henn and Fava, 1994), and for the dissemination of such information for its incorporation into decision-making using pro-ecological criteria.

Individual Level

Individuals will contribute to societal ecological sustainability in their roles as citizens, community members, consumers, family members and employees. As society interacts with individuals in these various roles, society can help assess and develop the ecological knowledge, skills and attitudes (KSAs) that individuals can then use as inputs to the decisions they make in their various roles. Evidence of inadequate ecological KSAs should prompt society to provide pro-environmental role-based education, although education alone is insufficient (Kollmuss and Agyeman, 2002). Literature from social psychology shows the effectiveness of increased knowledge for changing attitudes, but less so for behavior (McKenzie-Mohr and Smith, 1999). However, engaging entire communities in environmental project planning and implementation can foster commitment, promote community norms and better fit new behaviors to existing rituals and rhythms of daily life, thus bridging the gap between the everyday world and more abstract worldviews.

Individual decision-making processes will regularly incorporate gender and environmentally specific knowledge, understanding and concern for the environment, and society will provide both formal and informal environmental education that will facilitate ecologically sustainable decision-making and the development of pro-environmental worldviews and behaviors (Rands, 1990). Individuals will then generate outputs of pro-ecological decisions and behaviors. Individuals will need to have access to ecological feedback, and social institutions such as the media and education will help provide this feedback (Day and Smith, n.d.). Individuals in turn will provide these social institutions with feedback about their environmental experiences.

Along with pro-ecological values noted in our discussion of the ecological level, a critical value that must be held at the individual level is acceptance of individual responsibility for environmental quality (Hwang et al., 2000). An ESS must promote this value in its interactions with individuals. By defending and encouraging both 'diversity in nature and culture' (Shiva, 2005), an ESS will reinforce a basic ecological principle that diverse ecosystems (and societies) are more sustainable and resilient. An ESS will likely employ a variety of individual-oriented strategies, focusing on developing environmental knowledge, understanding and concern, and helping individuals overcome economic and social barriers to pro-environmental behavior (Rands, 1990). As noted earlier, self-efficacy (Taylor, 1989) is needed to encourage individuals to act consistently with their acceptance of personal responsibility. Empowering individuals to engage in pro-environmental behavior and providing opportunities for feedback to social institutions on these matters will also be important strategies.

Organizational Level

Starik and Rands (1995) identified several relevant characteristics ESOs would exhibit in their interactions with societies. Our focus here is on the other side of this relationship: the characteristics ESSs will exhibit in their interactions with organizations. The key inputs to ESS–organization interactions will be the degree of sustainability of the organization's past operating practices. If these have been becoming more sustainable, an ESS is likely to provide rewards such as praise and recognition; if becoming less sustainable, an ESS is likely to withdraw resources and otherwise impose negative sanctions. Key throughput processes involved in providing these inputs will involve accurate assessment and publicity of organizations' ecological performance. Organizations' throughput processes and outputs need to be understood and assessed, and actions will need to be taken to promote organizational transparency (Elkington, 1998). Such interactions should help organizations generate sustainable products and services, assimilable by-products and ecologically sensitive and aware employees and stakeholders. Outputs will include strong infrastructures for recycling and remanufacturing, for environmental education and for stakeholder–organization interaction. In short, ESSs will value and use various strategies to promote organizational responsibility, transparency and cooperation.

Political-Economic Level

An ecologically sustainable society will interact with entities at the political-economic level to create governance and market institutions that encourage, facilitate and reward individual and organizational engagement in ecologically sustainable behavior. Key inputs to societal activity at this level will be accurate assessment of the ecological impacts of existing governmental policies and activities, of existing market forces and of alternatives from other systems. Societal institutions will then engage with government and business to alter laws, policies, agency actions, and so on. The result of such engagement will be transformed legal and economic structures and instruments that provide a combination of high regulatory standards, market-based incentives, sustainable policy instruments such as subsidies, taxes, loan and investment criteria, and the use of techniques such as full environmental cost accounting by public and private institutions. Such instruments and practices will not only encourage sustainable and discourage unsustainable behavior, but will also generate substantial feedback to citizens, consumers and managers that makes the links between behavioral choices and ecological conditions much more rapid and transparent. As both a means and an end, such efforts will involve values such as openness, democratic participation, civic engagement and the primacy of societal interest over self-interest. Strategies for engaging in such efforts and bringing about such outcomes will entail educational and other civic forums, advisory commissions in both the public and the private sector, and the infusion of a sustainability orientation into organizations in sectors such as education, religion, the media and associations (for example, trade, professional).

Socio-Cultural Level

The initial creation of an ecologically sustainable society is achieved through its interaction with entities at all of the levels addressed above. As this occurs, the shared values and beliefs of an ESS will be integrated into its society through consensus, the quest for the supernatural and social order, and narratives constructed as a response to inputs from other systems. For example, the Itza Maya of Guatemala attribute intentionality to the forces of nature, which results in sustainable behavioral norms and expectations that span all levels of internal social organization (Atran et al., 2002). But shared values and beliefs of the Itza Maya are incompatible with dominant, unsustainable, global economic forces. Thus, the focus at the socio-cultural level is how an ESS will interact with other societies.

An ESS interacting with a non-sustainable society will self-organize to promote change in the non-sustainable society. Socio-cultural inputs from external societies could include, for example, economic environmental externalities generated by other societies and ideologies of competition or human domination over nature. Interaction between an ESS and other societies could include sharing the ESS's internal perceptions of external threats to its sustainability. Some societies are working towards reconciling deep-seated cultural values that are incompatible with the global market. Switzerland, in particular, is one country that has 'a long history of particularly strong local institutions, which allows us to examine the strategies of subnational actors facing change and to evaluate the adaptive capacity of a set of longstanding institutions and values' (Wiegnadt, 2004, p. 110).

ESS strategies could include using dominant information sources like the news media to link external threats to sustainability with shared traditional values, consensus and social stability. Interactions with other societies that are not ecologically sustainable can also include using sustainability as a form of resistance to domination through education, interaction with the natural environment, and construction of shared narratives with an ecological basis. Participants in Community Supported Agriculture often rely on narratives of opposition to the globalization of agriculture and the loss of ecological diversity as a main reason for involvement in the movement. Interactions with other societies that are not ecologically sustainable can also include attempting to help them move toward sustainability. The challenge is to find ideological commonalities, or to identify potential loci of miscommunication regarding sustainability (Casagrande, 2004). Interactions with other ESSs will likely focus on providing mutual reinforcement. The values emphasized at this level include the balance of stability versus adaptation, social consensus regarding sustainability and well-being, and multicultural tolerance.

TOWARDS AN ECOLOGICALLY SUSTAINABLE SOCIETY

We believe that the characteristics of an ESS that we identify in Table 2.2 can provide guidance for a society attempting to move toward sustainability.

Below we specifically illustrate the meaning of the attributes we have identified by developing some suggestions as to how these ESS concepts could be applied to the challenge of achieving societal sustainability in a specific case: the Republic of the Marshall Islands (RMI). Rather than being an 'ecotopian' (Callenbach, 1975) paradise, RMI is a lower-middle-income developing nation in the South Pacific facing significant problems such as rapidly growing population, limited resources (natural, financial and technological), declining resource stocks (fisheries) and potentially catastrophic ecological change (global warming). These are conditions that have led some to conclude that the concept of sustainable development may have little applicability to RMI in its present form (Ribbens and Ribbens, 1999). We are not so pessimistic. As an island nation, RMI may be more responsive to ecological change because it is a small, geographically secluded, and relatively homogeneous society, where environmental information is reasonably accessible at all levels of social organization. Also, citizens of RMI may share a more coherent belief system than other more complex societies. We believe that developing useful prescriptions for becoming an ESS in the case of RMI would provide support for the ESS attributes we have identified in this chapter, as well as for the initial approach of Starik and Rands (1995). This is not to deny, however, that Marshallese society may find it difficult nonetheless to withstand external threats (environmental and economic) or manage natural resources that cover a large geographic area.

THE REPUBLIC OF THE MARSHALL ISLANDS

The Republic of the Marshall Islands (RMI) consists of 29 coral atolls roughly organized into two chains in the western Pacific Ocean north of the equator between 4 degrees and 14 degrees north, and 160 degrees and 173 degrees east (Levy, 1996). The total land area of RMI is 180 km^2 (World Bank, 1997) which is comprised of approximately 1225 islets. Archeological finds suggest that the atolls were settled about 4000 years ago (RMI Online, 2005); all of Micronesia was claimed by Spain in 1494 under the Treaty of Tordesillas. While the RMI atolls were first 'discovered' by Spain in 1529, the Germans established the first outpost there in 1885 to trade in copra (dried coconut flesh) (US Department of State, 2005). Until the Japanese took control at the beginning of World War I, the traditional male chiefs (Iroj) maintained control as the governance mechanism.

Like many other Pacific Islanders, the traditional Marshallese subsistence patterns were based on a combination of swidden (slash and burn) agriculture and fishing. Swidden agricultural, as defined by agricultural economist Esther Boserup (1993), is a form of agriculture where land can be used intermittently, with heavy reliance on fire to clear fields and fallowing to restore soil fertility. This form of shifting cultivation requires a delicate balance of human population and natural resources. Ecologically diverse gardens produced food crops like giant taro *Alocasia maccrohiza*, breadfruit *Artocarpus mariannensis* and *Artocarpus altilis*, spider lily *Crinum bakeri*, swamp taro *Cyrtosperma chamissionis*, coconut *Cocos nucifer*, banana *Musa sapientum*, pandanus *Pandanus tectorius* and arrowroot *Tacca leontopetaloides* (Spennemann, 2000).

Traditional Marshallese agriculture required a deep knowledge of the environment. From a cultural perspective, agriculture is more than just food production. It also tells us much about the culture. The Marshallese were able successfully to practice swidden agriculture by balancing population density to natural resource availability through implementation of matrilineal, kin-based access to garden plots. Kinship networks were expanded to neighboring islands through marriage (Kiste, 1974; Mason, 1947). These extended networks afforded family units the opportunity to trade with neighboring kin for resources they were unable to produce or procure on their own. These forms of cultural adaptation are comparable to traditional Native North American Hopi agricultural practices, wherein the Hopi possessed a detailed understanding of their physical environment and garden plots, and kinship networks were based on matrilineal kinship ties (Vasquez and Kuwanwisiwma, 2001). Current ecological and cultural conditions in RMI make this form of agriculture an unsustainable option. Current levels of population density are much too high to support shifting cultivation and would result in ecological devastation. In addition, global climate changes have resulted in the loss of land mass and contamination of fresh water sources. Societal changes in the economy and gender roles, and the loss of cultural and ecological knowledge among the Marshallese, also reflect the change in traditional culture.

During World War II, the United States assumed control after fierce fighting with the Japanese, and post-war developed the Trust Territory of the Pacific Islands which included the Marshall Islands. The process toward independent status began in the late 1970s with the drafting of a constitution and organization of a government, and became complete in the mid-1980s with the change in name and recognition as an independent government by other nations and world organizations.

The official 2005 RMI population estimate is 59 071 people, with 38.2 percent of the population in that year under age 15 (RMI Online, 2005). The estimated annual population growth rate in 1988 was very high (4.3 percent) and by 2010 the population was predicted to be 91 411 people. However, by 1993, the growth rate had dropped to 3.6 percent after the government increased its health education and family planning resources (Cappelle, 1996). The estimated population growth rate currently is 2.27 percent (US Central Intelligence Agency, 2005). Another factor contributing to the decline in growth rate has been emigration; Pacific Profile (2005) suggests that out-migration to the United States has reduced the rate of natural increase to 1.5 percent. Some reports suggest that approximately one in five ethnic Marshallese now reside in the US (US Department of State, 2005). Approximately half of the population lives in two locations – Majuro, an atoll containing the capital city of the same name, and Ebeye, an islet adjacent to the US military base on Kwajalein Atoll.

RMI is classified as a lower-middle-income economy by the World Bank (1997), with a per capita GDP of $1487 in 1990 which has increased slightly to $1600 in 2001 (all money is stated in United States dollars). This increase in per capita GDP of approximately 0.6 percent annually was well less than inflation over the same period. The GDP is based primarily on direct aid from the United States government which accounts for 67.8 percent of the FY2006 national budget (State Department, 2005). Over half of the economy is service-based; in 2005, service is estimated to account for 57.7 percent of the economy (RMI Online, 2005). In 1994 RMI imported $70.4 million in goods but only exported $22.2 million, resulting in a negative balance of trade of $48.2 million (RMI Online, 2000). This pattern is fairly consistent across time with imports in 2000 of $54 million and exports of $9 million (US Central Intelligence Agency, 2005). About 64 percent of all jobs in RMI are in the public sector (US Department of State, 2005).

According to the World Health Organization (WHO) high population growth and crowded conditions in urban areas have resulted in diseases such as tuberculosis and leprosy among the Marshallese people. In addition, changes in traditional culture have brought about a rise in levels of adult obesity, non-communicable diseases, teenage pregnancy, suicide, alcoholism and tobacco use (WHO, 2005).

Ribbens and Ribbens (1999) examined RMI and found a spectrum of issues which have kept sustainability an illusory goal. These issues include overpopulation, fragile and damaged ecosystems, and a lack of both financial and human resources. In addition, RMI faces some cultural difficulties due to its history. The citizens have been widely exposed to Western ideals and thus have shifted from a more traditional set of goals and desires to a more materialistic Western lifestyle. However, some attitudinal issues, such as time management and resource use, remain more traditionally Marshallese. The President of RMI has recently begun to enforce work hours for government employees to ensure that government services are provided, and has begun an examination of reducing the government workforce by expecting individuals to fulfill a 40-hour work week (*Marshall*

Islands Journal, 2000). Another attitudinal challenge is moving the mindset of the population from survival to conservation. For example, marine resources in RMI are not fully protected and the focus remains on exploitation, not conservation (Harding, 1992).

The government is young – full independence came in 1986 – with little tradition of setting or managing environmental policy. The national environmental protection authority (RMIEPA) was created in 1984. A great deal of legal and administrative work remains to be done within RMIEPA and other government ministries before a strong national assessment program is put into place (Harding, 1992, p. 18). As of 1992, its 12 employees focused on solid waste, earthmoving, water quality and pesticide use (Harding, 1992), leaving scant resources for larger strategic issues or education. Marshallese individuals focus on jobs and economic issues, and the RMI government is preoccupied with the overall economic difficulties which are exacerbated by the fact that it has little or no power to influence its global partners.

Furthermore, the low atolls that comprise RMI are highly susceptible to damage if climate change produces any significant increase in sea level. The average height above sea level on most islands is 2 meters, so an increase of the sea level of just 30 cm would significantly encroach on the already limited land mass. The vulnerability to waves and storm surges is at the best of times precarious. Although the islands have by no means been free from weather extremes, they are more frequently referred to in folklore as *jolet jen Anij* (gifts from God). The notion that the Marshall Islands are a God-given sanctuary away from the harshness of other areas is a crucial part of the socio-cultural identity of the people.

The recent El Niño event of 1997–98 created a temporary sea level rise of 2 cm (Environmental News Network, 1998). The ambassador to the United Nations from RMI, Jackeo Relang, in a speech on the floor of the United Nations stated that RMI has already lost meters of useable and habitable land to climate change and sea level rise (Relang, 2000). Additionally, changes in climate patterns could substantially lengthen the drought season and increase the severity of typhoons (Connell and Maata, 1992). Given the increasing frequency and severity of storms and the physics of storm surges, the Marshall Islands will likely be at even greater risk, placing the Marshallese among the first of many environmental refugees (Embassy of the Republic of the Marshall Islands, n.d.).

An additional complicating factor to achieving an ESS in RMI deals with the historical use of the island nation as a nuclear testing and now waste depository site. Nuclear testing in RMI began in 1946 with the famous test at Bikini Atoll and continued until 1996. Currently, RMI and other island nations are being targeted by both state and private commercial enterprises as ideal locations for the disposal of nuclear waste. 'Islands have always been seen as good laboratory sites because of their isolation within vast oceanic regions. Here the "inputs" and "outputs" of the organic system are perceived to be more easily observed and controlled' (Kuletz, 2002, p. 137).

While on an ecological and on a human level these events have been devastating, ranging from the vaporization of an entire islet to the emergence of birth defects known as 'jelly-fish babies' – fetuses born without eyes, heads, or legs (Kuletz, 2002, p. 128), the nuclearization of RMI has forged the links of resistance among RMI and other Pacific Island nations in the formation of a 'pan-islander identity politics' which emerged in the late 1970s and peaked in 1996 surrounding the French nuclear tests (Kuletz, 2002). The formation of a new socio-cultural identity may be one of the variables useful in achieving an ESS.

Ribbens and Ribbens (1999) conclude that serious and substantial obstacles exist which are unlikely to be successfully overcome using traditional conceptualizations of sustainable development in RMI. The high rate of population growth, increasing demand for consumable goods, severely limited ecological resilience and the need to transform decision-making are all serious challenges to any successful implementation of sustainable development.

APPLICATION OF ESS CHARACTERISTICS TO THE REPUBLIC OF THE MARSHALL ISLANDS

Given this background on the current social, environmental, economic and cultural conditions in RMI, we will now attempt to apply the attributes of an ecologically sustainable society identified earlier in this chapter (see Table 2.2) to the case of the Marshall Islands. The various applications of these attributes are summarized in Table 2.3. Our examples necessarily cross levels, but are introduced within the level in which they are most directly applicable.

Ecological Level

At the ecological level, the entities with which Marshallese society is interacting are the ecosystems of the Marshall Islands, Micronesia as a whole, and the global climate system. Accordingly, input levels to monitor include energy production and utilization, fish stocks, coconut and biomass production, and soil nutrient levels.

A current fundamental impediment to RMI sustainability is that most energy, food and other goods must be imported from outside of the

Table 2.3 Application of ESS characteristics to the Republic of the Marshall Islands

	Inputs	Throughputs	Outputs	Feedback	Values	Strategies
Ecological	Extractable resources such as fisheries, nutrients. Ocean, sunshine, wind, wave, tidal, biomass energy	Sustainable aquaculture and agriculture practices. Solar, wind, wave and tidal energy generation. Neighborhood recycling/reuse	Recycled/remanufactured aluminum, steel, glass, plastics. Zero waste. Sustainable extractive resource exports	Comprehensive monitoring and analysis of both terrestrial and marine environments	See importance of clean terrestrial/ marine environment for health, economic well-being and aesthetics	Develop system-wide policies for recycling and waste reduction. Provide support for small business which remanufacture plastics, etc.
Individual	Provide information, promote norms and teach skills such as: organic gardening, exercise, nutritious diet, initiative, creativity, wise reproductive choices	Encourage individual decision-making in each realm of life which acknowledges the importance of ecosystem protection and waste minimization	Recognize and praise sustainable outputs such as: town meeting participation, neighborhood recycling projects, sustainable consumption, kin-based gardening, ideas for innovative resource use (e.g. coconut bio-diesel)	Disseminate environmental knowledge about the effects of pollution and the effects of their decisions via town meetings, interviews, media, sermons	Identify and promote values that integrate sustainability and traditional norms, community self-reliance and self-confidence	Increase educational opportunities, lifelong learning. Empowerment, sustainable economic opportunities, access to healthy lifestyles
Organizational	Recruit organizations which bring environmentally friendly policies	Provide incentives to 'green' practices of current organizations, infuse	Better locally produced goods and services which involve less waste and less energy use for	Request more funding for EPA to support better monitoring and enforcement of	Hold companies and individuals responsible for acts of environmental	Invest in green Abeta@ testing: companies, international development

	and knowledge, including kinship and chiefdom-based social networks	organizations with sustainable values	transport to RMI. Use organizational policies to educate workers about non-employee green decision-making, entrepreneurship tied to kin-based resource management, community-based energy production	current laws, develop publicity system to provide information about greener practices and successes using them, monitor household economic productivity and social capital	destruction, create a forum for resolving conflict between different priorities such as economic development and environmental protection	agencies, national governments. Build coalitions with international environmental groups to build support for RMI's plight and gather ideas to improve internal environmental practices
Political-Economic	NGOs	Remove corruption from legal process	Improve the efficiency and effectiveness of government processes, free resources for environmental protection, economic integration of islands	Provide timely monitoring and reporting of economic and ecological indicators	Open the behaviors of government officials to public scrutiny, set high standards of behavior for government employees, grassroots monitoring of ecological issues	Hold public meetings to discuss revisions of: RMI laws and policies, trade/fishing treaties, Compact of Free Association (US)
Socio-Cultural	Traditional norms, knowledge and historical narratives. Religious	Multicultural environmental education. Ecological	Recognition of external threats to sustainability and internal social	Information about changes in external awareness of threats to internal	Traditional values in opposition to external ideologies. Relevance of	Dominant information sources focus on history and

Table 2.3 (*continued*)

	Inputs	Throughputs	Outputs	Feedback	Values	Strategies
	environmental worldviews. External market ideologies	narratives of resistance	stability. Recognition of others of need to adapt to change	sustainability. Information about norms, values and consensus regarding sustainability	bilingual environmental education. Historical tradition-based sustainability. Economic independence. Ecological interdependence	traditional values as sustainable. Global publicity of ecological plight. Involvement in global pro-sustainability coalitions

country. Waste from these products is not recycled and accumulates in the environment. The trade deficit creates a dependence on foreign assistance, while a low internal energy production capacity combined with lack of capital and technology exacerbates unsustainable resource extraction (for example, fish and copra) required to pay for imported necessities. Furthermore, the global market devalues traditional knowledge, norms and subsistence, completing a positive feedback loop of dependency. The current welfare-oriented social system is incompatible with traditional values, social organization and diet. Sustainable intervention, as we define it here, requires combining traditional knowledge, social organization and ecologically sustainable production with new technologies in a manner that breaks the dependency feedback loop. The four main foci of intervention are education, health, energy and technology. Table 2.3 identifies various ecological-level characteristics that must be developed. We briefly summarize these here, but develop examples more fully in the discussion of the levels that follow based on their primary level of implementation.

Marshallese society must utilize extractable resources at sustainable yield levels. Particular use should be made of renewable sources of energy (for example, sun, tide, wind, wave and biomass). Local energy generation, sustainable aquaculture and agriculture, and extensive recycling and reuse must form the basis for throughputs. This will yield dramatically lowered levels of waste and provide material outputs. This may also require reduction of exports of locally extracted resources. Extensive monitoring must occur to ensure production and use at sustainable levels. Initiating such practices requires the establishment and reinforcement of the value of a sustainable natural environment. Promoting and achieving sustainable values and practices will require strategies that support broader individual, political, economic and social goals. Chief among such strategies should be locally based extraction, recycling and remanufacturing business which are controlled by and will benefit the Marshallese people first and foremost.

Individual Level

Entities at the individual level include Marshallese citizens as well as others who visit or occupy RMI including tourists, US military personnel and foreign fishermen. Change at the individual level may be the easiest and most rewarding for the Marshallese people. Expanding waistlines and associated health problems like diabetes are among the most pressing health concerns for many in RMI and other developing countries. According to Yamada and Palafox 'diabetes is not simply a metabolic problem of elevated serum glucose. Our examination reveals the manner in which diabetes . . . is socially produced – that at its roots are economic interests, cultural disruption, and ecological destruction' (2001, p. 704).

The link between health and ecological sustainability derives from traditional subsistence, which formally linked diet with kin-based social cooperation and sustainable use of natural resources. The declining health of indigenous populations undergoing cultural change through increased contact with Western cultures is widely documented. For example, extensive studies of the Native Americans in North and South America show alarming increases in diabetes and obesity with the adoption of a Western lifestyle that results in limited physical activity and high-fat, high-sugar diets (Venkat Narayan, 1997; Williams et al., 2000; Wing et al., 2001).

Traditional staple food crops in RMI consisted of taro and breadfruit, which have been displaced by imported white rice as the basic starch. The displacement of some of the islanders from their home atolls for employment and/or the abandonment of kinship-based garden plots means that traditional agriculture and marine-based foods have been abandoned for imported processed and canned foods. As a result of new economic forms, people lead more sedentary lives than in the past and depend less on their traditional kinship network. Many extended kin groups have been separated and cultural norms regarding diet and child rearing have been lost (Yamada and Palafox, 2001).

We advocate providing information and promoting traditional cultural norms related to organic kinship-based gardening, balanced nutrition, exercise and individual initiative. Encouraging and rewarding ecologically and nutritional sound decision-making in the form of 'neighborhood garden of the month' prizes and/or school garden projects that showcase valuable ecological knowledge increase physical activity, promote self-reliance and confidence, foster a sense of community and kin networks, and increase educational opportunities for lifelong learning, empowerment and sustainable economic activities. Other activities such as the establishment of a neighborhood-based recycling program foster the concept of sustainable consumption, reduce the effects of pollution and increase sustainable economic activities.

Bilingual (English and Marshallese) school curricula and public education campaigns could emphasize traditional knowledge, language, gardening and diet, as well as ecological sustainability. Community and private gardens and fishing cooperatives based on traditional subsistence could be promoted to emphasize nutrition. We are not suggesting that island ecosystems can support the current population using traditional subsistence strategies. However, relic knowledge of traditional gardening, fishing and maritime navigation provide powerful sources of national pride. New twists on traditional subsistence can also enhance nutrition on a local basis and reduce dependency on foreign foods to some extent.

Traditional practices and norms can provide the basis for adapting new sustainable food production strategies and techniques. For example, the use of intensive composting or mulching could be used as a substitute for the more traditional slash-and-burn form of agriculture, thereby resulting in a new form of slash-and-mulch agriculture. From a different angle, taro, which is a traditional food crop that is high in starch, could be reintroduced to replace imported rice which provides the same amount of starch and other nutrients, thereby reducing the need to import staple foods. The cultivation and processing of taro, if conducted in a sustainable practice, could lead to increased physical activity and better health.

Organizational Level

The central need at the interaction of the socio-cultural level with the organizational level is for societal institutions and structures to encourage the development of sustainable values, goals, skills and practices within large numbers of specific profit and non-profit sector organizations. Entities at the organizational level include individual businesses, government agencies, schools, churches, media organizations, NGOs, and so on. Businesses such as hotels, construction companies, food processors and producers, and households and residential communities must be formally and informally educated about the importance and viability of sustainable practices. Assistance from non-RMI organizations with sustainability expertise should be sought in order to help develop expertise in sustainability among local organizations. Due to the need for viable locally owned businesses, the emphasis should be on importing expertise, not supplanting local organizations with external ones. Similar development of expertise is needed among non-profit organizations such as schools, churches and particularly US military units and contractors.

As sustainability expertise and practices are developed, more sustainable outputs will emerge from organizations, both in the form of products and services, and also in the form of transmission of sustainability information and encouragement to individual employees, customers and members of organizations. Attempts to engage in sustainability practices should result in greater demands by organizations for facilitative activities by RMI government agencies, in the form of technical assistance, grants and stricter law enforcement. Interaction with organizations will depend upon values that hold businesses responsible for their environmental behavior, that recognize the necessity of individual non-profit organizations reinforcing the sustainability message, and that firmly uphold the essential compatibility of the economic, social and ecological components of sustainability.

Strategies for carrying out such interaction can include seeking assistance from the peak organizations to which individual organizations belong or relate (for example, the environmental committee of the diocese of the Catholic Church, or the National Council of Churches; a green small business association or environmental committee of a Pacific Island business association; an ecotourism organization). In addition, seeking assistance from the sustainability-promoting units of international development agencies, other Pacific Island governments, the RMIEPA, international environmental organizations, and so on will likely be needed. Such efforts should be led at the societal level by coalitions of leaders of societal institutions such as kinship networks, schools, churches, business owners, civic organizations and political leaders.

We advocate a nationwide private-, government- and NGO-funded sustainability initiative that could begin by using local, community-based energy production. The New Zealand-based NGO Empower Consultants Limited is exploring the introduction of small-scale, coconut-fueled, bio-diesel, electric generators on outer islands. This technology would be based on a renewable resource, would be accessible to all islands, and requires cooperation that can leverage traditional social organization. Coconut plantation management and harvesting are based on traditional political leadership, kinship and gender roles. Micro-credit programs could support entrepreneurial co-operatives involving traditional weaving co-operatives or manufacturing of hammocks and products for sale on other islands and to tourists. A comprehensive urban recycling program based on traditional ecological values could provide a resource for manufacturing plastic products when combined with simple technologies like injection molding and using energy from community-based bio-diesel generators. Such an initiative would reduce waste, strengthen community solidarity and economic links between the various islands, and weaken dependency on at least some imported products.

Political-Economic Level

As Table 2.2 notes, the existing laws and market forces that influence environmental behaviors and outcomes serve as a starting point for transformation of these laws and forces into more ecologically sustainable states. A key actor in this transformation at the intersection of the socio-cultural level and the political-economic level are social institutions, such as NGOs, religious, educational and kinship networks. Creation of an ESS in RMI therefore requires that such social actors begin to recognize the desirability of sustainability and the necessity of altering political-economic instruments, and begin to take such action. There is evidence that such action is beginning to take place. In 2001, a nationwide economic and social summit articulated a 'people's vision' of RMI as a country within an interdependent world, with an enhanced socio-economic self-reliance, an educated, healthy, productive, law-abiding and God-loving people in which individual freedom and fundamental human rights are protected, culture and traditions are respected, and development and environmental sustainability are in harmony (RMI News, 2005).

Recognition of the unsustainability of current practices and trends is noted, and the relationship of poor environmental and social conditions to economic malaise and poor governance is explicitly stated. The widespread absence of good governance, accountability and transparency is noted, and the presence of corruption and nepotism are specifically highlighted. The existence of weak domestic environmental management mechanisms is also identified as a problem. 'Improved integration of environmental issues into local and national planning and development is required. Moreover, far more attention and focus on environmental issues is needed from both political and traditional leaders' (RMI News, 2005).

Strengthening of socio-cultural institutions in RMI, and an increased commitment to sustainability on their part must continue in order to bring about the transformation in political and economic throughputs and, as a result, outputs and feedback called for in Table 2.3. The sustainability initiative we describe above includes economic and political integration of islands. Sustainability also requires grassroots networks that monitor and creatively work to resolve ecological issues. Variables of analysis for policy evaluation can include: (1) economic activity; (2) health parameters; (3) psychological satisfaction; (4) community solidarity (social capital); and (5) ecological parameters (fish stocks, coconut reproduction, pollution, and so on) as indicated in Tables 2.2 and 2.3. Establishing goals, monitoring variables and readjusting policies as needed could create a sustainable feedback.

Socio-Cultural Level

As noted previously in our discussion of socio-cultural level of Table 2.2, the focus at this level is the interaction of Marshallese society with other societies, particularly those of other Pacific islands, and of influential nations such as the United States, Australia, New Zealand, Japan and Taiwan. While Table 2.3 emphasizes these external interactions, we acknowledge that Marshallese society must initially develop the internal socio-cultural elements of an ESS. It can do so as it engages in the interactions with the

Marshallese ecosystems, people, organizations and government and market forces described above.

Internal inputs at the socio-cultural level include traditional norms that allowed more sustainable existence in the past, including kinship-based social networks, trade between islands, traditional diet, subsistence knowledge and historical narratives of past protection of resources. As noted in Table 2.2, these must be reconciled with external inputs at this level, including religious views regarding the environment, non-sustainable ideologies of market competition and of human dominance over nature, and economic principles that externalize environmental costs. Sustainability would require throughputs that reconcile conflicting internal and external values, norms and ideologies. As noted in our discussion of previous levels, these could include restructuring school curricula to include traditional ecological and nutritional education, the role individuals play in protecting the environment, and non-monetary costs of environmental degradation. Ecological narratives of traditional resistance to external threats could be adapted to emphasize threats to internal sustainability and could be promoted through the media. Outputs include widespread recognition of external threats to sustainability and social stability.

Feedback forums could bring together young and old to reshape old cultural norms into new environmentally friendly norms in response to external ideologies. Survey research could monitor norms and values across scales from individuals to the nation; in particular, consensus in public opinion regarding external, non-sustainable ideologies. The media could promote indigenous Marshallese spokespeople who link traditional lifestyle, ecological sustainability, recycling and health as an alternative to foreign resource extraction, waste, trade deficits and dependence on foreign assistance. Values emphasized at the socio-cultural level in a Marshall Islands ESS would include traditional values in opposition to external ideologies, including traditional ecological knowledge, economic independence, an appreciation of bilingual environmental education, and holding resources for future generations as opposed to resource export.

As described in our discussion of Table 2.2, sustainability at the socio-cultural level also requires an ESS to integrate sustainability into non-ESS external systems with which it interacts. In this case, such interaction with the United States, Australia, New Zealand, Japan and Taiwan may be particularly important. The US, for example, currently leads the world in carbon gas emissions and bears the responsibility of egregious past policies in RMI. The policies, practices and ecological values of these societies, along with those of RMI, serve as inputs. Throughputs emphasize acts of societal engagement designed to promote sustainability in other societies. Marshallese expatriates living in the US could serve as 'cultural brokers' to change US ideologies by articulating a new ecological narrative based on traditional values and resistance, and emphasizing the plight of sea level rise in RMI. RMI has also partnered with other Pacific island nations in climate change negotiations, bringing new ecological narratives to the world stage. Such throughput processes would hopefully bring about outputs of increased understanding in these societies of the extent to which they threaten the sustainability of Marshallese society (among others). This increased understanding would hopefully lead to the strengthening of pro-ecological and pro-responsibility values in these societies. The strategies used to promote these understandings and values could also include new mutually reinforcing relations with other nations that are showing signs of attempting to become ESSs, such as Switzerland and some of the Nordic countries.

CONCLUSION

In this chapter we have attempted to accomplish three goals: identify the essential systemic attributes of entities at five levels; develop an ideal type that identifies the characteristics that an ecologically sustainable society would have in its systemic interactions with entities at these five levels; and suggest how this framework could be applied in the case of a specific society that faces significant challenges to its ecological sustainability. In so doing we have attempted to demonstrate the broader relevance of the approach taken by Starik and Rands (1995) with respect to ecologically sustainable organizations, to specify the implicit assumptions underlying their work and thereby strengthen their approach, and to suggest the applicability of their general approach to the case of a particular entity. We believe that each of these attempts represents a meaningful contribution to the literature on sustainability, and provides opportunities for further theoretical and practical contributions.

Our identification of essential systemic characteristics of entities at each of the five levels provides a firmer basis for the approach taken by Starik and Rands, and can therefore aid those organizational researchers who in the future wish to draw upon and/or extend their work. In addition, it provides a basis for developing analogues of their ESO ideal type at other levels of analysis.

Our development of such an ideal type at the socio-cultural level demonstrates the robustness of this approach, and the ability to extend it to other disciplines beyond organizational scholarship. Development of similar ideal types at the individual level and the political-economic level should also be possible.

By applying this model to the case of the society in the Republic of the Marshall Islands we hope to have strengthened the case for the relevance of our ESS ideal type. We believe that it also demonstrates the practical relevance of applying the ESO ideal type to particular organizations. Most importantly, we believe that our suggestions for the creation of a sustainable Marshallese society can provide the basis for meaningful action that can enhance its sustainability. One of the Marshall Islands Millennium Development Goals is to 'Ensure Environmental Sustainability' (RMI-UNDP, 2005). We hope that our work can also encourage the Marshallese to think about the interconnections across the levels of their society in order to increase effective progress toward their goal and to broaden their perspective of directions to consider in pursuit of their goal.

While not a primary focus of this chapter, we believe that another contribution we have made is to broaden our understanding of the essential elements of sustainability, extending it beyond the '3 Es'. While the critical role of cultural acceptability has been pointed out by many scholars, it is too frequently ignored, particularly in the literature on organizational sustainability. Not surprisingly, the focus of this chapter on the socio-cultural level reveals the inextricable interconnectedness of cultural and social sustainability with ecological sustainability more clearly than would a focus on any other level.

Potentially more significantly, we may be the first to suggest that self-efficacy plays a critical role in motivating efforts to engage in sustainable activities, and that the degree to which an action is 'managerially sustainable' is therefore an essential component of the overall sustainability of an action. We believe that this is important at the individual, organizational, political-economic and socio-cultural levels. Further development of the notion that actions that are objectively sustainable must be perceived to be within an entity's managerial capabilities would seem to be warranted, and worthy of attention by scholars in various disciplines.

This chapter has two primary limitations. First, as acknowledged earlier, the concept of a society engaging in purposeful action is awkward. One could argue that all actions at the socio-cultural level will be engaged in by either individuals or organizations. While we acknowledge the logic of this argument, we believe that discussing action at the socio-cultural level has several benefits. It underscores the need for widespread changes in knowledge, skills and attitudes that are nonetheless perceived as consistent with traditional values and norms. This suggests the critical need for collaborative action by representatives of all societal institutions. As such it suggests that use of adversarial and competitive strategies by particular individuals or organizations cannot bring about a sustainable society, at least not by themselves.

A second limitation is that this chapter merely represents 'armchair theorizing'. Our application of ESS characteristics to Marshallese society have not been tested. Neither are they the work of members of Marshallese society. They do, however, reflect direct experience with and substantial familiarity with various data on RMI. The practical relevance of these suggestions remain to be demonstrated, however. The application of these ideas is clearly an area in which we hope to engage, in an action-research context. In a similar vein, we would encourage organizational scholars interested in sustainability to attempt increasingly to apply their theories and practical suggestions to actual cases.

We must again re-emphasize that we have not presented a framework of a fully sustainable society, but of an ecologically sustainable society. We have been guided by the assumption that moving toward ecological sustainability is not possible without attending to social, cultural, economic and managerial sustainability concerns. But the explication of a framework for a society that is sustainable in all of these ways is beyond the scope of this chapter.

A final comment is in order. We believe that this chapter underscores the benefit that can result from the interaction of organizational scholars with scholars from different disciplines. We believe that efforts to articulate, stimulate and study sustainability will require increased amounts of such interdisciplinary scholarship, and encourage those who have not yet ventured into such collaborative efforts to do so.

NOTES

1. In our treatment of inputs we include existing structural components as well as new entries into the system. We recognize that some real distinctions exist between these, but within the Katz and Kahn (1978) framework feel it is appropriate to treat these aspects together as inputs.
2. We express appreciation to Mark Cordano for this observation.

REFERENCES

Agrawal, Abinash (1997), *Community in Conservation: Beyond Enchantment and Disenchantment*, Gainesville, FL: Conservation and Development Forum.

Atran, Scott, Douglas Medin, Norbert Ross, Elizabeth Lynch, Valentina Vapnarsky, Edilberto Ucan Ek', John Coley, Christopher Timura and Michael Baran (2002), 'Folkecology, cultural epidemiology, and the spirit of the commons: a garden experiment in the Maya lowlands, 1991–2001', *Current Anthropology*, **43**, 421–50.

Boserup, Esther (1993), *The Conditions of Agricultural Change: The Economics of Agrarian Change Under Population Pressure*, New York: Earthscan Publications.

Browder, John O. (2002), 'Conservation and development projects in the Brazilian Amazon: lessons from the community initiative program in Rondonia', *Environmental Management*, **29**, 750–62.

Brown, Becky J., Mark E. Hanson, Diana M. Liverman and Robert W. Merideth Jr. (1987), 'Global sustainability: toward definition', *Environmental Management*, **11** (6), 713–19.

Brown, Lester R., Alan Durning, Christopher Flavin, Hilary French, Jodi Jacobson, Nicholas Lenssen, Marcia Lowe, Sandra Postel, Michael Renner, Linda Stark, Peter Weber and John Young (1993), *State of the World, 1993*, New York: Norton.

Bush, Mark B. (1997), *Ecology of a Changing Planet*, Upper Saddle River, NJ: Prentice Hall.

Callenbach, Ernest (1975), *Ecotopia*, San Francisco, CA: Banyan Tree Books.

Cappelle, D. (1996), 'Statement by the RMI Secretary of Health and the Environment to the Second United Nations Conference on Human Settlement', http://www.un.org/Conferences/habitat/eng~stat/14/mli14.txt, accessed 14 June 1996.

Casagrande, David G. (2004), 'Conceptions of primary forest in a Tzeltal Maya community: implications for conservation', *Human Organization*, **63**, 189–292.

Connell, John and Matakite Maata (1992), *Environmental Planning, Climate Change and Potential Sea Level Rise: Report on a Mission to the Republic of the Marshall Islands*, Apia, Western Samoa: South Pacific Regional Environmental Programme.

Day, B.A. and W.A. Smith (n.d.), 'The applied behavior change (ABC) framework for environmental applications', accessed at www.usaid.gov/environment/greencom/abcframe.pdf.

Dixon, John A. and Louise A. Fallon (1989), 'The concept of sustainability: origins, extensions and usefulness for policy', *Society and Natural Resources*, **2**, 73–84.

Doty, D. Harold and William H. Glick (1994), 'Typologies as a unique form of theory building: toward improved understanding and modeling', *Academy of Management Review*, **19**, 230–51.

Elkington, John (1998), *Cannibals With Forks: The Triple Bottom Line of 21st Century Business*, Philadelphia, PA: New Society Publishers.

Embassy of the Republic of the Marshall Islands (n.d.), http://www.rmiembassyus.org/, accessed 24 October 2005.

Environmental News Network (1998), 'El Niño spurs rise in global average sea level', accessed 9 December 1998 at http://cnn.com/TECH/science/9812/09/sealevel.yoto/index.html.

Escobar, Arturo (1992a), 'Imagining a post-development era? Critical thought, development, and social movements', *Social Text*, **31/32**, 20–56.

Escobar, Arturo (1992b), 'Reflections on "development": grassroots approaches and alternative politics in the third world', *Futures*, **24** (5), 411–36.

Espinosa, M. Cristina (1998), 'Differentiated use of wildlife resources by riberenho families of the northeastern Amazon', dissertation in anthropology, University of Florida, Gainesville, FL.

Farrell, Alex and Maureen Hart (1998), 'What does sustainability really mean? The search for useful indicators', *Environment*, **40** (9), 5–9, 26–31.

Feldstein, Hillary and Susan V. Poats (1990), *Working Together: Gender Analysis in Agriculture*, West Hartford, CT: Kumarian Press.

Gladwin, Thomas N., James J. Kennelly and Tara S. Krause (1995), 'Shifting paradigms for sustainable development: implications for management theory and research', *Academy of Management Review*, **20**, 874–907.

Harding, Elizabeth (1992), *Review of Environmental Law: Republic of the Marshall Islands (RETA 5403)*, in the Strengthening Environment Management Capabilities in Pacific Island Developing Countries series, Sydney, Australia: South Pacific Regional Environment Programme.

Hawkes, Jon (2005), *The Fourth Pillar of Sustainability: Culture's Essential Role in Public Planning*, Sydney, Australia: Humanities Press.

Henn, Carl L. and James A. Fava (1994), 'Life-cycle analysis and resource management', in Rao V. Kolluru (ed.), *Environmental Strategies Handbook*, New York: McGraw-Hill, pp. 923–70.

Holling, Crawford S. (2003), 'Foreward: the backloop to sustainability', in Fikret Berkes, Johan Colding and Carl Folke (eds), *Navigating Social-Ecological Systems: Building Resilience for Complexity and Change*, Cambridge: Cambridge University Press, pp. xv–xxi.

Hwang, Yeong-Hyeon, Seong-Il Kim and Jiann-Min Jeng (2000), 'Examining the causal relationships among selected antecedents of responsible environmental behavior', *Journal of Environmental Education*, **31** (4), 19–25.

Katz, Daniel and Robert L. Kahn (1978), *The Social Psychology of Organizations*, 2nd edn, New York: John Wiley & Sons.

Kaus, Andrea (1993), 'Environmental perceptions and social relations in the Mapimí Biosphere Reserve', *Conservation Biology*, **7** (2), 398–406.

Kiste, Robert C. (1974), *The Bikinians: A Study in Forced Migration*, Menlo Park, CA: Cummings Publishing Co.

Kollmuss, Anja and Julian Agyeman (2002), 'Mind the gap: why do people act environmentally and what are the barriers to pro-environmental behavior?' *Environmental Education Research*, **8** (3), 239–60.

Kuletz, Valerie (2002), 'The movement for environmental justice in the Pacific Islands', in Joni Adamson, Mei Mei Evans and Rachel Stein (eds), *The Environmental Justice Reader: Politics, Poetics, and Pedagogy*, Tucson, AZ: University of Arizona Press, pp. 125–44.

Leopold, Aldo (1948/1987), *A Sand County Almanac*, New York: Oxford University Press.

Levy, Neil M. (1996), *Micronesia Handbook*, 4th edn, Chico, CA: Moon Publications.

Marshall Islands Journal (2000), 'Marshall Islands President Note's action plan: show up, do your job', 4 February.

Mason, Leonard E. (1947), 'The economic organization of the Marshall Islanders', *Human Relations Area Files*, Washington, DC: US Commercial Co.

Mayer, Aubrey L., Hale W. Thurston and Christopher W. Pawlowski (2004), 'The multidisciplinary influence of common sustainability indices', *Frontiers in Ecology and the Environment*, **2** (8), 419–26.

McIlvaine-Newsad, Heather (2003), 'Ojalá que lluevé algo en el campo: cultural influences of development', *International Journal of Agricultural Resources, Governance and Ecology*, **2**, 153–66.

McKenzie-Mohr, Doug and William Smith (1999), *Fostering Sustainable Behavior: An Introduction to Community-Based Social Marketing*, Gabriola Island, Canada: New Society Publishers.

Meadows, Donella H., Dennis L. Meadows and Jorgen Randers (1992), *Beyond the Limits*, Post Mills, VT: Chelsea Green.

Natcher, David C. and Clifford G. Hickey (2002), 'Putting the community back into community-based resource management: a criteria and indicators approach to sustainability', *Human Organization*, **61**, 350–63.
Pirages, Dennis C. (1977), *The Sustainable Society: Implications for Limited Growth*, New York: Praeger.
Poats, Susan, Marianne Schmink and Anita Spring (eds) (1987), *Gender Issues in Farming Systems Research and Extension*, Boulder, CO: Westview Press.
Rands, Gordon P. (1990), 'Environmental attitudes, behaviors and decision making: implications for management education and development', in W. Michael Hoffman, Robert E. Frederick and Edward S. Petry, Jr. (eds), *The Corporation, Ethics, and the Environment*, New York: Quorum Books, pp. 269–86.
Redclift, Michael (1992), 'The meaning of sustainable development', *Geoforum*, **23** (3), 395–403.
Relang, Jackeo (2000), 'Marshall Islands Statement to the United Nations at the Fifty-Fifth Session of the General Assembly of the United Nations on September 21, 2000', accessed at www.un.org/ga/webcast/statements/marshallisland E.htm.
Ribbens, Barbara and Gordon P. Rands (2001), 'Greening society in the Marshall Islands: a vision of ecological sustainability', presentation to the Eastern Academy of Management International Meeting, 15-18 June, San Jose, Costa Rica.
Ribbens, Barbara and Eric Ribbens (1999), 'Searching for sustainability in the Marshall Islands: development dreams clash with ecological reality', in Walter Wehrmeyer and Yacob Mulugetta (eds), *Growing Pains: Environmental Management in Developing Countries*, Sheffield: Greenleaf Publishing, pp. 283–95.
RMI News (2005), 'Social and economic report 2005 – a summary of key findings and issues', accessed 17 November 2005 at www.yokwe.net/print.php?sid=1224.
RMI Online (2005), 'Website of the Embassy of the Republic of the Marshall Islands', accessed 3 November at www.rmiembassyus.org.
RMI-UNDP (2005), 'Republic of the Marshall Islands Millennium Development Goals National Progress Report', published September 2005, accessed at www.spc.int/prism/mdg/Countries_natrpts/MDG%20RMI%20Report%20Rev%20II.pdf.
Sen, Gita and Caren Grown (1987), *Development, Crises, and Alternative Visions: Third World Women's Perspectives*, New York: Monthly Review Press.
Shiva, Vandana (2005), *Earth Democracy: Justice, Sustainability, and Peace*, Cambridge, MA: South End Press.
Spennemann, Dirk H.R. (2000), 'Plants and their uses in the Marshalls – food plants', accessed 15 December 2005 at http://marshall.csu.edu.au/Marshalls/html/plants/food.html.
Starik, Mark and Gordon P. Rands (1995), 'Weaving an integrated web: multilevel and multisystem perspectives of ecologically sustainable organizations', *Academy of Management Review*, **20**, 908–35.
Stepp, John R., Eric C. Jones, Mitchell Pavao-Zuckerman, David Casagrande and Rebecca K. Zarger (2003), 'Remarkable properties of human ecosystems', *Conservation Ecology*, **7** (3), 11.
Taylor, Dorceta E. (1989), 'Blacks and the environment: toward an explanation of the concern and action gap between blacks and whites', *Environment and Behavior*, **21** (2), 175–205.
United Nations Population Fund (2005), '2005 country profiles for population and reproductive health: policy developments and indicators', accessed at www.prb.org/pdf06/2005UNFPA_CountryProfiles_AsiaPacific.pdf.

US Central Intelligence Agency (CIA) (2005), *The World Factbook, 2005*, accessed at www.cia.gov/cia/publications/factbook/index.html.
US Department of State (2005), 'Population' section of US Department of State Post Reports on Marshall Islands, updated 29 November, accessed at http://foia.state.gov/MMS/postrpt/pr_view_all.asp?CntryID=95.
Vasquez, Miguel and Leigh Kuwanwisiwma (2001), personal communication with H. McIlvaine-Newsad, 15 July, Kykotsmovi, AZ.
Venkat Narayan, K.M. (1997), 'Diabetes mellitus in Native Americans: the problem and its implications', *Population Research and Policy Review*, **16** (1–2), 169–92.
Vroom, Victor H. (1964), *Work and Motivation*, New York: Wiley.
Wiegnadt, Ellen (2004), 'Losing ground: challenges to mountain agriculture in Switzerland', *Culture and Agriculture*, **26** (1–2), 110–23.
Williams, Robert, Jeffrey Long, Robert Hanson, Maurice Sievers and William Knowler (2000), 'Individual estimates of European genetic admixture associated with lower body-mass index, plasma glucose, and prevalence of Type 2 diabetes in Pima Indians', *American Journal of Human Genetics*, **66**, 527–38.
Wing, Rena R., Michael D. Goldstein, Kelly J. Acton, Leann L. Birch, John M. Jakicic, James F. Sallis, Jr., Delia Smith-West, Robert W. Jeffery and Richard S. Surwit (2001), 'Behavioral science research in diabetes lifestyle changes related to obesity, eating behavior, and physical activity', *Diabetes Care*, **24**, 117–23.
World Bank (1997), *World Development Report 1997: The State in a Changing World*, New York: Oxford University Press.
World Commission on Environment and Development (1987), *Our Common Future*, New York: Oxford University Press.
World Health Organization (WHO) (2005), '*Marshall Islands: health situation*', accessed 16 November at www.wpro.who.int/countries/msi/health_ situation. htm.
Yamada, Seiji and Neal Palafox (2001), 'On the biopsychosocial model: the example of political economic causes of diabetes in the Marshall Islands', *Family Medicine*, **33** (9), 702–4.

3. A use-centered perspective on sustainability: a case-study of land use in the American Southwest

Christa Walck

The crafting of long-term ecological and societal solutions to the problems created by global and capital-intensive systems of mass production requires consideration of both temporal and spatial dimensions of development. Development occurs over time as well as over space. While it is relatively easy to map the rapidly increasing spatial reach of organizations and their impact on global ecosystems, their temporal reach is more problematic. Few organizations live beyond a few generations. Western corporations have routinely been scolded for short-sightedness and limited planning. Although organizations are encouraged to create visions that can withstand the unpredictability and uncertainties of global markets, the rapid pace of change can undercut attempts to craft long-term solutions.

This plants a seed of doubt: Can such short-lived phenomena as organizations be responsible for crafting solutions for long-term ecological and societal sustainability? As organizations transform at a rapid pace, are organizational memories sufficiently deep and robust to safeguard visions and plans for ecological and social sustainability? And, if organizations do not live long enough to carry out viable strategies, what can? Historically, governments and communities, with their longer lives and longer memories, have stepped into the breach to hold organizations accountable with evolving regulatory regimes and public policies. Yet contemporary failures of both, coupled with the enormity of problems facing societies grappling with ecological and social sustainability and the growing global reach of corporations, have led some to conclude that organizations themselves must be part of the solution through voluntary efforts to manage growth and use natural resources in sustainable ways.

Mihelcic et al. (2003) defined sustainable development as the design of human systems to ensure that the use of natural resources does not diminish quality of life or adversely impact the environment. This definition recognizes the importance of both societal and ecological sustainability, as well as the importance of natural resource use to sustainable development. Ecological and societal sustainability are intimately connected: when ecosystems fail to function, the societies that they support also fail. Ecological functioning is the bedrock of sustainability. Ecological functioning depends on judicious use of natural resources – sustainable use, if the resource in question is a self-replicating biological entity, or smart, clean and efficient (not wasteful) use of resources such as water and minerals.

To reduce environmental impacts that result from unsustainable natural resource use, managers and engineers have designed organizational systems such as environmental management systems. However, this organization-centric view of resource use offers a limited view of the sustainability mosaic. Organizations use natural resources (inputs) to produce goods and services (outputs) which improve the quality of life for their customers. While organizations sometimes consider their impacts on a broader range of stakeholders, their use of natural resources can generate social inequities by privileging access to resources for some, while precluding access to others. Organizations are embedded in larger human systems, and organizational decisions about natural resource use can have broad and unintended consequences for actors in that system, including reduced ecological functioning which imperils the way of life of some actors in the larger system.

In this chapter, I will frame the human system in which organizations operate as an evolving 'complex of use' that connects uses and users. I trace the use of one natural resource by an evolving complex of users in a specific place over time: land in the American Southwest from 1860 to 2004. Called either grasslands or rangelands depending on one's emphasis on the resource (grass) or use (range for domesticated animals), this land is largely a public commons appropriated for private use. By unraveling the ways in which organizations used the resource, examining the impact of these uses on the environment and mapping an evolving complex of use, I hope to shed some light on possibilities for crafting long-term solutions for sustainable resource use that also sustains diverse human communities.

THE LENS: A USE-CENTERED PERSPECTIVE

If the ways in which organizations use natural resources are critical to sustainability, then a theory of use would be helpful. Theories of land use have focused on two issues. First, researchers have studied the intersection of geography and economics, such as the application of spatial and location theories to land markets that vary by use (agriculture, forestry, housing) or transportation access. This enabled researchers to map geospatial communities and calculate market boundaries (Thrall, 2002). Second, researchers have developed schemes to classify and model the impacts of land use on land cover using sophisticated remote sensing technologies. This enabled researchers to improve assessment and planning.

While both of these approaches have been applied to rangeland use in the American Southwest from economic and ecological perspectives, neither situated use in a cultural complex in which users (such as organizations) use the natural resource of land. For this reason, I turned to Johnson (1998), who elaborated a user-centered theory (Figure 3.1) which connected use and user, albeit for the purpose of theorizing technology use and innovation, not land use.[1]

Johnson noted the primacy of a system-centered view of technology in which the artifact was primary and designers of technology knew best how to use it; this assumed an external end (*telos*) of technology such as social good or social control, and privileged both the system and the designer or expert over the user. Johnson reconfigured the end (*telos*) of technology in the user, calling for a user-centered theory of technology in which a technology and its design should be in the best interest of the user. The user, not the designer, became an 'integral, participatory force in the process' of technology development (p. 30) as Johnson, a rhetorician, placed the user, technology, designer and task (end-use) into a complex of use by applying rhetorical theory. Earlier studies of technology development had focused on the end-use of technology at the expense of the complex of use and user. Johnson believed the productive knowledge of users was critical

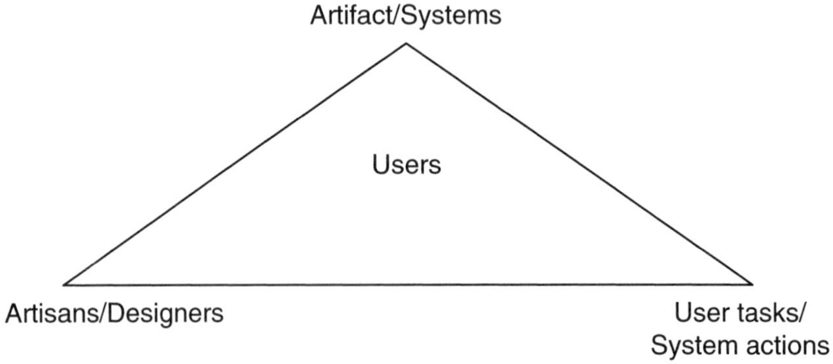

Source: Johnson, 1998, Figure 2.6, p. 36.

Figure 3.1 The user-centered rhetorical triangle

to developing appropriate technologies and placed the user of technology at the center of his model, closing the gap between expert and user and shifting power in the direction of the user through user participation in design. The designer was encouraged to engage in a dialogue with the user in order to create a better technology for use.

Johnson's model, although focused on technology use, offers an interesting way of thinking about land use in a complex of use in which users and uses, as well as technologies and experts, are interconnected. However, Johnson's placement of the user at the center of the model shifts our attention away from the end-use of the resource – how land is used and whether that use is sustainable. To re-emphasize end-use and posit the *telos* of land use to be sustaining the resource, I emphasize the relationship between user and use, the impact of use on the resource, and application of technologies and experts to mediate use by a user (Figure 3.2). Thus, while I adopt the components of Johnson's complex of use, I reconfigure the model as use-centered, rather than user-centered. While users may want direct and unmediated use of the resource, technology and experts often intervene to mediate use. In Figure 3.2, direct use and mediated use are differentiated. While some mediators increase unsustainable exploitation of the resource, others promote sustainable use. Mediators such as technology, experts or community activists may be a key to societal sustainability and equitable use.

Figure 3.3 shows how a use-centered approach can be applied to land use. In order for users such as farmers or conservationists to use land for crops or watershed protection, they need to acquire knowledge of the resource, often acquired from experts, and apply technologies, including management technologies.

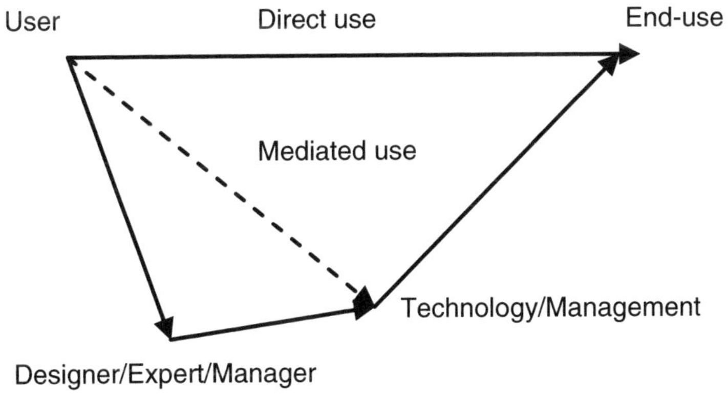

Figure 3.2 Use-centered perspective: end-use and mediated use

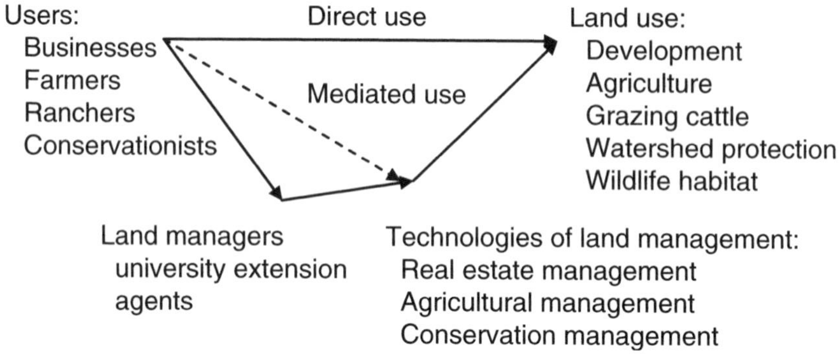

Figure 3.3 Use-centered perspective on land use

In the case-study which follows, the use-centered perspective will be used to frame historical changes in rangeland use, the emergence of experts and technologies to mediate it, and the impact of use on sustainability of the resource and of the social actors in the human system.

THE METHOD: HISTORICAL CASE-STUDY

Historians tend to take a narrative, atheoretical approach to their subjects. But history can also be used to discern patterns of behavior, and where there is pattern lurks theory. History can thus be used to develop theories and to some extent test them by revealing when, whether or how anticipated patterns emerge. Research for this chapter began as an historical narrative of land use and ranching in the grasslands of the American Southwest from 1860 to the present. However, as I started to view this history with a use-centered lens that emphasized a complex of use, I realized that I was tracing the use of a resource by a shifting set of users which was increasingly mediated by experts and technologies. The use-centered lens thus elicited an interesting pattern in the historical narrative.

The history that follows traces the use of rangeland in the American Southwest, the technologies that emerged to manage and mediate its use, both enabling and constraining it, and changing relationships among users, experts, technologies and land uses. Two caveats are in order. While ranching – cattle grazing by stockmen – has been the primary use of rangeland, this is not a history of the cattle industry. Moreover, since the majority of the grasslands studied were public lands, the expertise and technologies which emerged were developed by governmental agencies and public universities more so than private ranchers or the cattle industry, although the latter applied them (often under duress) to gain access to natural resource use. My understanding of the history of public lands ranching is grounded in research on the history of ranching in southwestern New Mexico and the Gila National Forest (MacLennan and Walck, forthcoming) as well as published studies of ranching in Arizona (Sheridan, 2001; Sayre, 2002; Sayre, 1999; Bahre and Shelton, 1996; Hirt, 1989) and excellent secondary sources for the history of public lands ranching in the West (Baker et al., 1988; Donahue, 1999; Foss, 1960; Graf, 1990; Jacobs, 1999; Jordan, 1993; Rowley, 1986; Stout, 1970).[2]

THE RESOURCE: RANGELAND OF THE AMERICAN SOUTHWEST

Before presenting the historical study, it is important to know something about the resource itself – in this case, the semi-arid grasslands which cover most of the American Southwest. It cannot be overemphasized that sustainable use of a natural resource requires specific and dedicated knowledge of the resource – expertise. The natural resource of land is defined by Aldo Leopold (1949/1970) as a community that includes soils, waters, plants and animals (p. 239). This concept of land requires knowledge of the interaction between soil types and hydrology, and the specific fauna and flora that have adapted to these conditions for life to function ecologically. The land of the Southwest is significantly shaped by one component: water, or more accurately, its scarcity. This scarcity determines the community of plants and animals that can adapt to the harsh conditions of little rain. The soils are surprisingly fertile when watered, but rain is confined to one short season and few rivers run through the land. In a land where margins for survival are razor-thin, small changes can wreak havoc. Introduction of exotic animals and plants create unintended consequences.

The American Southwest has been described as an 'ecological confusion zone' (Burgess, 1995), a grassland savannah sandwiched between arid desert scrub in the lower basins, and wetter woodland or forest on higher mountains. Soil moisture, coming in quick pulses of drenching rain separated by intervals of drought, governs plant growth. Different plants use different strategies to exploit the soil and water. Some store water (yucca, ocotillo); others use extensive root systems to access deeper soil moisture (woody brush plants with slow responses to rain, such as mesquite, juniper, acacia); and yet others use dense but intensive shallow root systems to respond rapidly to rain with fast growth and rapid colonization (grasses such as the annual red brome and herbaceous perennials such as black grama, as well as half-shrubs such as burro weed).

The opening of the semi-arid lands of the American Southwest to cattle ranching in the 1860s rapidly shifted the ecology of the region from perennial grassland to unpalatable woody shrubs, a successional shift in plant communities. Leopold observed this process and its attendant erosion first hand during his early days in the Forest Service in the American Southwest – brush has 'taken the country', he wrote – and he blamed grazing (Leopold, 1924). Recent studies have proved him right: numerous case-studies have established a strong link between livestock grazing and woody encroachment (Baker, 1996; Archer, 1994). They indicate that rates and patterns of succession have been rapid, non-linear, accentuated by climate fluctuation (periodic drought) and local factors, and are non-reversible over time-frames relevant to management. Moreover, once established, woody growth may redirect successional processes so that the new state persists even if grazing is reduced or eliminated (Archer, 1994). In addition to the change in plant communities, erosion in the form of deep gullies (arroyos) pockmarked the range. While extreme variability in climate in the Southwest makes it difficult to isolate natural erosion from erosion induced by human activity, and climate change may have facilitated the successional shift in plant communities, much of the severe erosion and sedimentation has been attributed to overgrazing by livestock in the nineteenth century. In other words, lack of understanding of the ecology of the region (expertise) led to an end-use (grazing) which was unsustainable.

After spending time in a relatively undamaged desert ecosystem in Mexico, Leopold poignantly observed 'that it is ironical that Chihuahua, with a history and a terrain so strikingly similar to southern New Mexico and Arizona should present so lovely a picture of ecological health, whereas our own states . . . are so badly damaged that only tourists and others ecologically color-blind, can look upon them without a feeling of sadness and regret' (Leopold, 1937, p. 201).

THE HISTORY OF RANGELAND USE IN THE AMERICAN SOUTHWEST, 1860–2004

Overview

While many have pondered the politics of grass (Foss, 1960) and implicated short-sighted ranchers in this 'waste of the West' (Jacobs, 1999), none have viewed the history of land use in the American Southwest from a use-centered perspective. Applying this perspective revealed three historical phases of natural resource use and users. The first phase, from 1860 to 1900, was characterized by a dominant land use, cattle grazing, and a single user, the ranch. Ranches were organizations for exploiting land; they responded to markets and developed little expertise in the ecology of rangeland. Rangelands were rapidly stripped of grass and suffered significant erosion which degraded the resource. In the second phase, from 1900 to 1960, grazing remained the dominant land use, but the use became mediated by technologies of range management developed and administered by experts to respond to land degradation resulting from unsustainable use. The third phase, beginning in 1960 and continuing to the present day, initiated a period of multiple use and multiple users mediated by increasingly sophisticated technologies for both range and ecological land management. Rangeland was used for development, recreation, wildlife and watershed values as well as grazing. Safeguarding multiple uses has enabled more equitable use of the land resource.

Phase One, 1860–1900: Ranches Rule the Range

In the mid-nineteenth century, the American Southwest was Apache territory. To the Euro-Americans who ventured there, it was a wasteland to be transformed by human labor. Unlike the Great Plains, the semi-arid grasslands of the American Southwest never supported large native herbivores such as bison, and were too dry for farming without intensive and costly irrigation. Forced removal of the Apaches by the US government after the Civil War to enable mining and homesteading ended a period of sustainable use by an indigenous population. Logging companies cut the pines from the high country, and mining companies dug silver and copper from the earth, but the main way to make this idle land productive was to exploit the natural resource by grazing cattle. The sparseness of native vegetation required huge tracts of land to support grazing by these exotic herbivores, yet land ownership was confined by law to small homesteads of 160 acres in a land which John Wesley Powell estimated required 2560 acres for a viable homestead (Donahue, 1999; Foss, 1960).

The predictable failures of legitimate homesteaders on the arid Western lands, compounded by illegal activities of land speculators, resulted in enormous cattle ranches – the 'robber barons' of the 1870s and 1880s – which ran hundreds of thousands of cattle onto Southwestern grasslands. If the farm was the organization for land use in the East, the ranch was the organization for land use in the West, created to take advantage of the opportunity of free grass. Ranches were corporations financed largely by Eastern US and European capitalists as speculative ventures (Sayre, 1999, 2002). Investors, merchants and banks invested capital in ranches to buy stock and land and financed the shipment of cattle to urban markets by rail. Although ranches had private landholdings, all grazed their stock heavily on the publicly-owned range, the use of which was free and open to all; this is why ranching in the West is characterized as 'public lands ranching', or the private use of public lands to graze cattle. By the 1880s, big ranches, commercialized and specialized to the point that they were risk-capital ventures, controlled the cattle industry; only large ranches could endure droughts and market fluctuations (Jordan, 1993; Sayre, 1999).

European capital seeking investment in the 1870s and 1880s was so great that ranches rapidly overstocked the range (Sayre, 1999). Cattle in the desert Southwest were estimated at 500 000 in 1830–40; by the late 1880s, they had increased to a peak of 1.5 million (Baker, 1996, p. 165). Overproduction saturated the beef market, which collapsed in 1884. The late 1880s were a disaster for the cattle industry. The severe drought of 1886–88 coincided with ferocious winters. Cattle were treated as commodities, and the conditions of exploitation were barbaric: cattle dehydrated, starved and froze to death.

Ranching success depends on knowledge of habitat and improvements made to habitat to support stock – it depends on expertise and technology. Unfortunately, mental models for animal husbandry were based on well-watered Eastern landscapes. Ranchers believed that 'if only' rains would come, grass would grow plentifully and all would be well. The fragile ecology of these semi-arid lands was not understood by Euro-American ranchers intent on the mass production of beef (Bahre and Shelton, 1996). Not only did they lack expertise about the land resource, they also 'knew nothing of grazing capacity and there was no fund of technical knowledge about forage management to rely on' (Baker et al., 1988, p. 92). Machine and management technologies were minimal: longhorns imported from Texas were not distinguished by selective breeding for the habitat (Jordan, 1993); they ranged freely over enormous tracts of land with no system of enclosure and rotation; cowboys on horseback rounded up stock for branding and drove cattle to railheads on unpaved roads; and watering systems remained primitive, dependent more on natural hydrology than innovative technology. The first application of modern technology to public lands ranching was the introduction of barbed wire in 1874 to fence off the open range illegally.

Uninformed and unconstrained use devastated the natural resource of grassland. Ignorance of the ecological dynamics of this semi-arid landscape led to rapid degradation of ecological functioning. Overgrazing by livestock, along with the plowing of river bottomland and channeling of rivers for irrigation (relatively small acreages compared to rangeland), extermination of beavers by trappers, and logging in the high country to support mines, all interacted with drought conditions to create exposed surfaces which permitted the torrential summer rains to run off quickly instead of seeping into the ground. Floods once restrained by beaver dams and forest cover roared down the mountainsides to cut deep gullies. Amplified by a severe drought, water sources dried up by 1893 and 65 percent of cattle on the range died. The drought ended by 1895 but overgrazing and flooding resulted in accelerated sheet and gully erosion throughout the region (Baker, 1996; Bahre and Shelton, 1996). The original perennial grasses were replaced by juniper, thistle and cheat grass. In the blink of an historical eye, the ecology changed from mature perennial grassland to a true wasteland of woody shrubs and annuals that offered meager graze.

This changed ecology could not support large numbers of cattle. By the end of the century, the large ranch organizations funded by external capital that had dominated the American Southwest were being broken up and sold off, often to small local ranches which supported only a few hundred head of cattle. Degradation of the resource by unsustainable use thus diminished the ability of ranches to survive.

Applying a use-centered perspective for this period is straightforward (Figure 3.4). From 1860 until about 1900, the dominant user was the livestock ranch and the dominant use was cattle grazing. Cattle were an exotic species, mass produced for market and profit. They enabled the ranch organization to make direct use of the natural resource – grass. Grasslands were seen simply as cattle forage, not an ecological system (Hirt, 1989). The absence of ecological expertise and sparse use of techniques and tools by rancher and cowboy suggests minimal mediation between user and end-use. By the end of this period, ranching was unsustainable; the primary

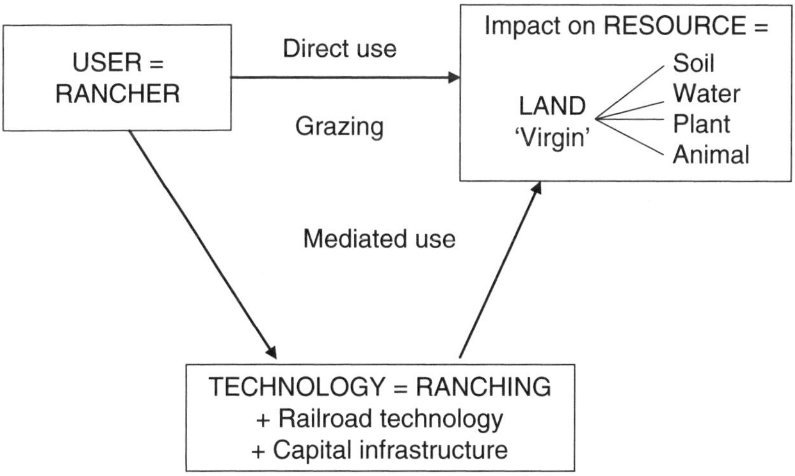

Figure 3.4 Phase One, 1860–1900: ranching

constraint on ranching was the nature of the land itself, which had been altered by misuse.

With respect to the larger human system in the sustainability mosaic, while the large ranch was the dominant organization which used rangeland in unsustainable ways, other organizations and their technologies contributed to this unsustainable use. Discoveries of metals, particularly silver and copper, lured miners. Railroads which arrived to transport ores also enabled mass export of cattle, which encouraged ranching. Successful miners often invested their capital in ranches, and banks provided additional capital for land speculation and stock. Mining contributed to deforestation of the highlands which upset the hydrology of the region (MacLennan and Walck, forthcoming). The US government was also strongly implicated in the devastation of rangeland. Government land policy emphasized social and economic development for Euro-Americans (but no comparable social equity for Native Americans), encouraging homesteaders to move onto wasteland and make it economically productive. Ignoring the ecological expertise contained in Powell's reports, the 'crazy-quilt landownership patterns' created by the General Land Office encouraged and invited overgrazing and cultivation of submarginal lands which accelerated erosion and increased siltage and floods (Foss, 1960, p. 37). Government agencies driven by economics and politics also turned a blind eye to ranches which illegally laid claims to large amounts of public land.

Hirt (1989) succinctly concluded that during this period Anglo-American ideologies placed a high value on resource production yet resulted in resource deterioration – 'A utilitarian society had created an environment of degraded utility' (p. 180). 'Powered by potent technologies, supported by an expanding capitalist economy, and buttressed by public policies endorsing unsustainable consumption of natural resources', this ideology created the environmental crisis which remains with us to this day (p. 183).

Phase Two, 1900–60: Range Management Expertise and Technologies Attempt to Recover the Resource and Sustain Ranching

In the early twentieth century, public policies of land conservation grounded in scientific advances in forestry, stockbreeding and grassland ecology attempted to recover the resource for grazing. Visible degradation of Western rangeland generated a growing public demand for land conservation and regulation. Congress responded in 1891 by placing 40 million acres of land nationwide into Forest Reserves (later called National Forests) for parks and watersheds. The Forest Service, established in 1905 in the Department of Agriculture, managed these lands, which in the American Southwest were used more for grazing than timber (Baker et al., 1988). The

Forest Service quickly developed extensive principles of range management to conserve and restore the resource for grazing. In 1934, Congress passed the Taylor Grazing Act (TGA), withdrawing the remaining 173 million acres of open range from the public domain and placing it under permanent management of the Department of the Interior (Stout, 1970). With the majority of rangeland in the American Southwest in the hands of federal or state governments, which in turn leased it to private organizations, it fell to these federal agencies to develop the expertise and technologies needed to manage land use.

The Forest Service under Gifford Pinchot favored integrated, scientific planning and centralized control of forest reserves for commercial purposes. Public policy favored large, efficient cattle ranches which obeyed regulations. The Forest Service quickly established an annual permit system for all livestock based on estimated grazing capacity. Allotments were surveyed to determine the annual amount of forage produced, and estimates were reduced by amounts needed for wildlife use, soil stability, watershed health and 'maintain[ing] a pleasing environment' (Baker et al., 1988, p. 93). Forest rangers then recommended the number of cattle that could graze the next year, which was incorporated into the ranch's permit (Wilkinson and Anderson, 1987). Grazing regulations were codified in the Forest Service's *Use Book*, which aimed to use 'forage resources' to the fullest extent consistent with 'good forest management', 'reduce waste of forage' and obtain a more 'judicious and profitable use of the range' (Wilkinson and Anderson, 1987, p. 93; Baker et al., 1988, p. 92). Baker opined that the 'grazing control system' in place by 1905 was a 'remarkably advanced administrative and land management system, given the time and state of technical knowledge' (1988, p. 92). The permit system quickly forced reductions in numbers of livestock grazing the reserves, which led to better forage on the reserves than on the unregulated open range. Ranches both competed for this land, and resisted agency management.

The early estimates of grazing capacity were not particularly scientific, and 'rule-of-thumb guesses of the early range managers had to be replaced by knowledge rooted in tests, experiments, and intensive analysis of the result data' (Rowley, 1986, p. 86). Forest rangers were originally untrained Westerners who knew the land, but increasingly they were selected from graduates of Eastern schools such as Yale School of Forestry (Leopold's Alma Mater), Cornell and Michigan (Baker et al., 1988). Forestry was becoming a profession which claimed scientific expertise and developed and utilized technologies. In 1910 the Forest Service embarked on an ambitious program of reconnaissance, inspections, inventories and research to enable better decision-making. Ranges were mapped to determine their 'carrying capacity, proper season of use, class of stock to which each portion is best adapted, and need of development' (Baker et al., 1988). By the 1920s range surveys merged with systematic analysis of grazing capacity led to the development of long-term range management plans. In 1930 the Southwestern Forest and Range Experiment Station was established to improve upon existing knowledge and to furnish answers to technical and practical problems (Baker et al., 1988, pp. 97–9). The extensive Forest Service range research and empirical studies culminated in 1936 in a 600-page report to the US Senate entitled *The Western Range*, which concluded that the public range was overstocked by 43 percent and recommended further conservation measures (Donahue, 1999, p. 44). This report led to the establishment of 'typical' management scenarios, or grazing systems, for ten specific vegetative types, in which it was averred that each vegetation type has its own environmental and physiological requirements which must be understood and provided for when grazing livestock (Baker, 1988, p. 98). Expertise and land management went hand in hand to mediate resource use.

The Department of the Interior (DOI) took a similar technical approach to range management when it inherited the TGA lands in 1934. It established a Grazing Service to determine grazing capacity – the maximum number of livestock which could be grazed without injury to the range, calculated in 'animal unit months' (AUMs) – and distributed permits and assessed grazing fees for use (Stout, 1970). However, unlike the centralized organization of Forest Service officials who were trained professionals implementing scientific research and gathering data, the DOI implemented a decentralized system of Grazing Districts run by ranchers elected by permit holders. With little funding for mapping and research, the carrying capacity of permits was determined by ranchers, not science, which perpetuated inefficient and outmoded forms of animal husbandry and generated stocking rates determined more by tradition and user preferences than science (Foss, 1960; Donahue, 1999, pp. 35–40). The rules and procedures that were supposed to govern use were captured by the users themselves, a common phenomenon in the history of regulation (Winner, 1996). In 1946 the Grazing Service merged with the General Land Office to form the Bureau of Land Management (BLM). The BLM had a staff of 86 to oversee 150 million acres and stockmen continued to overgraze the carrying capacity of their permits with little fear of reprisal (Foss, 1960).

While the range management expertise that emerged during this period was impressive – government-funded experts employed scientific techniques to determine more precise algorithms of use, embodied in allotments with annual operating instructions (AOIs), permits, AUMs and management plans – the on-the-ground techniques used to maintain and improve rangeland productivity in the face of changing conditions (the shift from grassland to woody shrubs) were relatively simple and mechanical: trenching, grubbing, chaining, railing, mowing, burning and check dams. Pick-up trucks and small tractors worked alongside horses and humans on the difficult terrain. Predator control, fire suppression and herbicides for noxious weed control in the 1950s added to the methods which attempted to halt or at least stabilize what was increasingly recognized by ecologists as the replacement of grasslands by shrublands and woodlands in a new steady state under the impact of grazing. This phase ended with a prolonged drought in the 1950s.

As in the prior phase, grazing continued to be the dominant use of rangeland. However, during this period, experts in federal agencies responded to land degradation resulting from unsustainable use by mediating use with technologies of range management informed by scientific expertise (see Figure 3.5). Although public policy shifted from a strategy of land disposal to a strategy of land management in order to improve and sustain the resource, federal land and water policies continued to emphasize resource productivity. Regulation and management based on scientific research were meant to create 'a sustained productive range on which to build a sound grazing enterprise and to provide economic family units' (Chapline, 1944, p. 131). Limits on use to enable range recovery were therefore as much an attempt to sustain a ranching economy on public lands as an attempt to

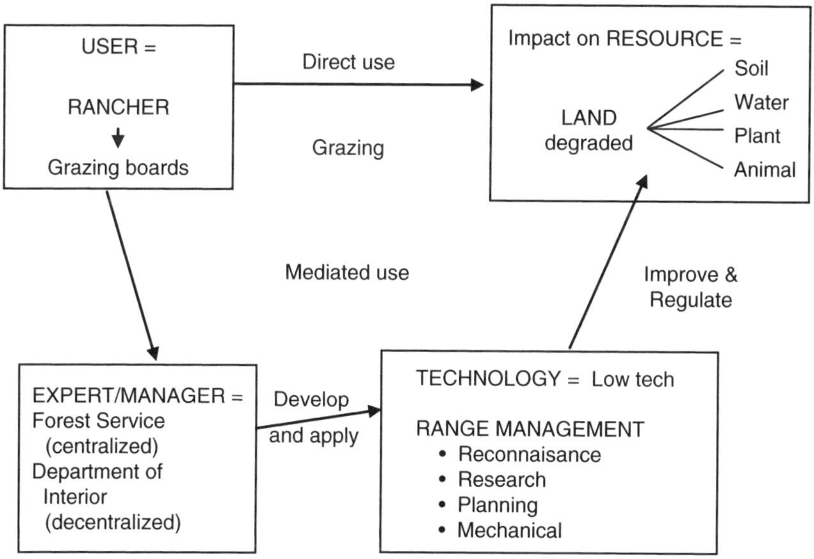

Figure 3.5 Phase Two, 1900–1960: range management

sustain the ecological functioning of rangeland. Although use by ranches was limited since fewer cattle were permitted to graze, prohibition of grazing was never the state's intent and ranching probably survived because of this shift in policy (MacLennan and Walck, forthcoming).

The ranch organization remained the dominant user of the land. However, as rangeland health failed to recover despite an increase in expertise and application of technologies, the number of cattle on the range remained small and so did the size of ranches, particularly during the lean years of the Depression and labor shortages of the World Wars. Expertise resided in government agencies more than in the ranches. Ranches consolidated and ranchers sought second incomes in town or in the mines which expanded in the American Southwest during this period. Ranchers often wanted it both ways – government assistance to control or mediate erosion and pests and sustain the resource, combined with higher allotments of cattle on the range to sustain the ranch organization. Recognizing that the economic sustainability of ranching depended on political clout, ranchers also formed professional cattlemen's associations to lobby state and federal governments.

While government agencies and ranches dominated the human complex of use on the grasslands during this period, advances in mining technologies also drew large mining corporations to the American Southwest. The economy of the region shifted from ranch income to mining income. Purchases of water rights for mining had a significant impact on the hydrology, and smelting of metals as well as dumping rock after removal of minerals created toxic wastes in localized areas (MacLennan and Walck, forthcoming). Tourism, formerly relegated to those seeking cures from ailments that benefited from a warm, dry climate, began to develop as the open spaces and climate attracted people from urban centers in search of recreation and renewal. By mid-century, a ranching culture still dominated the American Southwest, but ranchers' political power exceeded their economic power in a society that was poised to shift from rural to urban land use patterns.

Phase Three, 1960–Present: Multiple-Use Era and High-Tech Tools

As range conditions and market values for land and beef continued to create a bleak ranching economy, and decades of attempts by experts to improve the condition of rangeland with scientific management had little impact on the steady march of woody shrubs into the grasslands, the productive use of rangeland for ranching became marginal while urbanization generated a new set of users who valued rangeland for consumptive, non-wealth generating purposes such as wildlife habitat, watershed conservation, recreation and housing. A growing environmental movement prompted citizens and environmental groups in the American Southwest to contest the use of public lands for grazing, since grazing appeared to harm sensitive habitats harboring endangered species and also to diminish the aesthetics of a landscape now used for suburban housing or recreational wilderness (Donahue, 1999; Jacobs, 1999).

The American Southwest experienced a new boom after World War II – an urban boom of migrants who relocated, retired or built second homes there. While diminishing cattle production and ranch productivity should have led to declining value of ranches, the opposite occurred. Capital accumulation in the Southwest shifted from cattle production to real estate development and land speculation as rangeland looked like potential suburban lands for subdivision and home construction for the droves of migrants (Sayre, 2002). As land values rose into the 1980s, and estate taxes and capital gains made it difficult to keep land in ranching, many ranches sold out their private holdings to developers or subdivided land; those who continued to ranch did so because of a preference for the ranching way of life rather than its economic benefit, and old-time ranch families began to give way to hobby ranching (Smith and Martin, 1972).

Ecologically, urbanization poses a threat to the semi-arid environment that is less visible but nonetheless critical to the grasslands – it demands water supplies that strain groundwater levels (Sayre, 2002) and it also fragments and destroys critical habitats. Sale or subdivision of ranches for home sites increases population density which depletes scarce water resources and makes large-scale ecosystem management including wildlife corridors very difficult (Sheridan, 2001). On the other hand, urbanization also created a shift in values toward conservation of public lands which was reflected in changes in federal land use policies.

In 1960, Congress passed the Multiple Use-Sustained Yield Act (MUSY), authorizing the Department of Agriculture to develop and administer renewable resources on the National Forests not only for productive use (grazing, timber, mining) but also for uses associated with non-economic land values – outdoor recreation, watershed and wildlife. This shifted federal policy away from productive use and toward environmental protection and conservation biology.[3] The Bureau of Land Management shifted focus from animal husbandry to range and watershed management. Agencies had to prepare resource management plans (RMPs) and environmental impact statements (EISs) for use of public lands, including a plan for each grazing allotment. Many regulations required public input into the management process, and public input often generated conflict, pushing agency personnel to develop strategies for managing people as well as land. Regulations for water quality and endangered species generated ample opportunities for litigation by environmentalists who pointed to cattle as the source of water pollution, stream erosion, and fish and bird loss, and to the Forest Service and Bureau of Land Management as inadequate enforcers of federal laws and management plans. Habitat Conservation Plans (HCPs), a modification of the Endangered Species Act, were also developed for private lands.

The proliferating regulations coincided with advances in range science as well as the new sciences of ecology and conservation biology and the high-technology tools which support them including computer simulation modeling, global positioning systems, geographic information systems and remote sensing data. Experts in these new sciences have proliferated not only in government agencies but also in universities (often publicly funded) and environmental organizations. In addition, university departments of animal science developed expertise in the animal and its economics: breeding, feeding, parasite and disease control, the cost of raising cattle, and marketing of the beef product. Range science at universities began to emphasize specification of ecological conditions to determine optimal grazing systems, and the new science of ecology began to ask hard questions about the impacts of grazing on the ecosystem, using detailed scientific studies and new technologies to develop answers. New Mexico State University, for example, operates two large research centers to study livestock, grazing methods and range forage, collaborating with the US Department of Agriculture (USDA) at the Jornada Experimental Range to develop ecologically-based technologies for monitoring, remediation and grazing management in desert environments. Despite these new and sophisticated technologies for land management, true recovery of the presettlement grassland ecology was increasingly deemed an impossible task (Archer, 1994).

Ranchers have taken advantage of the advances in animal and range science, attending universities and working with university extension agents to determine better ways to use rangeland for grazing. Equally important, they also had to determine how to coexist with new urban neighbors who had not grown up around the ranching way of life and who wanted to use grasslands for more than grazing. Ranchers have been slow to accept the need to develop sustainable, holistic range management practices that enhance wildlife and watershed use (Sayre, 2001), putting them into conflict with environmental groups. One solution to the challenge of multiple use has been the development of cooperative management plans which include multiple stakeholders – ranchers, government and university scientists, and environmentalists. For example, the USDA Cooperative State Research, Education and Extension Service (US Department of Agriculture, 2004), conducts research and disseminates information to ranchers in partnership with land-grant universities and special interest groups such as the Grazing

Lands Conservation Initiative, Sustainable Rangelands Roundtable, and Society for Range Management. Another solution is being championed by environmentalists who see value in building partnerships with ranchers. As the grasslands are threatened by developers, non-profit groups like the Nature Conservancy and rancher-based land trusts have begun purchasing ranchland and development rights to protect ranches from development and preserve habitat. Collaborative groups like the Quivira Coalition, Malpai Borderlands Group and Arizona Common Ground Roundtable are forging bonds between ranchers and environmentalists, seeking what they call a 'radical center' (Johnson, 2003; Sterling, 2004). As they try to move 'from opinion-based to fact-based decision making' (Sheridan, 2001, p. 150), these collaborative groups depend on the expertise of scientists and their technologies.

Thus in the latter half of the twentieth century, the complexity of the system of users, experts and technologies has grown significantly as multiple uses of the grasslands are contested (Figure 3.6). Ranchers, federal agencies, university researchers, extension agents, developers, environmentalists and other special interest groups have all tried to use or mediate use of rangelands. The ranch's earlier monopoly on the range was contested by new users with different values and lifestyles, and federal agencies managed

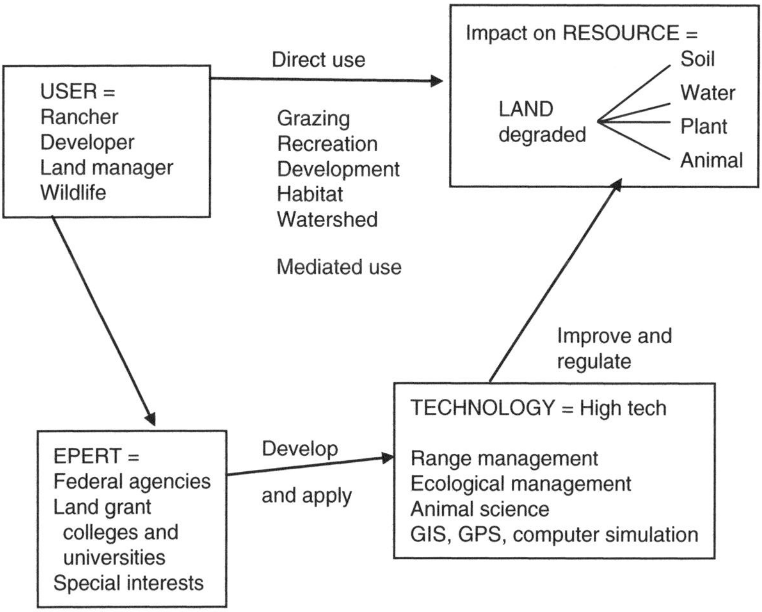

Figure 3.6 Phase Three, 1960–present: multiple-use management

public lands for multiple use. The balance appears to have shifted more toward sustaining the resource than sustaining the ranching economy, but the multiple uses of recreation and watershed maintenance also support the new urban economy of the Southwest. The complexity of the system of users, experts and technologies attempting to function within the web of regulation makes the neat lines of influence of earlier period begin to blur as users access technology to become experts, experts play multiple roles of regulator, manager and communicator, and a shift in popular values toward ecology puts pressure on ranches and developers to develop new expertise, use new technologies and learn how to collaborate if they want to survive.

CONCLUSION

What can we learn from the history of rangeland use in the American Southwest? That the short-term view of organizations that rapidly exploited a natural resource quickly shortened their own lives. In other words, loss of ecological sustainability quickly led to loss of societal sustainability. The large but short-lived ranches produced by the reach of global capital had no vision beyond untrammeled access to a natural resource. Mass production of beef for urban markets by ranches exploiting grasslands rapidly destroyed ecological functioning because these organizations failed to recognize or utilize ecological knowledge about semi-arid environments. The destruction was so profound that plant succession was reversed, and rearguard actions with technologies to mediate use have been successful primarily in reducing resource use, but not in restoring ecological function to presettlement viability. This has limited the human uses of the land, redistributing access over time from ranches trying to make productive use of the land to developers consuming the land for housing and recreation.

Because much of the grasslands have remained in public ownership and were leased to private ranches for use, public concerns about land conservation prompted public policies to manage the rangeland. For 50 years the public policy goal remained productive use, while managing for sustainability of the resource by protecting watersheds and wildlife took a back seat. As we enter the twenty-first century, the threat to sustainability of rangeland ecosystems is less the rancher than the developer with a new short-term vision for land use: divide, sell and build homes, straining the fragile water resources of the arid ecosystem. Paradoxically, the shift in values toward consumptive use of wilderness through outdoor recreation and vacation and retirement homes is creating a market for land that sets the stage for a new round of unsustainable use of rangeland.

If the end (*telos*) of technology has been construed as social good or social control, the end of land use could perhaps be construed as sustainability. We began this chapter by defining sustainable development as the design of human systems to ensure that the use of natural resources does not diminish quality of life or adversely impact the environment (Mihelcic et al., 2003). The case-study of rangeland use revealed a complex of use that was increasingly mediated by experts and technologies. Tracing this complex over time revealed a shift from single to multiple uses and users, and a growing awareness that if human use is to be sustainable, the resource must be sustained as well. A dramatically unsustainable use of rangeland at the end of the nineteenth century predicated on ignorance of the ecology of semi-arid grasslands prompted intervention by government agencies who acted in the public interest to balance competing human uses with the desire to keep the grassland ecosystem functioning.

The government's ability to mediate use depended on scientific and management expertise and technologies. As sociologists of knowledge have learned, experts have the power to shape how a problem is defined and who gets to use knowledge for what ends. While the government had the political power to demand change in rangeland use in the face of extraordinary devastation of the resource, the case-study suggests that it was the power of expert knowledge in the emerging science of forestry, as well as the development of a new profession of forestry wielding that knowledge and developing management technologies to impact land use, that truly changed how rangeland was used at the turn of the century. Embedding these professionals in federal agencies and funding new technologies to increase knowledge of the resource enabled the government to mediate use of public rangeland to sustain the resource while also attempting to sustain ranching as an economic activity. Even so, by the time the government was able to act, the resource was so significantly degraded that the large ranches of the 1880s were already collapsing and the government led a rearguard action to save the small rancher.

Use of rangeland in the twentieth century continued to be mediated by access to expertise and technologies, although diffusion of expertise and technologies to public and private organizations such as universities and special interest groups generated a new complex of use. When new users with new value systems arrived to compete for access to grasslands, the balance began to shift from expertise and management of the resource itself, to expertise and management of human systems which balanced the needs of multiple users in networks of collaboration. Both public and private interests played roles in the new complex of use, but they continued to depend on expanding expertise and emerging technologies to be part of the network.

The lesson for organizations is that the sustainability mosaic will be reflected in complexes of use. Competing uses will in some cases be decided by raw power in a contest between users, but in a technological age dominated by specialists arrayed in professions making knowledge claims, it seems more likely that use will be mediated by experts and technologies connected in complexes of use. Organizations that recognize their place in evolving complexes of use, and develop or share in the ongoing development of expertise and appropriate technologies that enable use while sustaining the resource, are more likely to sustain themselves in the process. Short-term solutions like environmental management systems can become longer-term solutions if these systems are predicated on using the best science, accessing the best expertise and utilizing the most appropriate technologies that are available in the larger human system. If the end of land use is a functioning ecosystem which can sustain human use of that land over time, then a sustainability mosaic centered on land use will require experts in diverse fields from conservation biology, human and physical geography, and animal science to experts in human conflict management and systems.

It will also require an understanding of evolving complexes of use in order to balance competing claims and search for opportunities for cooperation. Social equity in the sustainable use of natural resources will depend upon human political systems for managing competing claims to resources and identifying the points of leverage and opportunities for cooperation. In the nineteenth century, the Apache were never considered part of the political system, and were rapidly removed from the land by a federal government promoting the productive use of grasslands for a growing Euro-American population. Now it is those productive users – ranchers – whose needs are trumped by an urban agenda for both development and conservation. Balancing sustainable use of the resource with the need to sustain diverse human populations will require not only expertise and technology, but also a political will to invite everyone to the table when significant decisions are made about natural resource use.

Another implication of this study is the need to manage the public commons. Like rangeland, two resources that are likely to be contested during this century – water and air – are arguably public commons. They are subject to multiple uses by multiple users, and their unsustainable use will affect us all. While the use of rangeland was localized and the impact of its unsustainable use was limited to a specific region, unsustainable uses of water and air have much broader implications for social equity, since water moves across regions and air circulates globally. Scientific expertise and technologies, wielded by governmental bodies with broader scope, will increasingly mediate how water and air are used. Organizations which recognize the need for an equitable use of resources among multiple users, and which can cooperate to access and distribute resources equitably, are most likely to find themselves with a place at the global table over the long run.

This study is nonetheless one case, bound by culture, place, time and the limitations of our understanding of the past to serve as a viable guide for future courses of action. It is difficult to say whether the actions which led to destruction of the grasslands of the American Southwest are comparable to the forces destroying the Amazonian rainforest or the world's ocean resources, or whether an historical study of a natural resource such as petroleum will yield the same complex of mediated use. Case-studies of each resource will reveal different uses, users, technologies and mediators, and it may be difficult to generalize from multiple case-studies those factors that would have predictive validity across time and place. As the powers of governments and communities appear to be receding in the face of global corporations, it is also difficult to predict who or what will successfully mediate corporate access to natural resources in the future. The value of an in-depth study of a specific place across time, however, is its ability to correct our commonsense notions of what happened and why, reveal the unintended consequences of actions, and point us toward the larger system in which all action is embedded. While studies of the past do not necessarily provide specific guidance regarding what to do in the future, they chart the course we are now on, serve as cautionary tales, and sometimes give us hope that action for the social good can make a difference if we use the best tools available to us at the time, persist in our efforts and take a long-term view in which we learn from lessons of the past.

If sustainable development is the design of human systems to ensure that the use of natural resources does not diminish quality of life or adversely impact the environment, then a sustainability mosaic could be crafted as an evolving complex of use in which legitimate and powerful mediators can assure the sustainability of a natural resource while balancing competing claims to it in the interests of social equity. A long-term solution to sustainable resource use must be grounded both in the development of the best scientific knowledge of the resource itself and application of appropriate technologies, and also in a political process which gives communities affected by use – and particularly unsustainable use – a voice.

NOTES

1. Johnson's (1998) user-centered theory is itself an adaptation of rhetorical theory (p. 35) in which a system of 'readers-writers-and-reality' centered on a text was transformed into

a system of 'designers-artifacts-and-tasks' centered on a user. I have tweaked the model again to pull the end-use out of the system and make it visible.
2. From a historian's point of view, primary sources include original documents, eyewitness accounts and other materials, often housed in archives, produced during the period a historian is studying. Secondary sources are histories constructed at a later date by historians using primary sources.
3. MUSY was quickly followed by a raft of additional policies to protect the environment which agencies administered: 1964 Wilderness Act; 1968 Wild and Scenic Rivers Act; 1969 National Environmental Policy Act (NEPA); 1972 Federal Water Pollution Act; 1973 Endangered Species Act; 1974 Forest Rangeland Renewable Resource Planning Act (RPA); 1976 Amended National Forest Management Act; 1976 Clean Air Act; 1976 Federal Land Policy and Management Act (FLPMA); 1977 Clean Water Act; 1978 Public Rangelands Improvement Act (PRIA); and 1994 Rangeland Reform '94: Draft Environmental Impact Statement (DEIS).

REFERENCES

Archer, S. (1994), 'Woody plant encroachment into Southwestern grasslands and savannas: rates, patterns and proximate causes', in M. Vavra, W. Laycock and R. Pieper (eds), *Ecological Implications of Livestock Herbivory in the West*, Denver, CO: Society for Range Management, pp. 13–68.

Bahre, Conrad J. and Marlyn N. Shelton (1996), 'Rangeland destruction: cattle and drought in Southeastern Arizona at the turn of the century', *Journal of the Southwest*, **38** (1), 1–22.

Baker, M.B., Jr. (1996), 'Hydrology and watershed management in semi-arid grasslands', in USDA Forest Service, *The Future of Arid Grasslands: Identifying Issues, Seeking Solutions*, Tucson, AZ: USDA, pp. 158–70.

Baker, R.D., R.S. Maxwell, V.H. Treat and H.C. Dethloff (1988), *Timeless Heritage: A History of the Forest Service in the Southwest*, USDA Forest Service FS-409, August, Washington, DC: US Government Printing Office.

Burgess, T. (1995), 'Northwestern Apacherian savannas: a description, and review of issues concerning human inhabitation', in USDA Forest Service, *The Future of Arid Grasslands: Identifying Issues, Seeking Solutions*, Tucson, AZ: USDA, pp. 3–10.

Chapline, William (1944), 'The history of western range research', *Agricultural History*, **18**, 127–43.

Donahue, D. (1999), *The Western Range Revisited: Removing Livestock from Public Lands to Conserve Native Biodiversity*, Norman, OK: University of Oklahoma Press.

Foss, P. (1960), *Politics and Grass: The Administration of Grazing on the Public Domain*, Seattle, WA: University of Washington Press.

Graf, W. (1990), *Wilderness Preservation and the Sagebrush Rebellions*, Lanham, MD: Rowman & Littlefield.

Hirt, Paul (1989), 'The transformation of a landscape: culture and ecology in southeastern Arizona', *Environmental Review*, **13** (4), 167–89.

Jacobs, L. (1999), *Waste of the West: Public Lands Ranching*, Tucson, AZ: L. Jacobs.

Johnson, Barbara H. (ed.) (2003), 'Forging a West that works: an invitation to the radical center', *Essays on Ranching, Conservation and Science*, Santa Fe, NM: Quivira Coalition.

Johnson, R.R. (1998), *User-Centered Technology: A Rhetorical Theory of Computers and Other Mundane Artifacts*, Albany, NY: SUNY Press.
Jordan, T.G. (1993), *North American Cattle Ranching Frontiers: Origins, Diffusion and Differentiation*, Albuquerque, NM: University of New Mexico.
Leopold, Aldo (1924), 'Grass, brush, timber and fire in southern Arizona', *Journal of Forestry*, reprinted in D. Brown and N. Carmony (eds) (1995), *Aldo Leopold's Southwest*, Albuquerque, NM: University of New Mexico Press, pp. 179–90.
Leopold, Aldo (1937), 'Conservationist in Mexico', *American Forests*, reprinted in D. Brown and N. Carmony (eds), *Aldo Leopold's Southwest*, Albuquerque, NM: University of New Mexico Press, pp. 201–8.
Leopold, Aldo (1949/1970), *A Sand County Almanac*, NY: Ballantine Books.
MacLennan, Carol and Christa Walck (forthcoming), 'How mining, ranching, and state power changed the landscape of Southwestern New Mexico, 1850–2005', in Lisa Cliggett and Christopher Poole (eds), *Economies and the Transformation of Landscape*, Vol. 25, Walnut Creek, CA: Altamira Press.
Mihelcic, J.R., J.C. Crittenden, M.J. Small, D.R. Shonnard, D.R. Hokanson, Q. Zhang, H. Chen, S.A. Sorby, V.U. James, J.W. Sutherland and J.L. Schnoor (2003), 'Sustainability science and engineering: the emergence of a new metadiscipline', *Environmental Science and Technology*, **37**, 5314–24.
Rowley, William D. (1986), *US Forest Service Grazing and Rangelands: A History*, College Station, TX: Texas A&M University Press.
Sayre, Nathan (1999), 'The cattle boom in Southern Arizona: towards a critical political ecology', *Journal of the Southwest*, **41** (2), 239–71.
Sayre, Nathan (2001), *The New Ranch Handbook: A Guide To Restoring Western Rangelands*, Santa Fe, NM: Quivira Coalition.
Sayre, Nathan (2002), *Ranching, Endangered Species, and Urbanization in the Southwest: Species of Capital*, Tucson, AZ: University of Arizona Press.
Sheridan, Thomas E. (2001), 'Cows, condos, and the contested commons: the political ecology of ranching on the Arizona-Sonora borderlands', *Human Organization*, **60** (2), 141–52.
Smith, Arthur H. and William E. Martin (1972), 'Socioeconomic behavior of cattle ranchers, with implications for rural community development in the West', *American Journal of Agricultural Economics*, **54** (2), 217–25.
Sterling, Terry Greene (2004), 'Radical center tries to shield ranch land: diverse interests unite behind common goals', *Washington Post*, 13 November, p. A03.
Stout, Joe A. (1970), 'Cattlemen, conservationists, and the Taylor Grazing Act', *New Mexico Historical Review*, **65** (4), 311–32.
Thrall, Grant (2002), *Business Geography and New Real Estate Market Analysis*, London and New York: Oxford University Press.
US Department of Agriculture (USDA) (2004), Cooperative State Research, Education and Extension Service document, accessed May 2004 at www.csrees.usda.gov.
Wilkinson, C.F. and H.M. Anderson (1987), *Land and Resource Planning in the National Forests*, Washington, DC: Island Press.
Winner, L. (1996), *The Whale and the Reactor: A Search for Limits in an Age of High Technology*, Chicago, IL: University of Chicago Press.

4. Changing practice on sustainability: understanding and overcoming the organizational and psychological barriers to action

Andrew J. Hoffman and Max H. Bazerman

Sustainable development (or sustainability) suffers from many definitions. For most, that definition starts with the Bruntland definition: 'meeting the needs of present generations without compromising the needs of future generations to meet theirs' (World Commission on Environment and Development, 1987). From there, many turn to the triple bottom line (Elkington, 1998) – the 'three Es' of economy, environment and social equity or the 'three Ps' of people, planet and profits. Others go further to focus on eco-efficiency, corporate social responsibility, transparency and inclusion (Holliday et al., 2002). And still others incorporate considerations for inter-species, inter-racial and inter-generational equity as well as equity between North and South via development that strengthens the capacity of both rich and poor to enhance their welfare while preserving the environment (Farrell and Hart, 1998). Ehrenfeld (2004) sums all this up by saying that sustainability is an issue of human 'flourishing'. In truth, sustainability encompasses all these considerations and more. The definition of sustainable development is still in development, so to speak.

Because of this ambiguity, there are a large number of critiques that challenge the notion of sustainability. Some question the concept on its efficacy for meaningful action relative to topics with more longevity, such as corporate social responsibility (CSR) (Norman and MacDonald, 2003). Others question the extent to which the sustainability agenda could be injurious to corporate survival (Murray, 2005). So ambiguous and contentious is the concept that some have suggested that the term 'sustainable development' should be jettisoned, since it means everything to everyone and therefore nothing at all (Goodman, 2000).

That this term is so contentious and ambiguous is not cause for abandonment. Instead, this represents the extent to which the term evades clarity, embodies complexity and, in the end, requires a change in many of our underlying cognitive and cultural beliefs (Bazerman and Hoffman, 1999). It requires an alteration in the way we conceive of the purpose of the firm, its connection with the natural environment and the ways in which it serves human communities. In fact, while each of these three issues requires 'an internal change in our intellectual emphasis, loyalties, affections and convictions' (Leopold, 1949, p. 210), it is the interconnections among the three that truly make it such a challenge.

These interconnections are both positive and negative, intertwined in a series of multi-directional feedback loops that require a systemic approach to be resolved (Meadows et al., 2004). Firm activity impacts social communities for the positive when economic growth serves human prosperity. Its impacts are negative when widening income disparities mean that not all people share in that material and economic progress (Crossette, 1998). Firm activity impacts the natural environment negatively through the massive resource extractions and pollution emissions that are utilized to fuel that economic growth. It creates positive outcomes when new technologies or services are developed, which reduce or eliminate that ecosystem strain.

Firm activity aside, the natural environment is directly linked to human well-being. Environmental improvements can improve the food yield of land and sea resources, decrease toxic hazards from pollution and maintain these attributes for generations to come. Conversely, environmental degradation affects the quality of life for human populations, sometimes affecting all (Beck, 1992), but most often affecting the poor or under-represented disproportionately (Bryant, 1995). And vice versa, social responses to environmental problems can have both detrimental and advantageous affects on human populations through impacts on sector employment, productivity and economic activity. These affects can be exacerbated negatively through poorly timed or poorly executed interventions (such as the protection of the spotted owl in the Pacific Northwestern United States) and positively through responses that are inclusive and efficiently designed (such as the Montreal Protocol to eliminate ozone-depleting substances). In all such linkages among the three parts of the sustainability triad – economy, environment and social equity – there is a need to change our conceptions of each part individually, and the whole in its entirety.

In this chapter, we argue that the change in thinking required of the sustainability agenda will never come to fruition within practical domains unless proper attention is given to the sources of individual and social resistance to such change. The implementation of wise management practices cannot be accomplished without a concurrent set of strategies for surmounting these barriers. We will briefly discuss how sustainability has emerged as a phenomenon in the real world, thrusting corporations into addressing this issue. Next, we will illustrate how contributions from the fields of behavioral decision research and organizational behavior can enrich this shift in corporate practice, offering greater insights into the necessary ingredients for wise sustainability management to make it into practice. We will close with a discussion of strategies for overcoming barriers to action.

SUSTAINABILITY IN CONCEPT

Over the past 100 years, society has witnessed unprecedented economic growth and human prosperity. Our industrial and intellectual pursuits have created a tripling in global per capita income (World Business Council for Sustainable Development, 1997), an increase in average life expectancy of almost two-thirds (World Resources Institute, 1994), and a populace that is significantly more literate and educated than our predecessors (World Business Council for Sustainable Development, 2002). These advancements have all been enabled by industrial sector developments in medicine, materials, transportation, communication and food production.

In the latter half of the twentieth century, however, society has begun to question some of the commonly held assumptions of that development. On one front, people have challenged the belief that the environment can be treated as an endless source of resources and a limitless depository for waste. On another, concerns have been raised that all people do not share equally in this economic prosperity, leaving many without access to the opportunities our advancing world has to offer. This questioning has resulted both in the recognition of corporate activity as the source of environmental and social problems, and in a more recent recognition that industry can also be a part of the solution. Out of this recognition, concerns for sustainable development were born.

In our increasingly globalized world, the impact of industrial and commercial activities has become more vivid and severe. For several reasons, the environmental and social problems that society faces cannot be considered, much less resolved, without the inclusion of business as a central factor (Hoffman, 2005). Five of these reasons are noted here.

First, business decisions concerning what material, labor and energy inputs to use and how to manage product and waste outputs ultimately determine environmental and social quality. Therefore, industry is often directly responsible for problems related to sustainability, and is thus most vulnerable to social and political challenges for change. Second, companies are generally the sources of technological evolution within society. As such, companies often best understand the technical trade-offs that innovation choices may involve. While corporate critics and others may appreciate the impact of systemic change, companies understand the underlying technical and economic aspects of innovation. Third, governments no longer possess the full array of resources and knowledge necessary to dictate solutions to companies. Many within policy circles now agree that companies must become participants in the regulatory process if sustainable and economically efficient solutions are to be found. Fourth, the power of business organizations to determine the structures of social, economic and political activity has grown to such enormous proportions that industry, both individually and through markets, now possesses the most resources needed to create more efficient coordinating mechanisms. Indeed, businesses have been developing solutions to emerging environmental and social problems with a number of products and services, such as: alternative mobility systems, including gas–electric hybrid vehicles, fuel-cell vehicles and car-sharing in urban centers; alternative energy sources including wind energy, fuel cells and micro-turbines; and alternative manufacturing materials, including bio-materials (to replace fossil fuel based fabrics such as nylon, polyester and lycra) and composite woods (to replace large-stock timber). Fifth, as society demands that environmental and social problems be addressed, companies can earn new profits by finding solutions (Hoffman, 2005; Prahalad, 2004).

Clearly, there is a strong logic behind the need for business to play a more active role in supporting the goal of a sustainable society. But to date, the evidence points to a slow diffusion of industry-led ideas and actions. Given that an industry will be profoundly affected by and contribute to the ongoing concerns for sustainability, there is a great need and opportunity for a better understanding of this slow diffusion. We argue that while the visionaries who have generated new ideas for sustainable development offer important and vital insights, they too often seem to assume that, 'If we write about it, they will follow.' Extensive research on the diffusion of innovation makes it clear that this view is naive. We need to understand the barriers that exist to implementation and offer new insights concerning how to put wise insights into practice. Here, organizational theory and behavioral decision research have much to offer.

TURNING SUSTAINABILITY INSIGHTS INTO PRACTICE

Research in the organizational behavior disciplines focuses on how social and psychological processes influence the perception and development of managerial and market structures, including managerial and market structures relevant to the natural and human environments. Organizational behavior's interdisciplinary, multi-level focus makes it well suited to addressing the human side of management behaviors. Organizational behavior research offers multiple lenses for viewing the complexities of the intersection of business and sustainability. More importantly, this research sheds light on tactics that can be used to integrate the insights of broader managerial research into practice.

At the individual level, behavioral decision research offers insights into how the social perception and enactment of issues occurs (Cordano and Frieze, 2000) and, therefore, highlights the fundamental mechanisms by which change can be undertaken. Behavioral research posits that individuals attempt to act rationally, but are bounded in their ability to achieve rationality (Simon, 1957; March and Simon, 1958). Armed with four decades of behavioral decision findings, researchers now are able to predict, a priori, how people will make decisions that are inconsistent, inefficient and based on normatively irrelevant information. Individuals rely on simplifying strategies, or cognitive heuristics. While these heuristics are frequently useful shortcuts, they also lead to a wide variety of decision biases (Kahneman and Tversky, 1973, 1979; Bazerman, 2005).

At the collective level, organizational theory views individuals as part of larger systems of organizations and institutions (Hoffman, 1999). It examines the political and economic root causes of environmental and social disruption and develops a systematic approach that shows how organizations, institutions and individuals can both push for and resist reforms (Schnaiberg and Gould, 1994). It attends to the rise of social movements, addressing how change occurs within social systems and why. Central to this stream is a consideration of risks as they relate to the macro-sociological change (Beck, 1992) and the reasons why social structures will resist that change, focusing on the 'social, political and cultural processes' by which issues, problems and solutions are given attention, defined and resolved (Hannigan, 1995, p. 30).

At both the individual and organizational level of analysis, behavioral research has much to contribute toward the resolution of contemporary problems of practical relevance. The next section will discuss specific ways in which behavioral scholarship can help practitioners in policy, business and non-profit communities put sustainable development into practice.

Cognitive Biases that Perpetuate Unsustainable Practices

A great deal of research has examined the patterns of thinking that lead to suboptimal outcomes. In this section, we will highlight one cognitive limitation, the mythical fixed pie, and end the section with an overview of how other decision biases prevent us from adopting wise innovations.

We begin with the story of Ben Cone, a forester in North Carolina. When he feared that the presence of endangered red-cockaded woodpeckers on his property would make him a target of the US Fish and Wildlife Service, Cone shifted from a 60-year tradition of sustainable forest management to massive clear-cutting of trees (Baden, 1995). Clearly, this is not the type of solution intended by the Endangered Species Act (ESA), which protected the woodpecker. Why did Cone destroy his forest? He assumed that any outcome desired by the government or environmentalists would be bad for him – an assumption referred to as the mythical fixed pie of negotiation, which is the belief that negotiators are fighting over a finite pool of resources (Bazerman, 1983). The most common reason negotiators fail to find optimal outcomes is that they do not look for trade-offs that can enlarge the pool of resources to be distributed.

It is important to note that it was not the ESA's implementation that caused Mr. Cone's hasty and drastic actions, but rather his misperceptions of it. After the story became a touchstone for ESA critics, it was revealed that endangered species considerations influenced only 15 percent of Cone's land. He was free to continue thinning trees on the remaining land as he had done for years. Furthermore, the US Fish and Wildlife Service repeatedly offered Cone proposals that would have insulated him from future ESA responsibilities. He refused to cooperate, however, believing that whatever the government and environmentalists desired must be bad for his business. Cone's fear of the complete economic loss of his assets led him toward a radical protective strategy (Bazerman et al., 2001). His belief in the win–lose nature of endangered species protection guided his unfortunate actions. It is tempting to assume that if we were in Ben Cone's position, we would reach more sophisticated conclusions. Yet, prior to the work of Walton and McKersie (1965), many brilliant negotiation scholars committed errors similar to Cone's. And we surmise that similar beliefs by many protagonists in disputes related to sustainable development continue to result in similar dysfunctional results.

The mythical fixed pie and sustainability

To this date, competing perspectives on the relationship between economic competitiveness on the one hand and environmental protection and social equity on the other remain part of an active, highly visible debate. Splitting into polarized camps, protagonists argue whether this relationship is inherently 'win–lose' or 'win–win'. Win–lose proponents argue that environmental protection (Walley and Whitehead 1994; Palmer et al., 1995) and social responsibility (Meckling and Jensen, 1983; *The Economist*, 2005) reduce economic competitiveness. Win–win proponents argue that this framing of the issue is a false dichotomy and that economic competitiveness improves through sustainability initiatives (Porter and van der Linde, 1995a, 1995b; Holliday et al., 2002). These bright thinkers argue for one incomplete process or the other, overlooking the symbiotic nature of these alternatives.

The present debate has hardened into an ideological conflict between intractable positions. Pro-sustainability advocates have begun asking whether existing models of corporate practice must be redefined (Post et al., 2002), while pro-business advocates have asked in reply whether 'social responsibility will harm business' (Murray, 2005, p. A2). Critics of the sustainability agenda opine that those advocating for corporate action on social and environmental issues are really promoting an agenda that will bring those very corporations to collapse; that the advocates for action possess a 'basic failure to understand why capitalism works' (*The Economist*, 2001, p. 70). As such, the challenge to sustainability advocates within the corporate regime becomes one of inconsistent values and objectives; a contest between the tenets of capitalism and the tenets of sustainability. The two are presented as orthogonal; they cannot be simultaneously achieved. In the end, the debate is framed as a win–lose debate in which social and economic objectives cannot be simultaneously met (*The Economist*, 2005).

Once this tension is framed in such terms, advocates of one agenda are immediately suspect by those who represent the other agenda – most vividly displayed by the recent criticism of companies that have acknowledged climate change and adopted voluntary greenhouse gas reduction goals. Termed 'Kyoto capitalists' or the 'carbon cartel', they are charged with unscrupulously seeking financial gain from the climate change issue by embracing a 'cynical approach to regulation', an effort to reap financial benefits while the 'costs can be foisted on the backs of others' (*Wall Street Journal*, 2004, p. A16). In response, these companies see those resisting climate action as ill-informed, selfish or destructive to the stability of the economy and ecology. As long as this win–lose mindset prevails, creative and wise outcomes will be obscured.

The negotiations literature teaches us that the contrasting win–lose or win–win frames of reference are not only unnecessarily polarized, but also fundamentally incomplete (Thompson, 2004). And it offers an alternative model that integrates elements of both positions for a more productive outlook on the issue. Conflict between economics and sustainability is a mixed-motive situation (Walton and McKersie, 1965); in other words, the balancing of environmental, human and economic interests is neither purely cooperative nor purely competitive. Within this mixed-motive perspective, we argue that protagonists on all sides of the debate miss too many opportunities to transform the contentious debate into an efficient set of solutions. That is, it would be healthier for protagonists to move beyond win–lose and argue over a more optimal set of possible solutions.

When win–win sustainability advocates argue that environmentalism or social responsibility is good business, pro-business win–lose advocates can too easily point to poor environmental regulations or misguided CSR initiatives that harm profitability. And when pro-business advocates in the win–lose camp argue their case, those in the win–win camp counter with singular examples of sustainability initiatives creating new profitability. The key to resolving this circular and contentious debate is the recognition that sustainable development is sometimes profit-compatible and sometimes not. When parties acknowledge this simple fact, it becomes easier to analyze specific initiatives more carefully and convince corporations to adopt measures that are mutually beneficial. This thinking moves us beyond the simple question, 'Does it pay to be green?' (King and Lenox, 2001; Margolis and Walsh, 2001) or 'Does it pay to be sustainable?' Instead, it asks us to consider 'How and when does it pay to be sustainable?' for specific companies in specific circumstances (Howard-Grenville and Hoffman, 2003).

Other cognitive biases

Thus far in this section, we have focused on one bias, the mythical fixed pie, and specified what it tells us about how to encourage parties to move beyond their limiting mindsets and adopt sustainability friendly ideas. But many other biases are also socially and environmentally dysfunctional. Positive illusions (the tendency of people to see themselves, their future and the world in a better condition than what is reality), self-serving interpretations of fairness (the tendency of people to make egocentric judgments of what is fair), and overconfidence (the tendency of people to be overconfident in their estimation abilities and not acknowledge the true uncertainties in those assessments) are other culprits that explain destructive behaviors (Hoffman et al., 1999).

Similarly, we know that people and organizations tend to overly discount the future. As a result, individuals (and organizations) too often forego upfront capital expenditures that would offer huge annual returns. Perhaps one of the most obvious examples of the harmful impact of overly high discount rates with regards to the future is the global fishing crisis. Worldwide, 11 of the 17 largest fishing basins have been depleted in recent decades. With the aid of high-tech equipment and government subsidies, fishermen have depleted the oceans of once-plentiful species. This emerging catastrophe has economic, environmental and social implications. Subsidies for the global fishing fleet have helped produce enough boats, hooks and nets to catch twice the number of available fish. Quite simply, too many boats are chasing too few fish, leading to fisheries collapse, destroyed capacity to feed human populations and severe economic loss through both lost revenue and misplaced government resources. In the extreme, international skirmishes over borders and poaching have emerged, further exacerbating the level of human suffering. Disputes over fishing rights have turned violent in recent years: Canadian fishermen blockaded a US ferry and shot at a Spanish ship; Russians shot at Japanese fishermen; Iceland forced a Danish boat from its waters; Australian forces have seized Indonesian boats; and the Portuguese Navy fired on a Spanish boat.

Economic, social and environmental disruption such as this – for example, the depletion of freshwater supplies, environmental pollution and the exhaustion of natural resources – will become increasingly common as the world continues to exhaust global ecosystems (Millennium Ecosystem Assessment, 2005). This will have tremendous implications for both the natural environment from which materials are drawn and the human populations that rely on those materials for both sustenance and economic income.

Given these woes, why do governments continue to subsidize fish over-harvesting? The psychological tendency to overly discount the future is largely to blame. The immediate need for maintaining domestic fishing fleets blinds policy-makers (and fishermen) to the pending collapse that their very actions are creating. Political scientists, sociologists, social psychologists and decision researchers have offered unique insights into the management of social dilemmas. Yet policy-makers have failed to apply these insights to the management of fishery crises around the world. The diffusion of wise practices must include strategies for confronting these cognitive obstacles.

Organizational Biases that Perpetuate Unsustainable Practices

The adoption of wise innovation is limited not just by cognitive obstacles, but also by the ways in which organizations have evolved based on market pressures and adaptive organizational responses. In this section, we focus on one such organizational limitation, the over-reliance on regulatory standards. By regulations, we refer to any form of coercive influence, both those established by governments as well as other forms of regulatory bodies (such as trade associations, standard-setting bodies and others). We conclude the section with an overview of how other organizational properties keep us from adopting wise innovations.

While regulations for sustainable behavior are not fully developed, regulations are the most apparent source of pressure for organizational action on sustainability in the United States and elsewhere (including, we argue, ineffective and counter-productive action as well). While recent regulatory innovations have been based on cooperative or voluntary formats, regulatory pressure is still largely seen as coercive in nature, forcing compliance by threat of penalty or sanction. But regulatory standards are also symbolic, uncertain, contested and constitutive. Courts frequently measure compliance against 'industry standards', 'business necessity' and 'the limits of current technology'. Without overlooking the coercive aspects of standards (Scott, 1995), we must also consider how they are supported by contending logics of cognitive values and beliefs (Powell, 1996). Edelman (1990), for example, shows how abstract coercive legal mandates are typically enacted in organizational practices via mechanisms of translation and adaptation based on these supporting cognitive institutions.

Regulatory standards and sustainability

Consider that present regulations and standards for enforcement around the world are largely founded on a 'command-and-control' format, which perpetuates an adversarial relationship between industry and the enforcing body. These enforcing bodies can be local, state, national or international governments as well as international standard-setting bodies such as ISO, the United Nations or the World Bank. This adversarial relationship supports the belief that regulators and industry decision-makers cannot find solutions that offer mutual gain. Unfortunately, any solutions to sustainable development will have to consider the 'inherent' trade-offs among regulators, industry and activist communities.

Some have begun to argue that existing standard and enforcement programs may be the biggest challenge faced by sustainability proponents today. While they can force behaviors that are easily monitored by oversight agencies, they perpetuate perceptions about the relationship between economics and sustainability that may be contrary to the goals of both. They are based on institutions that perpetuate the view that the three interests of the triple bottom line are mutually exclusive. While government standards have historically produced results consistent with broad environmental and social objectives (Easterbrook, 1995), many now view this paradigm as out of date and overly restrictive of corporate initiatives beyond strict compliance (Schmitt, 1994). But to change them will require alterations in multiple levels of systemic policy structures, individual and collective organizational cultures, and the cognitive biases of individual managers.

Tenbrunsel et al. (1997) argue that strict standards lock organizations into a focus on compliance rather than the attainment of the overall societal goals and interests they are intended to promote. They suggest that decision-makers may evaluate suboptimal choices (economic, social or environmental) that better adhere to a standard than optimal choices that are tangential to, or violate, the standard. Once standards are written, program managers within government and corporations become constrained by a compliance mindset and by bureaucratic procedures that attenuate the search for creative solutions to complex problems. Standards direct attention and embody a theory of cause, effect and solution that is often received as accepted wisdom. Across a broad spectrum of disassociated industries, a given rule structure dictates which actions are appropriate, by what measure, to what extent and through which means. It often ignores the technological and logistical issues associated with overlapping regulatory programs, as well as the multi-media and multi-objective impacts of a particular rule of policy (Raffle and Mitchell, 1993).

This stifling of multi-level solution development is particularly problematic for a sustainability agenda which is, by definition, multi-level in nature. Standards can explicitly restrict optimal solutions. Tenbrunsel et al. (1997) for example, suggest a motivational explanation for the 'misdirected attention' effect: namely that standard-based systems can change the incentive systems for individuals and promote self-interested behaviors that are at odds with wider societal interests (Tenbrunsel et al., 1997). Suboptimal outcomes are the product of both unintentional and intentional actions on the part of a decision-maker, within a context that frames incentives and defines options. Unintentional actions may result from individuals 'just following the rules', creativity not being rewarded, a 'use it or lose it' rationale, intrinsic motivation being replaced with extrinsic motivation, or a 'no law against it' mentality. Intentional actions include trying to 'beat the system'.

As we noted earlier, standards are supported by contending logics and project-symbolic activity. To alter the meaning behind regulatory standards and the tensions that exist between such mandates and organizational processes (Edelman, 1990; Mezias, 1995), we must change both the overt (regulative) and the taken-for-granted (cognitive) institutions upon which they are based (Scott, 1995). In essence, a standard is an artifact of the wider regulatory cultures, structures and traditions from which it originates. But existing cognitive aspects of such standards are anchored in the constellation of beliefs, organizational routines, policies and practices that have accumulated over decades of organizational and programmatic routines. They have defined both the nature of the problem and the form of the solution. This insight has critical implications as we move forward and consider regulations that address issues of sustainability.

In particular, the introduction of the social elements of the triple bottom line into political and economic systems may pose a serious cognitive challenge, significantly more daunting than the integration of environmental values over the past 40 years. The underlying institutions that support regulations and standards on this front may be (actually or perceptually) divergent from the presently accepted measures and objectives of economic growth and business strategy (Hoffman, 2000). Where environmental problems are highly visible and clearly threatening to almost everyone, not just a small percentage of the population, the social equity components of sustainable development are less visible and inherently about distributing resources from those who presently have to those who are presently without. This will invite resistance.

For example, one of the objectives of sustainability is the distribution of environmental costs and benefits fairly among people in all economic and cultural classes. This is underlain by the pragmatic concern that poverty resulting from inequitable resource distribution leads to the degradation of the ecosystem and could lead to destabilized economic and political regimes (Farrell and Hart, 1998). Regulations that seek to offset these concerns could be at serious odds with the individualistic, self-interested, profit-seeking, resource-utilizing beliefs that underlie the present capitalistic system (Allenby, 1998). Regulations designed to tackle social equity issues may continue to face the kinds of ideological opposition that frames the tension as a win–lose debate.

Other organizational biases

Regulatory standards are not the only source of environmentally and socially detrimental behavior that has become established within organizations over time. Multitudes of accompanying organizational arrangements can shield managers from perceiving opportunities to satisfy environmental and social interests to the betterment of the organization and society. Organizational silos keep multiple elements of organizations from seeing and implementing wise strategies that cut across the organization. Such silos are often based on political divisions and protective departmental interests that shield organizations from identifying the potential economic benefits of sustainability initiatives. Segmented responsibilities within these multiple departments can also separate economic cause from effect, thereby leaving opportunities on the table (Lovins and Lovins, 1997).

Capital budgets keep plant managers from making wise long-term decisions regarding total lifespan costing of plant equipment. Capital planning is supported by economic metrics that perpetuate behaviors that damage the environment or ignore social consequences. For example, the gross domestic product (GDP), the foremost indicator of a nation's economic progress, measures all financial transactions of products and services in the country, but does not acknowledge or value a distinction between those transactions that add to a country's environmental or social well-being and those that actually diminish it (Redefining Progress, 1996). Other metrics, such as return on investment, net present value and return on equity, are built upon beliefs and assumptions that overlook measures that include environmental and social concerns. Financial markets often encourage short-term goals, undervalue environmental resources, disregard human impacts and discount the future in favor of accounting and reporting systems that do not reflect true environmental and social risks and opportunities (Schmidheiny, 1996). Economic return on investment must support the debt load expected by lending institutions and corporate investors. These pressures will lead companies to harvest resources at rates that exceed maximum sustainable yield, thereby diminishing the stability of the ecosystem as well as the natural capital asset base upon which future generations must depend for their livelihood. The short-term payback periods of financial markets take precedent over the long-term time horizons of ecological and social systems.

Coordinating mechanisms within the organization, such as established reward and incentives systems, often mask the opportunities available through change. Where a company may claim to hold sustainability as important in its mission statements, misaligned reward systems can lead individual managers toward fulfilling immediate personal goals that diverge from the broader, long-range goals of the sustainable organization (Kerr, 1995). Rewards exist on the systemic level as well. Architects and engineers are compensated with a percentage of the cost of the building or equipment that is specified at construction, not over its lifetime. There are few incentives to seek out and include the input of those who will live, work and play within or around the built structure. Further, these professionals are often penalized for eliminating equipment that may be costly at the beginning of the project, but cheaper over the long term. This has led the US government to misallocate about $1 trillion to air-conditioning equipment that would not have been necessary had the buildings been optimally designed to produce the same or better comfort at lower cost (Houghton et al., 1992).

At the deepest level, certain unquestioned assumptions are implanted in managers in their earliest education at business schools and then perpetuated through managerial structures. These assumptions include: the notion that the firm is socially and physically autonomous; the idea that profit motive is the singular objective of the firm; the omission of natural capital from market accounting systems; the perception of the natural environment as a limitless source of resources and a limitless sink for wastes; and the unquestioned necessity of economic growth (Capra, 1982; Daly, 1991; Daly and Cobb, 1994; Gladwin et al., 1995). These assumptions support actions that are detrimental to the stability of environmental and social systems surrounding the organization.

Within organizations, the changes needed to help employees overcome these biases happen slowly and invite resistance. Resistance can come in the form of habitual routines that perpetuate behaviors that employees may know are damaging the environment. Often the perpetuation of habit stems from an individual's realization that changing an established habit will involve some form of short-term costs in the form of resources, effort or discomfort. While inefficient or inconsistent with long-term objectives, these established routines can become familiar, comfortable and reliably predictable (Clark, 1985). Habitual routines often grow out of taken-for-granted engineering or managerial practice. Fear of the unknown can also drive both organizational inertia and the continued reliance on basic underlying assumptions. Both external and internal change can be upsetting for organizational constituents, particularly when the outcome or consequences of change cannot be predicted. Of course, in the real world, outcomes or consequences can never be predicted. Resource limitations can restrict the ability of an organization to overcome sunk costs of plant, equipment and personnel. Sunk costs can become psychological roadblocks that prevent managers from adequately addressing demands for change. Short-term costs predominate, thus biasing the manager to over-discount the future. Finally, threats to established power bases can cause resistance to organizational change. Organizational culture establishes a structure of power that will bias the perceptions of those whom the existing system benefits. Any attempts to restructure the system will likely undermine these power structures and invite organizational confusion, interdepartmental rivalry or organizational resistance (Mintzberg, 1979). Self-preservation may override concerns for environmental, social or economic objectives in managerial decision-making.

In summary, organizational arrangements and cultural beliefs tend to perpetuate unsustainable behavior. Individuals within organizations deviate from rational and sustainable behavior through the individual biases discussed in the last section, coupled with the organizational-level biases discussed in this section. Overcoming these obstacles will require alterations in the organization that integrate environmental and social concerns into the organization's basic underlying beliefs, recasting them in ways that are mutually beneficial to the objectives of the organization and the sustainability of human and natural systems on which it depends.

OVERCOMING COGNITIVE AND ORGANIZATIONAL BARRIERS: THE ENDANGERED SPECIES ACT AND HABITAT CONSERVATION PLANS

We would like to close this chapter with an example that illustrates a way to overcome the biases we have discussed. It centers on the Endangered Species

Act (ESA), the most controversial of US environmental laws and one that seemingly pits corporate interests against those of environmental protection, with local, regional and national communities impacted by the outcome. The mission of the ESA is to create a mechanism for the US government to designate any animal or plant species as 'endangered' or 'threatened' and prohibit its 'take' (for example, any harm to a member of the species or its habitat). Once listed, recovery plans are drafted to serve as a guide to ensure the species' long-term survival. The standard frame that ESA debates have taken is win–lose. The mythical fixed pie leads to prototypical conflicts in which neither side of the debate trusts or engages the other.

To critics, the idea of giving up jobs and crippling a regional economy to save individual species sounds absurd. Protection of the human economy is paramount. To proponents, such economic sacrifices are unfortunate but necessary to protect the 1516 species of flora and fauna listed as threatened or endangered. Protection of natural ecosystems is priceless. This is how ESA debates most often play out. Economic and development interests form intractable positions and fight a win–lose battle over concessionary agreements. But this polarization is unnecessary and, in fact, counterproductive to wise outcomes that seek to resolve interests on multiple sides of the debate. The mythical fixed pie bias coupled with perverse incentives and rewards lead participants to conceal or destroy evidence of listed species on private lands; in the words of one landowner, to 'shoot, shovel, and shut up' (Crismon, 1998). It yields outcomes that are suboptimal for all three parts of the triple bottom line: economic, environmental and equitable.

By most accounts, the listing of the spotted owl represents the most controversial 'train-wreck' of ESA implementation. This Pacific Northwest controversy epitomizes the tensions in which cognitive and organizational barriers can lead to suboptimal outcomes. Each side of the debate viewed beating the other as the path to achieving its goals. Environmentalists wanted a better environment and were willing to sacrifice economic development toward that end. Development interests wanted economic growth and considered it unacceptable to forfeit jobs or economic prosperity in the name of species protection. In the end, protection of the spotted owl removed large tracts of federal lands from logging, leading to a decrease in the supply of raw timber, elimination of mill capacity, job loss and price increases. Local and regional economies were impacted.

But, it did not need to play out this way. While the spotted owl controversy represents a costly effort to protect an endangered species, it is also an example of a mistake, one that could have been avoided had the corporations, agencies and interest groups dealt with the underlying issues early in a proactive fashion (Yaffee, 1994). But the mythical fixed pie perspective prevented the parties from engaging with each other early. Because a response was delayed through mistrust and confrontation, costs increased. As plants and animals become scarce, the costs of protecting them rise exponentially. We are better off investing small amounts of resources to proactively to avoid such catastrophes as the spotted owl controversy, rather than face the impasses so evident in recent years. The costs of sustainability are now, and the benefits accrue to future generations.

But solutions exist to this ESA dilemma. In an attempt to move beyond these supporting beliefs and the perverse behaviors they provoke, Congress amended the ESA in 1982 and introduced Habitat Conservation Plans (HCPs) as a mechanism to encourage creative solutions that balance conservation, community and economic imperatives. HCPs provide the opportunity to enlarge the pie by giving private landowners a permit to violate the specifics of the ESA through 'incidental taking' of listed species in the course of lawful development activities, provided that the landowner follows certain steps to provide for conservation of that species. Those steps, as laid out in the HCP, must be developed in cooperative engagement with all impacted parties to the debate. This promotes transparency and inclusiveness as a democratic process brings economic, environmental and social issues to the table. HCPs can overcome the win–lose mentality by creatively developing plans that satisfy endangered species protection, community concerns and economic interests. They break the existing mold of coercive command-and-control regulation and form creative public–private partnerships that loosen regulatory strangleholds, enhance long-term regulatory predictability and species protection, improve conservation science and technology and include impacted human populations.

But in spite of the opportunities that voluntary programs such as HCPs present, barriers to change still exist. Key economic and environmental stakeholders have historically been slow to adopt this shift in regulatory relations (Troast et al., 2002). In the first ten years of the HCPs' existence (from 1982 to 1991), only 12 HCP plans were approved by the federal government (US Fish and Wildlife Service, 1999). By viewing HCPs through the lens of behavioral scholarship, we can assess how to overcome these barriers (Troast et al., 2002).

There are many reasons for this institutional resistance. We will list four here:

- Resource constraints. The responsible federal agencies have been understaffed and constrained by limited resources (such as for site visits, scientific review, program development).
- Fear of the unknown. Most companies affected by the ESA know little about the HCP process, and many prefer the 'devil they know' in command-and-control regulations to the 'devil they don't know'.

- Threats to political interests and a fixed pie perspective. Poised for battle with commercial interests, environmental activists have condemned HCPs as overly permissive and fundamentally flawed in their long-term design (Sabel et al., 1999); industry interests view them as yet another costly web of government bureaucracy.
- Habitual distrust. All parties possess a degree of historic, ingrained distrust for others in this negotiation process.

To overcome some of this resistance, the Department of Interior introduced the 'No Surprises' policy in 1991, reassuring private landowners that the government would stand by the terms of any HCP negotiated. This policy stimulated interest in companies to engage stakeholders in resolving species protection issues more fully and led to more adoption of HCPs. By the end of 1997, there were 243 HCP agreements in 16 states, covering 6.2 million acres of land.

But while the shift from command-and-control implementation of the ESA to the negotiated implementation of HCPs brought about many creative new efforts, the number of HCPs remains much smaller than the number of conflicts in which an HCP could be used as a tool to generate a better solution for landowners, the community and the environment. Ongoing organizational and cognitive barriers explain this contradiction. First, despite the potential of HCPs to enlarge the pie and create value for landowners and environmental interests, many parties continued to view their conflicts as win–lose and zero-sum, adopting the view that 'If it's good for the other side, it can't be good for me.' In addition, the branch of government that created the HCP legislation did not give the government employees in charge of implementation the budget or the skills needed to implement HCPs effectively. The government employees charged with negotiating HCPs were overworked and were not trained to negotiate against wealthy landowners who could heavily finance their negotiations. Finally, the political tendency of the administration of George W. Bush to focus on economic over social and environmental interests in its policy-making allowed economic interests simply to conquer alternative interests, rather than seeking wise agreements with them. Collectively, HCPs represent an excellent prototype of a sustainable development innovation that was limited by cognitive, organizational and political factors (see Troast et al., 2002 for a more detailed analysis).

We will face many similar challenges in the future, in which we can pit social and environmental interests against the short-term economic interests of a special interest group or a specific company, or we can start overcoming barriers to developing sustainable solutions earlier in the process. For example, in Puget Sound, killer whales (or orcas) are close to being listed under the Endangered Species Act. If they are listed, there will be a significant impact on waterborne travel – shipping, ferries, fishing companies as well as the communities that rely on them. Stakeholders should come together now to understand the migration and living patterns of these animals so as to protect them proactively and avoid listing. Or, more likely, the parties can fight a political battle over their listing, where we either suffer the loss of the species or incur significant economic losses.

CONCLUSION

The field of management research has made great strides in the past quarter-century, building a body of research and literature that can help us understand and improve the environmental and social impact of corporate activity. Yet much can be done to bring this research into the realm of practice and change corporate behavior for the better. Tremendous opportunities for making wise changes lie ahead of us; low-hanging fruit still remains.

To bring about wise changes, we must confront the barriers to individual and organizational implementation. As an issue of practical action, sustainability has become much more complex and requires a more sophisticated view to be managed effectively. This is an area to which organizational research can contribute. Organizational research attends to the psychological and organizational sources of unsustainable behavior and helps us identify solutions through alterations in systemic control structures and individual interests and biases (Winn and Angell, 2000). Research on decision-making and organizational theory has implications for managers who now recognize that, to improve global conditions of the environment and people, we need to understand how to change the behavior of individuals and organizations. In addition, policy-makers need to understand how to incorporate business thinking into policy development to foster the most effective and efficient response from business.

REFERENCES

Allenby, B. (1998), 'USA vs. SD: can American values and sustainable development live together in peace?', *Tomorrow*, **4** (8) 61.

Baden, J. (1995), 'The adverse consequences of the ESA', *Seattle Times*, 25 October, p. B5.

Bazerman, M. (1983), 'Negotiator judgment: a critical look at the rationality assumption', *American Behavioral Scientist*, **27**, 618–34.

Bazerman, M. (2005), *Judgment in Managerial Decision Making*, New York: John Wiley & Sons.
Bazerman, M. and A. Hoffman (1999), 'Sources of environmentally destructive behavior: individual, organizational and institutional perspectives', *Research in Organizational Behavior*, **21**, 39–79.
Bazerman, M.H., J. Baron and K. Shonk (2001), *You Can't Enlarge the Pie: Six Barriers to Effective Government*, New York: Basic Books.
Beck, U. (1992), *Risk Society: Towards a New Modernity*, London: Sage.
Bryant, B. (1995), *Environmental Justice: Issues, Policies and Solutions*, Washington, DC: Island Press.
Capra, F. (1982), *The Turning Point*, New York: Bantam Books.
Clark, K. (1985), 'The interaction of design hierarchies and market concepts in technological evolution', *Research Policy*, **14** (5), 235–51.
Cordano, M. and I. Frieze (2000), 'Pollution reduction preferences of US environmental managers: applying Ajzen's theory of planned behavior', *Academy of Management Journal*, **43** (4), 627–41.
Crismon, S. (1998), 'Pender County, North Carolina red-cockaded woodpecker habitat conservation plan and safe harbor', in L. Zucker *Improving Integrated Natural Resource Planning: Habitat Conservation Plans*, Washington, DC: National Center for Environmental Decision-Making Research, pp. 3–21.
Crossette, B. (1998), 'Most consuming more, and the rich consuming much more', *New York Times*, 13 September, Section 1, p. 3.
Daly, H. (1991), *Steady-State Economics*, Washington, DC: Island Press.
Daly, H. and J. Cobb (1994), *For the Common Good*, Boston, MA: Beacon Press.
Easterbrook, G. (1995), *A Moment on the Earth*, New York: Viking.
The Economist (2001), 'Economics focus: curse of the ethical executive', *The Economist*, 17 November, p. 70.
The Economist (2005), 'The good company', 22 January, pp. 3–22.
Edelman, L. (1990), 'Legal environments and organizational governance: the expansion of due process in the American workplace', *American Journal of Sociology*, **95**, 1401–40.
Ehrenfeld, J. (2004), 'Searching for sustainability: no quick fix', *Reflections: The SoL Journal on Knowledge, Learning and Change*, **5** (8), 1–13.
Elkington, J. (1998), *Cannibals with Forks: The Triple Bottom Line for 21st Century Business*, Oxford: Capstone.
Farrell, A. and M. Hart (1998), 'What does sustainability really mean? The search for useful indicators', *Environment*, November (4–9), 26–31.
Gladwin, T., J. Kennelly and T. Krause (1995), 'Shifting paradigms for sustainable development: implications for management theory and research', *Academy of Management Review*, **20** (4), 874–907.
Goodman, A. (2000), 'Down with SD, Long live SD!', *Tomorrow* (September/October), 64.
Hannigan, J. (1995), *Environmental Sociology: A Social Constructionist Perspective*, London: Routledge.
Hoffman, A. (1999), 'Institutional evolution and change: environmentalism and the US chemical industry', *Academy of Management Journal*, **42** (4), 351–71.
Hoffman, A. (2000), 'Integrating environmental and social issues into corporate practice', *Environment*, **42** (5), 22–33.
Hoffman, A. (2005), 'Business decisions and the environment: significance, challenges, and momentum of an emerging research field', in G. Brewer and P. Stern

(eds), *Decision Making for the Environment: Social and Behavioral Science Research Priorities*, Washington, DC: National Research Council, National Academies Press, pp. 200–229.

Hoffman, A., K. Wade-Benzoni, L. Thompson, D. Moore, J. Gillespie and M. Bazerman (1999), 'A mixed-motive perspective on the economics versus environment debate', *American Behavioral Scientist*, **42** (8), 1254–76.

Holliday, C., S. Schmidheiny and P. Watts (2002), *Walking the Talk: The Business Case for Sustainable Development*, San Francisco, CA: Berrett-Koehler.

Houghton, D., R. Bishop, R. Lovins, A. Stickney, J. Newcomb, M. Shepard and B. Davids (1992), *The State of the Art: Space Cooling and Air Handling*, Aspen, CO: Rocky Mountain Institute.

Howard-Grenville, J. and A. Hoffman (2003), 'The importance of cultural framing to the success of social initiatives in business', *Academy of Management Executive*, **17** (2), 70–84.

Kahneman, D. and A. Tverksy (1973), 'On the psychology of prediction', *Psychological Review*, **80**, 237–51.

Kahneman, D. and A. Tversky (1979), 'Prospect theory: an analysis of decision under risk', *Econometrica*, **47**, 263–91.

Kerr, S. (1995), 'On the folly of rewarding A while hoping for B', *Academy of Management Executive*, **9** (1), 7–16.

King, A. and M. Lenox (2001), 'Does it really pay to be green? An empirical study of firm environmental and financial performance', *Journal of Industrial Ecology*, **5** (1), 105–16.

Leopold, A. (1949), *A Sand County Almanac, And Sketches Here and There*, New York: Oxford University Press.

Lovins, A. and H. Lovins (1997), *Climate: Making Sense and Making Money*, Snowmass, CO: Rocky Mountain Institute.

March, J. and H. Simon (1958), *Organizations*, New York: John Wiley & Sons.

Margolis, J. and J. Walsh (2001), *People and Profits? The Search for a Link Between a Company's Social and Financial Performance*, Mahwah, NJ: Lawrence Erlbaum Associates.

Meadows, D., J. Randers and D. Meadows (2004), *Limits to Growth: The 30-Year Update*, Post Mills, VT: Chelsea Green Publishing.

Meckling, W. and M. Jensen (1983), 'Reflections on the corporation as a social invention', *Midland Corporate Finance Journal* (Fall), 6–15.

Mezias, S. (1995), 'Using institutional theory to understand for-profit sectors: the case of financial reporting standards', in W.R. Scott and S. Christensen (eds), *The Institutional Construction of Organizations*, Thousand Oaks, CA: Sage Publications, pp. 164–98.

Millennium Ecosystem Assessment (2005), *Ecosystems and Human Well-Being*, Washington, DC: Island Press.

Mintzberg, H. (1979), *The Structuring of Organizations*, Englewood Cliffs, NJ: Prentice-Hall.

Murray, A. (2005), 'Will "social responsibility" harm business?', *Wall Street Journal*, 18 May, p. A2.

Norman, W. and C. MacDonald (2003), 'Getting to the bottom of the "triple bottom line"', *Business Ethics Quarterly*, **14** (2), 243–62.

Palmer, K., W. Oates and P. Portney (1995), 'Tightening environmental standards: the benefit–cost or the no-cost paradigm?', *Journal of Economic Perspectives*, **9** (4), 119–32.

Porter, M. and C. van der Linde (1995a), 'Green and competitive: ending the stalemate', *Harvard Business Review* (September–October), 120–34.
Porter, M. and C. van der Linde (1995b), 'Toward a new conception of the environment–competitiveness relationship', *Journal of Economic Perspectives*, **9** (4), 97–118.
Post, J., L. Preston and S. Sauter-Sachs (2002), *Redefining the Corporation: Stakeholder Management and Organizational Wealth*, Stanford, CA: Stanford University Press.
Powell, W. (1996), 'On the nature of institutional embeddedness: labels versus explanation', *Advances in Strategic Management*, **13**, 293–300.
Prahalad, C.K. (2004), *The Fortune at the Bottom of the Pyramid: Eradicating Poverty Through Profits*, Upper Saddle River, NJ: Wharton School Publishing.
Raffle, B. and D. Mitchell (1993), *Effective Environmental Strategies: Opportunities For Innovation and Flexibility Under Federal Environmental Law*, Chicago, IL: Amoco Corporation.
Redefining Progress (1996), *What's Wrong with GDP*, San Francisco, CA: Redefining Progress.
Royston, M. (1979), *Pollution Prevention Pays*, London: Pergamon.
Royston, M. (1980), 'Making pollution prevention pay', *Harvard Business Review* (November–December), 6–27.
Sabel, C., A. Fung and B. Karkkainen (1999), 'Beyond backyard environmentalism: how communities are quietly refashioning environmental regulation', *Boston Review*, **24** (5), 4–11.
Schmidheiny, S. (1996), *Financing Change*, Cambridge, MA: MIT Press.
Schmitt, R. (1994), 'The AMOCO/EPA Yorktown experience and regulating the right thing', *Natural Resources and Environment* (Summer) (11–13), 51.
Schnaiberg, A. and K. Gould (1994), *Environment and Society: The Enduring Conflict*, New York: Worth Publishing.
Scott, W.R. (1995), *Institutions and Organizations*, London: Sage Publications.
Simon, H.A. (1957), *Models of Man*, New York: Wiley.
Tenbrunsel, A., K. Wade-Benzoni, D. Messick and M. Bazerman (1997), 'The dysfunctional effects of standards on environmental attitudes and choices', in M. Bazerman, D. Messick, A. Tenbrunsel and K. Wade-Benzoni (eds), *Environment, Ethics, and Behavior: The Psychology of Environmental Valuation and Degradation*, San Francisco, CA: New Lexington Books, pp. 105–21.
Thompson, L. (2004), *The Mind and Heart of the Negotiator*, Upper Saddle River, NJ: Prentice-Hall.
Troast, J., A. Hoffman, H. Riley and M. Bazerman (2002), 'Institutions as barriers and enablers to negotiated agreements: institutional entrepreneurship and the Plum Creek Habitat Conservation Plan', in A. Hoffman and M. Ventresca (eds), *Organizations, Policy and the Natural Environment: Institutional and Strategic Perspectives*, Stanford, CA: Stanford University Press, pp. 235–61.
US Fish and Wildlife Service (1999), *Status of Habitat Conservation Plans*, Washington, DC: Government Printing Office.
Wall Street Journal (2004), 'Kyoto capitalists', 13 December, p. A16.
Walley, N. and B. Whitehead (1994), 'It's not easy being green', *Harvard Business Review* (May–June), 46–51.
Walton, R. and R. McKersie (1965), *A Behavioral Theory of Labor Negotiations: An Analysis of a Social Interaction System*, New York: McGraw Hill.

Winn, M. and L. Angell (2000), 'Toward a process model of corporate greening', *Organization Studies*, **21** (6), 1119–47.

World Business Council for Sustainable Development (2002), *Tomorrow's Markets: Global Trends and Their Implications for Business*, Geneva, Switzerland: World Business Council for Sustainable Development.

World Business Council for Sustainable Development (1997), *Exploring Sustainable Development: WBCSD Global Scenario*, London: World Business Council for Sustainable Development.

World Commission on Environment and Development (1987), *Our Common Future*, Oxford: Oxford University Press.

World Resources Institute (1994), *World Resources, 1994–1995*, New York: Oxford University Press.

Yaffee, S. (1994), *The Wisdom of the Spotted Owl: Policy Lessons for a New Century*, Washington, DC: Island Press.

5. Institutionalization as a prerequisite for sustainable corporate development

Frank Wijen

The notion of sustainable development has come into vogue, both in academia and in business circles. After its introduction in 1987 by the World Commission on Environment and Development (the 'Brundtland Commission'), the idea of meeting the needs of the present without compromising the ability of future generations to meet their own needs has been widely embraced in the management literature as the reconciliation of environmental, social and economic imperatives (Elkington, 1998; Hart, 1995; Hawken et al., 2000; Holliday et al., 2002). Quite a few companies have adopted principles of sustainable business or, similarly, corporate (social) responsibility (Husted, 2003; Smith, 2003; Van Tulder and Van der Zwart, 2006). The World Business Council for Sustainable Development (WBCSD), representing many such proactive companies, numbers some 165 members with aggregate annual sales of US$ 4000 billion (Stigson and Rendlen, 2005).

While the principles of sustainable business have thus been widely embraced, it is less clear to what extent this has materialized in more sustainable practices, especially since it concerns the realization of a systemic equilibrium over a longer period (Ehrenfeld, 2005; Roome, 1998). However, the question of whether sustainable business will be sustained is particularly relevant, since the notion may be subject to implementation problems and erosion owing to changing 'management fads' or unfavorable economic tides. This chapter examines whether efforts to conduct sustainable business are accompanied by more sustainable practices over a longer period. In particular, the chapter seeks to identify the critical conditions that lead to success or failure from the viewpoint of sustainable business development. In order to do so, I draw on an extensive case-study of a large multinational food company that had committed itself to the realization of environmentally sustainable development; the social dimension of sustainability was not an issue. This firm, for reasons of anonymity called

'Greenheart', was intensively studied over a five-year period. The case is particularly interesting because of its dynamics: an initially successful move towards sustainable business was reversed after some time due to the concurrence of critical events. I extensively describe the case in order to provide all relevant information, which serves as input for the subsequent analysis of the company's behavior through the conceptual lenses of stakeholder influence and organizational learning.

The chapter's main conclusion is that the successful pursuit of sustainable corporate development requires companies to institutionalize their environmental activities. The institutionalization of sustainable business has two dimensions: (1) companies must have a high and widely shared environmental ambition; and (2) firms must deeply embed their environmental practices. On the basis of these dimensions, I identify different types of corporate sustainability behavior. While the study has focused on the environmental dimension of sustainable corporate development, it is likely that institutionalization is also required for social sustainability. The conclusion has important implications for academia. Since the perspectives of stakeholder power and organizational learning show important parallels and complementarities, they should be used in conjunction. Besides, the proliferation of longitudinal studies would significantly further our understanding of the dynamics of sustainable business development. The study's outcomes also have significant managerial implications, since high environmental (and social) performance requires not only top-management ambition but also company-wide support, routinization and systemization, and tight integration with other activities.

CASE DESCRIPTION

The case-study is an appropriate technique to understand processes and causes of complex social phenomena (Ragin, 1987; Yin, 1994). A 'critical' case provides detailed insights and is representative of a focal phenomenon. The outcomes of such a study have implications going beyond the scope of the focal case (Gerring, 2001; Yin, 1994). The focal organization was selected because it had made an important commitment to the pursuit of corporate sustainability. Case information was collected at five points in time over the period 1999–2004, through in-depth, semi-structured interviews with the company's major internal and external actors, the perusal of firm-specific and other documents, as well as observations during site visits. Overall, some 60 information sources were used. All relevant data were transcribed and systematically coded with the help of Atlas/ti, an effective qualitative software package (Weitzman and Miles, 1995). The codes were based on contextual and theoretical issues, such as antecedents, environmental measures, stakeholder power and organizational learning. After removing redundant information, the coded transcripts were converted into the case description; they also provided the basis for the subsequent analysis.

The case description starts with the company's history in order to highlight the chronology of critical events that shaped the corporate identity and practices. I then describe the environmental measures and performance by the focal company, in order to assess the actual actions and outcomes in terms of environmental sustainability. The subsection on environmental management structure shows how the making and implementation of environmentally relevant decisions were officially designed. Next, I identify the most significant internal and external stakeholders, since their formal and informal influences critically shaped the company's sustainability voyage.

Case history

Greenheart was created around 1900. Starting as a small, craftsman-like Dutch food producer, it had evolved into a large corporation with over 20 subsidiaries on four continents, employing over 3000 people, by the end of the twentieth century. The last years of the previous century especially showed high increases of its sales and employees. Its branded food products were sold all around the globe. Greenheart had one particularly successful product, which was the second best-selling product of the sector worldwide. However, the company sensed that its sales were levelling off in an increasingly competitive market. This led to a radical decision. Early in 2001, the family that had, by and large, owned Greenheart for a century sold its shares to a foreign, family-owned company, which was also operating in the food industry; the buyer had already possessed a minority interest in Greenheart's equity for several years. All shares, including those that were traded on the public stock market, fell into the hands of the new owner.

Prior to the takeover, Greenheart was run by one and the same chief executive officer (CEO) for 25 years. This CEO, who retired after the takeover, shared with his family predecessors a deep, personal, religiously inspired conviction that nature is in a very critical situation. This conviction had far-reaching implications for the corporate values. Environmental concern was one of the four major values mentioned in the corporate mission statement and was a recurrent theme in the annual corporate report. In 1990, the CEO embraced the conclusions of the 'Brundtland report' on the worrying condition of globally interrelated ecosystems. The company created a fund for environmentally benign investments which did not meet the corporation's normal financial standards. It also started to transfer 1 percent of its net annual profit to societal initiatives that aimed at the creation of environmental awareness at large. Within the highest strategic forums, the CEO fulfilled the role of environmental value-keeper. The social dimension of sustainability was not articulated and no major initiatives were taken to promote social values within the company.

The new owner did not share this environmental sustainability drive. He had bought Greenheart because of its marketing and profit potential. After the takeover, which was formally a merger, the enlarged company ('Greenheart Plus') had more than doubled Greenheart's original sales volume, ranking among the global top ten producers in its sector, with some 30 subsidiaries and over 8000 employees throughout the world.

While the environmental value did not completely fade into the background, there was a significant shift in the corporate value attributed to the environment. This was reflected in a different mission statement. In 1995, Greenheart's mission was stated as follows: 'We care for the environment, and are dedicated to reducing our impact to a sustainable level.' Greenheart interpreted sustainability as conducting its business activities without negatively affecting the environment. The company had the ambition to realize its understanding of environmentally sustainable business by the year 2005. In 2002, after a year of negotiation between representatives of the former and the new owner, the following corporate mission was formulated: 'We, employees of [Greenheart Plus] . . . cherish the role that we play in our own [social and natural] environment[s], because we work for an organization that is dedicated to both society and the environment.' A statement of norms and values was created as a compromise, adding that 'We want to limit our impact on the environment as much as possible, and work towards long-term sustainability.' It should be noted, though, that no time period was added and that the highest corporate objective, reflected in a vision statement, did not mention the environment: 'We want to reinforce our position as a world leader in the [food] industry, and want to offer people added value by creating appealing quality products.' While care for the environment was therefore still an official objective, it was no longer one of the highest corporate values. Besides, the top management team (TMT) of Greenheart Plus interpreted environmental care differently, as stated in the 2003 environmental report of the main Dutch subsidiary: 'The aim is no longer sustainable management but control of the environmental load stemming from one's own business activities.'

Greenheart had a tradition of open communication with the outside world. It participated in several reflection platforms, for example, with the Dutch Ministry of the Environment and a business platform of food producers that had committed themselves to sustainable development. The new owner was much more reluctant to convey information to external parties. By the end of 2002, Greenheart Plus had ended its membership of the different reflection platforms and basically confined its external environmental contacts to those with regulative authorities. Financial and environmental performance figures, which were published on an annual basis until the year 2000, were no longer publicly announced.

By the end of 2000, an external crisis that affected one of the components of Greenheart's main product induced the company, for safety reasons, to conduct an overnight change in its product composition. This change led to significant production problems, including an extraordinarily high rate of defective products, which exceeded 20 percent instead of the 'normal' 10–15 percent waste rate. These production problems had a very negative effect on Greenheart's financial and environmental performance in 2001 and 2002. As a result, a major reorganization took place in 2003, in which 30 percent of the Dutch employees lost their jobs. Worldwide, many top managers with environmental commitment left the company and were replaced by people who were unfamiliar with the company's (environmental) antecedents.

ENVIRONMENTAL MEASURES AND PERFORMANCE

During the 1990s, Greenheart took a host of internal environmental measures to reduce the company's environmental impact, starting with measures that were easy to realize ('low-hanging fruit'). These included: the purification and recycling of effluent water; the use of surface water for cooling purposes; the separation and recycling of solid waste; a green office plan (the use of recycled paper, the use of LPG for company-owned cars, the separation of solid waste, and so on); the use of thinner packing materials; and the local procurement of materials by an overseas subsidiary to avoid long-distance transport. Greenheart also installed solar panels and wind turbines at some production sites, which yielded the public image of a highly proactive company. When further internal measures were not feasible within the existing technical frames, external compensation measures were taken. Examples are a reforestation project and the purchase of energy from renewable resources ('green electricity') to compensate for excess emissions of carbon dioxide.

Early in 2000, the arrival of a new corporate environmental coordinator gave an impetus to new technical measures, such as closing water loops through the use of advanced membrane systems and reverse osmosis. Besides, additional measures were studied: stocktaking of short-term environmental improvement possibilities; product chain management, involving qualitatively and quantitatively different supplies (this was important because 60 percent of the environmental impact of Greenheart's main product was situated elsewhere in the product chain); the development of a sustainability management system in which managerial bonuses were related to environmental performance; and the replacement of the existing batch technology production method, leading to a 'normal' 10+ percent rate of defective products, by continuous process technology, including closed systems and better process control. Continuous production would involve lower energy and water consumption, and lower emission levels of solid waste and effluent water.

Apart from these actual and envisaged technical measures, Greenheart engaged in initiatives to create environmental awareness. This was stimulated at all levels, ranging from the highest strategic levels to the shop floor. Awareness recurred on the agenda of the company's strategic forums, was part of corporate training programs, and was propagated through an internal, bimonthly environmental pamphlet. Furthermore, special environmental days were organized to clean up the environment and there was social pressure among employees. A marketing manager noted: 'When I leave my office while the light is on, someone else will turn it off, and say: "Watch it."' It should be noted, however, that environmental values were upheld by a minority, which had to activate a benevolent but passive majority of employees. A field visit in 1999 left one with the impression that operating personnel in particular seemed to lack environmental awareness. In the early 2000s, the commitment to environmentally inspired actions decreased due to financial difficulties and the departure of many top managers with environmental commitment.

After the takeover, environmental actions were reoriented either towards those that were required by law or to cost-effective measures, which paid themselves back within less than two years owing to savings on raw materials or other inputs. Three environmental priorities were identified: enhanced energy efficiency, decreased volumes of (effluent) water and decreased production waste. This led to measures such as the refinement of production techniques, tracing and repairing leakages of compressed air, and the increased recycling of effluent water. Environmental projects that were not directly rewarding, such as awareness creation, research on continuous production and on product chain management, the conceptualization of sustainability, the elaboration of a sustainability management system, external compensation measures, and the development of renewable energy, came to an end. The annual budget of over 2 million euros for environmental actions, that had been agreed upon before the takeover, was frozen when the financial tide was rough and eventually faded into obscurity.

In the 1990s, Greenheart measured its environmental impact through a quantitative, tailor-made environmental barometer, which focused on five global areas of environmental disruption: greenhouse gases, acidification, water consumption, effluent water and solid waste. In each of these areas, the barometer measured the distance to the final target, which was a zero impact. Greenheart's environmental distance to target, as measured by the barometer, dropped from 25 in 1992 to 15 in 1996 and 12 in 1999. Afterwards, the exact score was unknown because environmental data were no longer systematically collected and analyzed. It was clear, however, that the distance to target had risen again because of the production-related problems and because of a higher automation rate. It was also felt that one overall figure was not very explanatory, because the indicator was built up of a large number of heterogeneous components. It was therefore decided to abandon the existing barometer and to use more specific indicators. After the dramatic year 2002, with its important production-related problems, the performance at the main Dutch production site showed, by and large, progress in the (newly) designated priority areas of energy efficiency, production waste rate, and fresh-water consumption and effluent-water production. At the same time, this subsidiary did not fully meet all regulative requirements, especially administrative obligations.

Environmental Management Structure

Prior to the takeover, the environmental objectives were initiated and ratified at Greenheart's strategic apex. Environmental issues used to be a recurrent agenda point of meetings between the CEO, who was the environmental value-keeper, and other members of the corporate TMT, each of whom represented either a geographic cluster of markets or a key functional area. An environmental policy group, consisting of representatives from different functional disciplines and headed by the corporate environmental coordinator, prepared advice for the corporate TMT. Once the TMT had ratified environmental proposals, its decisions were conveyed to the managers of the respective subsidiaries. The managers were formally responsible for the implementation of TMT decisions by their subsidiaries.

The corporate environmental coordinator then discussed the implementation of TMT decisions with the managers of the different subsidiaries. The subsidiary environmental coordinators, who combined this function with other activities, were subsequently supposed to convene environmental working groups. Such working groups consisted of representatives from the different functional disciplines concerned, as well as a corporate technical staff member and an external adviser. The environmental working groups brainstormed different options for improvement projects and retained the most viable ones. However, most environmental initiatives were taken on an ad hoc basis since these groups were never fully operational, apart from the one in Greenheart's largest production subsidiary, which started functioning well from 2000 onwards. Working groups obtained technical support from the corporate technical staff, which was also in charge of eco-efficient sourcing (saving both money and natural resources), environmental training, and setting up a company-wide environmental database. Subsidiaries needed to regularly report to and obtain approval from corporate bodies for projects with substantial financial implications. Approved proposals were converted into action plans for the next year. Figure 5.1 summarizes Greenheart's main structural tenets prior to the takeover. The solid lines indicate formal relationships, while the dashed lines represent information flows. The rectangular boxes are line functions, ovals represent staff functions, and octagons indicate (permanent or ad hoc) working groups.

After the takeover, the environmental management's centre of gravity progressively shifted from the corporate to the subsidiary level. The corporate

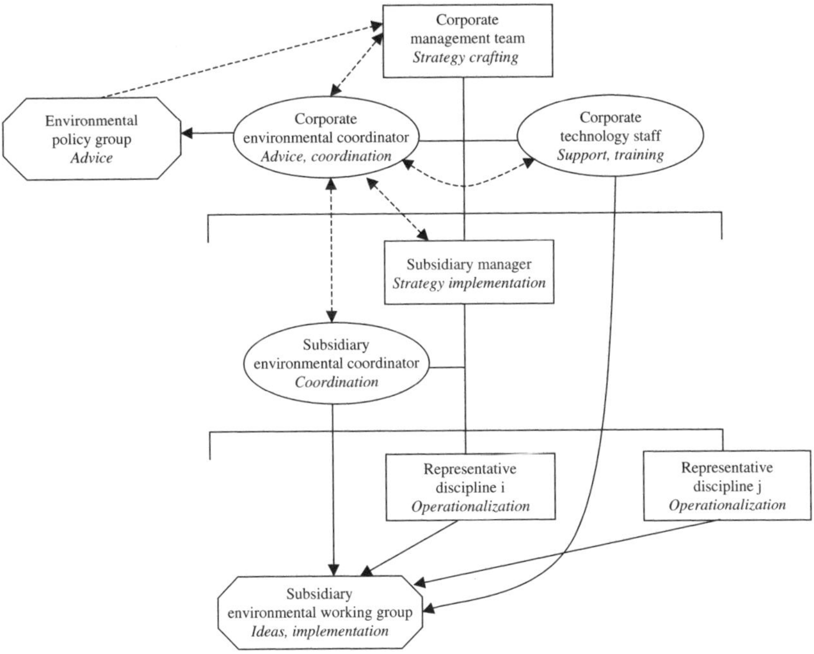

Figure 5.1 Environmental management structure of Greenheart (1999)

TMT, while still having a member representing the environmental value, focused on socio-economic targets and abstained, by and large, from launching new environmental initiatives. The new owner's 'lean and mean' organization philosophy was applied to the corporate environmental department in 2003 when it was completely dismantled; in its wake, company-wide activities such as the exchange of corporate environmental data and the alignment of local environmental policies halted. All environmental responsibilities were allocated to subsidiaries, which focused on locally relevant issues, particularly regulative compliance and cost savings with (positive) environmental side-effects. While a formal management system was not universally embraced, environmental issues were addressed in a more systematic way, at least in the Dutch subsidiaries. Operational teams (OTs) were created, consisting of the production manager, the heads of different functional areas (manufacturing, packing, engineering, logistics, and so on), the environmental coordinator, and other staff officers (personnel, finance, quality control) of the respective subsidiaries. The OTs were endowed with ample formal and financial authority as well as knowledge of different functional areas, but faced capacity constraints since all persons were involved on a part-time basis. The teams convened once a month to evaluate past environmental performance, trace (overt and hidden) problems, discuss new targets and formulate new action plans. These plans were subsequently implemented by the department(s) concerned and coordinated by the environmental coordinator, who had regular bilateral contacts with the persons involved. The aim was to set up a standardized plan–do–check–act system with parallels to quality management and leading to incremental but continuous performance improvements. The new environmental management structure is displayed in Figure 5.2.

Internal and External Stakeholders

The following actors were the most salient stakeholders of Greenheart (Plus) in the environmental area during the period 1999–2004.

CEO

The CEO who had led Greenheart for 25 years, until his retirement in 2001, was widely perceived as a very important stakeholder. He fulfilled two roles. As corporate value-keeper, he was in charge of guarding and stimulating environmental values within the company. His strong personal conviction regarding the necessity to stop environmental degradation was the driving force of Greenheart's pursuit of environmental sustainability. Besides, the CEO was the highest corporate decision-maker. He chaired the corporate TMT, and did not hesitate to use his formal power to put the environmental

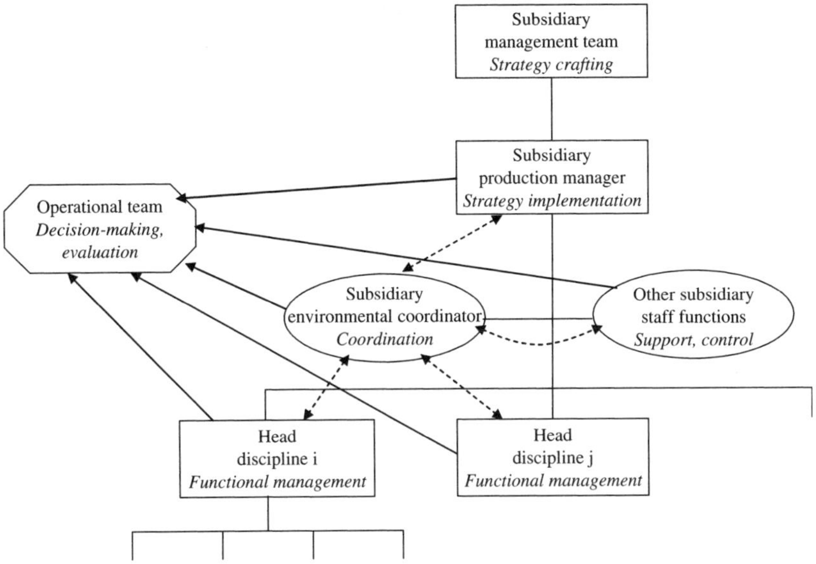

Figure 5.2 Environmental management structure of Greenheart Plus (2004)

agenda forward: 'Fortunately, I am the [CEO], which gives me a certain influence. If I had been any of the other colleagues, it would have been much more difficult.'

In 2001, the new owner appointed another CEO, who wielded his considerable formal power predominantly to enhance the company's financial performance. He did not attribute a high priority to environmental initiatives, except those which were financially rewarding. Whereas the former CEO was also the environmental value-keeper, the new CEO delegated this function to another TMT member, who was clearly less influential. As a result, top management commitment to environmental sustainability sharply declined after the takeover.

Corporate environmental coordinator

A main activity of Greenheart's corporate environmental coordinator during the period 1996–99 was to coordinate company-wide environmental actions. He conveyed information from subsidiaries to the corporate environmental policy group, which advised the corporate TMT. The environmental coordinator ('actually, I am a bridgehead') also had contacts with general managers and subsidiary environmental coordinators on the implementation of the corporate environmental policy and the exchange of new (technical) knowledge. Furthermore, he consulted with the corporate technical staff and had regular consultations with the CEO on environmental actions to be taken. The environmental coordinator's external contacts included a government-led brainstorm group on corporate sustainability, an open dialogue with environmental pressure groups, technology-related contacts with universities, and meetings with external advisers.

Early in 2000, a new corporate environmental coordinator was appointed. While his tasks were about the same as those of his predecessor, he had quite a different vision of this function, which was related to the fact that he came from the very different chemical industry. The new environmental coordinator heavily focused on technical innovation. Over a five-year period, he wanted to replace the existing batch-wise production system, engendering a high waste rate, by a continuous, closed-flow production process, as was usual in the chemical industry. The environmental coordinator also wanted to achieve short-term technical improvements, introduce biodegradable packing, improve employee mentality, and integrate backwards in order better to control the environmental performance of Greenheart's products over their entire life cycles. Early in 2003, the corporate environmental coordinator left the company when his position was abolished.

Subsidiary environmental coordinators

Greenheart's subsidiary environmental coordinators were characterized by the corporate coordinator as quite important actors, because they were in charge of implementing the corporate environmental strategy at the shop floor level, for which the commitment of the operational staff was indispensable. Commitment was, however, compromised because of different objectives, involving competitive time claims. In 1999, a subsidiary environmental coordinator observed: 'The main purpose of almost anyone in the production organization is to produce. When we come with our environmental activities, a choice has to be made: Do I let someone [make our products] . . . or save water? The choice, then, is made quickly: let the person make [a high volume of our products].' He concluded that there were conflicts of interest between targets at the corporate level and the subsidiary level as well as between environmental values embraced by blue-collar personnel ('who just come for the money') and white-collar employees.

After Greenheart Plus was restructured, the subsidiary environmental coordinators began to fulfil a central role by initiating and coordinating environmental actions. Several tensions disappeared. Since there was no more active corporate steering, the subsidiaries could largely formulate their own targets. Besides, different types of objectives were 'reconciled': environmental targets were formulated in economic terms, such as reduced waste rates leading to enhanced volumes of saleable products and reduced environmental load. In 2004, the environmental coordinator of a major subsidiary characterized this reorientation as 'a shift from idealism to realism', asserting that waste prevention and other eco-efficiency measures have a much higher environmental pay-off than any other measures.

OTs

Internal tensions also diminished because the targets between administrative and production personnel were aligned in the OTs, which became effective from 2004 onwards, at least in the Dutch subsidiaries. These teams were important because they provided complementary insights from different functional areas and, above all, management commitment to regularly establish, evaluate and revise environmentally relevant targets. The OT was regarded by a local coordinator as 'a pragmatic environmental management system that warrants structural attention to the environment'.

Corporate technical staff

The corporate technical staff was relatively important in 1999, because it formulated the company's technical standards and provided solutions for prevailing environmental problems. The technical staff also played a role in more eco-efficient materials procurement, investment decisions, and the introduction of an interactive environmental database.

After the takeover, the corporate technical staff was seriously downsized since the new owner regarded corporate bodies as an important source of indirect costs. The importance of the corporate technical staff to environmental issues progressively faded. By 2004, this body no longer played a significant role in the environmental area.

National government

National government was considered a very important actor. In the second half of the 1990s, a Dutch governmental representative coordinated a project on the application of the sustainability concept at the company level with three business organizations, including Greenheart, in divergent sectors. Greenheart's corporate environmental coordinator at the time highly appreciated this 'very good dialogue', because 'they are in the position to constantly lobby, within other governmental departments and internationally, as to what are or may be the possible developments in the area of sustainability. It concerns, then, the development of insights from which our own ideas can be distilled, our own strategy can be adjusted. From that perspective, it is often very meaningful.' In 2001, the Dutch Ministry of the Environment and Greenheart cooperated in a project on the development of a sustainability management system, which aimed at linking environmental performance to managerial incentives. In 2003, contacts with national government were broken when the corporate environmental department was dismantled.

Local governmental bodies
By contrast, contacts with local governmental bodies, including municipalities and local water boards, were intensified after the reorganization. It was acknowledged that regulatory compliance had too readily been taken for granted. Local environmental issues such as noise and odour, which had previously been ignored in the sustainability barometer, were given more attention. In some areas, in particular the storage of dangerous substances and the communication of environmental data, several subsidiaries had not acted in compliance with the regulatory requirements over the period 2000–2004. Priority was then given to restoring compliance from 2005 onwards, though understaffing of the environmental function remained a point of concern.

Environmental pressure groups
Environmental pressure groups were regarded as slightly important because of their capacity to harm the company's environmental image. An open communication was maintained with these groups. In 1999, an environmental representative viewed the company as very proactive indeed. 'For years, [Greenheart] has been an absolute leader in the field of environmental conditions.' The corporate coordinator viewed the attitude of the environmental movement as cooperative but devoid of inspiring ideas. After the disappearance of the corporate environmental department, contacts with the environmental movement ceased.

Transport companies
Transport companies were of some importance to the company. Greenheart (Plus) had concluded energy efficiency agreements with the government and its performance was affected by the energy impact of transport to customers. The marketing department had regular contacts with transport companies on logistic optimization. A representative of the carrier admitted that the environment was not an issue when distributing goods. The carrier did not necessarily use clean trucks. Delivery schedules were determined by customer demands and timely deliveries often entailed partial truck-loads. After the takeover, when cost savings became a dominant issue, efforts to enhance the energy performance of Greenheart Plus's distribution – through an enhanced loading degree, less frequent deliveries, and so on – were intensified, which engendered some environmental gains.

ANALYSIS

Greenheart (Plus) from a Power Perspective

During the 1990s, Greenheart's sustainability drive was initiated and sustained by the CEO's personal conviction that his company had to contribute to an environmentally sustainable world. The CEO incorporated the sustainability value into the company's mission. He also came up with, and provided ample support for, strategic objectives in the field of sustainability, which were implemented top-down through an elaborate environmental structure. Greenheart's corporate environmental coordinator functioned as an information interface between the corporate and the subsidiary levels, translating strategic objectives into operational targets and feeding subsidiary performance back to the apex. Greenheart's corporate technical staff provided know-how to implement and standardize environmental initiatives. In the late 1990s, the sustainability value was widely shared among higher managers and white-collar workers, but there was a lack of commitment at the shop-floor level. Despite persistent awareness-creation efforts, the blue-collar workers predominantly pursued primary production targets. Subsidiary environmental coordinators faced the difficulty of getting concrete environmental initiatives implemented since they faced competitive time claims and because environmental activities did not constitute an integral part of the shop-floor routines. National government served as an important external ally to conceptualize corporate sustainability. Other external stakeholders – in particular, environmental pressure groups and transport companies – did not have a significant impact on Greenheart's environmental behavior.

Power or influence has its origin in an actor (the influencer) holding resources such as authority, money, social norms and information to which another actor (the influencee) is sensitive, leading to behavior that the influencee would otherwise not display (Dahl, 1957; DiMaggio and Powell, 1983; Etzioni, 1964; French and Raven, 1968; Mintzberg, 1983). The importance attached to Greenheart's major stakeholders stemmed from the resources that they held, or to which they had access, and to which others were sensitive: formal authority (the CEO), economic resources (the CEO), environmental norms (the CEO), information (the corporate environmental coordinator, the corporate technical staff, national government), and the ability to implement initiatives (the subsidiary environmental coordinators as representatives of blue-collar workers). The CEO took the lead, and wielded his formal, economic and social power to push the environmental agenda. Most internal actors acquiesced in his authority. Only blue-collar workers showed a certain degree of passive resistance because of competitive time claims, personal indifference and a lack of embedding in their daily activities. The company's commitment to sustainability was initiated and spurred on top-down, and many environmental initiatives were supported. Ample formal, informational and financial resources were allocated to the conceptualization and implementation of the sustainability objective. There was a tension at the shop-floor level because operational influence was partially withheld from pursuing environmental targets, but still a significant number of concrete actions were taken. Thus, the dissimilar resources of different stakeholders were, by and large, used in a cooperative way, yielding synergetic effects. The ensuing rise of Greenheart's sustainability performance was evidenced by a halving of its negative environmental impact score, from 25 in 1992 to 12 in 1999.

Two factors marked a discontinuity in the company's environmental course of action. Following an external crisis in 2000, the composition of Greenheart's best-selling product was changed. This engendered important production problems and poor financial performance in major subsidiaries during the first years of the new millennium. The corporate TMT then attributed the highest priority to a short-term improvement of output and profit figures, ultimately involving a major reorganization. From 2001 onwards, many employees ranked the sustainability cause lower than before because they felt that their jobs were threatened. As a result, the drive of most internal actors to pursue environmental targets decreased significantly.

A second factor of significance was the change of CEO. The former CEO, who had led Greenheart for over 25 years, was succeeded by a person who attributed much less importance to the environmental value. The new CEO decided that environmental initiatives should be confined to those that were required by law or that paid themselves back. He dismantled the corporate environmental department and marginalized or replaced many (critical) higher managers with 'fresh', environmentally disinterested outsiders. At the same time, the new CEO grounded environmental aspects on a more structural basis into the organization by creating OTs at the subsidiary level. The perception of relevant external stakeholders also shifted from those actors contributing new conceptual insights into industrial sustainability (such as national government) towards those parties needed to comply with regulation (in particular, local governments).

As a result of these changes, internal stakeholders wielded their power towards externally required actions and (internal) measures with immediate economic pay-offs. Formal influence changed from fully-fledged, normative support for environmental actions to cautious, calculative endorsement. The nature of informational influence turned from external and global to internal and local. The operational support for environmental initiatives was fostered through a new structure and the concurrence of productive and environmental targets. In these new spheres of influence, the actions of different internal actors were no longer coordinated at the corporate level, giving rise to more divergent practices across subsidiaries. By contrast, environmental measures within subsidiaries were more coherent, consistent and structured than before, enhancing the efficiency of Greenheart Plus's environmental initiatives.

At the same time, the company's overall environmental ambition level had considerably decreased, since sustainability was no longer of primary importance. This suggests that the sustainability value was less deeply rooted than might be expected. Certain actors tried to uphold the ambitious objective and were subsequently marginalized. Most internal stakeholders, though, showed little resistance towards the erosion of this value, suggesting that the pursuit of environmental sustainability was neither firmly embedded in the tissue of influential internal actors nor in the company's routines. While a direct comparison between the period before the major changes and the epoch afterwards is delicate owing to a change of environmental yardsticks, it seems obvious that the altered balance of power led to a regression of the company's environmental behaviour.

Greenheart (Plus) from a Learning Perspective

Throughout the 1990s, Greenheart's environmental performance, such as evidenced by the environmental barometer, improved dramatically. This progress was not necessarily the consequence of increased insights into environmental issues. Measures such as financing reforestation projects and procuring renewable electricity favoured the company's environmental performance but not per se its understanding of their technical nature. However, a substantial part of Greenheart's enhanced environmental performance was induced by the accumulation of new insights pertaining to the conceptualization and implementation of industrial sustainability. The company continued acquiring new environmental insights after the turn of the millennium, albeit at a reduced pace, but the nature of newly acquired knowledge changed from predominantly strategic and conceptual to exclusively operational and applied.

Organizations learn when they increase their behavioural capacities owing to information processing, which involves the acquisition, sharing and retention of new knowledge (Argote, 1999; Huber, 1991; Kim, 1993). Greenheart (Plus) acquired new information from a variety of sources: experimenting with new production practices such as reducing production waste, enhancing energy efficiency and recycling effluent water; participating in reflective platforms on the conceptualization of sustainability; and adopting externally developed insights, such as those on continuous production. Greenheart shared new knowledge through: employees, in particular, environmental coordinators and corporate technical staff members; documented information, including a (not fully operational) environmental database and an environmental magazine; and technical equipment and practices, such as the use of solar panels and the recycling of effluent water. The sources of information sharing largely coincided with those of information storage: employees, documents, equipment, and so on.

New insights that are related to cues like discovery, effectiveness and innovation give rise to explorative learning, whereas insights that are strongly linked to existing practices – involving terms like adaptation, efficiency and implementation – lead to exploitative learning (March, 1991; Weick and Westley, 1996). Greenheart's search for conceptual clarity, its engagement with a variety of heterogeneous, strategically significant actors, and the consideration of new types of production methods in the late 1990s are all indicators of explorative learning. Operational measures were largely taken on an ad hoc basis. Well-functioning environmental routines, firmly embedded in an integrative structure, were largely absent. After the two major events, the company ceased its quest for 'business as unusual'. While its explorative learning came to a halt, Greenheart Plus focused on exploitative learning. Existing practices were refined through minor adaptations of its production methods. This occurred on a systematic basis and was relatively well embedded at the operational level.

Organizational learning is most effective when different roles concur: idea generators who creatively combine technologies, markets and products; internal entrepreneurs who apply new knowledge to concrete settings; boundary spanners who link local colleagues to external information sources; and sponsors who provide senior management support for new ideas (Tushman and Nadler, 1996; Nonaka, 1996; Senge, 1999). In the 1990s, different actors fulfilled key roles in Greenheart's learning process. Reflection platforms (with national government, with other companies in the food sector) as well as the last corporate environmental coordinator functioned as idea generators on the conceptualization of industrial sustainability. Greenheart's corporate environmental coordinators diffused salient environmental information, both from outward in, and from the strategic forums to the subsidiaries, thus acting as boundary spanners. Greenheart's CEO provided ample top management support for sustainability initiatives, thus fulfilling the role of sponsor. Only the role of internal entrepreneur was not well articulated within the company. The concurrence of three major learning roles led to a fairly effective organizational learning process.

The events of the early 2000s had major implications for learning roles. The change of CEO led to the disappearance of a major sponsor since formal top management support became weak and financial resources dried up. This was, to a certain extent, compensated by an increased formal commitment of subsidiary TMTs to local environmental initiatives. Idea generators were no longer considered since contacts with external reflection platforms were broken and the corporate environmental coordinator was dismissed. By contrast, the role of internal entrepreneur became more articulated through the OTs, who had to come up with concrete solutions. The role of boundary spanner shifted from the corporate environmental coordinator to the subsidiary coordinators, whereby it should be noted that the latter faced significant time constraints. Greenheart Plus thus showed the concurrence of three critical learning roles, though these roles were not highly articulated. Consequently, the company learned efficiently but at a lower pace than before.

Learning requires the allocation of sufficient resources for the acquisition and processing of new insights (Cyert and March, 1992; Nonaka, 1994; Senge, 1999). In the late 1990s, relatively ample resources were available at Greenheart, with the exception of the shop-floor level. The availability of these resources, secured by top management support, enabled the company to progress on a highly ambitious learning path. After the two discontinuities, in the early 2000s, Greenheart Plus lowered its environmental ambition level. The budget for environmental initiatives was frozen, the corporate environmental department was eliminated, the corporate technical staff and external reflection platforms were marginalized, and no additional environmental staff was hired at the subsidiary level. The scarcity of resources for environmental initiatives slowed down the company's learning process.

Greenheart's quest for environmental sustainability is summarized in Table 5.1. Analytical insights from the two perspectives (stakeholder influence and organizational learning) are summarized using two major dimensions that emerged from the data: (1) the relative importance that organizational members attribute to environmental sustainability ('ambition'); and (2) the degree to which environmental practices are an integrative part of the company's business as usual ('embeddedness'). The table shows largely divergent outcomes for Greenheart's subsequent stages of rise and regression.

DISCUSSION AND CONCLUSION

Summary and Discussion

The case-study shows the evolution of a company in its quest for environmental sustainability. Greenheart initially made great strides: the

Table 5.1 Analysis of the Greenheart (Plus) case

Perspective	Stakeholder influence		Organizational learning	
Stage / Dimension	Rise	Regression	Rise	Regression
Ambition	Sustainability of primary importance, especially at higher and middle levels	Sustainability company-wide subordinate to economic objectives	Substantial resources for learning and concurrence of three articulated learning roles	Few resources for learning and concurrence of three less prominent roles
Embeddedness	Environmental issues not integrated and not core part of routines	Start of integrating and routinizing environmental activities	Conceptualization and ad hoc environmental measures (mainly explorative learning)	Systematic implementation of environmental activities (exploitative learning)

organization embraced sustainability as a core value, sought to reconceptualize its business activities, was open to a variety of (external) stakeholders, and allocated ample means to reduce its environmental impact. This venture lost momentum after a change of ownership and economic difficulties: the sustainability value was interpreted in a more restricted sense and became of secondary importance, environmental activities had to fit within the existing business frame, a more restricted number of predominantly internal stakeholders were considered, and the environmental budget largely evaporated; at the same time, environmental activities were undertaken on a more structural basis.

These findings suggest that the focal company went through subsequent phases of rise and regression during its sustainability voyage. The literature has described different levels of progress on the corporate sustainability path, ranging from early stages involving eco-efficiency and pollution control measures to more advanced stages of business process reconceptualization and product redesign (Sharma and Henriques, 2005). Alternatively, different corporate attitudes to environmental issues have been identified: from defensive and reactive, as evidenced by resistance to environmental initiatives, via compliance with regulatory requirements to offensive and proactive, with a prominent role for discretionary (that is, not legally required) environmental initiatives and ample top management commitment (Henriques and Sadorsky, 1999; Kolk and Mauser, 2002; Zadek, 2004). Similarly, companies can be classified on the basis of their environmental management styles: from laggards, trying to evade environmental measures, via compliers to true believers, who take far-reaching measures on moral grounds (Thornton et al., 2003). Indeed, it has been argued that the 'normative case' for environmental initiatives, consisting of morally driven actions, tends to be associated with higher levels of proactiveness than the 'business case', where fear of regulatory retaliation and economic self-interest are more dominant considerations (Garriga and Melé, 2004; Smith, 2003).

While the focal company can easily be accommodated within the different classification schemes, the extant literature tends to assume, sometimes explicitly but mostly implicitly, that companies either adopt and maintain a particular environmental attitude or show increasing levels of proactiveness over time (Porter and Van der Linde, 1995; Hart, 1995; Hawken et al., 2000; Holliday et al., 2002; Shrivastava, 1995). This assumption seems to be based on the following line of reasoning. Companies generally ignore environmental issues until they are forced to comply with regulatory requirements. Once they are forced to take environmental actions, they 'discover' their economic benefits, in terms of improved reputation, enhanced sales potential, cost savings and/or avoided liability claims. A final step is taken when business leaders make their organizations behave like good corporate citizens and take far-reaching measures on moral grounds, regardless of their immediate pay-offs. This pattern of rising proactiveness may have occurred in quite a few instances, but is by no means an iron law. The Greenheart case shows that a company's rise in environmental performance may be followed by a period of regression.

The analysis in the previous section identified two reasons for this regression. The first pertains to the company's ambition level. When Greenheart Plus entered economically turbulent waters, the environmental objective became less prominent. The economic difficulties encountered and the change of ownership were important reasons for this lower priority. Saliently, the environmental regression met with hardly any internal resistance. Virtually all employees acquiesced in the reshuffling of corporate values. They accepted the new top management priorities and preferred job security to the pursuit of environmental objectives. The vulnerability of the environmental value feeds the critique that corporate environmental or social initiatives should be regarded with suspicion since the primary *raison d'être* is an economic one (Hertz, 2001; Klein, 2001). An alternative argument is that since the sustainability drive had been largely imposed top-down, the environmental value had been neither widely nor deeply embraced throughout the organization. Change initiatives based on hierarchical power are unstable: they tend to fade over time since they lack wide (internal) support (Lawrence et al., 2001). Widespread endorsement is thus key to sustained progress, especially when it concerns new initiatives. From a learning perspective, the withdrawal of resources required to involve organizational members fulfilling critical roles leads to reduced progress on learning paths entered (Senge, 1999). It can thus be concluded that the pursuit of corporate sustainability requires high ambition, not only at the top management level but also throughout the organization. High ambition shows similarities with the related notion of shared vision (Senge, 1990; Shrivastava, 1995), since both highlight the importance of organization-wide support. High ambition, however, goes beyond shared vision, since the former also connotes commitment to (environmental) challenges that are hard to realize (Simon, 1976; Vergragt and Van der Wel, 1998).

The second reason for regression was the lack of well-embedded environmental practices. Greenheart used to take a variety of environmental initiatives, but they were largely adopted on an ad hoc basis. Had these actions been more firmly embedded in ongoing routines, they would probably have been more resistant to changed top management priorities. Routinized practices, which have been adopted throughout the company and which have persisted for some time, are particularly inert. They are likely to meet with fierce resistance when attempts to change them are undertaken (Cyert and March, 1992; Nelson and Winter, 1982; Tushman and Romanelli, 1985). Besides, Greenheart's environmental activities were largely taken in isolation, without benefitting from the synergies and 'protection' of intertwined activities. The integration of environmental and economic activities leads to the exploitation of common grounds and avoids, at least to a certain extent, the need to prioritize one type of activity over another when resource limitations would call for such choices (Porter and Van der Linde, 1995). Furthermore, systematically implemented activities that lead to measurable results, including environmental management systems such as ISO 14001, are more resistant to unfavourable economic tides and changing top management priorities than conceptual and ad hoc measures (Bansal and Bogner, 2002). Therefore, environmental practices must be deeply embedded in corporate practices in order to sustain the pursuit of sustainable business. Embeddedness is related to structure (Argote, 1999; Mintzberg, 1979), since both pertain to the way in which (environmental) activities are organized. Embeddedness is more related to permanence, though, since structure concerns the officially designed and readily changeable modus operandi, whereas embeddedness expresses the actual degree of ingrained commitment to existing cognitive frames and practices (Uzzi, 1996, 1997).

Conclusion and Implications

The above results should be interpreted with some caution, since they are based on a single case-study. An important conclusion from the analysis is thus that companies can only display environmentally sustainable behaviour over a longer period if they have: (1) a high and widely shared environmental ambition; and (2) well-embedded environmental practices. The behaviour of such organizations can be labelled as 'institutionalized sustainability' (cf. Ackerman, 1973). Institutions refer to collectively taken-for-granted behaviour, materialized through widely accepted practices, rules and technologies (Greenwood et al., 2002; Lawrence et al., 2001; Tolbert and Zucker, 1996). The two dimensions identified are critical to understanding the behaviour of organizations over a longer period. Sustaining corporate sustainability efforts requires both deeply held and widely embraced values (the 'ambition' dimension) and the adoption of ingrained, routinized practices (the 'embeddedness' dimension). Companies scoring high on the ambition dimension but low on the embeddedness dimension, such as tended to be the case with Greenheart prior to the critical events, are engaged in an 'idealist sustainability quest'. Their actions are conceptual, ad hoc and symbolic. By contrast, companies with a low ambition level but a high degree of embeddedness, as tended to be evidenced by Greenheart Plus, are characterized by 'realist environmental management'. They are concerned with the systematic implementation of technically feasible measures, the scope of which is not to attain environmentally sustainable levels. The different types of behaviour related to corporate environmental sustainability are displayed in Table 5.2.

The present study has mainly focused on the environmental dimension of sustainable corporate development, though the outcomes may also be relevant for social sustainability. Many social and environmental issues in business share features such as a systemic nature, a dual (normative and business) character, and a 'natural subordination' to economic imperatives. Therefore, institutionalization would seem to be critical for

Table 5.2 Typology of corporate sustainability behavior

Ambition / Embeddedness	Low	High
Low	Unsustainable business	Idealist sustainability quest
High	Realist environmental management	Institutionalized sustainability

both the environmental and social dimensions of sustainable corporate development.

An important managerial implication is thus that maintaining environmental (and social) sustainability requires high degrees of ambition and embeddedness. Sustained excellence in environmental (and social) performance requires not only top management ambition but also company-wide support; this invalidates top-down decision-making models which overlook the implementation side. Routinization and systemization are imperative since ad hoc measures are ephemeral. Formal environmental management systems such as ISO 14001 are instrumental in this respect (Epstein and Roy, 2001), though such systems have no built-in ambition level (Bansal and Bogner, 2002) and the tacit knowledge of employees should also be mobilized (Boiral, 2002). Furthermore, tight integration with other activities is required, implying that isolated environmental (and social) departments are counter-productive.

The analysis of the focal company was performed from two different perspectives: organizational learning and stakeholder influence. Both paradigms are rooted in extensive bodies of literature (for overviews of the organizational learning literature, see Argote, 1999; Baum, 2002; and Dierkes et al., 2002; synopses of the stakeholder influence literature can be found in Baum, 2002; Hardy and Clegg, 1996; and Kramer and Neale, 1998). Notwithstanding the substantial number of writings proliferated by each body, the crossroads of learning and influence have hardly been explored (Contu and Willmott, 2003; Weick and Westley, 1996). However, the outcomes from both analyses, which were summarized in Table 5.1, showed striking parallels when related to the dimensions of ambition and embeddedness. Both perspectives are also complementary (Gladwin, 1993). On the one hand, stakeholder influence shapes organizational learning; the latter becomes effective when influential actors allocate the resources needed to learn (Senge, 1999; Roome and Wijen, 2006; Tushman and Nadler, 1996). Besides, actors have to be sufficiently powerful to fulfil critical learning roles effectively (Contu and Willmott, 2003; Coopey, 1996; Roome and Wijen, 2006). On the other hand, organizational learning affects a company's power relations: the more insights are acquired concerning the desirability or necessity to consider certain actors, the more an organization will perceive these actors as important and become sensitive to their resources (Nooteboom, 2000; Pfeffer and Salancik, 1978). Using the complementary perspectives of stakeholder power and organizational learning in conjunction with each other, therefore, significantly enhances our insights.

Besides, it is important to study organizations over a longer period in order to observe unfolding dynamics, especially in the field of sustainable development. Longitudinal studies show not only the mechanisms leading to changes but also reveal the degree to which intended changes are sustained over a longer period. Many academic studies have focused on inertia and resistance to change (Baum, 2002; Gersick, 1991; Tushman and Romanelli, 1985; Valley and Thompson, 1998). Sustaining environmentally (and socially) relevant behavioral changes against all odds over a longer period has received far less attention, though this issue is particularly relevant when organizations have not yet institutionalized environmentally (and socially) relevant practices (Senge, 1999). Indeed, institutionalization is a prerequisite for sustainable corporate development, key to understanding the conditions under which sustainable development can turn from well-intended management by exception into widely practised business as usual. Longitudinal studies focusing on how attempts to conduct more sustainable business are initiated, leveraged and maintained would further our understanding of such institutionalization processes.

The present chapter has unpacked the mechanisms underlying the dynamic behaviour of a company pursuing environmental sustainability. Many writings pertaining to drivers of sustainable development or corporate social responsibility point to isolated factors such as enlightened leadership, a competitive edge and societal pressure. By contrast, this chapter suggests that the development of corporate sustainability requires the concurrence of ambition and embeddedness. The higher the scores on these dimensions and the more systemic the corporate orientation, the more a company has institutionalized its sustainability endeavor and the higher the probability of sustained progress. Companies highlighting only one dimension have a lower performance and are vulnerable to (economic and managerial) vagaries. A systemic view, collective drive and routinized practices are, therefore, indispensable companions of companies on their sustainability voyage.

REFERENCES

Ackerman, Robert (1973), 'How companies respond to social demands', *Harvard Business Review*, **51** (4), 88–98.

Argote, Linda (1999), *Organizational Learning: Creating, Retaining and Transferring Knowledge*, Boston, MA: Kluwer.

Bansal, Pratima and William Bogner (2002), 'Deciding on ISO 14001: Economics, Institutions, and Context', *Long Range Planning*, **35**, 269–90.

Baum, Joel (ed.) (2002), *The Blackwell Companion to Organizations*, Oxford: Blackwell.

Boiral, Olivier (2002), 'Tacit knowledge and environmental management', *Long Range Planning*, **35**, 291–317.

Contu, Alessia and Hugh Willmott (2003), 'Re-embedding situatedness: the importance of power relations in learning theory', *Organization Science*, **14** (3), 283–96.

Coopey, John (1996), 'Crucial gaps in "the learning organization": power, politics, and ideology', in Ken Starkey (ed.), *How Organizations Learn*, London: Thomson.

Cyert, Richard and James March (1992), *A Behavioral Theory of the Firm*, 2nd edn, Cambridge: Blackwell.

Dahl, Robert (1957), 'The concept of power', *Behavioral Science*, **20**, 201–15.

Dierkes, Meinolf, Ariane Berthoin Antal, John Child and Ikujiro Nonaka (eds) (2001), *Handbook of Organizational Learning and Knowledge*, Oxford: Oxford University Press.

DiMaggio, Paul and Walter Powell (1983), 'The iron cage revisited: institutional isomorphism and collective rationality in organizational fields', *American Sociological Review*, **48** (April), 147–60.

Ehrenfeld, John (2005), 'The roots of sustainability', *MIT Sloan Management Review*, **46** (2), 23–5.

Elkington, John (1998), *Cannibals with Forks: The Triple Bottom Line of 21st Century Business*, Gabriola Island: New Society Publishers.

Epstein, Marc and Marie-Josée Roy (2001), 'Sustainability in action: identifying and measuring the key performance drivers', *Long Range Planning*, **34**, 585–604.

Etzioni, Amitai (1964), *Modern Organizations*, Englewood Cliffs, NJ: Prentice Hall.

French, John and Bertram Raven (1968), 'The bases of social power', in Dorwin Cartwright and Alvin Zander (eds), *Group Dynamics*, 3rd edn, New York: Harper & Row.

Garriga, Elisabet and Domènec Melé (2004), 'Corporate social responsibility theories: mapping the territory', *Journal of Business Ethics*, **53**, 51–71.

Gerring, John (2001), *Social Science Methodology: A Critical Framework*, Cambridge: Cambridge University Press.

Gersick, Connie (1991), 'Revolutionary change theories: a multilevel exploration of the punctuated equilibrium', *Academy of Management Review*, **16** (1), 10–36.

Gladwin, Thomas (1993), 'The meaning of greening: a plea for organizational theory', in Kurt Fischer and Johan Schot (eds), *Environmental Strategies for Industry: International Perspectives*, Washington, DC: Island Press.

Greenwood, Royston, Roy Suddaby and Bob Hinings (2002), 'The role of professional associations in institutional change', *Academy of Management Journal*, **45**, 58–80.

Hardy, Cynthia and Stewart Clegg (1996), 'Some dare call it power', in Stewart Clegg, Cynthia Hardy and Walter Nord (eds), *Handbook of Organization Studies*, Thousand Oaks, CA: Sage.

Hart, Stuart (1995), 'A natural-resource-based view of the firm', *Academy of Management Review*, **20** (4), 986–1014.

Hawken, Paul, Amory Lovins and Hunter Lovins (2000), *Natural Capitalism: Creating the Next Industrial Revolution*, London: Earthscan.

Henriques, Irene and Perry Sadorsky (1999), 'The relationship between environmental commitment and managerial perceptions of stakeholder importance', *Academy of Management Journal*, **42** (1), 87–99.

Hertz, Noreena (2001), *The Silent Takeover: Global Capitalism and the Death of Democracy*, London: Heinemann.

Holliday, Charles, Stephen Schmidheiny and Philip Watts (2002), *Walking the Talk: The Business Case for Sustainable Development*, Sheffield: Greenleaf.

Huber, George (1991), 'Organizational learning: the contributing processes and the literatures', *Organization Science*, **2** (1), 88–115.

Husted, Bryan (2003), 'Governance choices for corporate social responsibility: to contribute, collaborate or internalize?', *Long Range Planning*, **36**, 481–98.
Kim, Daniel (1993), 'The link between individual and organizational learning', *Sloan Management Review* (Fall), 37–50.
Klein, Naomi (2001), *No Logo: No Space, No Choice, No Jobs*, Flamingo: London.
Kolk, Ans and Anniek Mauser (2002), 'The evolution of environmental management: from stage models to performance evaluation', *Business Strategy and the Environment*, **11**, 14–31.
Kramer, Roderick and Margaret Neale (1998), *Power and Influence in Organizations*, Thousand Oaks, CA: Sage.
Lawrence, Thomas, Monika Winn and Deveraux Jennings (2001), 'The temporal dynamics of institutionalization', *Academy of Management Review*, **26** (4), 624–44.
March, James (1991), 'Exploration and exploitation in organizational learning', *Organization Science*, **2** (1), 71–87.
Mintzberg, Henry (1979), *The Structuring of Organizations: A Synthesis of the Research*, Englewood Cliffs, CA: Prentice-Hall.
Mintzberg, Henry (1983), *Power In and Around Organizations*, Englewood Cliffs, NJ: Prentice-Hall.
Nelson, Richard and Sidney Winter (1982), *An Evolutionary Theory of Economic Change*, Cambridge: Belknap.
Nonaka, Ikujiro (1994), 'A dynamic theory of organizational knowledge creation', *Organization Science*, **5** (1), 14–37.
Nonaka, Ikujiro (1996), 'The knowledge-creating company', in Ken Starkey (ed.), *How Organizations Learn*, London: Thomson.
Nooteboom, Bart (2000), *Learning and Innovation in Organizations and Economies*, Oxford: Oxford University Press.
Pfeffer, Jeffrey and Gerald Salancik (1978), *The External Control of Organizations: A Resource Dependence Perspective*, New York: Harper & Row.
Porter, Michael and Claas Van der Linde (1995), 'Green and competitive: ending the stalemate', *Harvard Business Review* (September), 120–34.
Ragin, Charles (1987), *The Comparative Method: Moving beyond Qualitative and Quantitative Strategies*, Berkeley, CA: University of California Press.
Roome, Nigel (ed.) (1998), *Sustainability Strategies for Industry: The Future of Corporate Practice*, Washington, DC: Island Press.
Roome, Nigel and Frank Wijen (2006), 'Stakeholder influence and organizational learning in corporate environmental management', *Organization Studies*, **27** (2), 235–63.
Senge, Peter (1990), *The Fifth Discipline: The Art and Practice of the Learning Organization*, New York: Doubleday.
Senge, Peter (1999), 'The life cycle of typical change initiatives', in Peter Senge, Art Kleiner, Charlotte Roberts, Richard Ross, George Roth and Bryan Smith (eds), *The Dance of Change: The Challenges to Sustaining Momentum in Learning Organizations*, New York: Doubleday.
Sharma, Sanjay and Irene Henriques (2005), 'Stakeholder influences on sustainability practices in the Canadian forest products industry', *Strategic Management Journal*, **26**, 159–80.
Simon, Herbert (1976), 'From substantive to procedural rationality', in Spiro Latsis (ed.), *Method and Appraisal in Economics*, Cambridge: Cambridge University Press.

Shrivastava, Paul (1995), 'The role of corporations in achieving ecological sustainability', *Academy of Management Review*, **20** (4), 936–60.

Smith, Craig (2003), 'Corporate social responsibility: whether or how?', *California Management Review*, **45** (4), 52–76.

Stigson, Björn and Britta Rendlen (2005), 'Drivers of business behaviour in the realm of sustainable development: the role and influence of the WBCSD, a global business network', in Frank Wijen, Kees Zoeteman and Jan Pieters (eds), *A Handbook of Globalisation and Environmental Policy: National Government Interventions in a Global Arena*, Cheltenham, UK and Northampton, MA, USA: Edward Elgar.

Thornton, Dorothy, Robert Kagan and Neil Gunningham (2003), 'Sources of corporate environmental performance', *California Management Review*, **46** (1), 127–41.

Tolbert, Pamela and Lynne Zucker (1996), 'The institutionalization of institutional theory', in Stewart Clegg, Cynthia Hardy and Walter Nord (eds), *Handbook of Organization Studies*, London: Sage.

Tushman, Michael and David Nadler (1996), 'Organizing for innovation', in Ken Starkey (ed.), *How Organizations Learn*, London: Thomson.

Tushman, Michael and Elaine Romanelli (1985), 'Organizational evolution: a metamorphosis model of convergence and reorientation', in L. Cummings and Barry Staw (eds), *Research in Organizational Behavior*, Greenwich, CI: JAI Press.

Uzzi, Brian (1996), 'The sources and consequences of embeddedness for the economic performance of organizations: the network effect', *American Sociological Review*, **61** (4), 674–98.

Uzzi, Brian (1997), 'Social structures and competition in interfirm networks: the paradox of embeddedness', *Administrative Science Quarterly*, **42**, 35–67.

Valley, Kathleen and Tracy Thompson (1998), 'Sticky ties and bad attitudes: relational and individual bases of resistance to change in organizational structure', in Roderick Kramer and Margaret Neale (eds), *Power and Influence in Organizations*, Thousand Oaks, CA: Sage.

Van Tulder, Rob and Alex Van der Zwart (2006), *International Business–Society Management: Linking Corporate Responsibility and Globalization*, Abingdon: Routledge.

Vergragt, Philip and Marjan Van der Wel (1998), 'Backcasting: an example of sustainable washing', in Nigel Roome (ed.), *Sustainability Strategies for Industry: The Future of Corporate Practice*, Washington, DC: Island Press.

Weick, Karl and Frances Westley (1996), 'Organizational learning: affirming an oxymoron', in Stewart Clegg, Cynthia Hardy and Walter Nord (eds), *Handbook of Organization Studies*, London: Sage.

Weitzman, Eben and Matthew Miles (1995), *Computer Programs for Qualitative Data Analysis: A Software Sourcebook*, Thousand Oaks, CA: Sage.

World Commission on Environment and Development (1987), *Our Common Future*, Oxford: Oxford University Press.

Yin, Robert (1994), *Case Study Research: Design and Methods*, 2nd edn, Thousand Oaks, CA: Sage.

Zadek, Simon (2004), 'The path to corporate responsibility', *Harvard Business Review* (December), 125–32.

6. Stakeholder salience, issues management and mapping new ways to sustainability

David Saiia[1]

Organizations that depend on community acceptance and support, such as non-profit service NGOs (non-governmental organizations) are particularly influenced by the power, legitimacy and urgency, or salience, of key stakeholders (Mitchell, Agle and Wood, 1997; Balser and McCluskey, 2005). As with all organizations, NGOs have multiple stakeholders with varying degrees of salience embedded in a network of stakeholder connections; these stakeholders interact with the organization on multiple levels affecting people, planet and prosperity. Sustainability is often defined as the balance among people, planet and prosperity; thus stakeholder management is a natural fit with sustainability because stakeholders inhabit these levels and interact among them. This insight into sustainability is particularly discernible in non-profit service NGOs because of their direct reliance on salient stakeholder support: NGOs depend not only on donors, but also on managing the interaction among service recipients and various facilitators.

Nearly 20 years ago, the World Commission on Environment and Development (WCED, 1987) provided a definition of sustainability that, in the final analysis, is not much different from the Haudenosaunee's (often referred to as the 'Iroquois') decision-making rule contained in their '*Gayanashagowa*' or 'Great Binding Law': a decision is good when it serves the present and all those it affects through the seventh generation (Murphy, 1996; Roland, 1989). This comparison brackets nearly 400 years of organizational and societal decision-making but regrettably signifies little progress in furthering the realization of sustainability. A great insight is not a strategy, nor does an understanding of sustainability ensure its implementation. Nevertheless, it can be argued that the ideas of both the WCED and the Haudenosaunee suggest a form of stakeholder management: taking into account intergenerational stakeholders as well as critical and immediately salient stakeholders. This stakeholder salience concept (Mitchell et al., 1997) provides some direction for the management of conflicting stakeholder demands by helping to balance people, planet and prosperity. But the determination of the degree of salience at a particular time or towards a particular issue is complex and often dynamic. This chapter offers a technique to interpret the often bewildering array of stakeholder data that may be collected to determine salience, network embeddedness and/or engagement. A better way to organize and understand this information will allow for more effective and responsive stakeholder management, leading to superior strategic management and a more informed approach to sustainability.

The purpose of this chapter is to describe both the process used to create a numerical assessment of stakeholder salience that can be rendered graphically, and the motivations to develop this technique. A case-study of an Ecuadorian NGO provides the context for this research. Through this process of creating and graphically displaying a representation of stakeholder salience, ideas of issues management are integrated with stakeholder management to provide focus and order to the predictable cascade of hard-to-manage stakeholder information that is too often the outcome of stakeholder information-gathering. As an outcome of this chapter, a relational stakeholder map is offered as a technique to organize a wide range of stakeholder information so managers can better understand and manage stakeholders relative to organizational interests and long-term sustainability.

The initial data for this chapter were the result of a stakeholder survey conducted in Ecuador for Fundación Maquipucuna (FM), in the summer of 2000, to facilitate strategic planning and restructuring of the organization. Context for data analysis was provided by an extensive case-study and subsequent documentary research.

In the following sections, this chapter will bring the reader through an initial case description of Fundación Maquipucuna (FM) to provide a context for an application of stakeholder theory in the form of a 'salience map'. This application of mapping stakeholder salience is not simply an academic exercise but an ongoing effort to create a sustainable future for FM. A theoretical overview is provided to explain and connect work on stakeholder salience, issues management, stakeholder networks and constructivist theory. It will be suggested that the integration of issues management into stakeholder thinking can provide focus for what is often an unwieldy conglomeration of stakeholder data. A short explanation of how the concept of sustainability is particularly important for an organization like FM is also included. The methods section then explains why the use of an iterative case-study approach (Yin, 1994) best captures complex socio-economic interactions in evolving and uncontrolled settings. The first iteration of the case provides the reader with a context for the first proposition, data collection, analysis and results. A second iteration of the case presents an emergent proposition based on unforeseen changes in the stakeholder network. Subsequent data collection and analysis led to an 'adjusted' relational stakeholder map offered as a way to record and understand recent events at FM. Some general insights into stakeholder management and sustainability will be offered in conclusion.

BACKGROUND INFORMATION

At the time of data collection (summer 2000), Fundación Maquipucuna (FM) was preparing for a review by the World Bank as a condition for gaining access to a $3.3 million grant through the Global Environment Fund (GEF). Since FM's mission includes both conservation of rare cloud-forest and sustainable development in communities that border the protected areas, it was already known that issues concerning land use and land consolidation were of primary concern for most of FM's stakeholders. The intent of the survey was to collect rich qualitative data on the stakeholders who could affect FM's mission or be affected by the pursuit of this mission. As described in the methods section below, these initial stakeholder data were collected using structured interviews over a six-week period (Yin, 1994). In these interviews stakeholders were each asked to assess their own salience over the three dimensions – power, urgency and legitimacy – set out by Mitchell et al. (1997). FM's land acquisition and management or, more generally, FM's land-tenure was used as a focal issue. Data provided by these stakeholders, and other sources, informed an organizational restructuring of FM as part of the foundation's strategic management process. The GEF grant was awarded by the World Bank to FM for the period 2001–2004.

While these stakeholder data were useful in many ways, their usefulness was limited by the difficulty in organizing the information gathered about FM's stakeholders. More specifically, the stakeholder data initially yielded information that could not easily be compared across stakeholder groups. Furthermore, there was no formal technique to organize data so as to anticipate which groups were likely to support FM's work, which groups might obstruct the work, or which groups may be inactive or 'dormant'. This lingering confusion regarding the organization of the collected stakeholder information became particularly troublesome for FM's management team and its board of directors as they tried to keep these different groups in mind during planning sessions. The study that follows is a direct result of this unmet need for greater clarity about stakeholders. This chapter presents an innovative way to map stakeholder data: 'stakeholder salience mapping'. Stakeholder salience mapping is a marriage of issues management and stakeholder salience information. As is true of so many new ideas, this technique is a product of frustration and of dire necessity. The initial map of FM's stakeholders, created from the data collected in the stakeholder interviews, seemed accurate and descriptive, but when unexpected stakeholder actions became a serious threat, there was a need to revise and further FM's understanding of its stakeholders. 'Salience mapping' was created in response to this need.

THEORETICAL BACKGROUND

Stakeholder Theories, Issues Management and Sustainability

Stakeholder theory is an important paradigm in the research of social issues in management. Indeed, in some ways, stakeholder theory has supplanted the idea of issues management over the past 20 years. Issues management is a method used to identify critical organizational issues and the influential constituencies related to those issues to manage external affairs. Stakeholder theory gave management scholars a conceptual way to consider concerns that were often seen as external to the operation of the firm until they erupted as a critical issue that could interfere with the pursuit of objectives, goals and mission. Therefore, stakeholder management provided an alternative to issues management because it helps managers to identify critical issues through better stakeholder engagement practices. The stakeholders identified the issues rather than the issues identifying the interest groups. Stakeholder theory is informed by the contributions of stakeholder salience (Mitchell et al., 1997) and stakeholder networks (Rowley, 1997), which help practitioners and scholars to: (1) identify, weigh and rank the interests of different stakeholder groups; and (2) understand managerial discretion as it relates to a firm's embeddedness in a stakeholder network.

Other writers have re-examined issues management and shown its relevance in helping to focus organizational action relative to critical events or issues (see Ansoff, 1979; Hoffman and Ocasio, 2001; Huegens, 2002; Wartick and Rude, 1986). At its roots issues management has been used to help organizations manage surprise and external threats (Ansoff, 1979). This chapter builds on insights from issues management and further operationalizes stakeholder management through the salience concept by using focal events to map stakeholders in terms of critical organizational issues of strategic significance. Because critical strategic issues often broach the question of firm survival and the continued support of salient stakeholders, the fit between an issues management focused stakeholder approach and organizational sustainability seems apt.

Sustainability requires that we consider business and society in terms of salient stakeholders and multilayered and interconnected networks (Starik and Rands, 1995). Sustainability presupposes an understanding of organizational embeddedness and making decisions within the organization that are communally acceptable and beneficial to highly salient stakeholders now and into the future.

Stakeholder Salience and Network Ideas in Stakeholder Management

Stakeholder salience and network ideas in stakeholder management are currently limited because they provide us with static views of what is often a fluid situation. Practical experience and anecdotal evidence from case-studies offer abundant evidence of how networks and salience can shift as issues gain ascendancy and clarity (Pasquero, 1996; Saiia, Schmitt and Beaulieu, 2003). This observation indicates that stakeholder relationships are not objective conditions of the stakeholder environment that can be easily grasped and managed in terms of stable and established networks. Stakeholders enter and exit the operational milieu, they may reorganize, the nature of their interactions may change, or they may build new coalitions (Pasquero, 1996). These are all signs of relationships that are in a formative stage that is not yet stabilized. Freeman's (1984) stakeholder theory points towards capturing dynamic behavior of stakeholders, but is less helpful in understanding potentially shifting stakeholder networks. However, a theoretical core addressing stakeholder dynamics is now emerging (for example Gray, 1989; Pasquero, 1996; Saiia et al., 2003). In the next section, some theoretical background for stakeholder dynamics and identifying salient stakeholders is discussed and developed.

From Freeman's early work on stakeholder management there was an implicit awareness of the dynamic nature of stakeholder relations. More recent work has begun to focus explicitly on the nature of these dynamics and how better to understand them (Gray, 1989; Pasquero, 1996; Schmitt, Saiia and Beaulieu, 2003). A technique to help visualize these relationships would provide managers with a useful tool for strategic decision-making.

Much research on stakeholder networks is based on theories that explain a firm's discretion as a result of the structure of the stakeholder environment. They infer from these structures a set of stakeholder influence strategies (Frooman, 1999; Rowley, 1997). This assumes that the members of a network can be objectively identified and that their network is relatively stable. Following the logic of these studies, the actions of stakeholders and the interacting firms are determined to a large extent by network structures, and the actors within these networks (Gray, 1989; Pasquero, 1996; Saiia et al., 2003) have little discretion relative to their position in the network.

When addressing well-defined issues and objectives, this body of research offers valuable insight into management decision-making and discretion. However, these network theories are less helpful as an aid for understanding fragile and formative stakeholder networks. Such networks exist in a highly uncertain situation in which the issue is incompletely defined or not fully understood (such as sustainability). Social constructivist theories, such as negotiated order theory (for example Nathan and Mitroff, 1991; Strauss et al., 1963), actor-network theory (for example Callon, 1986) and constructivist discourse (for example Best, 1995) can provide a starting point for developing insights into dynamic stakeholder relations, and in particular, the hard-to-pin-down issue of sustainability.

Social Constructivist Theories

Constructivist theory posits that relationships are actively shaped within (stakeholder) interactions (Callon, 1992). Stakeholder relations do not simply exist; they are formed over many encounters between a firm and its stakeholders when dealing with specific issues. In other studies of social science this focus on a specific issue or relationship has been referred to as a 'focal event'. The importance of context as a means to 'properly understand, interpret appropriately, or describe in a relevant fashion' a focal event is not under dispute among researchers (Goodwin and Duranti, 1992, p. 3). Indeed, it can be argued that the context determines the appropriate resources directed at a given stakeholder, and what context we consider appropriate depends on the event under focus. This point provides an important re-visioning of stakeholder theory: in this representation, the firm is not at the center of the stakeholder map as suggested by Freeman (1984), but the issue, as pursued by the firm, becomes the organizing principle, the focal event (Saiia et al., 2003).

Network connections are formed while stakeholders try to make sense of the focal event: an issue within a specific context. The network does not eclipse its stakeholders or the firm; it both adds structure to firm–stakeholder interactions while at the same time the network is itself an outcome of the issue definition process. As the actors encounter each other and negotiate issues, they build a common understanding of a situation (Nathan and Mitroff, 1991; Strauss et al., 1963) and commit themselves to certain 'rules of the game' (Callon, 1986) which might be understood as temporary agreements for acting upon an issue. These agreements may be subject to change at any time. However, the more they are carried out, the more the commitments will be solidified, and it thus becomes less likely that the stakeholder relationships or the structure of the network will change in an unpredictable manner (Callon, 1992). By understanding the process of how stakeholders encounter and negotiate emergent issues with the firm and other stakeholders, a more complete picture can be offered of network formation and behavior and thus of stakeholder dynamics. A complex and multilayered issue such as sustainability provides a good example of this point.

The more sensitive the environment and the issue being considered, the more critical the network: drilling in the Arctic National Wildlife Refuge (ANWR) is a good recent example of an issue that has created changeable or dynamic stakeholder relations. This issues-based orientation represents a refocus of the consideration of stakeholders, the focal organization and their network embeddedness. If we can identify the core similarities characterizing firm–stakeholder interactions relative to critical issues, we might be able to understand factors contributing to the dynamics of stakeholder relations and what elements are important for influencing these networks.

Therefore, if we have a technique whereby a variety of stakeholder data can be integrated into a single graphical interface; managers will have a better opportunity to gain a clear vision of their organization and its actions in the context of a web of stakeholders. With such a tool, the following propositions can be addressed:

Proposition 1: *If relevant data concerning FM's stakeholders could be integrated into a single graphical interface then more effective decisions can be made.*

Proposition 1a: *FM will become more sustainable if it is able better to understand how its stakeholders are likely to behave and interact.*

Proposition 1b: *The exercise of mapping out an organization's stakeholders relative to a specific issue can provide a valuable tool for strategic management and sustainability of the focal organization.*

CONTEXT

Fundación Maquipucuna (FM), founded in 1988, is an Ecuadorian nonprofit organization devoted to conservation and sustainable development of the rural communities bordering the Maquipucuna Ecological Reserve. FM currently owns and manages a 7500-hectare reserve northwest of Quito, Ecuador. FM management has extensive experience in working with multiple stakeholders (including local, federal and international governments, local farmers, business owners and NGO officers), assisting them in microenterprise development (such as shade-grown coffee and eco-tourism lodges) that improve local living conditions without contributing to the destruction of the natural environment. The funding to support FM's conservation activities is dependent upon international donor groups and private sources. FM is the originator and motivating force behind the Choco-Andean Ecological Corridor Project that has been partially funded by the World Bank's Global Environmental Fund (GEF) and designed to protect two of the Earth's top five biodiversity hotspots (Webster and Rhode, 2001).

The success of FM's sustainability efforts depends on cooperation, collaboration and an appreciation of the inherently complex interrelationships of ecology on multiple levels from natural ecological systems to human-built ecological systems. From FM's beginning in 1988, it has engaged various researchers at different times in strategic management, agriculture, education, marketing, systems ecology and public policy to explore the interrelationships required for sustainability. Examples of FM's commitment to engage a wide range of stakeholders can be identified in terms of research grants, doctoral dissertations, data sets and published articles. However, the collective result of FM's application of its ecological perspective can be understood as a radical reconceptualization of the conventional organizational structure. FM strives to transcend not only the for-profit–non-profit boundaries, but also community–group boundaries, national–international boundaries, academic–disciplinary boundaries, research–praxis boundaries, and human–environmental boundaries. These instances of spanning conventional network boundaries are the true markers of sustainable organizational practice but they require a high level of stakeholder awareness and participation. In order to achieve the expected economic and social outcomes required for sustainability, multi-level, multi-stakeholder network spanning is necessary (Dunphy et al., 2003). FM's organizational structure is based on an interpretation of corporate ecology (Saiia and Cyphert, 2003, Saiia, 2007).

In an attempt to manifest its commitment to stakeholder inclusion and sustainability, FM redesigned its organizational structure to embody corporate ecology. Corporate ecology is a term used to describe the process through which resources are collected and transformed by corporate entities for use by citizens in modern, free-market societies. Through this term the idea of systems interdependence is brought into clearer focus and made conscious. As with all systems of ecology, corporate ecology represents a mindset directed toward deeper understanding and appreciation of the dynamic processes through which resources are concentrated and redistributed. This redistribution occurs throughout the interlinked elements of modern systems including living organisms, naturally occurring physical cycles and corporate activities. More specifically, as corporations act in pursuit of their missions they have direct and indirect impact on a variety of people, communities, governments and the natural environmental systems (that is, air, water, soil, biodiversity, and so on). Corporate ecology examines the corporate entity as a system nested within larger systems and therefore dependent on those other larger systems (Saiia, 2007). FM's new structure better represented the close relationship that would have to be created between conservation efforts and local business practices to pursue sustainability.

In 2002, FM became a hybrid organization that retained its traditional non-profit (for-purpose) unit, separated its administrative functions as a stand-alone unit, and created a new for-profit unit. This three-part structure allows FM to function as a more complete, adaptive and responsive institution within its multilayered network. FM must function within Ecuador, conserving and managing protected cloud-forest and critical watershed resources, with a wide variety of other stakeholders with competing interests ranging from local farmers to local governments, to national business interests, to the Ecuadorian national government, to multinational corporations, to international agencies and associations. Each of these groups has interests that intersect with FM through issues and initiatives influenced through FM's operations. In order for FM to be effective as an organization it needs better administration and more predictable cash flow. FM has long been praised for its success as a 'for-purpose' organization; indeed, FM has achieved a greater than 80 percent reduction in logging in the protected areas under its management. However, 14 years of financial uncertainty and budgetary crises due to over-reliance on too few donors have created continued administrative turnover and inefficiency that is emblematic of small NGOs. In response to this, FM's three-unit structure (non-profit (for-purpose), administrative and for-profit) was designed as a self-reinforcing system that attempts to mimic the symbiosis of naturally occurring systems: the non-profit activities incubate for-profit ideas for micro-enterprise that give economic incentive to support the non-profit objectives, while the administrative costs are increasingly paid for by the for-profit activities making it easier for the non-profit to raise funds for projects with competitively lower administrative overheads.

The first unit, FM's for-purpose unit (the traditional non-profit activities), continues the research and conservation activities that have been part of FM since its inception. Included in these activities are fundraising for land purchase and research projects, and the development and incubation of sustainable micro-enterprises for village populations that border the reserve and the ecological corridor areas. The second unit is the administrative unit. This unit is now oriented to serve both the for-purpose and for-profit units. Costs of the administrative unit are paid for by the for-purpose unit currently, but are gradually being shifted to the for-profit unit as it begins to generate cash flow. The for-profit unit follows the same mission FM has always followed, but it adds to that mission providing value to customers and its suppliers. The for-profit unit operates as an export company that collects, consolidates, quality-checks, brands, markets and sells products that are sustainably produced in the villages in which FM works. The products marketed by FM represent a physical manifestation of its mission: they must be sustainably produced and represent high value-added output given the locally available knowledge and technology. It should be mentioned that FM is not encouraging high-volume production.

What is not immediately evident is how this system achieves a positive feedback and indeed creates sustainable competitive advantage that may be literally sustainable. There are two common issues with which 'for-purpose' organizations must contend. The first common issue with any conservation-oriented organization is demonstrating and distributing the value of the resource being protected. FM's approach as a hybrid organization is to create a brand image that uses the uniqueness of the protected area as the central brand identifier, creating and marketing products that are appealing to a target market that values biodiversity. As mentioned above, the areas being protected are truly unique on our planet and represent endemic plant and animal species that exist nowhere else on Earth. The second issue commonly faced by non-profit organizations is constant cash-flow problems. This issue causes a great number of organizational problems including program rescissions, loss of community trust (when programs are under-funded or discontinued), constant fundraising, low wages and loss of critical personnel (and the loss of organizational memory). By adding the for-profit unit and generating cash flow, these problems can be addressed more systematically. As the for-profit unit absorbs more of the administrative costs, FM gains a competitive advantage in fundraising also: the non-profit side can demonstrate that a higher proportion of donor-dollars are going to the program and not to administration. This is a very convincing argument for many donors that object to funding overheads.

The more important strategic advantage is still hidden. FM's mission to establish ecological corridors will require a huge land area being left uninhabited and to a large extent unwatched. Fencing is pointless and destructive. By including the village stakeholders in the strategic system, FM seeks to create a community of reserve wardens. FM markets the products under a brand name that is connected with the reserve, but the villages own the means of production and create the products. FM teaches and trains the producers in sustainable production techniques and the selection of high value-added products, but the villagers gain a better standard of living. The product value is tied to the success of FM's mission to protect this unique remnant of Choco-Andean biodiversity: as the reserve succeeds the products succeed, as the products get distributed the reserve becomes more well known and thus can fundraise more effectively. The citizens of the villages begin to experience the value of the reserve through the brand value attributed to their products. Thus the positive feedback is demonstrated and, in a perfect world, this chapter would go on to describe the outstanding results achieved through the application of stakeholder inclusion in the strategic management process. However, not all stakeholders play by the rules, and some stakeholders have very different priorities.

METHODS

A case method is often used to capture embedded data from a complex socio-economic context such as a business or an organization that engages in an activity that can influence or is influenced by a large number of stakeholders. Moreover, an iterative case method can capture emergent issues and the changing nature of a complex societal interaction (Yin, 1994). Therefore, an iterative case study of Fundación Maquipucuna (FM) can best capture the evolving and multilayered nature of the land-tenure issue and its impact on FM and its stakeholders. Understanding the role of the stakeholders in constructing the land-tenure reality (Callon, 1992; Herman and Renz, 1998) was of great significance for FM in creating a strategic plan and a structure that could effectively conserve unique areas within and around which these community stakeholders live. Therefore, the first part of this study was designed to collect and analyze stakeholder data for FM (Miles and Huberman, 1984; Yin, 1994) to be used in its strategic management process. Ninety-two hours of interview data were collected, transcribed, coded and analyzed. As a check on reliability of our coding of the salience dimension assessments, a Scott's Pi test for intercoder reliability was conducted. When new developments came into sudden and sharp conflict with FM's past experience it was clear that new data were needed. It was determined that a new technique to organize and interpret FM's stakeholder data was needed. Developing this new technique offered an opportunity to make a practical contribution to stakeholder theory and issues management in the form of 'stakeholder salience mapping'.

Data Collection

Data were collected in two rounds: first, 92 hours of structured stakeholder interviews (Yin, 1994) were conducted over a six-week period (27 May – 14 July 2000; see Table 6.1); second, data were collected from documentary sources and through approximately 20 more hours of informal discussion with FM staff and board members (2001–2006).

Table 6.1 List of stakeholders

Stakeholder group	Number of interviews
Government representatives (agency officers)	7
Ecologists (researchers)	5
Domestic NGOs (Ecuadorian)	4
International NGOs	4
Community (farmers, shop-owners, etc.)	17
Outcasts (squatters, poachers, etc.)	8
Multinational corporations (operating in Ecuador)	3
World Bank (Ecuador office)	2
Media (people in Ecuador)	5
Fundación Maquipucuna (members of the organization)	9
Total	64

Structured interviews were conducted with representatives of each category of stakeholder. These interviews contained questions that addressed FM's land acquisition and management activities. These interviews revealed the stakeholder's self-assessment of their power, urgency and legitimacy (Mitchell et al., 1997) relative to FM's land-tenure. Stakeholder groups interviewed were purposefully conducted in the first language of the participant, either English or Spanish. Each interview was recorded and then transcribed and translated into English when appropriate while the researcher was on-site, so follow-up and confirmation inquiries were conducted as they became necessary. Purposefully selected to create a comprehensive representation of the stakeholders with whom FM had had numerous dealing over the previous 18 years. The specific representative of each stakeholder group was a convenience sample, though care and effort was invested in identifying, contacting and meeting those stakeholders we interviewed. All the interviews were guided by a specific set of questions, though the conversation was allowed to progress as naturally as possible, and follow-up questions were asked of participants. The interview was completed when all the questions were asked and the stakeholder had self-assessed their salience in terms of power, legitimacy and urgency relative to FM's land acquisitions and subsequent land management policies. A total of 64 interviews were conducted resulting in 92 hours of interview data; 57 interviews (89 percent) were conducted in Spanish and seven interviews (11 percent) were conducted in English. These interviews lasted an average of 45 minutes, with a range from 22 minutes to 1.5 hours; 57 (89 percent) of the interviews took place at the informant's place of work or home, while the remaining seven interviews (11 percent) were conducted at FM's

Table 6.2 Relative size and network connectedness

Stakeholder group	Relative size[1] (Ranked largest to smallest)	Network ties[2]
Government	1	HI
Multinational corporations (industrial sector/agribusiness)	2	HI
Community (farmers, small business, etc.)	3	LO
World Bank (presence in Ecuador)	4	HI
Media (Ecuador)	5	HI
International NGOs (presence in Ecuador)	6	M
Domestic NGOs	7	HI
Outcasts (squatters, poachers, etc.)	8	LO
Ecologists (researchers)	9	M
Fundación Maquipucuna	10	HI

Notes:

1. Rank ordered from an estimated contribution to GDP. Ecuador's GDP was $45.65 billion (the country adopted the US dollar as the national currency in 2000). Officially, the general contribution to GDP is divided as follows: 8.7 percent Agriculture, 29.7 percent Industry and 61 percent Service. However, the labor force is divided thus: 30 percent Agriculture, 25 percent Industry and 45 percent Service, with 9–10 percent Unemployment and approximately 47 percent Underemployment. External debt is listed at $15.69 billion – with imports at $6.22 billion and exports at $6.073 (a growing trade deficit).
2. These are consensus estimates collected from members of the Fundación Maquipucuna staff.

Sources: PUCE-Ecuador Labor Market Survey; Central Bank of Ecuador and Bolsa de Valores; Central Bank of Ecuador. Monthly Statistical Information.

research station. These interviews were conducted in the first language of the participant, either English or Spanish. Each interview was recorded and then transcribed and translated into English when appropriate while the researcher was on-site, so follow-up and confirmation inquiries were conducted as they became necessary.

In response to the findings from the first data collection and the subsequent change in the critical land-tenure issue (the emergence of a powerful 'squatter' and a renegade government minister), it was decided that strategic action needed to be taken and more data about FM's stakeholders were needed. Table 6.2 represents the additional data FM's stakeholders gathered through documentary sources (such as the World Bank and the Ecuadorian Central Bank publications) and through numerous email and telephone conversations with the FM staff over a period from 2001 to 2005.

Our first impulse had been to consider follow-up stakeholder interviews. However, funding, timing and immediate need led us to reconsider the information we already had and what we could gather from existing sources. Table 6.2 provides some estimates of the relative size and network ties of the stakeholder groups we had previously interviewed. The size is an estimate of the contribution to GDP of each of the groups in rank order, 1 being the largest. The network ties data are based on the emails and conversation with FM staff.

These rankings were best-guess estimates based on data from the Ecuador Labor Market Survey, the Central Bank of Ecuador, the USA Central Intelligence Agency report on Ecuador and reports from the World Bank.

Data Analysis

Each stakeholder was asked to assess their own perceived salience relative to FM's land tenure using a Likert-type scale from 0 to 4 over the three dimensions of salience: power, legitimacy and urgency (0 = none, 4 = strong). The scale was adjusted to 0–4 using the Likert methodology of a five-point scale, thus providing for a '0' response if a respondent felt they had no influence upon one of the dimensions. The responses from the representative stakeholders from each group were tallied and then averaged for each of the dimensions of salience. These numbers were then totaled to create an overall salience number to create a salience number for comparison among FM's stakeholder groups. These data appear in Table 6.3. The three dimension numbers were added together for a maximum score of 12. Since the mean of each dimension for each stakeholder group was used, the extent of dispersion for each sample mean was carefully studied along with box-plots of the group data-points to make sure that the mean was not a misrepresentation of what was being presented as a unitary 'stakeholder group' assessment of power, legitimacy or urgency (Neuendorf, 2002; Patel, 1996). An Excel formula within the data spreadsheet was used to calculate the sample standard deviation for each of the stakeholder-specific salience dimensions (though the sample size for the 'multinational corporations' and the World Bank were so small that is was not useful for these two samples). The standard deviations generally fell between 0.2 and 0.4 for the three dimensions for each group. However, these simple tests did prove useful as discrepancies were noted within the 'community' stakeholder group.

What started out as a grouping of 19 interviews in the community stakeholder group was altered in two ways. First, two of the community respondents appeared to be outliers on two of the three dimensions within the group and were clearly negative towards FM's land-tenure activities.

Table 6.3 Ratings of stakeholder salience related to land-tenure of Maquipucuna

Stakeholder: Government Positive	Perceived influence
Legitimacy	4
Power	3.5
Urgency	2
Total	9.5
Stakeholder: Domestic NGOs Positive	**Perceived influence**
Legitimacy	2.75
Power	2
Urgency	3.75
Total	8.5
Stakeholder: Ecologists Positive	**Perceived influence**
Legitimacy	3
Power	2.2
Urgency	4
Total	9.2
Stakeholder: International NGOs Positive	**Perceived influence**
Legitimacy	3.5
Power	2.75
Urgency	3.5
Total	9.75
Stakeholder: FM Positive	**Perceived influence**
Legitimacy	3.75
Power	3.25
Urgency	4
Total	11
Stakeholder: Community Positive/Negative (17%)*	**Perceived influence**
Legitimacy	3.85
Power	1.75
Urgency	2.2
Total	±7.8

Note: * This was the only split group.

Table 6.3 (continued)

Stakeholder: Outcasts Negative	Perceived influence
Legitimacy	3.25
Power	1.25
Urgency	4
Total	−8.5

Stakeholder: Multinational Corporations Negative	Perceived influence
Legitimacy	3
Power	3.75
Urgency	2
Total	−8.75

Stakeholder: World Bank Dormant	Perceived influence
Legitimacy	3.45
Power	3.75
Urgency	2
Total	9.2

Stakeholder: Media Positive	Perceived influence
Legitimacy	3.6
Power	3.2
Urgency	3
Total	9.8

This contrasted with the 14 stakeholders strongly in support of FM. A closer examination of the interview transcripts and further questioning of FM's staff resulted in these two stakeholders being reassigned with the 'outcast' group that included squatters and poachers as their numbers were consistent with the three other dimensions within that group. The second change resulted from the observation that three respondents within the 'community' stakeholder group were a mirror image of the larger group. These stakeholders expressed greater urgency and a lower perception of power relative to FM's land-tenure activities and they were negative towards FM. While these respondents are still grouped with the community stakeholder they are a mirror image of the group that supports FM's land-tenure activities.

For this study FM's stakeholders were ultimately grouped into ten groups, Table 6.3 contains their average salience numbers relative to FM's land tenure.

Among the ten stakeholder groups there is a relatively small range of average salience numbers (7.8 to 11). The stakeholders that were a part of the FM organization feel strongly salient about FM's land tenure with a score of 11 and the stakeholders representing the community had a score of 7.8. In the separate dimensions there was much greater variability than in the averaged group scores. This is very informative because it lends some insight into how these stakeholders do feel or do not feel salient, as suggested would be the case by Mitchell et al. (1997). The government representatives expressed a high degree of legitimacy (4), as one respondent explained, 'It is our job to create secure and orderly rules and procedures for land issues and the foundation [FM] has been very careful to follow both the spirit and the letter of the law.' People in the community that were in support of FM (83 percent) felt a high degree of legitimacy (3.85), but did not feel very powerful to effect FM's land-tenure activities; they did not express much urgency about these issues either. A common theme in the community was, 'They [FM] have done so many good things in the area. We have learned how important the forest is to keep our water – it's good they're here.' The remaining community stakeholders (17 percent) were opposed to FM's control of 'so much' land and felt much more urgency but less power and legitimacy. One community stakeholder expressed his opposition to FM's land-tenure because 'it [FM] is controlled by foreigners who are trying to buy up all the land'. Ecologists (researchers working in and around FM's ecological reserve) and international NGO stakeholders were predictably in strong support of FM with strong numbers in the urgency and legitimacy dimensions. 'Maquipucuna is protecting some of the richest areas of endemic biodiversity in the world. Most people have no idea how important this work is.' The domestic NGOs were also very much in support of FM though they felt their legitimacy and power were not strong. One stakeholder in that group commented, 'We sometimes feel like our views about the land don't carry much weight when FM gets so much attention.' Finally the multinationals were consistently opposed to FM's land-tenure activities although they did not attach a particularly high degree of urgency to these activities. Their views were summed up in this excerpt: 'As long as they [FM] stay in the hilly parts of the Andes, we are not so concerned, but if groups like them [FM] get their way – everything will be untouchable. How will anybody be able to make a living if that happens?'

We were also careful to make sure that we only included data from stakeholders for which there was a completed structured survey. These data were used to determine the orientation of the stakeholder group toward FM: positive (for), negative (against) or dormant (unwilling to act). The 'dormant' axis can be best understood as representing a stakeholder's potential to act in a positive or negative way given the proper motivation. We also based these designations on historical data (Beckerman and Solimano, 2002; Gerlach, 2003) and on experience from FM staff members that indicated the orientation of the groups.

An example of the case-based evidence used to infer orientation is: the World Bank has given FM a large grant ($3.3 million) but has repeatedly refused to intervene in legal or political disputes that involved commercial and political interests that could or did involve other investments. Currently (as of June 2006) FM is in negotiation with the World Bank for a grant in excess of $8 million. This history of actions earned the World Bank a 'dormant' designation in Table 6.3. The multinational corporations (MCs) have consistently found themselves at odds with the policies and orientation of FM and other NGO organizations that promote conservation and community resource control. This history of behavior earned the MCs a 'negative' designation.

The 'salience' numbers in Table 6.3 are only useful if these numbers represent a reliable expression of salience to people looking at the same issue. To test for reporting bias or misunderstanding of the dimensions recorded in the self-reported stakeholder salience numbers we triangulated the assessment in Table 6.3 with the assessments of a research assistant familiar with the FM case (naive expert 1), the president and co-founder of FM (naive expert 2), and the researcher. Each of the two naive experts was asked to rate the power, urgency and legitimacy of the ten stakeholder groups relative to FM's land-tenure issues in the same way the stakeholders has rated themselves. Reliability of coding was assessed using Scott's Pi to test for the statistical significance of the agreement or disagreement.

The agreement noted in Table 6.4 is a good indication that the salience numbers are being interpreted in a consistent and reliable manner. Scott's Pi determines whether consistent application of the rating system, in this case the Likert-type scale for the salience dimensions, is being applied or is attributable to chance agreements. By comparing the observed agreements to the expected agreements the researcher can better assess how consistent the rating outcomes are or if the outcomes are attributable to chance. These outcomes are regarded as significant because they indicate agreement in assessment considerably beyond chance and help us to conclude that we are getting a reliable snapshot of our stakeholders' perceived salience relative to FM's land acquisition and management activities.

However, a larger number of interviews would give us a higher degree of certainty and with a larger sample a more sophisticated statistical model could be used to confirm the appropriateness of the dimensions. The com-

Table 6.4 Salience reliability and Scott's Pi for each pair of coders

Coder pairs	Agreement	Disagreement
Researcher and Stakeholder	71	4
Researcher and Naive Expert 1	62	13
Researcher and Naive Expert 2	64	11
Naive Expert 1and 2	60	15
Naive Expert 1 and Stakeholder	66	9
Naive Expert 2 and Stakeholder	67	8
Total	390	60
Simple agreement across all four coders	390/450 = 87%	
Simple agreement for researcher against three other coders	197/225 = 87%	

$$\text{Scott's Pi} = \frac{\%OA - \%EA}{1 - \%EA}$$

OA = Observed agreement, EA = Expected agreement

Coder pairs	Expected agreement	Observed agreement	Scott's Pi
Researcher and Stakeholder	31	94.6	92.17
Researcher and Naive Expert 1	28	82.6	75.8
Researcher and Naive Expert 2	27	85.3	79.8

bination of the case material and these simple statistics, however, allow us to make some statements about FM's position among its stakeholders and perhaps to speculate a bit further.

RESULTS

As indicated earlier, the initial purpose of this project was to gather salience data from stakeholders to map out their positions for FM management relative to FM's land-tenure. Table 6.3 represents an important outcome for this purpose because it helps us to understand how salient each of the stakeholder groups feel and to be able to draw some comparisons based on these ratings. This section further explicates the results of the salience assessment laid out in Table 6.3. Moreover, it introduces the unexpected developments regarding FM's land-tenure and how those events provide the stimulus for further refinement of our mapping tool.

For the most part, the general salience numbers were not very surprising. The orientation of some of the groups (such as the multinational corporations) −8.75 was consistent and predictable. Some of the subtle differences such as the negative salience numbers for the sub-group of community stakeholders may provide rich areas for further investigation. As expected, the oil extraction and pipeline, lumber, mining and agribusiness firms find FM's land acquisitions and management problematic and at times antithetical to multinational corporate organizational objectives and activities. We can see this reflected in the strong negative salience numbers (−8.75). On the other hand, we can see that the expected allies of FM, such as the domestic NGOs and the ecologists, have strong positives (8.5 and 9.2 respectively).

These salience numbers provide a solid basis for comparing and organizing our insights about FM's stakeholders. Table 6.3 provides one way to organize one type of data but a graphical representation of this information would make these data far more accessible. Therefore the data tabulated in Table 6.3 was used to map out the stakeholders to give FM's management an idea of the array of these groups and their relative salience. A 'hub and spoke' type of stakeholder map (Figure 6.1) was created as an extension of the maps Freeman (1984) used in his work. This map was intended to give FM's management a visual idea of who FM's stakeholders were, their orientation toward FM's activities, and their stakeholder salience relative to the land-tenure issue.

This map represents the relative salience of the stakeholders from the data we collected through our structured interviews. It is helpful to FM's management in their decision-making responsibilities because it helped the managers visualize relationships between the land-tenure issues and the clusters of stakeholders. The salience of these stakeholders was kept in mind as FM created a new organizational structure to professionalize its organization, in preparation for the World Bank interactions. However, FM's unpredictable relationship with the World Bank was the first indication that there was more to stakeholder salience than we could capture using the 'hub and spoke' maps.

A CRITICAL THREAT TO FM's SUSTAINABILITY – CASE (PART 2)

In the additional case data provided in this section, further context is provided for the emerging stakeholder mapping technique that was used to map and

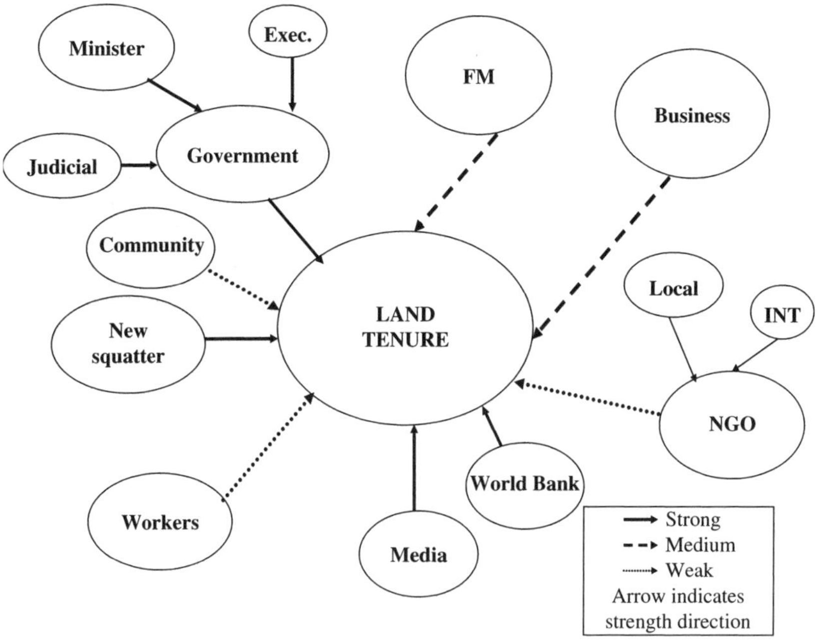

Figure 6.1 Issues-centered stakeholder map for Maquipucuna's land-tenure, 2004

present a simplified expression of stakeholder salience, network connections and group orientation. The facts of the FM case provide a context through which the strategic significance of careful stakeholder data-gathering and interpretation can be better understood. The issues' focus and a focal event can help us identify triggers of change in the relationship among the organizational stakeholders. These moments of triggered readjustment are strategic opportunities for prepared stakeholders within a network system.

Background

In 2002 potent, critical and unexpected threats to FM's sustainability developed around the issue of land-tenure. One involved 'squatters'. The squatter problem that had previously been considered to be a nuisance problem, but a relatively stable stakeholder network relationship situation, suddenly became a mission-threatening issue. The normal policy solution employed by FM for squatter problems was well established and a law firm in Quito familiar with FM was on retainer. The question of land-tenure is well covered in Ecuadorian law, but has a troubled history with the citizenry, especially for poor farming communities (Gerlach, 2003). Farmers who cannot afford to buy land will sometimes expropriate uninhabited land and cultivate it as their own. This is called 'squatting' and if it goes unchallenged for an extended period of time (usually more than five years) the land becomes the property of the squatter. Squatter claims have been an occasional but manageable problem for FM (about seven or eight claims against land owned by FM in the last decade or so). However, this new type of squatter combined with a new land-tenure challenge instigated by a government minister energized this strategic issue and thus reordered the stakeholder landscape relative to FM. These developments necessitated a re-examination of the data gathered in our stakeholder interviews at FM in an attempt to find strategic options to address these new problems. These emergent strategic imperatives, in the form of these new problems, reveal how critical issues for focal organizations *vis-à-vis* their stakeholders can realign, thus changing the dynamics among the stakeholders affected by a particular issue. The organization must be able to use its knowledge of its stakeholders to leverage influence within a stakeholder network to achieve a sustainable outcome. Further case material is presented below to explicate the two critical issues that emerged suddenly for FM: (1) the threat to lease out FM's privately held ecological reserve; and (2) the new squatter claim. These issues threaten FM's land-tenure, but they also help contextualize the use of the newly revised stakeholder map and its importance for FM's sustainability.

Critical Land-Use Issues

Using the GEF grant from the World Bank, FM began to implement a series of projects that included the promotion of eco-tourism, and the development of shade-grown coffee and cocoa. FM also began to investigate other types of sustainable economic activities that were consistent with the conservation of the ecological corridors FM is helping to design. As part of the grant agreement FM allowed World Bank representatives full access to the project sites and to FM's financial records. FM received glowing reviews from the World Bank for its management of these GEF projects and was held out as a model of what sustainable conservation should be. However, as FM operated under the impression that it had stable and sustainable relationships with its salient stakeholders, critical events were about to challenge that perception.

- Problem 1: In the early part of 2003, a new squatter claim emerged in a particularly mountainous and seldom visited part of the FM ecological reserve. As has been FM's practice, their lawyer filed a formal challenge in the appropriate court. On the face of this squatter's claim, it had no validity because there had been no changes made to that area, there are no roads and no possibility that someone could have been secretly living off the land there continuously for over five years as required by Ecuadorian law for a valid squatter claim. On these grounds, it was a particularly weak claim. Therefore, it was shocking when FM lost the case in court. It soon became clear that the claimant was both politically and personally connected to powerful national leaders. The judge in charge of adjudicating the case interpreted the law in such a way that appeared to negate FM's legal land title. The decision was immediately appealed against, but this crisis put most of FM's other activities on hold.

- Problem 2: Several months after the loss in court, a powerful government official began to make statements about the concentration of land in foreign hands. It was claimed that foreign-funded foundations were acquiring land in Ecuador to the detriment of the people of Ecuador. Several foundations including FM were targeted for possible land sales or lease agreements. While this type of action would be in violation of the constitution of Ecuador it created great uncertainty with FM's donors and project partners.

These two problems represented a survival threat to FM. Suddenly an issue – land-tenure that had a specific procedure and a perfect record of success, was now an all-consuming crisis. The well-constructed strategy of sustainable product development, targeted marketing and cloud-forest preservation had to be put on hold while new strategies were created to address this radical change in the stakeholder environment.

This redefinition of the land-tenure issue had serious implications not only for FM but for several other highly salient stakeholders. Understanding how a few stakeholders can redefine an issue and reshape the stakeholder landscape is a critical sustainability question. Because this issue threatened the existence of FM and its ability to pursue its mission, suddenly the issue of FM's strategic direction and its sustainability all had to be reconsidered. In order for FM's management better to understand the new reality for FM and its stakeholders, some new propositions had to be generated to explore possible strategic responses. What began as a preplanned research project suddenly took on an emergent quality. The following propositions were created to help the researcher look back through the stakeholder data and present some possible response options for FM based on what could be discerned about the stakeholders.

Proposition 2: *A focal event can trigger a change in the stakeholder status quo and signal an opportunity to renegotiate existing relationships with stakeholders. (In this case, some multinational corporation stakeholders saw their interests align with FM's around the issue of land ownership rights.)*

Proposition 2a: *Dormant stakeholders may be activated by a focal event. (The World Bank is interested in providing another large grant to FM through the Global Environment Fund – GEF.)*

STAKEHOLDER MAPS

FM has been actively engaged with its stakeholders throughout its 18-year existence (1984–2006). The salience numbers of FM's stakeholders collected in the 2000 survey (as reported in Table 6.3) were used in a process to help FM plan and implement the Choco-Andean Corridor project as part of its overall mission. However, while the 'hub and spoke' map introduced by Freeman (1984), and adapted in the first part of this chapter as an issue-focused stakeholder map, provided a good start for prioritizing FM's efforts at stakeholder engagement, it did not consider a great deal of information (such as orientation, relative size and network connections) that would be useful to know about FM's stakeholders (Figure 6.1).

When the two critical land-tenure issues emerged, it became clear that FM's understanding of key stakeholders was incomplete and needed revision. Indeed, an earlier episode in 2002 involving the World Bank provided an early warning regarding FM's quixotic understanding of its stakeholders and their motivations.

In the second year of the GEF project funding (2002), an oil pipeline project was announced that would locate a new pipeline (*oleoducto de crudos pesados* or OCP) along the southern border of the Maquipucuna Ecological Reserve. The OCP posed a potential hazard to FM's mission and important watershed areas critical to FM's ecological reserve. FM's management assumed that the World Bank's generous support coupled with the glowing reports and reviews of FM's work would make them a strong ally in FM's opposition to the routing of the OCP. The World Bank, however, refused to get involved or even to render an objective opinion about the project or a proposed alternative route of less impact. This event should have been an indication that the insight regarding FM's stakeholders gained from Figure 6.1 was inadequate to deal with complex issues management. Note that the map in Figure 6.1 simply indicates the number of stakeholders concerned with FM's land-tenure and their relative strength.

It became clear that including the relative size of the stakeholder group and the degree of network embeddedness of each stakeholder as well as the salience number described in the analysis section (see Table 6.2) would improve the usefulness of the salience mapping because it helps managers visualize their stakeholders. Three dimensions were then created to represent the salience component based on the numbers and orientations presented in Table 6.3. These dimensions are positive, negative and dormant, to describe the stakeholder orientation, and are numbered from 0 to 12 to represent the relative salience numbers as described in the analysis section. The 'dormant' axis was added to represent stakeholders unwilling to act on a given issue. Size was represented by that stakeholder's 'bubble'. Note that the size data are based on estimated contributions to the GDP of Ecuador (Table 6.2). Published sources such as UN, World Bank and IMF reports as well as Ecuadorian sources such as reports from Instituto Nacional de Estadistica y Censos (Ministry of Economic Development, 2004) were employed for comparisons of GDP contributions for each of the stakeholder groups.

The intention was not to create a definitive number representing size for this first exploration, but rather to arrive at a number that would be close enough for comparison. The network connections estimate is also quite imprecise and is based on the best guess of FM's management based on email exchanges and telephone interviews. Using this information, the dimensions are divided into Hi and Lo quadrants to indicate the degree of network embeddedness. While these are imprecise estimates, this new mapping technique offered an insightful graphical interface for a wide variety of pertinent stakeholder information.

As with the map in Figure 6.1, by replacing the organization with the defining issue at the center of the map the number of salient stakeholders is reduced because some issues are of greater concern for fewer stakeholders. By focusing only on those stakeholders with salience *vis-à-vis* FM's land-tenure, FM's managers were better able to see critical stakeholders and their network connections.

In rethinking the mapping idea, a technique to represent as much stakeholder information as possible in a visual manner was desired. Figure 6.2 represents the results of this technique as applied to FM's stakeholders. FM was faced with issues that threatened its existence. The first proposition in this chapter suggested that better decisions could be made if FM had a better technique for interpreting stakeholder data. Furthermore, the first sub-proposition stated that FM would be more sustainable by understanding what was critically important to its most salient stakeholders.

In the next part of this chapter the use of such stakeholder maps will be discussed. This visual aid for decision-making integrates multiple types of

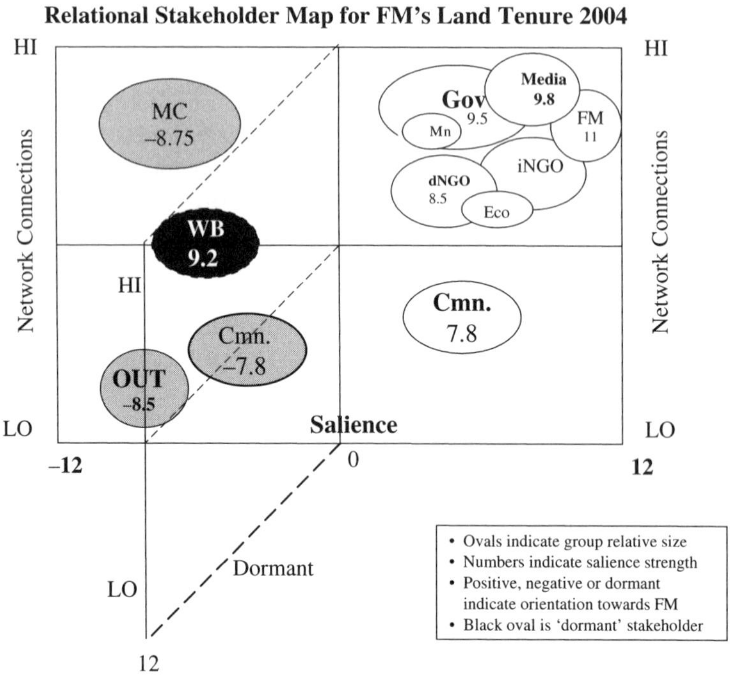

Notes:

MC	Multinational corporation
WB	World Bank
Cmn.	Community stakeholders
OUT	'Outcasts'
Gov	Ecuadorian government
Mn.	Minister
dNGO	Domestic non-governmental organizations
iNGO	International non-governmental organizations
FM	Fundación Maquipucuna
Eco	Ecologists

Figure 6.2 Stakeholder salience map

stakeholder analysis. It provides a way to look at clusters of stakeholders in opposition and in support of the organization's position on a particular issue.

DISCUSSION: OPTIONS AND ACTIONS

Figure 6.2 has proven to be very useful as a technique to help FM consider its strategic options in response to changes in the threats to its land-tenure. This stakeholder salience map presents a collection of stakeholders and shows how they grouped in terms of salience and connectedness, thus helping FM's managers to think of new ways to engage salient stakeholders. Previous to this land-tenure crisis, FM's challenge has been to raise money and manage the support of community stakeholders. While these issues are still very important, the threat to its land-tenure had greater urgency. FM generally had good support from the press, but land-tenure is not a 'headline' issue and was hard to keep in the headlines. Our map indicates that multinational corporations (MCs) were in opposition to FM, however, as a result of FM's land-tenure crisis; it became possible to seek cooperation between FM and the MCs.

The pre-crisis reality mapped out in Figure 6.1 made FM's response to a new squatter claim simply a matter of policy. The squatter is taken to court and the matter is resolved. Likewise, when a politician starts to make unsubstantiated claims about FM, it would be wise either to ignore the allegation until people lost interest or to find a way to get some good media coverage on one of its successful projects. But what happens when the facts no longer fit the newly reconstructed reality – when suddenly the 'landmarks' on your map change?

FM's management began to formulate strategic actions using the insights gained from the stakeholder data and the stakeholder orientation shown in the new map (Figure 6.2). These actions included the following. First, FM managed to get some very favorable media coverage in the periodicals, on the radio and on the television by pushing this story through allied stakeholders. Second, several meetings were held with MCs to discuss the importance of constitutional property rights, an impartial judiciary and an executive branch that would follow and enforce the existing law. Third, FM had to confront diplomatically and indirectly powerful political forces threatening its existence. Fourth, FM tried to enlist the support of its largest single donor, the World Bank, to help influence and counter these threats, but learned that the World Bank would not act on what it considered to be 'internal politics'. Fifth, FM managers used Figure 6.2 to create the projections in Figure 6.3 regarding stakeholder salience, orientation and connections reflecting the evolving land-tenure issues to understand better the newly constructed reality.

In this 'projected' stakeholder salience map presented in Figure 6.3, note how much more powerful the squatter group is perceived to be (squatters are included in the 'outsiders' with illegal loggers and poachers). The MCs also moved to the positive side as they realized that it was now in their interest to act to protect their legal rights to own assets and property, and that the government had to follow the law in order to guarantee those rights.

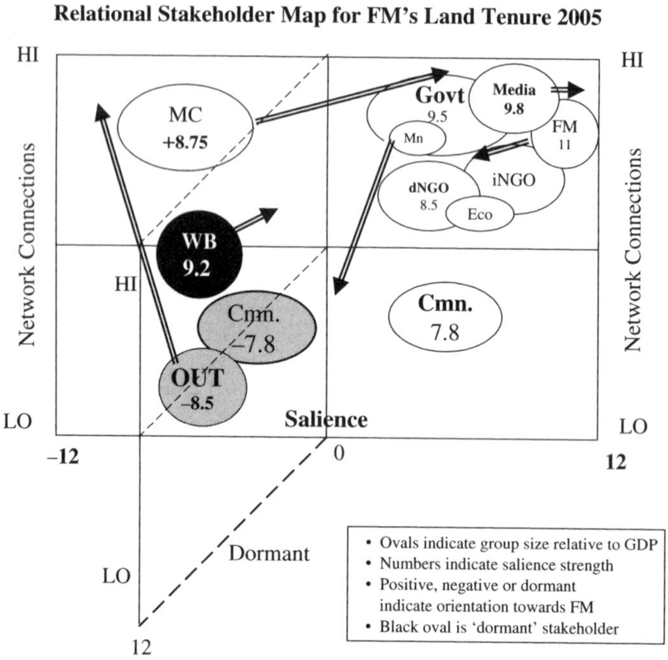

Notes:

MC	Multinational corporation
WB	World Bank
Cmn.	Community stakeholders
OUT	'Outcasts'
Gov	Ecuadorian government
Mn.	Minister
dNGO	Domestic non-governmental organizations
iNGO	International non-governmental organizations
FM	Fundación Maquipucuna
Eco	Ecologists

Figure 6.3 Adjusted stakeholder map indicating group movement

Stakeholders outside of Ecuador mounted efforts to put pressure on the Ecuadorian government to protect FM (see Appendix 6A). Several prominent ecological researchers, a couple of universities, aid agencies as well as national and international societies contacted the Ecuadorian government on behalf of FM. Finally, a US national center for conflict resolution was asked to begin a formal process of inquiry as a first step in helping FM negotiate with the Ecuadorian government.

While this challenge to the legal rights to own property and to have those rights protected by the government did allow FM to gain support from the

MCs, this land-tenure crisis was not threatening enough for the World Bank to get involved. The World Bank had to weigh other interests against FM's sustainability.

Truth and Consequences

As a result of the pressure applied on the Ecuadorian government by the media, the MCs and other interested stakeholders (see Appendix 6A), in December 2004, the government official who had threatened to lease or sell land consolidated by foundations (particularly focusing on FM) resigned. Thus, the first problem regarding land-tenure was resolved after almost two years of struggle. While this was a great first step, it still left the much more difficult issue of the newly powerful squatter.

Meanwhile, the political environment in Ecuador was increasingly unstable (Solano, 2005) after Ecuador's Supreme Court was dissolved by an Act of the Ecuador's President and 52 congressional allies (Forero and Bass, 2004). These events help the reader to understand the growing distrust and suspicion of the independence of the judicial rulings and activities of various agencies of the government (*The Economist*, 2005). An organization cannot be sustainable without the rule of law and the support of salient, well-connected and stable stakeholders. While a change in regime (see O'Grady, 2005) brought changes in government ministries that resolved FM's right to legally own land, as of June 2006, FM did not have resolution on the still active squatter's claim appeal.

While the judicial branch has been reshuffled, and various ministries have upheld FM's title, the survey of this particular parcel of land has now been called into question and the squatter has posted guards on the land they have now occupied. The squatter law was created as a remedy for landless farmers to be able to improve their lives through their own hard work on abandoned or neglected land (Hanratty, 1989). The still unsolved question in this ongoing land-tenure issue is how the 'new' squatter is connected to other stakeholders and who they might be. FM's experience has been that squatters do not have money to buy land through a legitimate sale, so they simply occupy remote uninhabited parcels. This squatter has money to pay for court fees and lawyers, and now hires guards to keep FM's surveyors out.

Some General Conclusions

It is again recognized that this is a specific case-study and, as such, generalizations are not possible. However, the details of this case indicate some useful insights that may apply to other organizations. First, issues management proved very useful when integrated with stakeholder information-gathering to bring focus and clarity to the stakeholder process used. This approach, however, is not without cost: it requires that the organization map its most salient stakeholders over a number of its top priority issues. In the past this may have presented an insurmountable obstacle, yet today we have the computing capacity to use database management to organize the data needed to create these maps more efficiently. Second, even relatively simple maps, like the one generated for FM, can help managers visualize the network of stakeholders around a particular issue. Third, augmenting the idea of salience with each stakeholder group's disposition to the focal organization, the relative size and the network connections is a synthesis of ideas that gives management useful insight into stakeholder disposition and ability to act. The end result of the synthesis represented by this salience map is a management-friendly representation of highly salient stakeholder groups and their potential to act and their likelihood to act. This can be critical input for management to make informed, insightful and ultimately more sustainable decisions.

Future Direction and Study Limitations

We are anxious to return to Ecuador to interview more stakeholders and collect new salience numbers for comparison with the data represented in this chapter. FM needs to develop new ways to address its squatter problem and will need to establish a more substantial legal defense fund to plan for a sustainable future.

This new stakeholder map is a promising visual tool, but it needs refinement in terms of its metrics for relative size and network connections. While acknowledging the need to understand network characteristics better, the data for a systematic network study were not available for this chapter. Our interpretation of stakeholder connectedness is impressionistic at best and represents more of a place-holder than a metric at this point. Good computer skills in database and programming could further develop this map into a truly dynamic tool for mapping and monitoring stakeholders and the networks that form around issues. Finally, it seems clear that the question of sustainability is a careful balance between good definition and the approach used to represent a socially constructed reality that must by careful definition depend on critical stakeholders. This approach involves organizing our stakeholder data into a knowledge tool to help us interpret this socially constructed reality. The technique captured by the salience map can help organizations better understand their stakeholders and thus what it will take to serve competing interests equitably. Organizing stakeholders according to critical issues will move more organizations towards sustainability as they begin to visualize how they can make decisions that consider the impact of their action on their stakeholders through the seventh generation.

NOTE

1. The author would like to thank his interpreter Ivan Raiklin for his diligence and clarity and his assistant Krasimira Georgieva. I would also like to thank the University of Northern Iowa, and Dean Farzad Moussavi of the Business School for his support of my field work.

REFERENCES

Ansoff, H.I. (1979), 'The changing shape of the strategic problem', in D.E. Schendel and C.W. Hofer (eds), *Strategic Management: A New View of Business Policy and Planning*, Boston, MA: Little, Brown, pp. 30–43.

Balser, D. and J. McCluskey (2005), 'Managing stakeholder relationships and nonprofit organization effectiveness', *Nonprofit Management and Leadership*, **15** (3)(Spring), 295–315.

Beckerman, P. and A. Solimano (2002), 'Longer-term origins of Ecuador's "Predollarization" crisis', in Paul Beckerman and Andres Solimano (eds), *Crisis and Dollarization in Ecuador: Stability, Growth, and Social Equity*, Washington, DC: World Bank, pp. 1–47.

Best, J. (1995), 'Constructionism in context', in J. Best (ed.), *Images of Issues: Typifying Contemporary Social Problems*, New York: Aldine de Gruyter, pp. 337–54.

Callon, M. (1986), 'Some elements of a sociology of translation: domestication of the scallops and the fishermen of St Brieuc Bay', in J. Law (ed.), *Power, Action and Belief*, London: Routledge & Kegan Paul, pp. 196–233.

Callon, M. (1992), 'The dynamics of techno-economic networks', in R. Coombs, P. Savitotti and V. Walsh (eds), *Technological Change and Company Strategies: Economic and Sociological Perspectives*, London: Academic Press, pp. 72–102.

Dunphy, D., A. Griffiths and S. Benn (2003), *Organizational Change for Corporate Sustainability: A Guide for Leaders and Change Agents of the Future*, New York: Routledge.

The Economist (2005), 'The Americas: confused in the Andes – Ecuador', **377**, 40.

Forero, J. and C.D. Bass (2004), 'Firings on Ecuador's top court stir opposition's wrath', *New York Times*, 18 December, p. A3.

Freeman, R.E. (1984), *Strategic Management: A Stakeholder Approach*, Boston, MA: Pitman/Ballinger.

Frooman, J. (1999), 'Stakeholder influence strategies', *Academy of Management Review*, **24** (2), 191–205.

Gerlach, A. (2003), *Indians, Oil, and Politics: A Recent History of Ecuador*, Wilmington, DE: Scholarly Resources.

Goodwin, C. and A. Duranti (1992), 'Rethinking context: an introduction', in A. Duranti and C. Goodwin (eds), *Rethinking Context: Language as an Interactive Phenomenon*, New York: Cambridge University Press, 1–42.
Gray, B. (1989), *Collaborating: Finding Common Ground for Multiparty Problems*, San Francisco, CA: Jossey-Bass.
Hanratty, D. (ed.) (1989), *Ecuador: Land Use and Tenure*, Federal Research Division, Library of Congress, Washington, DC: Government Printing Office.
Herman, R.D. and D.O. Renz (1998), 'Nonprofit organizational effectiveness: contrasts between especially effective and less effective organizations', *Nonprofit Management and Leadership*, **9** (1), 23–8.
Hoffmann, A.J. and W. Ocasio (2001), 'Not all events are attended equally: toward a middle-range theory of industry attention to external events', *Organizational Science*, **12** (4), 414–34.
Heugens, P. (2002), 'Strategic issues management', *Business and Society*, **41** (4), 456–68.
Miles, M.B. and A.M. Huberman (1984), *Qualitative Data Analysis: A Sourcebook of New Methods*, Beverly Hills, CA: Sage.
Ministry of Economic Development (2004), Instituto Nacional de Estadistica y Censos economic data, Government of Ecuador.
Mitchell, R.K., B.R. Agle and D.J. Wood (1997), 'Toward a theory of stakeholder identification and salience: defining the principle of who and what really counts', *Academy of Management Review*, **22** (4), 853–86.
Murphy, G. (1996), '7th generation: the great law', National Public Telecomputing Network (NPTN), accessed 15 March 2006 at www.indigenouspeople.net/iroqcon.htm.
Nathan, M.L. and I.I. Mitroff (1991), 'The use of negotiated order theory as a tool for the analysis and development of an interorganizational field', *Journal of Applied Behavioral Science*, **27** (2), 163–80.
O'Grady, M. (2005), 'Americas: Ecuadorians say, "no mas", to Gutierrez', *Wall Street Journal*, 22 April, p. 13.
Pasquero, J. (1996), 'Stakeholder theory as a constructivist paradigm', in J. Logsdon and K. Rehbein (eds), proceedings of the 7th Annual Conference of the International Association for Business and Society, Santa Fe, NM, pp. 584–9.
Patel, J.K. (1996), *Handbook of the Normal Distribution*, Statistics, a Series of Textbooks and Monographs, Thousand Oaks, CA: Sage.
Roland, J. (1989), 'Gayanashagowa: the great binding law', Constitution Society, accessed 15 March 2006 at www.constitution.org/cons/iroquois.htm.
Rowley, T.J. (1997), 'Moving beyond dyadic ties – a network theory of stakeholder influences', *Academy of Management Review*, **22** (4), 887–910.
Rowley, T. and S. Berman (2000), 'A brand new brand of corporate social performance', *Business and Society*, **39** (4), 397–418.
Saiia, D. (forthcoming), 'Corporate ecology', in Robert Kolb (ed.), *Encyclopedia of Corporate Social Responsibility*, Thousand Oaks, CA: Sage.
Saiia, D. and D. Cyphert (2003), 'Public discourse of the corporate citizen', *Corporate Reputation Review*, **6** (1), 47–57.
Saiia, D., R. Schmitt and S. Beaulieu (2003), 'Stakeholder salience dynamics', proceedings of the CSR Conference, London, England.
Solano, G. (2005), 'Tear gas ends sit-in by lawmakers in Ecuador', *Houston Chronicle*, 24 March, p. 13.

Starik, M. and G. Rands (1995), 'Weaving an Integrated Web: Multilevel and Multisystem Perspectives of Ecologically Sustainable Organizations', *Academy of Management Review*, **20** (4), 908–35.

Strauss, A., L. Schatzman, D. Ehrlich, R. Bucher and M. Sabshin (1963), 'The hospital and its negotiated order', in E. Friedson (ed.), *The Hospital in Modern Society*, New York: Free Press, pp. 147–69.

Schmitt, R., D. Saiia and S. Beaulieu (2002), 'Exploring dynamic stakeholder relations: an application to three case studies', *Proceedings of the 13th Annual Conference of the International Association for Business and Society*, Yellowstone, WY: IABS, 231–37.

Wartick, S.L. and Rude, R.E. (1986), 'Issues management: corporate fad or corporate functions', *California Management Review*, **29** (1), 124–40.

Webster, G.L. and R.M. Rhode (2001), *Plant Diversity of an Andean Cloud Forest: Inventory of the Vascular Plants of Maquipucuna, Ecuador*. University of California Publications in Botany, 82, Berkeley, CA: University of California.

Yin, R.K. (1994), 'Case study research: design and methods', *Applied Social Research Methods Series*, vol. 5, 2nd edn, New York: Sage.

APPENDIX 6A: LETTER FROM FM's STAKEHOLDER ENGAGEMENT CAMPAIGN

Quito, April 5th, 2004

[redacted]

[redacted]

I, ..., am entirely opposed to and wish to protest the awarding of lands within the Maquipucuna Reserve to shady economic interests. Mr. [redacted], the lands that belong to Maquipucuna Reserve were bought by legitimate owners in order to protect a natural human heritage. Four percent of all bird species in the world are found in Maquipucuna and 10% of all the plants in Ecuador are protected there. Moreover, dozens of endangered animals and plant species, which are listed in the red book of the IUCN, are found in Maquipucuna as well.

The Maquipucuna Foundation not only protects the area within the confines of the reserve, but actively implements economic alternatives to deforestation, in turn generating sustainable job opportunities and supporting the development of local communities.

Thousands of Ecuadorian children; thousands of ecotourists that visit the region; many renowned scientists; hundreds of volunteers from many countries; friendly Governments; Embassies; the World Bank; the Global Environment Facility (GEF); SKAL – the biggest international association of tourism professionals; the Ecuadorian Ecotourism Association, ASEC; hundreds of people who consume Choco-Andes coffee, organic jams, and other products from the conservation projects of the region; and National Geographic and the Discovery Channel have not been mistaken in recognizing, and applauding, the innovative conservation model of the Maquipucuna Reserve.

Mr. Minister, put an end to this wrongful course of action.

I ask you, [redacted], to stop these abuses against the Maquipucuna Reserve. Do not allow INDA (Instituto Nacional de Desarrollo Agrario) to award land titles illegally within the Maquipucuna Reserve. Those who would receive this illegally-granted land are known to have personal economic interests, with audacious ambitions that run counter to conservation and community development objectives.

What is perhaps worst of all, [redacted], is that by illegally awarding lands within the reserve, you would endanger neighboring communities to the Maquipucuna Reserve, which are among the few communities in our nation to have accepted and embraced the global challenge to responsibly pursue economic development in a truly sustainable fashion.

Sincerely yours,

cc:

[redacted]

Note:
This letter was used as part of a strategic action to apply pressure from a broad cross-section of stakeholders in support of FM's land-tenure rights. Thousands of these letters were sent in. The names have been removed to avoid the possibility of further complications.

7. Stakeholder management and sustainability evaluation and reporting system (SERS): a new corporate performance management framework

Francesco Perrini and Antonio Tencati

Value creation is a company's ultimate goal (Rappaport, 1986; Mills and Weinstein, 2000; Jensen, 2001; Grant, 2002). To achieve this, the firm must be attentive to the context in which it operates. In fact a network of relationships connects the company to a large number of interrelated individuals and constituencies, called stakeholders (Freeman, 1984; Donaldson and Preston, 1995; Post et al., 2002; Ulrich and Krieg, 1973; Dierkes, 1976). These relationships influence the way a company is governed and, in turn, are influenced by the company's behavior. Post et al. (2002) emphasize that 'the capacity of a firm to generate sustainable wealth over time, and hence its long-term value, is determined by its relationships with critical stakeholders' (p. 9) and 'any stakeholder relationship may be the most critical one at a particular time or on a particular issue' (p. 8).

Convincing examples are provided by the protesting and boycotting campaigns carried out by non-governmental organizations (NGOs) against various companies operating in different industries and countries (Klein, 2000; Hertz, 2001; Bandura et al., 2002; Bakan, 2004). Managers of these firms changed their strategic choices under the pressure of some specific stakeholder groups, and because they did not perceive this pressure soon enough, the consequences for both company reputation and business development were in some instances harmful.

The gauge of corporate success cannot be limited to the creation of value for only one stakeholder group, that is, the shareholders (Clarkson, 1995, p. 112). Especially since 1990, many proposals were developed to integrate and supersede the traditional methodologies focused on the financial dimension of corporate performance. Tools such as the balanced scorecard

(Kaplan and Norton, 1992, 2004), environmental and social reports (Bennett and James, 1999), sustainability reports defined according to the triple bottom line (TBL) agenda (Elkington, 1994, 1997) and international standards like the Sustainability Reporting Guidelines (Global Reporting Initiative, 2002, 2006) are all implemented in response to the challenges posed by new information requirements for decision-making processes and communication policies (Wagner and Schaltegger, 2003; Schaltegger and Wagner, 2006).

But how many companies have really changed their perspectives? How many companies measure and assess their own performance by considering the impact of their own activities, for example, on human, social and natural capitals? Even if we focus only on the listed companies worldwide, how many of these firms have really replaced the shareholder approach with a more comprehensive stakeholder approach? And if the largest companies do not, what about the small and medium-sized enterprises (SMEs), which comprise the majority of firms in every nation of the world?

The purpose of this chapter is to address this need for change by presenting a relational view of the firm, based on the strategic value of the linkages with stakeholders, and its implications for corporate performance evaluation and reporting systems. The focus will therefore be on a new proposal relevant to sustainability accounting, defined according to this stakeholder framework in order to support companies' strategic and managerial efforts – especially those of SMEs.

We begin by considering the ultimate goals of a company and propose sustainability as key to the long-term survival of firms. This model, which combines economic prosperity, social cohesion and environmental protection, is viable and consistent with the corporate objective of long-term value creation. A sustainability-oriented company is fully aware of its responsibilities towards the different stakeholders and adopts methods and tools to improve its social and ecological performance. Thus new sustainability accounting systems are needed.

In the next section, we advance our proposal, SERS (sustainability evaluation and reporting system), which we created from theoretical analyses and empirical experiences. The framework, consistent with the stakeholder view of the firm, can aid all corporate categories in managing and integrating stakeholder relationships, which are crucial for long-term success.

The last section discusses the details of this approach and the further steps needed to improve the measurement of business success and to go beyond the traditional financial and management accounting.

STAKEHOLDER VIEW, CORPORATE SUSTAINABILITY AND PERFORMANCE MANAGEMENT

According to the stakeholder view of the firm (Donaldson and Preston, 1995; Clarkson, 1995; Post et al., 2002), a company can endure if it builds and maintains sustainable and durable relationships with its entire stakeholder network. 'These relationships are the essential assets that managers must manage, and they are the ultimate source of organizational wealth' (Post et al., 2002, p. 8).

A company creates value when it adopts a sustainability-oriented managerial approach. In general, corporate sustainability is defined as 'a broad approach that includes various characteristics, in particular relating to the *contextual integration* of economic, environmental and social aspects' (Schaltegger and Burritt, 2005, p. 189). According to AccountAbility's (1999, p. 94) definition, 'sustainability is the capability of an organization to continue its activities indefinitely, having taken due account of their impact on natural, social and human capitals'. A sustainability-oriented company develops over time by considering the economic, social and environmental dimensions of its processes and performance. Therefore financial and competitive success, social legitimacy and efficient use of natural resources are interrelated according to a synergetic and circular perspective on the company's aims. Value creation processes are broad and shared and meet, in different ways, stakeholder expectations. We can therefore replace the generally adopted theory of value and introduce the concept of stakeholder value (Figge and Schaltegger, 2000).

Thus the sustainability of a firm depends on the sustainability of its stakeholder relationships: it must consider and engage not only shareholders, employees and clients, but also suppliers, public authorities, local (or national, according to a firm's size) community and civil society in general, financial partners and so on. Today, and more and more into the future, the quality, that is, the sustainability of stakeholder relationships must guide the managerial decision-making process and support a more comprehensive corporate strategy.

Adopting this stakeholder view of the firm requires rethinking the nature and purposes of businesses and their managerial tools. The success of managerial efforts cannot be measured from a shareholder perspective, but rather by means of a more holistic and comprehensive stakeholder framework. Companies need appropriate systems to measure and control their own behavior in order to assess the effectiveness of their response to stakeholder concerns and to communicate and demonstrate the results achieved. These new evaluation and reporting systems should broaden, integrate and improve the traditional financial and economic corporate performance measurement, emphasizing stakeholder needs in this process.

In more than 15 years, more than 100 standards and management solutions were developed to evaluate and report the economic, social, environmental and sustainability performance of companies (ISO Advisory Group on Corporate Social Responsibility, 2003). These tools provide qualitative, quantitative and economic information, influencing the interactions between a firm and its stakeholders. Lacking a clear reference system, this multiplicity and complexity nevertheless produce undesirable effects for companies and their own stakeholders:

- Confusion for companies and lack of management and organizational innovation. The existence of several standards and acronyms, the development of different and at the same time similar proposals, especially focused on big firms' expectations, can complicate companies' attitudes towards sustainability and corporate social responsibility (CSR). This can, in turn, slow down the adoption and implementation of more advanced managerial models, especially in SMEs, rather than supporting and promoting them.
- Confusion and lack of clarity for the companies' stakeholders. If firms lack an effective and clear approach toward managing, assessing and reporting their own performance, the stakeholder groups experience difficulties in analyzing and appreciating the company's sustainability efforts.

Furthermore this absence of shared, sound and recognized processes and methods can reward free-riders that behave fraudulently and communicate unfair and false results.

And even if we consider the most advanced methods of sustainability management (Figge et al., 2002), they are not designed to take into account explicitly, clearly and completely the different relationships between companies and their stakeholders. The concept of extended enterprise, based on a relational view of the firm focused on stakeholder linkages (Post et al., 2002, p. 25), goes beyond 'previous work on the "triple bottom line" and "balanced scorecard" ': 'The key to solving the core strategic problem is to understand the firm's entire set of stakeholder relationships' (Post et al., 2002, p. 8).

Furthermore the traditional environmental, social and sustainability reports are defined more as public relations products than as effective methodologies to control and manage corporate performance (Cerin, 2002a, 2002b).

Moreover the balanced scorecard, the GRI Sustainability Reporting Guidelines and the Sustainability Integrated Guidelines for Management

(SIGMA Project, 2003) are inappropriate for SMEs because of their complexity, limited flexibility and need for formal procedures. So far, for example, only some hundred companies all over the world have adopted the Sustainability Reporting Guidelines, which is far from a significant corporate involvement. Up until now also, approaches and guidelines have been designed to support SMEs in their managerial efforts (for example Rayner and Raven, 2002; CSR Europe, 2002; United Nations Industrial Development Organization, 2002; Deloitte Touche Tohmatsu Emerging Markets, 2004; Global Reporting Initiative, 2004) – important steps towards a greater engagement of SMEs, but without solutions which can be considered as reference points in the management of sustainability.

In conclusion, in order to face the strategic challenge of managing stakeholder relationships and meeting managerial needs, especially those of SMEs, we believe that there is a strong need for a clear and modular methodology to create a sustainability accounting system. We next present and describe our system of monitoring and tracking, qualitatively and quantitatively, the overall corporate performance according to a stakeholder view of the firm and based on a flexible structure suitable for companies of different industries, sizes and countries.

ANALYZING THE FRAMEWORK: SUSTAINABILITY EVALUATION AND REPORTING SYSTEM (SERS)

The goal of the proposal, called the sustainability evaluation and reporting system (SERS) and developed by SPACE (the Research Centre of Bocconi University on Risk, Security, Occupational Health and Safety, Environment and Crisis Management) is to aggregate different management tools (for example social reporting, environmental reporting and key performance indicators) into a comprehensive model (Perrini and Tencati, 2006). This integrated approach derives from theoretical analyses and experiences that span almost 15 years of research into the management of sustainability and the evaluation of and reporting on social, environmental and sustainability performance in collaboration with companies and institutions (SPACE, 1993; Pogutz and Tencati, 1997; De Silvio and Tencati, 2002; Tencati, 2002; Perrini and Tencati, 2003; Tencati and Perrini, 2006). The goal is to build an efficient and effective methodology for an overall assessment of corporate sustainability in order to support new accounting and reporting efforts (with a particular focus on SMEs), integrate financial and non-financial performance measures, improve the quality of decision-making processes and of the overall business management and strengthen corporate accountability and responsiveness towards the different stakeholder groups.

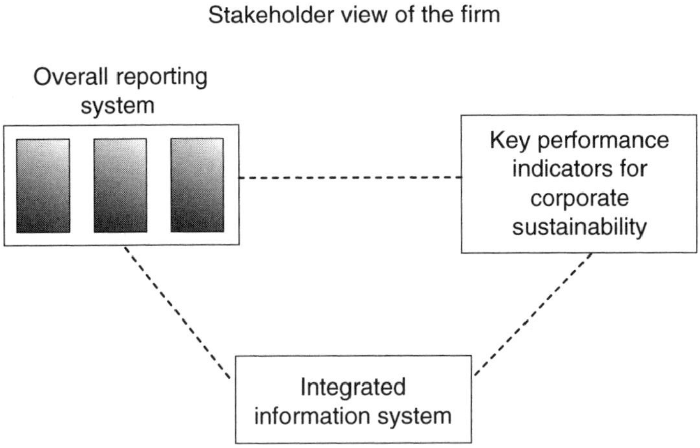

Figure 7.1 The sustainability evaluation and reporting system (SERS)

The SERS framework is composed of three modules (see Figure 7.1):

- the overall reporting system (or the sustainability reporting system), which comprises:
  - the annual report;
  - the social report;
  - the environmental report;
  - a set of integrated performance indicators;
- the integrated information system;
- the key performance indicators for corporate sustainability.

The Overall Reporting System

The annual report

The annual report comprises the profit and loss account, the balance sheet and the statement of cash flows. Ratios and indicators should be included to check corporate competitiveness in the finance, marketing, operations, technology and quality fields. Furthermore significant social and environmental information on risk management, potential liabilities, research and development policies and so on is presented in annual reports. Every country has specific regulations regarding the annual report. As a result of the most recent financial disasters, policy-makers strengthened the rules to require higher levels of transparency and fairness in financial accounting and reporting activities. However, from a stakeholder view, this tool does not cover all aspects of corporate performance, social and environmental among them.

The social report

The social report measures the impact of the company and its activities on the different stakeholder groups. It can support the management decision-making process and the corporate communication and engagement policies. According to the SERS approach, it is composed of the ethical policy, the value-added statement and the analysis of stakeholder relationships (see Table 7.1).

The ethical policy encompasses specific corporate commitments to the stakeholder groups in accordance with the relational view of the firm. On the basis of these commitments, corporate social performance is assessed by means of the other two instruments.

The value-added statement is a traditional tool in social reporting: for example, it was adopted in the 1970s by the group of German companies called Sozialbilanz-Praxis (Rusconi, 1988, pp. 84–8) and links traditional financial accounting with social reporting. It measures the (financial) value-added generated and distributed by the company to the different stakeholder groups (employees, financial partners, state and local authorities, community, shareholders) or invested into the firm. It is a first picture of the (stakeholder) value created and distributed (Figge and Schaltegger, 2000).

The goal of the analysis of stakeholder relationships is to assess the sustainability of the interactions between a company and its stakeholders through qualitative and quantitative information. This analysis also comprises forms of social accounting in order to understand the economic costs and benefits related to social activities and policies (for example

Table 7.1 The social report according to the SERS scheme

1. *Corporate identity*
- Brief description of the company
- Ethical policy
  - ➔ Charter of values and principles (Ethical Code)
  - ➔ Mission
  - ➔ Charter of commitments towards stakeholders
    - ➢ Employees
    - ➢ Members/shareholders, financial community
    - ➢ Clients/customers
    - ➢ Suppliers
    - ➢ Financial partners (banks, insurance companies and financial services)
    - ➢ State, local authorities and public administration
    - ➢ Community
2. *Economic wealth created and distributed by the company: the value added*
3. *Relationships with stakeholders*

internal costs and benefits associated with occupational health and safety management).

An interesting example of social reporting used as a fundamental tool to improve stakeholder management is provided by the Banca Lombarda experience (see Box 7.1).

BOX 7.1 BANCA LOMBARDA: SOCIAL REPORT AND IMPROVEMENT OF THE STAKEHOLDER MANAGEMENT STRATEGY

The Banca Lombarda Group is the result of a merger and some acquisitions realized between 1998 and 2000. From 31 December 1997 to 31 December 2003, it increased its total assets from 8.8 billion euros to 31.5 billion euros, and changed from a local banking group into one of the leading Italian banking groups operating mainly in the regions of Lombardy and Piedmont.

As of 31 December 2003, the Banca Lombarda Group had about 1.3 million customers, primarily composed of individuals and small and medium-sized companies, and it carried on its operations through 783 branches and a network of about 600 financial consultants. Banca Lombarda is listed by the Milan Stock Exchange (Banca Lombarda, 2005).

Between 2002 and 2003, the Group decided to develop a social report as an internal information system to assess and improve its stakeholder management strategy. As the long-term success of Banca Lombarda, also in financial terms, depends on the quality of the relationships with the stakeholder network and, in particular, with the local communities in which the Group operates, the development and adoption of an instrument capable of mapping the critical stakeholder groups and assessing the related corporate social performance became crucial. The scheme proposed by SPACE according to the SERS framework was adopted by the company to design and elaborate the social report. First of all the corporate identity was defined through the explicit identification of the ethical policy, that is, the principles and values at the basis of the corporate behavior, and the commitments towards the stakeholders. At that time, the most critical stakeholder groups were employees, stockholders, clients and the community(ies). The commitments, which represent the ultimate goals of a real social/societal strategy, were used to assess the value creation and distribution processes and the quality of stakeholder relationships. Initiatives relevant to stakeholder engagement (for example questionnaires, satisfaction surveys) were carried out. The outcomes of this long and demanding process, which involved representatives of the controlled banks operating at the local level, coordinated by top managers of the holding company, were used to build a clear and shared organic strategy to achieve effective management of the stakeholder relationships.

Therefore the implementation of the social report awarded the Group with the following benefits:

1. clear definition of the role of the firm in the community through a map of the different stakeholder groups and the development of an explicit social and societal strategy;
2. control and assessment of the value added and distributed;
3. support of planning and decision-making processes;
4. improvement of the quality of the company's relationships with stakeholders and consequent enhancement of the corporate reputation;
5. increase in and strengthening of the social consensus and license to operate.

The environmental report

In general the corporate environmental report is used to manage and control corporate activities and support communication with stakeholders, especially those interested in environmental issues (Azzone et al., 1997). Although a single, definitive model of an environmental report does not yet exist because of the special features of the tool (persistence of voluntary approach, focus on the national, industrial, corporate specificities and so on), we can attempt to define the boundaries that should characterize a comprehensive environmental information system. According to the nature of the environmental information (physical data or financial items) and the object to which these measurements refer (processes or products), it is possible to classify the principal methodologies developed up to now to monitor the relationships between corporate activities and the natural capital as follows (see Table 7.2).

The goal of the environmental reporting framework within SERS is to include all the methodologies identified and combine an accounting system that collects physical data with the measurement of (internal) costs and benefits related to the environmental management of processes and products (Burritt et al., 2002). The environmental report comprises input–output analysis, LCA and a cost–benefit account of the environmental management

Table 7.2 Environmental accounting: main methodologies

	Types of environmental information	
	Energy and material flows	Financial items
Object of analysis		
Processes	Ecobalance or input–output analysis	Cost–benefit accounting related to environmental management of processes
Products	Product ecobalance or life-cycle assessment (LCA)	Cost–benefit accounting related to environmental management of products

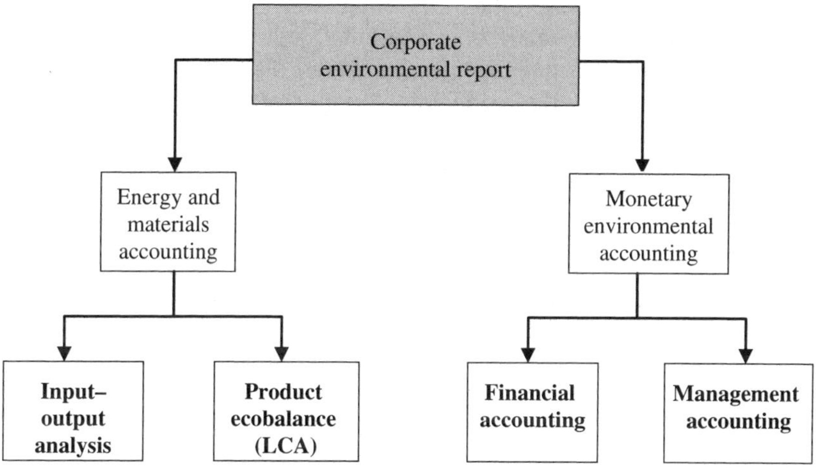

Figure 7.2 The environmental report: the SERS model

of products and processes. Therefore the environmental reporting system focuses on two important kinds of information flows: those related to physical data – energy and materials accounting – and those related to financial items – monetary environmental accounting (see Figure 7.2).

Energy and materials accounting (Hallay, 1990; Beck, 1993) collects information on the environmental impact of company activities. Input–output analyses gather and organize the information on energy and material consumption and the related emissions. Ecobalances (life-cycle assessment – LCA) measure the environmental impact of the main products of the firm in terms of resources consumption and pollution along their entire life cycle (the 'from-cradle-to-grave' approach).

BOX 7.2 ENEL: ENVIRONMENTAL COST ACCOUNTING IN A POWER PLANT (DE SILVIO AND TENCATI, 2002)

Between 1999 and 2000, a pilot project on monetary environmental accounting was carried out in the thermoelectric power plant of La Casella, near Piacenza, in Northern Italy. This plant is owned by the Italian Enel Group, one of the most important power companies in Europe. Because of a program to improve the eco-efficiency of the plants and a more and more pressing environmental regulation, the measurement of the environmental costs, that is, of the costs associated with environmental management, became strategic. Therefore, this project was implemented in order to develop an innovative environmental cost accounting system, which could be applied also by other plants in the Group. According to the achieved results, the environmental costs represent about 18 percent of the overall operating costs, that is, purchasing costs + salaries, wages and employee benefits. This information supported the introduction of an Environmental Management System, developed according to the requirements of the Eco-Management and Audit Scheme (EMAS) Regulation, with the purpose of improving the environmental performance of the plant as well as local relationships.

Monetary environmental accounting (Bundesumweltministerium and Umweltbundesamt, 1995; United States Environmental Protection Agency, 1995), which determines the financial costs and benefits borne by the company and associated with its environmental management activities, represents the second important dimension of developing a corporate environmental report. The goal is to build a tool to improve decision-making. This monetary environmental accounting has to be well integrated with the existing financial and management accounting systems (Burritt, 1997). Therefore because the definition of this kind of environmental accounting is complex, few companies in the world have introduced an advanced system of measuring environmental costs and benefits (see Box 7.2).

A set of integrated performance indicators

The sustainability reporting system allows a company to check and report its annual overall performance. Its goal is to build a true and fair view of the business situation to strengthen, improve and manage stakeholder relationships in a sustainable way. It is fundamental to the information needs of different stakeholder groups and corporate social accountability. Thus, in order to achieve a more complete view of its behavior, a company should also define and present a set of integrated performance indicators, that is, cross-cutting indicators (Global Reporting Initiative, 2002, pp. 45, 82–4). In general, cross-cutting indicators relate physical and technical quantities to financial ones (for example an indicator could relate the total amount of waste generated during the year to the value added). A firm thus goes beyond a simple triple bottom line approach to adopt a more comprehensive and integrated perspective, capable of defining a more reliable and material picture of the corporate activities and related implications. Further reflections upon this topic will be presented in the next paragraphs.

The Integrated Information System

The Integrated Information System is the core of performance evaluation and reporting processes. Based on the new ICT (information and communication technologies) solutions such as the enterprise resource planning (ERP) systems, it enables an organization to collect, process and share physical, technical and financial data. Programs to introduce environmental and social accounting systems to integrate and improve existing financial and cost accounting methodologies have to start from this level. The goal is to build a satellite accounting system (United Nations, 1993; United Nations et al., 2003) focused on social and environmental performance, capable of collecting and organizing all the relevant data (including financial) and connected with the other specific accounting and information systems.

A satellite of the existing management information system, this information system considers qualitative, quantitative (physical and technical) and economic-monetary data relative to social and environmental performance. These data are organized according to the three-level framework, which will be described in the next paragraph. For its own purposes, this satellite system also takes, from the management information system of the firm, data and information which are relevant to the good management of corporate sustainability. Thus, through the integration of the different databases (that is, regarding financial, cost, social and environmental accounting), it is possible to extract and provide to operators and decision-makers the necessary information to assess the overall performance of the company and its sustainability.

The Key Performance Indicators for Corporate Sustainability

The Key Performance Indicators for Corporate Sustainability are specific indicators developed according to the corporate information requirements. The aim is to provide a tool to monitor an organization's performance trends continually. Number and types of measures should be defined on the basis of real corporate needs. The key performance indicators (KPIs) thus represent a 'Dashboard of Sustainability' (International Institute for Sustainable Development, 2001) supporting management decision-making processes. Sets of indicators proposed by many organizations, such as the Global Reporting Initiative (2002, 2006), the World Business Council for Sustainable Development (2000, 2003), Eurostat (2001a, 2001b, 2005) and the European Environment Agency (2002, 2003) can be used to draw up an organization's specific measurements, but they cannot limit its choices. Indicators can focus on the financial, operating, marketing, environmental, social and cross-cutting (for example related to the eco-efficiency and the socio-efficiency of the organization: Schaltegger et al., 2002, p. 9; Schaltegger and Burritt, 2005, pp. 188–92) aspects of business management. KPIs are also used in the overall reporting system, and in order to define them the company should carry on stakeholder engagement activities (Stakeholder Research Associates Canada et al., 2005; AccountAbility, 2005).

KPIs are the crucial element of the SERS methodology. SMEs would not have sufficient time and resources to define a long and complicated sustainability reporting system. But this kind of firm certainly needs a map for an ongoing assessment of its performance and of the related quality (that is, degree of sustainability) of its relationships with stakeholders. This map is really provided by a set of KPIs. And this consistent and clear dashboard of sustainability could also be used to communicate the information required by the different stakeholder groups. Therefore, in line with the adopted stakeholder view of the firm and the sustainability concept, KPIs should be organized according to stakeholder categories (see Box 7.3).

This type of structure allows a company to focus on the relationships and the related performance which firms, and especially SMEs, develop through their activities and behavior. In particular, for SMEs, networks between companies and local stakeholders (community, public authorities, financial partners and so on) directly influence the overall corporate performance. An interesting example is the link between the social capital and success of Italian districts (Lipparini, 2002).

We provide a tool to exemplify the best approach for companies that design their own set of KPIs – a broad set of indicators, which cover the most important areas of social and environmental performance (Wood, 1991;

BOX 7.3 COOP ADRIATICA: KPIs AND SUSTAINABILITY REPORT (COOP ADRIATICA, 2004)

Coop is the largest Italian retail chain, with more than a 17 percent market share in the grocery market. It is owned by 5 300 000 members, grouped in around 175 territorial consumers' cooperative societies. The retail network is composed of 1280 points of sale, comprising 1 320 000 square meters and around 50 000 employees. The 2003 turnover was more than 11 000 million euros. Its leadership position on the market is supported and strengthened by efforts towards sustainability along its entire stakeholder network.

Coop Adriatica is one of the most important territorial cooperative societies. The 2003 turnover was 1700 million euros. Coop Adriatica has 760 000 members and 8130 employees. In 2004, it issued its second sustainability report. A set of KPIs is presented as a fundamental part of the document. Besides the financial/economic measures, the social and environmental indicators are organized according to stakeholder categories. The identified stakeholder groups are:

1. members/consumers;
2. employees;
3. environment;
4. local community.

The relationships with other stakeholder groups are also analyzed in the report: they are suppliers, the Coop system, unions, the cooperative movement and public authorities. In Coop Adriatica the sustainability report supports decision making and allows the company to deeply involve the stakeholders and especially the different local communities in the assessment of past results and in the definition of future goals of the social/societal strategy.

Clarkson, 1995). These indicators have been identified with the help of companies, public institutions and civil society at large (NGOs, trade unions and so on), to build a shared and comprehensive map of social and environmental issues related to corporate sustainability (Tencati et al., 2004). They are organized according to a three-level framework (World Business Council for Sustainable Development, 2000, p. 8; Global Reporting Initiative, 2002, pp. 36–7):

- Categories: stakeholder groups which are specifically affected by clusters of indicators.
- Aspects: thematic areas monitored by groups of performance indicators related to a given category of stakeholders.
- Indicators: measurements that supply information on a given aspect. They can be used to check and demonstrate organizational performance. The information can be qualitative, quantitative (physical and technical) or economic-monetary.

The stakeholder categories identified are:

1. employees;
2. members/shareholders, financial community;
3. clients/customers;
4. suppliers;
5. financial partners;
6. state, local authorities and public administration;
7. community;
8. environment.

The complete set of indicators is presented in the Appendix.

SMEs especially could refer to this set as a model, drawing only on the indicators most suited to their information needs, and building their own shared map, through a specific stakeholder engagement process, to assess and communicate their performance (see Box 7.4).

BOX 7.4 USING KPIs IN A SMALL COMPANY (ITALIAN MINISTRY OF LABOUR AND SOCIAL AFFAIRS, 2005)

Clan des Team Challenge (+39) is a service sector company founded in 2004. Its mission is 'to take the America's Cup challenge above and beyond the traditional rules, providing a model of ethical, responsible practice for all the actors involved. To respect and protect the environment, contributing to sustainable development, in all sporting, organizational, planning, and commercial activities, consistently adopting the good practices available and encouraging all partners and stakeholders – teams, partners, shareholders, and sponsors – to work for constant improvement'. In 2004 the turnover was around 2.8 million euros and the company had three employees. To pursue its mission and realize its values, +39 adopted a basic set of indicators (around 15), selected among the measurements presented in Appendix. These indicators, along with other specific ones (that is, medical and scientific parameters for employees and co-workers), are used to monitor, assess and report social responsibility performance, in the following areas:

- employees: hours of training by category; employees' benefits; injuries at work;
- shareholders: communication and reporting activities;
- suppliers: supplier management policy;
- financial partners: relations with banks and insurance companies (promotion of socially responsible practices);
- community: prevention of corruption (adoption of a code of conduct); corporate giving;
- environment: environmental policies (for example material and energy consumption and emissions, environmental management system, training, reporting and so on).

The socially responsible behavior developed by +39, also through the adoption of a specific set of KPIs, distinguished the company as one of the best Italian CSR practitioners. These cases of best practices were identified and selected by the working group put together by the Ministry of Labour and Social Affairs in Spring 2005 and composed of experts from Adiconsum (an Italian consumers' association), Anima and Sodalitas (two organizations promoted by companies to support the collaboration between business and not for profit organizations) and Unioncamere (the Italian Union of chambers of commerce). The task of the working group was to produce a volume entitled *Corporate Social Responsibility : Examples of Best Practices in Italy*, describing firms that have decided to support sustainability by adopting socially responsible practices. The volume was presented during a celebratory public event, hosted by Ferrari in Maranello on 14 July 2005, which was a first initiative to recognize and promote cases of excellence in the CSR field. The aim of the event was to stimulate the adoption of socially responsible practices and encourage participation in CSR activities, especially by SMEs.

CONCLUSIONS

Today, and more and more into the future, one of the keys to successful strategic management is the availability of sustainability accounting tools capable of monitoring and tracking qualitatively and quantitatively the overall corporate performance and, in particular, the state, that is, the sustainability, of the different stakeholder relationships. There is thus an urgent need for new systems to measure corporate outcomes according to a stakeholder framework consistent with a more suitable and correct strategic approach.

The final goal is to guarantee the long-term development of a company through a strong commitment to sustainability throughout its stakeholder network. Radical and innovative changes in corporate performance measurement, control and evaluation systems and significant improvement of the managerial paradigms are essential. Therefore, we believe it is necessary to go beyond traditional approaches to corporate performance management systems – even the most advanced forms such as the balanced scorecard, or complicated and not so flexible models based on the triple bottom line agenda, such as the Global Reporting Initiative or the SIGMA Project. In this chapter we have presented SERS, a sustainability evaluation and reporting system, based on a stakeholder view of the firm and therefore really aimed at balancing and integrating financial and non-financial performance indicators – supporting planning, implementation and control activities of a sustainability-oriented and responsive organization. Our proposal provides, especially through the set of KPIs on social and environmental performance, a broad map to help companies to understand stakeholder requirements and assess their own performance. The goals of the resulting system are, through an integrated perspective:

1. To aggregate different management tools (for example social reporting, environmental reporting, and KPIs) into a comprehensive model – methodological integration.
2. To map and monitor the entire set of a company's stakeholder relationships – integration of different perspectives into the sustainability accounting system towards a *multiple bottom* line approach.
3. To supply information, which can be qualitative, quantitative (physical and technical) and economic-monetary, through the performance measurements – integration of data and information. These indicators build a sort of dashboard of sustainability, that is, an effective *tableau de bord*, which goes beyond the traditional financial data. Moreover the availability of this broad range of measures allows a company to build integrated performance indicators by relating physical and technical

> quantities to financial ones. The environmental intensity ratio presented in the previous section is only an example of a methodology, applicable by all companies, which could develop many other measures according to their specific information needs. For example, in the occupational health and safety management field, an indicator could relate the trend of the injury rate during the last three years to the costs connected with the projects implemented to improve work conditions; with regard to R&D policies, another indicator could relate the achieved results – that is, new patents, the launch of new products, the introduction of new labeling schemes and so on – to investments during a specific period identified on the basis of industry-wide competitive dynamics. Such information support helps management to assess the effectiveness of their choices and to review their strategies and define next steps.

In this way, according to a relational view of the firm, the SERS methodology enables a company and its management to manage stakeholder relationships and address the information needs and the economic, social and environmental concerns of various stakeholder groups. This point is crucial for every kind of firm and especially for SMEs, whose success is deeply rooted in stakeholder networks.

Moreover the SERS structure, composed of different modules (the overall reporting system, the integrated information system and the key performance indicators), is flexible enough to be used by businesses of different sizes operating in different sectors and countries.

However, further steps in the field of sustainability accounting are expected: if stakeholder relationships are essential to the creation of sustainable wealth, not only the company-centered, but also the stakeholder-centered performance should be measured. In other words, for example, the degree of stakeholder trust and the stakeholder satisfaction generated by the corporate strategy and behavior should be carefully evaluated (Ghoshal and Bartlett, 1999; Lev, 2001; Castaldo, 2002; Nelli and Bensi, 2003). This calls for the development of further methodologies that could broaden the available set of measures, but also problematize the use of specific performance indicators.

Therefore, if we adopt a stakeholder view of the firm to design sustainability accounting systems, we should also understand how the stakeholder relationships and the related engagement processes could impact the quantity and quality of performance indicators aimed at monitoring corporate sustainability. This perspective could dramatically change the way managers and stakeholders assess firms, their success and their role in society.

REFERENCES

AccountAbility (1999), *AccountAbility 1000 (AA1000) Framework: Standard, Guidelines and Professional Qualification*, London: AccountAbility, accessed 24 August 2005 at www.accountability.org.uk.

AccountAbility (2005), *AA1000 Stakeholder Engagement Standard. Exposure Draft*, London: AccountAbility, accessed 14 November 2005 at www.accountability.org.uk.

Azzone, G., M. Brophy, G. Noci, R. Welford and W. Young (1997), 'A stakeholders' view of environmental reporting', *Long Range Planning*, **30** (5), 699–709.

Bakan, Joel (2004), *The Corporation: The Pathological Pursuit of Profit and Power*, New York: Free Press.

Banca Lombarda (2005), 'Company profile: history', accessed 11 September 2005 at www.bancalombarda.it.

Bandura, Albert, Gian-Vittorio Caprara and Laszlo Zsolnai (2002), 'Corporate transgressions', in Laszlo Zsolnai (ed.), *Ethics in the Economy: Handbook of Business Ethics*, Oxford and Bern: Peter Lang Academic Publisher, pp. 151–64.

Beck, Michael (ed.) (1993), *Ökobilanzierung im betrieblichen Management*, Würzburg: Vogel Buchverlag.

Bennett, Martin and Peter James (eds) (1999), *Sustainable Measures: Evaluation and Reporting of Environmental and Social Performance*, Sheffield: Greenleaf Publishing.

Bundesumweltministerium and Umweltbundesamt (eds) (1995), *Handbuch Umweltcontrolling*, Munich: Verlag Franz Vahlen.

Burritt, R.L. (1997), 'Corporate environmental performance indicators: cost allocation – boon or bane?', *Greener Management International*, **17** (Spring), 89–100.

Burritt, R.L., T. Hahn and S. Schaltegger (2002), 'Towards a comprehensive framework for environmental management accounting: links between business actors and environmental management accounting tools', *Australian Accounting Review*, **12** (2), 39–50.

Castaldo, Sandro (2002), *Fiducia e Relazioni di Mercato*, Bologna: il Mulino.

Cerin, P. (2002a), 'Communication in corporate environmental reports', *Corporate Social Responsibility and Environmental Management*, **9** (1), 46–66.

Cerin, P. (2002b), 'Characteristics of environmental reporters on the OM Stockholm Exchange', *Business Strategy and the Environment*, **11** (5), 298–311.

Clarkson, M.B.E. (1995), 'A stakeholder framework for analyzing and evaluating corporate social performance', *Academy of Management Review*, **20** (1), 92–117.

Coop Adriatica (2004), *03 Bilancio di Sostenibilità*, Villanova di Castenaso – Bologna: Coop Adriatica, accessed 12 September 2005 at www.e-coop.it.

CSR Europe (2002), *The SME Key. Unlocking Responsible Business*, accessed 20 January 2003 at www.smekey.org.

De Silvio, M. and A. Tencati (2002), 'I costi della gestione ecologica: il caso della Centrale Termoelettrica Enel di La Casella', *Economia and Management*, **3** (May–June), 107–22.

Deloitte Touche Tohmatsu Emerging Markets (2004), *Partnerships for Small Enterprise Development*, New York: United Nations Development Programme (UNDP), accessed 13 November 2005 at www.unido.org/doc/4364.

Dierkes, Meinolf (ed.) (1976), 'Künftige Beziehungen zwischen Unternehmen und Gesellschaft', *Veröffentlichungen der Stiftung Gesellschaft und Unternehmen*, vol. 5, Cologne: Hanstein.
Donaldson, T. and L.E. Preston (1995), 'The stakeholder theory of the corporation: concepts, evidence, and implications', *Academy of Management Review*, **20** (1), 65–91.
Elkington, J. (1994), 'Towards the sustainable corporation: win–win–win business strategies for sustainable development', *California Management Review*, **36** (2), 90–100.
Elkington, John (1997), *Cannibals with Forks: The Triple Bottom Line of 21st Century Business*, Oxford: Capstone Publishing.
European Environment Agency (EEA) (2002), *Environmental Signals 2002: Benchmarking the Millennium*, Luxembourg: Office for Official Publications of the European Communities.
European Environment Agency (EEA) (2003), *Europe's Environment: The Third Assessment*, Luxembourg: Office for Official Publications of the European Communities.
Eurostat (2001a), *Environmental Pressure Indicators for the EU*, Luxembourg: Office for Official Publications of the European Communities.
Eurostat (2001b), *Measuring Progress Towards a More Sustainable Europe*, Luxembourg: Office for Official Publications of the European Communities.
Eurostat (2005), 'Sustainable Development Indicators', accessed 2 June 2005 at http://epp.eurostat.cec.eu.int.
Figge, F., T. Hahn, S. Schaltegger and M. Wagner (2002), 'The sustainability balanced scorecard: linking sustainability management to business strategy', *Business Strategy and the Environment*, **11** (5), 269–84.
Figge, Frank and Stefan Schaltegger (2000), *What is 'Stakeholder Value'? Developing a Catchphrase into a Benchmarking Tool*, Lüneburg: Universität Lüneburg, Pictet & Cie, UNEP.
Freeman, R. Edward (1984), *Strategic Management: A Stakeholder Approach*, Boston, MA: Pitman Publishing.
Ghoshal, Sumantra and Christopher A. Bartlett (1999), *The Individualized Corporation: A Fundamentally New Approach to Management*, New York: HarperBusiness.
Global Reporting Initiative (GRI) (2002), *2002 Sustainability Reporting Guidelines*, Boston, MA: Global Reporting Initiative, accessed 10 September 2005 at www.globalreporting.org.
Global Reporting Initiative (GRI) (2004), *High 5!*, Amsterdam: GRI.
Global Reporting Initiative (GRI) (2006), *G3 Sustainability Reporting Guidelines. Version for Public Comment: 2 January 2006 – 31 March 2006*, Amsterdam: Global Reporting Initiative, accessed 15 January 2006 at www.grig3.org.
Grant, Robert M. (2002), *Contemporary Strategy Analysis: Concepts, Techniques, Applications*, 4th edn, Oxford: Blackwell Publishers.
Hallay, Hendric (ed.) (1990), *Die Ökobilanz. Ein betriebliches Informationssystem*, Berlin: Schriftenreihe des IÖW.
Hertz, Noreena (2001), *The Silent Takeover: Global Capitalism and the Death of Democracy*, London: Heinemann.
International Institute for Sustainable Development (IISD) (2001), 'The dashboard of sustainability', accessed 23 November 2001 at www.iisd.org.

ISO Advisory Group on Corporate Social Responsibility (2003), *Technical Report (TR) Terms of Reference (TOR)*, Geneva: ISO.
Italian Ministry of Labour and Social Affairs (2005), *Corporate Social Responsibility: Examples of Best Practices in Italy*, Rome: Italian Ministry of Labour and Social Affairs.
Jensen, M.C. (2001), 'Value maximization, stakeholder theory, and the corporate objective function', *Journal of Applied Corporate Finance*, **14** (3), 8–21.
Kaplan, R.S. and D.P. Norton (1992), 'The balanced scorecard: measures that drive performance', *Harvard Business Review*, **70** (1), 71–9.
Kaplan, Robert S. and David P. Norton (2004), *Strategy Maps: Converting Intangible Assets into Tangible Outcomes*, Boston, MA: Harvard Business School Press.
Klein, Naomi (2000), *No Logo: Taking Aim at the Brand Bullies*, Toronto: Knopf-Random House of Canada.
Lev, Baruch (2001), *Intangibles: Management, Measurement, and Reporting*, Washington, DC: Brookings Institution Press.
Lipparini, Andrea (2002), *La Gestione Strategica del Capitale Intellettuale e del Capitale Sociale*, Bologna: il Mulino.
Mills, R.W. and B. Weinstein (2000), 'Beyond shareholder value: reconciling the shareholder and stakeholder perspectives', *Journal of General Management*, **25** (3), 79–93.
Nelli, Roberto P. and Paola Bensi (2003), *L'Impresa e la sua Reputazione. L'Evoluzione della Media Coverage Analysis*, Milan: Vita e Pensiero.
Perrini, F. and A. Tencati (2003), 'Corporate social responsibility and firm performance: managing sustainability and the need of a new corporate evaluation and reporting system in a knowledge economy', paper presented to the *2003 Academy of Management Conference*, 1–6 August, Seattle.
Perrini, F. and A. Tencati (2006), 'Sustainability and stakeholder management: the need for new corporate performance evaluation and reporting systems', *Business Strategy and the Environment*, **15** (5), 296–308.
Pogutz, Stefano and Antonio Tencati (1997), *Ambiente, Competitività e Innovazione: Teoria e Casi*, Milan: Egea.
Post, J.E., L.E. Preston and S. Sachs (2002), 'Managing the extended enterprise: the new stakeholder view', *California Management Review*, **45** (1), 6–28.
Rappaport, Alfred (1986), *Creating Shareholder Value. The New Standard for Business Performance*, New York: Free Press.
Rayner, Jenny and Walter Raven (eds) (2002), *Corporate Social Responsibility Monitor*, London: GEE.
Rusconi, Gianfranco (1988), *Il Bilancio Sociale d'Impresa. Problemi e Prospettive*, Milan: Giuffrè Editore.
Schaltegger, Stefan and Roger Burritt (2005), 'Corporate sustainability', in Henk Folmer and Tom Tietenberg (eds), *The International Yearbook of Environmental and Resource Economics 2005/2006*, Cheltenham, UK and Northampton, MA, USA: Edward Elgar, pp. 185–222.
Schaltegger, Stefan, Christian Herzig, Oliver Kleiber and Jan Müller (2002), *Sustainability Management in Business Enterprises. Concepts and Instruments for Sustainable Organisation Development*, Bonn: Federal Ministry for the Environment, Nature Conservation and Nuclear Safety (BMU).
Schaltegger, S. and M. Wagner (2006), 'Integrative management of sustainability performance, measurement and reporting', *International Journal of Accounting, Auditing and Performance Evaluation*, **3** (1), 1–19.

SIGMA Project (2003), *The SIGMA Guidelines. Putting Sustainable Development into Practice – A Guide for Organisations*, London: BSI, accessed 15 July 2005 at www.projectsigma.com.

SPACE (1993), *Le Politiche Ambientali delle Prime Cento Imprese Italiane*, Milan: Bocconi University.

Stakeholder Research Associates Canada, United Nations Environment Programme and AccountAbility (2005), *The Stakeholder Engagement Manual, Volume 1*, Cobourg: Stakeholder Research Associates Canada, accessed 20 November 2005 at www.uneptie.org.

Tencati, A. (2002), *Sostenibilità, Impresa e Performance. Un Nuovo Modello di Evaluation and Reporting*, Milan: Egea.

Tencati, Antonio and Francesco Perrini (2006), 'The sustainability perspective: a new governance model', in Andrew Kakabadse and Mette Morsing (eds), *Corporate Social Responsibility: Reconciling Aspiration with Application*, Houndmills, UK and New York, USA: Palgrave Macmillan, pp. 94–111.

Tencati, A., F. Perrini and S. Pogutz (2004), 'New tools to foster corporate socially responsible behaviour', *Journal of Business Ethics*, **53** (1–2), 173–90.

Ulrich, Hans and Walter Krieg (1973), *Das St Galler Management-Modell*, Bern: Verlag Paul Haupt.

United Nations (1993), *Integrated Environmental and Economic Accounting*, New York: United Nations.

United Nations, European Commission, International Monetary Fund, Organisation for Economic Co-operation and Development and World Bank (2003), *Integrated Environmental and Economic Accounting 2003. Handbook of National Accounting*, New York: United Nations.

United Nations Industrial Development Organization (UNIDO) (2002), *Corporate Social Responsibility. Implications for Small and Medium Enterprises in Developing Countries*, Vienna: UNIDO.

United States Environmental Protection Agency (EPA) (1995), *An Introduction to Environmental Accounting as a Business Management Tool: Key Concepts and Terms*, Washington, DC: US EPA Office of Pollution, Prevention and Toxics, accessed 10 May 1996 at www.epa.gov.

Wagner, M. and S. Schaltegger (2003), 'How does sustainability performance relate to business competitiveness?', *Greener Management International*, **44** (Winter), 5–16.

Wood, D.J. (1991), 'Corporate social performance revisited', *Academy of Management Review*, **16** (4), 691–718.

World Business Council for Sustainable Development (WBCSD) (2000), *Measuring Eco-Efficiency. A Guide to Reporting Company Performance*, Geneva: WBCSD.

World Business Council for Sustainable Development (WBCSD) (2003), *Sustainable Development Reporting. Striking the Balance*, Geneva: WBCSD.

APPENDIX 7.1

Table 7A.1 Set of performance indicators

		Q	R	E
1	Employees			
1.1	*Composition of employees*	✓		
1.1.1	Category		✓	
1.1.2	Age		✓	
1.1.3	Seniority		✓	
1.1.4	Geographical region		✓	
1.1.5	Nationality		✓	
1.1.6	Contract type		✓	
1.1.7	Level of education		✓	
1.2	*Turnover*	✓		
1.2.1	Hiring		✓	
1.2.2	Employees and non-employees		✓	
1.2.3	Employment cessation (by type)		✓	
1.3	*Equal opportunity*	✓		
1.3.1	Gender ratio (by seniority, hiring, etc.)	✓	✓	
1.3.2	Gender salary differentials (by category and seniority)		✓	✓
1.3.3	Policies towards the disabled and minorities in general	✓	✓	✓
1.4	*Training*	✓		
1.4.1	Programs of training (by type)	✓	✓	✓
1.4.2	Hours of training by category	✓	✓	
1.4.3	Internships	✓	✓	
1.5	*Working hours by category*	✓	✓	
1.6	*Compensation of employees*	✓	✓	✓
1.6.1	Average gross compensation	✓	✓	✓
1.6.2	Career tracks	✓	✓	
1.6.3	Incentive systems	✓		✓
1.7	*Absence from work*	✓		
1.7.1	Days of absence		✓	
1.7.2	Cause	✓		
1.8	*Employee benefits*	✓	✓	✓
1.9	*Industrial relations*	✓	✓	
1.9.1	Respecting the rights of free association and collective bargaining	✓		
1.9.2	Percentage of employee union members		✓	
1.9.3	Other (hours on strike, employee participation in company management)	✓	✓	
1.10	*Internal communication*	✓	✓	
1.11	*Occupational health and safety*	✓	✓	
1.11.1	Injuries and diseases	✓	✓	
1.11.2	Projects	✓	✓	✓
1.12	*Employee satisfaction*	✓	✓	
1.12.1	Internal employee satisfaction research	✓	✓	
1.12.2	Projects	✓	✓	✓

Table 7A.1 (continued)

		Q	R	E
1.13	*Protection of workers' rights*	✓		
1.13.1	Child labor	✓		
1.13.2	Forced labor	✓		
1.14	*Disciplinary procedures*	✓		
2	Members/Shareholders, financial community			
2.1	*Composition of corporate capital*	✓		
2.1.1	Number of shareholder, by share type	✓	✓	✓
2.1.2	Member segmentation by category	✓	✓	✓
2.2	*Shareholder remuneration (ratios and share indicators)*	✓		
2.2.1	Share profit	✓	✓	✓
2.2.2	Dividends	✓	✓	✓
2.2.3	Price/earning per share	✓	✓	✓
2.2.4	Other	✓	✓	✓
2.3	*Stock price fluctuation*	✓	✓	✓
2.4	*Ratings*	✓	✓	
2.5	*Corporate governance*	✓		
2.6	*Member services and benefits*	✓		
2.7	*Investor relations*	✓		
2.7.1	Communication and reporting activities	✓	✓	
2.7.2	Institutional presentations and documents	✓	✓	
2.7.3	Roadshows	✓	✓	
2.7.4	One-to-one meetings	✓	✓	
2.7.5	Development of internet communication	✓	✓	
2.7.6	Other	✓	✓	
3	Clients/customers			
3.1	*Client characteristics*	✓		
3.1.1	Client division by category	✓	✓	✓
3.1.2	Client division per products	✓	✓	✓
3.2	*Market development*	✓		
3.2.1	New clients	✓	✓	✓
3.2.2	New products	✓	✓	✓
3.3	*Customer satisfaction and customer loyalty*	✓		
3.3.1	Customer satisfaction initiatives (surveys, market researches, call center, handling complaints)	✓	✓	✓
3.3.2	Customer loyalty initiatives	✓	✓	✓
3.4	*Product information and labeling (product safety, LCA, voluntary initiatives)*	✓	✓	✓
3.5	*Ethical and environment-friendly products*	✓	✓	✓
3.6	*Promotion policies (for example respecting self-disciplinary codes)*	✓	✓	
3.7	*Privacy protection*	✓	✓	
4	Suppliers			
4.1	*Supplier policy*	✓		
4.1.1	Supplier division per category	✓	✓	✓
4.1.2	Supplier profile	✓	✓	✓

Table 7A.1 (continued)

		Q	R	E
4.1.3	Communication and information	✓	✓	✓
4.2	*Procurement conditions*	✓	✓	✓
5	Financial partners			
5.1	*Relations with banks*	✓	✓	✓
5.2	*Relations with insurance companies*	✓	✓	✓
5.3	*Relations with financial services*	✓	✓	✓
6	State, local authorities and public administration			
6.1	*Taxes*	✓	✓	✓
6.2	*Relations with state, local authorities and public administration*	✓		
6.3	*Policies and codes to comply with law*	✓		
6.3.1	Norms and codes of conduct and internal auditing	✓		
6.3.2	Compliance checks and inspections	✓	✓	
6.4	*Contributions, fiscal benefits or financing received*	✓	✓	✓
7	Community			
7.1	*Corporate giving*	✓	✓	✓
7.2	*Direct contributions to social programs*	✓		
7.2.1	Education and training	✓	✓	✓
7.2.2	Culture	✓	✓	✓
7.2.3	Sports	✓	✓	✓
7.2.4	R&D	✓	✓	✓
7.2.5	Social solidarity (even international)	✓	✓	✓
7.2.6	Other (for example promoting employee volunteer work)	✓	✓	✓
7.3	*Stakeholder engagement*	✓		
7.4	*Relations with media*	✓		
7.5	*Virtual community*	✓		
7.5.1	Contacts (characteristics and analysis)	✓	✓	
7.5.2	Security	✓	✓	
7.5.3	Relationship management tools	✓	✓	
7.6	*Prevention of corruption (existence of policies and codes of conduct)*	✓		
8	Environment			
8.1	*Material and energy consumption and emissions*	✓	✓	
8.1.1	Energy	✓	✓	
8.1.2	Water management	✓	✓	
8.1.3	Raw materials, MRO and packaging	✓	✓	
8.1.4	Air emissions	✓	✓	
8.1.5	Waste management	✓	✓	
8.2	*Environmental strategy and relations with the community*	✓	✓	✓
8.2.1	Environmental management system and certification	✓	✓	✓
8.2.2	Training and education	✓	✓	✓
8.2.3	Environmental report	✓	✓	✓
8.3	*Environmental rating*	✓	✓	

Note: Q = Qualitative; R = Quantitative; E = Economic.

8. Who can act on sustainability issues? Corporate capital and the configuration of organizational fields

Jennifer A. Howard-Grenville, Andrew J. Hoffman and C.B. Bhattacharya

In 1997, John Browne set the British Petroleum Corporation (BP) on a new course, acknowledging that climate change was a significant issue, vowing to control the corporation's carbon footprint by reducing greenhouse gas emissions and devoting resources to the development of renewable energy sources. For this bold plan, the company received tremendous accolades from the press, non-governmental organizations (NGOs) and world governments. What is most exceptional about this event is that the company was seen as credible when the oil industry as a whole was suffering from some of the lowest public perceptions of any industrial sector (Cambridge Research, 1992). Soon after BP made its announcement, Shell and other large multinationals followed suit and the trade association opposing action on climate change – the Global Climate Coalition – collapsed. Why was BP able to do this? Could other competitors, such as Exxon, do the same? What are the attributes of a company that allow it to be seen as a valid spokesperson on issues of environmental and social sustainability? This is one form of the question we address in this chapter.

Another form of the question goes to more fundamental aspects of strategic success in an increasingly globalized marketplace, one where corporate actions must increasingly address social and environmental issues in developing countries (London and Hart, 2004; Hart and London, 2005). How do companies credibly enact new ways of doing business that engage new stakeholders? Consider the following example.

When electronics giant Hewlett-Packard (HP) decided to pilot a new solar-powered digital camera/printer that was small enough to fit into a backpack, it went not to California but to Kuppam, India, where it put the equipment into the hands of young women with grade-school education.

More than 100 miles from Bangalore, Kuppam and its rural surroundings are home to 300 000 people, half of whom live below the poverty line, and one-third of whom are illiterate (Dunn and Yamashita, 2003). In addition to turning these women into entrepreneurs running their own photography businesses, HP provided equipment and designed web-based services for locally-run community information centers. Why is a leading technology company like HP developing such products and services in a poor community like Kuppam? Leaders on the Kuppam initiative acknowledge that the project has significant social benefits. HP is changing the lives of people in the Kuppam region. The women photographers now have an income that will provide an education for their children and a water tap for their homes. And further, these women now have the self-confidence to seek further loans for larger initiatives.

While some within the company argue that it is simply pursuing business as usual – applying HP's core capabilities of discovering customer needs, deploying a diverse management team, creating a leading technology platform, and partnering with others to make it work (Dunn and Yamashita, 2003) – this is more than business as usual. HP's actions are different from other corporate initiatives in that they directly engage non-traditional beneficiaries in new ways. Kuppam's residents and local leadership gain access to information and economic development opportunities that are different from the products and services traditionally provided by an electronics company. In short, HP is creating new 'rules of the game' (Friedman, 1970, p. 126), challenging traditional conceptions of market expansion by introducing concerns for sustainable development.

HP is not alone in pursuing new social initiatives as an emerging part of its core business. Numerous other companies are taking actions to address social and environmental needs around the globe. With these efforts, companies are expanding who they influence and how that influence is felt; they are redefining who they see as key stakeholders for the company. For example, Anglo American, a global mining company, announced in 2003 that it would provide anti-retroviral drugs to its HIV-infected employees in South Africa, estimated at nearly one-quarter of its 130 000-person workforce, and that it would fund 900 rural clinics to enable employees' families and others to obtain HIV and tuberculosis treatment (*The Economist*, 2003). To accomplish this objective, Anglo American found itself engaging with unfamiliar constituencies including local community groups, rural healthcare workers, pharmaceutical providers and government leaders. Or, more specifically, Anglo American had redefined its organizational field (Scott, 2002) shifting from a relatively stable set of relationships with suppliers, regulators, competitors and customers to a less structured set of relationships in an enlarged and emergent field (Rao et al., 2000; Maguire et al., 2004).

These examples raise several questions that are critical for understanding the role of corporations in moving towards environmental and social sustainability. What capabilities do firms possess that enable them to take on the challenges associated with moving towards environmental and social sustainability? Why are firms differently positioned to address these challenges? While more traditional methods for environmental management, like pollution prevention, life-cycle analysis, and others, demand a technical, engineering focus largely within firm boundaries, moving towards environmental and social sustainability demands the company think beyond its borders in new ways, pursuing sustainability by engaging with non-traditional stakeholders and using non-traditional business logics and methods. To do this, they must have amassed a pre-existing cache of the appropriate social, political and cultural standing that enables them to pursue these actions credibly and to influence others.

In this chapter, we draw on recent work in institutional theory (Fligstein, 1997; Greenwood et al., 2002) and the related theory of fields (Bourdieu and Wacquant, 1992) to argue that corporate actions on social and environmental sustainability must be understood as embedded in a field of other actors with differential power to influence broad norms. We argue that companies that will successfully move towards environmental and social sustainability are those that possess distinct forms of social, cultural and economic capital. In the rest of this chapter, we first review the literature on environmental sustainability and organizations. We then outline recent developments in institutional theory and the theory of fields that can inform work on environmental and social sustainability. We consider different field conditions corporations may face when initiating actions that address sustainability, and discuss the role of various forms of capital in overcoming the associated challenges. Finally, we discuss implications for theory and practice of corporate actions towards sustainability.

ENVIRONMENTAL AND SOCIAL SUSTAINABILITY

Sustainability is a concept that has acquired many definitions over the years and continues to be mired in debate over what it really is, how to achieve it, and whether and how modern corporations have a role in achieving it. Many begin with the definition offered by the World Commission on Environment and Development (the Bruntland Commission) which states that 'sustainability is development that meets the needs of the present without compromising the ability of future generations to meet their own needs' (WCED, 1987, p. 43). Those who focus on environmental sustainability incorporate more specific ecological concepts such as carrying capacity and a systems view of natural resource extraction, consumption and recovery (Jennings and Zandbergen, 1995) and point to limitations in the Bruntland definition such as its lack of specificity on needs, their prioritization, and the role of entities in balancing such needs (Starik and Rands, 1995). One definition of environmental sustainability developed to apply to individual companies reads:

> Ecological sustainability is the ability of one or more entities, either individually or collectively, to exist and flourish (either unchanged or in evolved form) for lengthy time-frames, in such a manner that the existing and flourishing of other collectivities of entities is permitted at related levels and in related systems. (Starik and Rands, 1995, p. 909).

While this definition is focused only on environmental sustainability, it importantly draws attention to the embeddedness of companies within larger systems of industrial production and social systems. Adding social sustainability to the discussion demands a broader view of the need for existence and flourishing beyond the needs to sustain ecological and natural resource systems (Ehrenfeld, 2004). Indeed, social sustainability brings questions of social equity and economic prosperity into the debate (Bansal, 2005; Hart, 2005), suggesting that major corrections are needed to the considerable gaps between developed and developing nations, and rich and poor within those nations. Further, social sustainability demands attention to the maintenance of differing cultural systems and the lifestyles with which they are associated. Our goal here is not to offer a definitive definition of sustainability, but to highlight key issues that have been identified in the literature as important to understanding and assessing actions by companies along paths to sustainability. There are three issues that are particularly relevant to our analysis: first, sustainability is a construct that is socially defined and ever evolving; second, sustainability demands a multilevel view of organizations as embedded in larger systems; and third, addressing issues of sustainability involves considering the concerns of new stakeholder groups.

On the first point, sustainability, like other social constructs, has meaning only in a particular social and historical context. Its meaning emerges from dialogue and practices of numerous entities, such as governments, non-governmental organizations (NGOs) and corporations, over time and it therefore can be understood through the lens of institutional theory which focuses on the processes by which concepts and norms are developed, maintained or changed (DiMaggio, 1995; Jennings and Zandbergen, 1995; Greenwood and Hinings, 1996; Hoffman and

Ventresca, 2002). While earlier work on ecological sustainability from an institutional theory perspective has emphasized that the theory enables us to understand 'how consensus is built' around the meaning of sustainability and how it takes on a 'rule-like' quality (Jennings and Zandbergen, 1995, p. 1016), we emphasize that sustainability is an emergent concept. It is subject to considerable debate and simultaneously allows multiple meanings. A key focus of recent institutional theory addresses questions of how meanings emerge in concert with practices, and how differentially powerful actors influence that debate over meaning. Precisely because sustainability is an emergent concept, it is well suited to institutional analysis.

On the second point, a key insight from the literature on sustainability and organizations is that no single organization can be sustainable on its own. Sustainability is inherently a more systemic view, invoking multiple levels of action – individual, organizational, political and cultural – and interactions between these levels (Starik and Rands, 1995). The most appropriate level of analysis may not be the level of the individual organization; for example, industry-level analysis has proved fruitful for understanding the conditions that lead to environmentally sustainable companies (Russo, 2003). Others have argued that no company has the 'capability or market power to alter unilaterally entire socio-technical systems' (Hart, 1995, p. 1003), observing that environmentally favorable technologies often require associated changes in infrastructure. Our focus on institutional theory, and in particular on the theory of fields and the embeddedness of companies in fields, incorporates this inherently systemic view of sustainability.

Finally, recent work on sustainability identifies a wide range of stakeholders who are influencing corporate actions towards sustainability, and a wide range of tactics used by these stakeholders (Christmann, 2004; Sharma and Henriques, 2005). This suggests that the drivers for change on the issue are coming from a broader set of social interests, not simply from the traditional regulatory and economic drivers that have strongly influenced environmental or labor practices in the past. As departments within a company engage with different external stakeholder groups and issues, new types of stakeholder demands can challenge traditional ways of doing business, bringing the concerns to the core of marketing, research and development, or product development groups as never before (Howard-Grenville and Hoffman, 2003). This marries the multilevel challenges and changes associated with sustainability with the core capabilities of a business, suggesting that we need to understand the interaction between the broader organizational fields and the company's own actions and history within the field.

ORGANIZATIONAL FIELDS, CAPITAL AND CORPORATE ACTIONS

Institutional theory offers several key constructs for understanding the interaction of firms within and between their broader social environments. First, the 'organizational field' is defined as a community of organizations whose members interact with each other and share common norms or rules (Scott, 1995). Until recently, organizational theory has depicted a limited role for agency and change within fields (DiMaggio and Powell, 1983, 1991; Hoffman and Ventresca, 2002). Early institutional theory, in particular, focused on homogeneity of organizational forms or isomorphism as its primary phenomenological emphasis (DiMaggio and Powell, 1983). Organizational and other actors were regarded as 'passive recipients' (Fligstein, 2001, p. 110) of the norms operating within fields rather than active contributors to them.

More recent work has focused on the formation and change of institutions by analyzing the role of institutional entrepreneurs (Fligstein, 1997; Lawrence, 1999) in shaping the discourse, norms and structures that guide organizational action (Maguire et al., 2004), the importance of the distribution of power among actors within a field (DiMaggio, 1988; Brint and Karabel, 1991; Fligstein, 1991; Beckert, 1999), and the idea that fields are arenas of debate and contestation (Hoffman, 1999). Others add that fields can remain conflicted even when institutional norms are apparently settled, because powerful actors are continually working to maintain their legitimacy (Lounsbury and Glynn, 2001).

These two concepts directly parallel the issues identified from the literature on sustainability. First, like the meaning of sustainability itself, organizational field-level norms are socially defined and ever evolving. Second, understanding organizational action demands a multilevel view of organizations as embedded in larger fields, including attention to the range of stakeholders who are active in these fields.

In contrast to earlier work on institutional theory that depicted fields as having strong tendencies towards homogeneity, Bourdieu's theory of fields has always portrayed fields as dynamic. Organizations within fields continuously act to defend or improve their relative positions, so a field is always a field of struggles (Bourdieu and Wacquant, 1992). Organizations 'increase or . . . conserve their capital . . . in conformity with the tacit rules of the game . . . but they can also . . . transform, partially or completely, the immanent rules of the game' (Bourdieu and Wacquant, 1992, p. 99). The domain of sustainability is a perfect example of field-level jockeying. Who gets to define the term, assign status, or measure progress? Is it NGOs like the World Resources Institute, trade associations like the Chemical

Manufacturer's Association, industry groups like the World Business Council on Sustainable Development, government organizations like the EPA or companies like DuPont? As in all field-level debates, organizations vary individually and as groups in their ability to reshape the rules of the game (Fligstein, 1990). Some occupy positions of domination (Oakes et al., 1998) or possess superior skills with which to enact change (Fligstein, 1997). Rewording the question that opened this chapter: Why did BP's position in a field allow it to reframe the debate over corporate responses to climate change?

Even powerful actors cannot simply impose new logics and norms on a field because, at some level, the norms must be accepted by other actors (Beckert, 1999). And for action on social and environmental issues, traditional forms of power are insufficient because of the value-based nature of the norms at play (Wade-Benzoni et al., 2002) and the critical role that cultural and social credibility plays in influencing those values. Only certain firms that are entrepreneurial in nature, skilled at implementation, and credible within critical field-level constituencies can 'seek to differentiate through innovation and gain competitive advantage from opportunities in environmental [and social] strategies' (Troast et al., 2002, p. 249). Two key variables that determine whether a firm can act credibly and effectively on social and environmental issues are its position within an organizational field, and the level of economic, cultural and social capital it possesses.

Position and Capital within the Field

Each corporation occupies a unique position in a field. A key starting point for our discussion is the observation that not all positions in a field are equivalent. Some will be inherently more valuable than others because in every field there is a struggle for limited or scarce resources, be they economic, cultural or social (Bourdieu, 1986). There are relatively few valued positions within a field (Maguire et al., 2004) and those who occupy them will be continually working to maintain their position (Lounsbury and Glynn, 2001) while others may challenge the dominant positions or seek to establish new positions that are valued (Aldrich and Fiol, 1994). This dynamic suggests that companies can initiate change from a number of positions in the field, not just those traditionally regarded as powerful or dominant (Maguire et al., 2004; Smith, 2003). However, the ability to do so relies heavily on the capital or resources a company can muster and exchange, and the value that is ultimately placed on this capital by others. At any given point in time, some positions will be more valuable than others, shaping the strategies available to companies as they attempt to maintain, improve or capitalize on their unique position.

An organization's position in a field is inseparably related to the quantity and types of capital it holds (Bourdieu, 1985; Bourdieu and Wacquant; 1992). Capital exists in several forms – economic, cultural and social – and 'represents a power over the field (at a given moment)' (Bourdieu, 1985, p. 724). But beyond reflecting power, capital also draws attention to a variety of modes of influence an organization may possess, the relative value of these different modes, and their interaction with each other. Each type of capital is necessary, but on its own insufficient, for a corporation to engage in actions directed toward sustainability. Some combination of economic, cultural and social capital is essential and the type, as well as quantity, of capital is important.

Economic capital is perhaps the most familiar form and is represented by the possession of monetary resources, or other material resources that enable a company to detect and pursue particular goals. A company's revenues, size (number of employees), geographic distribution (number of locations and global spread of locations), and market share can be considered indicators of its economic capital. These factors can affect how a company undertakes actions towards sustainability by influencing both demand and supply conditions. On the supply side, companies with sufficient revenues and employees are more likely to have both the organizational slack and the specialized expertise (for example departments for community relations, corporate social responsibility, and so on) that enable them to detect social needs, generate responses and implement solutions. On the demand side, companies that are more highly geographically distributed and have a higher market share will be more visible to critical stakeholders – customers, regulators, suppliers and diverse communities. This increases their exposure to a range of social needs and stakeholder concerns, possibly making them more aware of sustainability concerns.

Cultural capital is the competence or authority to define and defend expertise in a particular arena of social life (Bourdieu, 1986). Like economic capital, it derives value from its scarcity and is unevenly distributed. Unlike economic capital, cultural capital is rarely represented in material form. The erosion of a corporation's cultural capital is perhaps more obviously observable than its existence, for erosion of cultural capital is accompanied by the loss of broad social legitimacy (Oakes et al., 1998) which may be marked by media exposure of a corporation's practices, lawsuits, boycotts of products or increased regulatory scrutiny (Smith, 2003).

The importance of cultural capital for acting on sustainability cannot be overstated; a corporation must possess a particular type of cultural capital in order to initiate credible actions on social and environmental issues. A corporation with appropriate cultural capital will hold broad socio-political legitimacy which may be manifested in public acceptance, government approval (for example, provision of subsidies or reduction of close scrutiny by government bodies), and public prestige of its leadership (Aldrich and Fiol, 1994; Rao, 1994). A clearly articulated identity of being socially responsible, a strong reputation among competitors, suppliers and customers, high brand equity, and relative transparency in a company's reporting practices are also indicators of the type of cultural capital that is valued for action on social and environmental issues (Scott and Lane, 2000; Smith, 2003; Bhattacharya and Sen, 2003).

Cultural capital, however, can be quite ambiguous. For example, if a brewer which produces alcoholic beverages has a strong reputation for its sound and progressive environmental management, and embraces social and environmental causes, will it hold valuable cultural capital? Or will its cultural capital be dominated by the fact that its core product, if abused, is harmful to individuals and their families? The answer depends on the composition and concerns of other participants in the various fields in which the company participates, and the answer may differ across fields. This example is a reminder that cultural capital has many facets, and the value of cultural capital is always judged relative to a complex and ever-shifting set of social standards. As a result, sustaining broadly valued cultural capital across a range of fields involves consistent actions by the company on a range of issues, over a long period of time. The cultural capital needed to act credibly on issues of sustainability may well rely on capital built up by actions on issues that have little to do with sustainability per se.

Finally, social capital is the 'sum of resources . . . that accrue to an [actor] by virtue of possessing a durable network of . . . relationships of mutual acquaintance and recognition' (Bourdieu and Wacquant, 1992, p. 119). Companies with high social capital gain greater access to information and have greater potential to notice opportunities in the environment (Davis, 1991). They may be more likely to initiate actions directed towards sustainability simply because they are well connected to other actors – either stakeholders who bring new demands, or other companies who share ideas of best practices. Even without direct contact between organizations in a network, membership in diverse networks will expose companies to a variety of possibilities because they will be able to observe structurally equivalent organizations and possibly imitate them (Burt, 1987; Galaskiewicz and Burt, 1991). A large number of relatively weak network ties may be more important in this regard than a smaller number of strong ties (Granovetter, 1973), particularly when it is desirable to access new organizational fields and the ideas and norms circulating within them.

Indeed, social capital is a key asset needed by companies seeking to operate in multiple, diverse fields. Whereas cultural capital lends reputational authority to a company and is critical to its credibility in acting on issues of social and environmental sustainability, social capital is what actually enables the company to implement its actions. Social capital yields the connections and contacts that allow members of a company to deeply understand local issues, and to identify those who will assist and those who may block efforts at change. Building and maintaining valued social capital involves attention to both the quantity and quality of relationships with others, with emphasis on building trusting, reciprocal relationships that endure meaningfully. There is a connection between the quality of cultural capital a company possesses and the social capital it can build through its members' interactions. A company with little cultural capital will not likely build social capital with stakeholders, who may be skeptical of the company's aims or sensitive to 'selling out'. On the other hand, a company with valued cultural capital may more easily build or maintain valued social capital. The relationship between social and cultural capital works the other way too, with social capital contributing to cultural capital (or not).

In the next section we consider several different field conditions in which corporations may act to alter institutional norms as they address issues of social and environmental sustainability.

FOUR FIELD CONDITIONS FOR CHANGE

While all fields may be arenas of struggle (Bourdieu and Wacquant, 1992), they need not all be highly uncertain domains. Certain fields are mature or stable, with the dominant actors holding the majority of valued resources. Change in these fields will involve the destruction of old ways of acting and interacting, as well as the reconstruction of new action patterns and logic (Greenwood et al., 2002). In contrast, there is likely to be much greater uncertainty in emerging or fragmented fields where norms and relationships are still in flux (Fligstein, 1997) or mature fields in crisis where relatively stable relationships and norms have been sharply disrupted (Hensmans, 2003; Maguire et al., 2004). In each type of field, the strategies and skills used by individual organizations to shape the field will be quite different (Fligstein, 1997; Rao et al., 2000; Fligstein, 2001).

Issues of sustainability may be manifested in different ways, sometimes precipitated by critical events (Hoffman and Ocascio, 2000) which can thrust a field into crisis, and at other times precipitated by gradual shifts in attention to emerging concerns. How a corporation fosters change in a particular instance will depend on the conditions of the field and the nature of the issue itself. Institutional entrepreneurship can take place within each of at least four field conditions: capturing an issue within a mature field, bridging between fields, creating a new field and defending a mature field in crisis.

Each is described below, along with the particular challenges it presents for companies and the type of capital needed to act in such field conditions. Table 8.1 summarizes the four field conditions, key challenges and the types of capital needed under each field condition.

Capturing an Issue within a Mature Field

First, members of a mature field may 'capture' a social or environmental issue, bringing it within the domain of the existing field. This move involves expanding the norms and rules that operate in a field, but not fundamentally altering the membership of the field or relationships among members. An example of this is the adoption by chemical manufacturers of Responsible Care® codes of environmental, health and safety practices to which all members of the industry's dominant trade association must adhere. In this case, there was generalized coercive pressure for the industry to improve public confidence in its operations, but there was no specific single event that triggered this move, nor did the membership of the field change significantly (Howard et al., 2000). The largest corporations in the industry initiated the change, with the explicit goal of gradually changing the field while maintaining their existing positions of power. They recognized this would need, in their words, 'long term investment of effort and the painstaking cultivation of various audiences, opinion formers, and decision makers on whom we depend' (Simmons and Wynne, 1993, p. 203).

The challenge for corporations in these situations is credibly to attain moral authority on an issue that was once considered outside their purview. They must have or work hard to build the cultural capital which enables them to be seen as credible leaders on the issue in a field where others have prior claims. For example, regulators were the key actors that set the norms for environmental practices in the chemical industry, so in introducing Responsible Care®, chemical manufacturers had to demonstrate collectively that their voluntary standards went beyond compliance, were meaningful and were diligently adopted. To bolster and maintain the cultural capital of its members and enable it to take this unilateral action, the American Chemical Council (ACC, formerly Chemical Manufacturers Association) launched an extensive print and television advertising campaign, and hundreds of individual manufacturing facilities formed community advisory panels to communicate directly with local communities. A few years later, following criticism of the extent of adoption and effectiveness of its standard, the ACC implemented mandatory third-party verification of Responsible Care® compliance.

This example demonstrates that such a move of capturing an issue within an existing field demands building new forms of cultural capital, which may

Table 8.1 Four field conditions for corporate action on social and environmental sustainability

Field condition	Key challenges	Types of capital needed
Capturing an issue within a mature field	• Establishing authority over a new issue • Shifting capacity of others to define the issue	Cultural capital Perhaps economic capital Relatively less social capital
Bridging between fields	• Building resources, expertise, and legitimacy in a peripheral field while remaining successful in traditional field(s)	Social capital
	• Managing possible internal conflicts arising from operating in multiple fields	Cultural capital
Creating a new field	• Breaking from old field logics and relationships and credibly building new ones	Social capital
	• Managing high uncertainty within the emerging field	Economic capital in proportion to scope of change Relatively less cultural capital (for start-ups in new fields)
Defending a mature field in crisis	• Restore trust and regain social 'license to operate' without significantly reshaping the norms and relationships in the field	Economic capital Relatively less cultural and social capital

involve the use of considerable economic capital to carry through on claims over time. Social capital is important in these cases to make connections that bring others within the field, for example in the case of community advisory panels. But social capital is not the most critical form of capital as interactions with new stakeholder groups may be quite limited in this case.

Bridging Between Fields

This move recognizes that corporations are simultaneously members of multiple, partially overlapping fields (Hoffman, 2001) and that, particularly when complex social issues are concerned, there will be interstices between fields (Rao et al., 2000). In these cases, corporations may act by bridging between fields. Rather than expanding the norms of an existing mature field (as in the case above), corporations act and seek to influence action in a peripheral field where they may hold little in terms of resources, expertise or legitimacy. The corporation does not abandon a valued position in a mature field and create or move into an emerging one, but it does deliberately engage a new set of actors, form new relationships and adopt new strategies while at the same time retaining many of the old ones.

For example, Anglo American bridged into a peripheral field by taking responsibility for aspects of healthcare in rural African communities. It worked to improve existing clinics, influencing government agencies and policy, but it did not capture the issue. In fact, while Anglo American's actions were seen as 'vital to the country's development model' they were not intended as a substitute for government action (*South Africa Quarterly Forecast Report*, 2002, p. 18). Indeed, they were intended to send a strong message for more government involvement. Similarly, BP moved into, and helped create, a field in which companies from many industries interacted with governments and NGOs around the issue of climate change. While this triggered internal change at BP and some redirection of strategy, BP continued to operate as a dominant player in the mature field of petroleum producers.

The challenge for corporations in these situations is to remain successful and credible in the mature field while simultaneously building resources, expertise and legitimacy in a peripheral or emerging one. Along with this comes the challenge of managing the possible internal conflicts between the logics of the two fields, and the opportunities afforded by the possible emergence of new organizational forms (Rao et al., 2000). Social capital is particularly important in overcoming these challenges and bridging to new fields. Establishing and maintaining a diverse network of relationships enables a company to learn about and effectively and credibly operate within fields that might be quite different from the traditional fields surrounding their core business. It may actually be more effective for companies to work in partnership with others in peripheral fields, as such partnerships can bring them capabilities and contacts that they do not possess and would not be effective at developing, For example, a nuclear power plant operating company engaged the help of a non-profit environmental group when it embarked on the years-long process of decommissioning the plant. Decommissioning involved a series of actions that required interaction with the community and with regulators in agencies the plant had no prior involvement with. In this situation, the environmental group brought credibility and experience in interfacing with these stakeholders, skills that the plant did not (and one could argue could not or should not) possess on its own. While social capital is critical, broad cultural capital is also valuable for companies seeking to bridge between fields. Cultural capital within a mature field will enable the company to maintain its position within that field while also credibly acting in a new field or fields.

Creating a New Field

Less frequently, corporations may strategically exit a mature field and/or attempt to create or move into an entirely new one. This type of move is often precipitated by a renunciation of the logic of the old field. New, small or less powerful actors may take on this role, drawing a stark contrast between the old norms and those they seek to establish (Rao et al., 2000; Hensmans, 2003). Corporations have been founded with the explicit goal of advancing a social agenda and perhaps disrupting the operation of a mature field in the process. For example, the No Sweat company sells clothing and running shoes produced only at factories that meet high labor standards. It includes details of laborer's wages and benefits on its shoe boxes and has challenged leading apparel companies like Nike to do the same (English, 2004). Creating a new field in which issues of social and environmental sustainability are central is not always the work of upstart corporations. For example, chemical giant Monsanto literally and symbolically shed its chemical operations and embraced the goal of being a life science company in the late 1990s. It strategically reshaped relationships in this emerging field, engaging farmers, scientists, regulators and governments in developing nations, while much less skillfully influencing public opinion (Simanis and Hart, 2001).

The challenge for corporations attempting to create new fields oriented around social and/or environmental sustainability is to break successfully from the old logic and relationships and credibly build new ones, particularly when there is high uncertainty in the emerging field and a large number of new stakeholders need to be taken into consideration. The type of capital most valued will likely be social capital, again because it enables access to a wide range of stakeholders and ideas. Cultural capital may be relatively less valued in an entirely new field with high uncertainty, as there is likely little consensus around what is expected of various players. As a result, a company in such a field may be able gradually to build its own distinctive reputation over time and define for itself and others that follow a new logic for business and for engaging outsiders. Sufficient economic capital is required and it must be held in proportion to the scope of change. For example, small start-up companies founded with social or environmental goals often have low economic capital, but a company like Monsanto held and used considerable economic capital to exit its chemical manufacturing field and attempted to enter, by acquiring a large number of biotech companies, the new field of agricultural biotech.

Defending a Mature Field in Crisis

Finally, companies may be members of a mature field in crisis. This is perhaps the most familiar case, with companies acting to respond to damaging external events caused by their past (or current) social or environmental actions. The recursive effects of a corporation's actions (or inactions) are felt in the field as a whole. For example, in the critical hours immediately following the *Valdez* shipwreck, Exxon was reluctant to acknowledge responsibility or take action to rectify the situation. The company resisted external pressure, endured public condemnation and faced significant financial penalties (which are now approaching $7 billion). But this very resistance empowered interest groups and the government to push through the Oil Pollution Prevention Act of 1990, further increasing regulatory restrictions on crude oil shipping which influenced Exxon and others' subsequent actions (Hoffman, 2001).

In another example, the Coca-Cola Corporation is facing mounting criticism for alleged environmental abuses in India and alleged labor rights abuses in Colombia (Stecklow, 2005). Coca-Cola has continued to argue that it has no control over the labor situation in Colombia and has full government approval to draw water from local aquifers. But activists have been able to control the form of the debate, engaging college students in pressing administrators for campus boycotts of Coca-Cola products and union representatives in filing lawsuits. Coca-Cola has been hesitant to engage these activists and, therefore, has ceded the field-level debate.

The challenge for companies, like Coca-Cola, in these situations is to regain their social 'license to operate' and restore trust without significantly reshaping the norms and relationships in the field. In these situations, high economic capital serves as a way to launch public relations campaigns designed to discredit detractors and affirm the norms of the company and its operations. Direct engagement with stakeholders through the use of cultural or social capital is relatively limited. As such, a company with economic clout but little cultural or social capital might engage in this kind of defensive action. Ironically, if allegations become widespread through the mainstream media, they may be quite damaging to the cultural and social capital of the company, at a point when it is already relatively low. This vicious cycle of low cultural and social capital can act against a company's efforts to address sustainability issues; in other words, defending a mature field in crisis is a reactive rather than proactive strategy, unlikely to result in effective, credible actions towards sustainability.

PATHWAYS TO SUSTAINABILITY: IMPLICATIONS AND FUTURE RESEARCH DIRECTIONS

While there is a long-standing academic debate about the objectives of the corporation (Freeman et al., 2004; Sundaram and Inkpen, 2004) and the connection between social performance and financial performance, these questions remain largely unresolved (Margolis and Walsh, 2001). Empirical evidence suggests that their resolution is not critical, however, as many corporations do act in ways that advance social issues while at the same time improving strategic position (Porter and van der Linde, 1995; Margolis and Walsh, 2003). In this chapter, we have sought to shift attention away from the question of why companies undertake actions on social and environmental issues, and towards outlining different ways that corporations do so as members of different types of organizational fields. Our goal has been to use recent insights from institutional theory to consider the dynamics of a firm's interactions with its external environment, recognizing that a company's actions can be both the product and, more importantly, the perpetrator of broader social change. To do this, our discussion has built on ideas of institutional entrepreneurship, using insights from Bourdieu's theory of fields to show how some corporations hold valued positions and capital that enable them to act credibly on issues of sustainability.

Our analysis makes both theoretical and practical contributions. First, our attention to companies as embedded in organizational fields captures the co-evolution of corporate actions, the fields in which companies reside, and issues of social and environmental sustainability themselves. Attending to field-level dynamics enables one to see issues of social and environmental sustainability as shifting rather than static, in accordance with how they are actually experienced by companies. The importance of a given issue at a given time is almost impossible to predict as there are many contributing factors from catastrophic events like oil spills or toxic releases, to geopolitical shifts that result in the displacement of people. Therefore, seeing a corporation as embedded in and possibly capable of shaping fields is essential to understanding its actions in such a complex environment.

A second theoretical contribution is the use of the notion of capital to enrich the institutional conception of fields, thereby giving us a language with which to discuss what is being exchanged, shared, accrued or contested within a field. Using the constructs of economic, cultural and social capital, we offer a way to distinguish why different organizations can act differently from their respective field-level positions. Those who hold certain quantities and types of capital may have the ability to act effectively and credibly on issues of sustainability, while others may not. The possession of cultural and social capital, in particular, are especially important for action on social and environmental issues, replacing economic capital as the central determinant of dominance in more traditional field-level interactions. Importantly, both social and cultural capital can not only be further enhanced by successful action on issues of sustainability, but they can also be dramatically eroded as a result of failures, highlighting the fragility of a company's ability to act effectively on issues of sustainability.

Finally, we contribute to theory on emerging fields by suggesting that corporations traditionally regarded as less powerful (for example, those that do not possess large quantities of economic capital) may nonetheless be able to develop and capture cultural and/or social capital by skillfully framing the debate, bridging disparate interests, or seeing and creatively developing new ways of acting. The result may be the emergence of entirely new fields or effective bridging to peripheral fields. Socially oriented start-ups such as Tom's of Maine, Ben & Jerry's and The Body Shop are all examples of firms that created new fields centered explicitly on social issues and offered alternatives to traditional products.

For practitioners, our discussion gives greater depth to the importance of managing a company's external interactions for taking action towards sustainability. External stakeholders that go far beyond traditional supply chain relationships hold ever-increasing power and influence on corporate action. Companies are subject to demands for greater transparency created by NGOs; consider the impact such demands have had on the actions of Nike, Wal-Mart, McDonald's, Coca-Cola, Monsanto, Shell and others. From a more proactive stance, companies expanding into new regional markets within developing countries are finding that successful implementation requires engagement with new forms of business partners. These may include local suppliers, distributors, NGOs and governments to help create opportunity for on-the-ground action (London and Hart, 2004; Prahalad, 2004; Hart, 2005; Hart and London, 2005). By engaging with such new forms of business partnerships, new types of activities are initiated, ones that have impacts that diverge from traditional forms of corporate action. Companies are developing hospitals, HIV clinics, community centers, water treatment facilities and housing facilities.

While managers cannot necessarily predict or control how issues of social or environmental sustainability relevant to their businesses arise, they can certainly understand the fields they operate in and the type of change they seek to undertake (or the type of change imposed upon them by others), and thereby cultivate the appropriate capital to act appropriately. Capturing an issue within an existing field, bridging between fields or creating a new field all invoke social and cultural capital in particular, though in different measures. The reactive stance of defending a mature field in crisis may rely less on these non-traditional forms of power. Our framework provides a starting point for understanding the competencies that must be developed to address issues of sustainability proactively. We forewarn practitioners that such assets are acquired over the long term, through persistent and patient internal development. But conversely, there is also an element of spontaneity in such actions – effective change agents act opportunistically to take advantage of the situation at hand and improvise and negotiate creatively to appeal to diverse interests and actors. And where the necessary capital cannot be developed by one company alone, it can partner with others in order to 'borrow' their capital. This is evidenced by the increasing number of alliances between businesses and NGOs on complex environmental and social issues.

Future Research

Several questions and directions for further research are raised by our discussion. First, while we identify a number of field conditions and suggest types of capital that would be particularly important in each, a more rigorous mapping between field conditions and the capitals necessary for acting on sustainability issues would be helpful. Empirical work in this area could confirm whether these field conditions are accurate descriptors, and which types of capital are critical under which conditions. Further, empirical work could assess whether different forms of capital are valued across field conditions between different geographical or cultural contexts. For example, are there settings in which social capital is always significantly more valuable than economic capital? In Western industrialized countries we are accustomed to thinking of economic capital as critical to gaining traditional power within an organizational field, but this may not be the case in other countries or market systems. In such settings, the capital necessary to act on issues of environmental and social sustainability may be more closely aligned with the capital needed to participate in commerce in general, and acting on sustainability may therefore not demand such a shift from 'business as usual' as it appears to demand in Western industrialized economies.

Second, future research might explore the skills necessary to take action. Mustering cultural and social capital in moments of flux and ambiguity is a necessary but not sufficient condition for effective change. Even the most respected and effectively connected corporations can make missteps, create inadvertent outcomes or even misread the situation. More work is needed on connecting the innate traits of the sustainable corporation to the active skill set necessary to carry out successful initiatives.

Third, our contribution towards examining the role of capital in determining a corporation's ability to act on social and environmental issues opens new research questions. How is cultural and social capital measured? How is it developed? How is it spent or, more importantly, lost? And if it is easily lost, will companies perhaps show a more conservative approach towards expending it on social issues since they may have more to lose? These kinds of questions offer a new direction in organizational research that has parallels to issues of brand equity in marketing while also incorporating issues of agency and action. Corporations with high cultural capital may not necessarily be the most likely to act because they may see actions on sustainability as risky, making leaders on possibly controversial social and environmental issues into lightning rods for criticism. Companies with very high social capital might be less open to possibilities for acting because they do not want to 'rock the boat' among their valuable network ties (Davis, 1991) and do not want to attract attention in a highly interconnected field.

Finally, longitudinal case-studies of corporations addressing issues of sustainability, both successful and unsuccessful, would be valuable in identifying how capital is accrued and used in acting on issues of sustainability. Longitudinal studies would also allow one to consider the recursive effects of action over time. Such a study would require either extended real-time study through interviewing, observation and document analysis, and/or extensive archival research. Because of the co-evolution of issues, fields, and a corporation's capital and actions, particularly when dealing with social or environmental issues, teasing out causality would be challenging in any such study. However, one need not establish absolute causality in order to contribute to understanding of the dynamics of change agency around sustainability. Indeed, in certain conditions, corporations can inadvertently trigger actions that result in change in a broader field, suggesting that intention to create change is not even an essential precursor.

In conclusion, corporate actions towards sustainability represent a unique type of change that is firmly embedded within field-level dynamics.

To understand how corporations are effective at making change in this area, that is, why some corporations can act credibly on social and environmental issues while others cannot, we need a way to describe the corporation's position in a field and its relevant economic, cultural and social capital. This chapter contributes to this understanding by outlining four field conditions in which issues of social and environmental sustainability are manifest, discussing the challenges associated with each and suggesting ways in which different forms of capital are used to address the challenges. Attention to field dynamics and the embeddedness of companies in multiple, complex fields highlights the fact that social and cultural capital, not merely economic capital, are essential assets for companies to possess on the journey towards sustainability.

REFERENCES

Aldrich, H. and C. Fiol (1994), 'Fools rush in? The institutional context of industry creation', *Academy of Management Review*, **16**, 645–70.

Bansal, P. (2005), 'Evolving sustainably: a longitudinal study of corporate sustainable development', *Strategic Management Journal*, **26**, 197–218.

Beckert, J. (1999), 'Agency, entrepreneurs, and institutional change: the role of strategic choice and institutionalized practices in organizations', *Organization Studies*, **20**, 777–99.

Bhattacharya, C.B. and S. Sen (2003), 'Consumer-company identification: a framework for understanding consumers' relationships with companies', *Journal of Marketing*, **67**, 76–88.

Bourdieu, P. (1985), 'The social space and the genesis of groups', *Theory and Society*, **14**, 723–44.

Bourdieu, P. (1986), 'The forms of capital', in J. Richardson (ed.), *Handbook of Theory and Research for the Sociology of Education*, New York: Greenwood Press, pp. 241–58.

Bourdieu, P. and L. Wacquant (1992), *An Invitation to Reflexive Sociology*, Chicago, IL: University of Chicago Press.

Brint, S. and J. Karabel (1991), 'Institutional origins and transformations: the case of American community colleges', in W. Powell and P. DiMaggio (eds), *The New Institutionalism in Organizational Analysis*, Chicago, IL: University of Chicago Press, pp. 337–60.

Burt, R. (1987), 'Social contagion and innovation: cohesion versus structural equivalence', *American Journal of Sociology*, **92**, 1282–1335.

Cambridge Research (1992), *Corporate EQ Scores 1992: Americans Rate Corporate Environmental Performance*, Cambridge, MA: Cambridge Research, Research International.

Christmann, P. (2004), 'Multinational companies and the environment: determinants of global environmental policy standardization', *Academy of Management Journal*, **47** (5), 747–60

Davis, G. (1991), 'Agents without principles? The spread of the poison pill through the intercorporate network', *Administrative Science Quarterly*, **36**, 583–613.

DiMaggio, P. (1988), 'Interest and agency in institutional theory', in L. Zucker (ed.), *Institutional Patterns and Organizations*, Cambridge, MA: Ballinger, pp. 3–21.
DiMaggio, P. (1995), 'Comments on what theory is not', *Administrative Science Quarterly*, **40**, 391–7.
DiMaggio, P. and W. Powell (1983), 'The iron cage revisited: institutional isomorphism and collective rationality in organizational fields', *American Sociological Review*, **48**, 147–60.
DiMaggio, P. and W. Powell (1991), 'Introduction', in W. Powell and P. DiMaggio (eds), *The New Institutionalism in Organizational Analysis*, Chicago, IL: University of Chicago Press, pp. 1–38.
Dunn, D. and K. Yamashita (2003), 'Microcapitalism and the megacorporation', *Harvard Business Review*, August, 46–54.
The Economist (2003), 'Follow my lead', 11 October, p. 68.
Ehrenfeld, J. (2004), 'Searching for sustainability: no quick fix', *Reflections: The SoL Journal on Knowledge, Learning and Change*, **5** (8), 1–13.
English, B. (2004), 'No sweat leader is passionate about Newton company's union-only apparel', *Boston Globe*, 1 May, p. C1
Fligstein, N. (1990), *The Transformation of Corporate Control*, Cambridge, MA: Harvard University Press.
Fligstein, N. (1991), 'The structural transformation of American industry: an institutional account of the causes of diversification in the largest firms: 1919–1979', in W. Powell and P. DiMaggio (eds), *The New Institutionalism in Organizational Analysis*, Chicago, IL: University of Chicago Press, pp. 311–36.
Fligstein, N. (1997), 'Social skill and institutional theory', *American Behavioral Scientist*, **40**, 397–405.
Fligstein, N. (2001), 'Social skill and the theory of fields', *Sociological Theory*, **19**, 105–25.
Freeman, R., A. Wicks and B. Parmar (2004), 'Stakeholder theory and the corporate objective revisited', *Organization Science*, **15**, 364–9.
Friedman, M. (1970), 'The social responsibility of business is to increase its profits', *New York Times Magazine*, 13 September, 32–3, 122, 124, 126.
Galaskiewicz, J. and R. Burt (1991), 'Interorganization contagion in corporate philanthropy', *Administrative Science Quarterly*, **36**, 88–105.
Granovetter, M. (1973), 'The strength of weak ties', *American Journal of Sociology*, **78**, 1360–80.
Greenwood, R. and C. Hinings (1996), 'Understanding radical organizational change: bringing together the old and the new institutionalism', *Academy of Management Review*, **21**, 1022–54.
Greenwood, R., R. Suddaby and C. Hinings (2002), 'Theorizing change: the role of professional associations in the transformation of institutionalized fields', *Academy of Management Journal*, **45**, 58–80.
Hart, S. (1995), *Capitalism at the Crossroads: The Unlimited Business Opportunities in Solving the World's Most Difficult Problems*, Upper Saddle River, NJ: Wharton School Publishing.
Hart, S. and T. London (2005), 'Developing native capability: what multi-nationals can learn from the base of the pyramid', *Stanford Social Innovation Review*, **3** (2), 28–33.
Hensmans, M. (2003), 'Social movement organizations: a metaphor for strategic actors in institutional fields', *Organization Studies*, **24**, 355–81.

Hoffman, A. (1999), 'Institutional evolution and change: environmentalism and the US chemical industry', *Academy of Management Journal*, **42**, 351–71.
Hoffman, A. (2001), *From Heresy to Dogma: An Institutional History of Corporate Environmentalism*, Stanford, CA: Stanford University Press.
Hoffman, A. and W. Ocascio (2001), 'Not all events are attended equally: toward a middle-range theory of industry attention to external events', *Organization Science*, **12** (4), 414–34.
Hoffman, A. and M. Ventresca (2002), *Organizations, Policy and the Natural Environment: Institutional and Strategic Perspectives*, Stanford, CA: Stanford University Press.
Howard, J., J. Nash and J. Ehrenfeld (2000), 'Standard or smokescreen? Implementation of a voluntary environmental code', *California Management Review*, **42**, 63–82.
Howard-Grenville, J. and A. Hoffman (2003), 'The importance of cultural framing to the success of social initiatives in business', *Academy of Management Executive*, **17**, 70–84.
Jennings, P. and P. Zandbergen (1995), 'Ecologically sustainable organizations: an institutional approach', *Academy of Management Review*, **20** (4), 1015–52.
Lawrence, T. (1999), 'Institutional strategy', *Journal of Management*, **25**, 161–88.
London, T. and S. Hart (2004), 'Reinventing strategies for emerging markets: beyond the trans-national model', *Journal of International Business Studies*, **35** (5), 350–70.
Lounsbury, M. and M. Glynn (2001), 'Cultural entrepreneurship: stories, legitimacy, and the acquisition of resources', *Strategic Management Journal*, **22**, 545–64.
Maguire, S., C. Hardy and T. Lawrence (2004), 'Institutional entrepreneurship in emerging fields: HIV/AIDS treatment advocacy in Canada', *Academy of Management Journal*, **47**, 657–79.
Margolis, J. and J. Walsh (2001), *People and Profits? The Search for a Link Between a Company's Social and Financial Performance*, Mahwah, NJ: Lawrence Erlbaum Associates.
Margolis, J. and J. Walsh (2003), 'Misery loves companies: rethinking social initiatives in business', *Administrative Science Quarterly*, **48**, 268–305.
Oakes, L., B. Townley and D. Cooper (1998), 'Business planning as pedagogy: language and control in a changing institutional field', *Administrative Science Quarterly*, **43**, 257–92.
Porter, M. and C. van der Linde (1995), 'Toward a new conception of the environment–competitiveness relationship', *Journal of Economic Perspectives*, **9** (4), 97–118
Prahalad, C.K. (2004), *The Fortune at the Bottom of the Pyramid: Eradicating Poverty Through Profits*, Upper Saddle River, NJ: Wharton School Publishing.
Rao, H. (1994), 'The social construction of reputation: certification contests, legitimation, and the survival of organizations in the American automobile industry, 1895–1912', *Strategic Management Journal*, 15 (Winter special issue), 29–44.
Rao, H., C. Morrill and M. Zald (2000), 'Power plays: how social movements and collective action create new organizational forms', *Research in Organizational Behavior*, **22**, 237–81.
Russo, M. (2003), 'The emergence of sustainable industries: building on natural capital', *Strategic Management Journal*, **24**, 317–31.

Scott, S. and V. Lane (2000), 'A stakeholder approach to organizational identity', *Academy of Management Review*, **25**, 43–62.
Scott, W.R. (1995), *Institutions and Organizations*, London: Sage Publications.
Scott, W.R. (2002), 'Organizations and the natural environment: evolving models', in A. Hoffman and M. Ventresca (eds), *Organizations, Policy and the Natural Environment: Institutional and Strategic Perspectives*, Stanford, CA: Stanford University Press, pp. 453–61.
Sharma, S. and I. Henriques (2005), 'Stakeholder influences on sustainability practices in the Canadian forest products industry', *Strategic Management Journal*, **26** (2), 159–80.
Simanis, E. and S. Hart (2001), 'The Monsanto company: quest for sustainability', Management Institute for Environment and Business Case, Washington, DC: World Resources Institute.
Simmons, P. and B. Wynne (1993), 'Responsible Care: trust, credibility, and environmental management', in K. Fischer and J. Schot (eds), *Environmental Strategies for Industry*, Washington, DC: Island Press, pp. 201–26.
Smith, N. (2003), 'Corporate social responsibility: whether or how?', *California Management Review*, **45**, 52–76.
South Africa Quarterly Forecast Report (2002), 'Chapter 3: Key economic sectors', *South Africa Quarterly Forecast Report*, (4th quarter), 18–24.
Starik, M. and G. Rands (1995), 'Weaving an integrated web: multilevel and multisystem perspectives of ecologically sustainable organizations', *Academy of Management Review*, **20** (4), 908–35.
Stecklow, S. (2005), 'How a global web of activists gives Coke problems in India', *Wall Street Journal*, 7 June, p. A1.
Sundaram, A. and A. Inkpen (2004), 'The corporate objective revisited', *Organization Science*, **15**, 350–63.
Troast, J., A. Hoffman, H. Riley and M. Bazerman (2002), 'Institutions as barriers and enablers to negotiated agreements: institutional entrepreneurship and the Plum Creek Habitat Conservation Plan', in A. Hoffman and M. Ventresca (eds) *Organizations, Policy and the Natural Environment: Institutional and Strategic Perspectives*, Stanford, CA: Stanford University Press, pp. 235–61.
Wade-Benzoni, K., A. Hoffman, L. Thompson, D. Moore, J. Gillespie and M. Bazerman (2002), 'Barriers to resolution in ideologically based negotiations: The role of values and institutions', *Academy of Management Review*, **27**, 41–57.
World Commission on Economic Development (WCED) (1987), *Our Common Future*, New York: Oxford University Press.

9. The political-institutional dimension of socio-environmental strategies: the game of Aracruz Celulose S.A. versus Tupiniquim and Guarani Indians

Celio Andrade

Since the 1990s corporate environmentalism has been challenged by the appearance of socio-environmental actors in the process of creating corporate strategies. Numerous studies have been carried out into the formulation of socio-environmental strategies in which the profit-maximizing rational choice is seen as one of the main driving forces. However, there remains an area concerning the relations between companies and their political-institutional space which has been little explored. This area is where the rules of the game are defined by pressure exerted by the companies' multiple stakeholders.

Stakeholders are individuals, entities or interest groups which exert pressure on the strategic direction of an organization in that they affect and/or are affected by them. In this context, the legitimacy of the company is seen as its capacity to construct socio-environmental strategies which take into consideration the demands of these actors. A socio-environmental strategy is a socially structured process, the result of conflict mediation between the organization and the various socio-environmental actors, rather than a rational strategy.

Given that the socio-environmental stakeholders present numerous conflicts of interest and have differing commitments and diverse objectives, this chapter focuses on the following issues: how a company can construct socio-environmental strategies which can mediate the inherent tension present among stakeholders with varying rationalities and interests, however legitimate, and how to encourage the right climate for cooperation in conflict, turning opponents into satisfied adversaries.

The answer to these questions has to do with recognizing the political-institutional dimension of socio-environmental strategies. In other words, an understanding that the formulation of strategies goes beyond the classical limits of planning and extends into the institutional space of a company, requiring constant political mediation and the construction of negotiation mechanisms between a company and its various stakeholders. This negotiation involves the accommodation and administration of differences as well as the elaboration of successive agreements and conventions, a game of mutual dependence, without losers, interspersed with episodes of conflict and cooperation.

The objective of this chapter is to analyse the way in which socio-environmental strategies have been drawn up by Aracruz Celulose S.A. to deal with specific conflict–cooperation situations. The main protagonists were, on the one hand, Aracruz Celulose S.A. and on the other, one of their groups of socio-environmental stakeholders: the Tupiniqim and Guarani Indians. In this case-study we used an analytical framework based on the perception of organizational strategy as a socially constructed process or product, from the sociology of French organizations, called the *logiques d'actions* approach (Amblard et al., 1996).

METHODOLOGY

The use of case-studies has been recommended by various social scientists as a way to understand contemporary phenomena better. Yin (1991), for example, suggests using them in research dealing with issues concerning the 'how and why' and where boundaries of context and phenomena are not necessarily clearly defined. This method provides a dynamic understanding of the political-institutional dimension of the strategic socio-environmental process of Aracruz, making use of the specific case of a conflict over land rights.

For this study, secondary data from internal documents, reports and publications from the two key actors were analysed. Primary data were collected in the field using non-participatory observation and semi-structured interviews. It is important to point out that this research adopted an epistemological position which attaches greater importance to facts rather than to making value judgments about those facts. In other words the researchers worked with the justifications and arguments of the actors when explaining their actions (Livian and Herreros, 1994). However, given the complexity of the observed phenomena, involving numerous actors and situations, the focus is on the essential facts that reveal the dynamics of the situation.

ORGANIZATIONAL ACTORS

Aracruz Celulose S.A.

Aracruz Celulose S.A. is the world's biggest producer of cellulose in the eucalyptus short-fibre market with a production capacity of 1.2 million tons a year and supplying approximately 20 percent of the global demand for eucalyptus cellulose and about 7 percent of short-fibre cellulose (Citicorp, 1998). The company is highly capital-intensive, produces a global commodity, competes in a cyclical market and is subject to increasing socio-environmental pressure (Aracruz, 1996). It leads in low pulp production costs. While the average production costs for the nine main producing countries is about US$389/ton, Aracruz boasts the world's lowest cellulose production costs: US$279/ton (Andrade et al., 1998).

The company operates an integrated system based on the forest–factory–port trichotomy and occupies an area of 203 000 hectares. It generates around 5000 direct and indirect jobs (Aracruz, 1996). Its eucalyptus forests cover a total area of 132 000 hectares in the north of Espirito Santo (63 percent) and the extreme south of Bahia (37 percent). Of the remaining area, 56 000 hectares are native forest reserves and 15 000 hectares are used for other purposes: roads, factories, port, and so on (Aracruz, 1998c). The headquarters of the company are located in Rio de Janeiro while the factory and the port are located in the municipality of Aracruz, in the state of Espirito Santo. In 1997 Aracruz exported 90 percent of its production, 39 percent to Europe, 36 percent to North America, 17 percent to Asia and 8 percent to Latin America. Between 1993 and 1994 its main clients included the United States, Belgium, England, France, Italy, Japan, South Korea, China, Indonesia, Thailand, Mexico and Argentina (CIMI, 1996). The main shareholders are the Norwegian group Lorentzen (28 percent), the South African group Mondi-Minorco Paper (28 percent), Banco Safra (28 percent) and BNDES (12 percent).

Indigenous Associations: Tupiniquim and Guarani and Tupiniquim de Comboios

About 1470 Tupiniquim and Guarani Indians live in three indigenous reserves in the municipality of Aracruz, Espirito Santo: Caeiras Velhas (2804 hectares), Pau Brasil (1498 hectares) and Comboios (2759 hectares) (Brasil, 1998). The indigenous reserve of Caeiras Velhas, the most densely populated, is made up of four villages: Irajá, Boa Esperança, Três Palmeiras and Caeira Velha (Aracruz, 1998d). About 70 Guarani Indians inhabit the villages Boa Esperança and Três Palmeiras. Another 1400

Tupiniquim Indians are spread over the three reserves: about 300 Indians live on the Comboios reserve, 200 live on the Pau Brasil reserve and another 900 live in the villages on the Caeiras Velhas reserve (CIMI, 1996). In 1998, after the signing of agreements between Aracruz Celulose S.A. mediated by FUNAI, the Indians began to organize themselves into Indigenous Associations to manage the technical and financial resources and strive towards self-sufficiency in the areas of education, health and agriculture (Aracruz, 1998b).

THE POLITICAL-INSTITUTIONAL DIMENSION OF SOCIO-ENVIRONMENTAL STRATEGIES: ANALYTICAL FRAMEWORK

For Carrieri (1998) the word 'strategy' has two basic interpretations which complement each other. The first explores the military origin of the concept where the notion of overwhelming, conquering or exterminating the opponent prevails. As far as allies are concerned, if taken into consideration, they are mere executors of orders. A sequence of actions is carefully thought through, step by step, to achieve predetermined objectives. Organizational and contextual differences are ignored, generalizing everything and everyone.

The second meaning deepens the maximizing perspective, directed at the fulfilling of economic objectives, as in cost–benefit analysis. For Chaffee (1985), Knights and Morgan (1991), Whipp (1996), Bensédrine (1997), Machado-da-Silva et al. (1998), among others, this meaning adds little new to the original military concept as it still exploits the predominance of a rational model of strategy formulation based firmly on traditional planning criteria. This perspective is used in game theory in its traditional version and is used to prescribe formulae for the mathematical modeling of anticipated solutions in situations marked by a conflict of the 'win–lose' type where there is no possibility for mutual gains for both parties (Von Neumann and Morgenstern, 1944).

There are numerous authors for whom strategy is a set of rational techniques used to gain control over the environment (Ansoff, 1977; Hofer and Schendel, 1978). For Avenier (1996) such authors can be grouped under the epistemological category of 'strategic planning' which is characterized by the treatment of strategy as a linear concept focusing on the carrying out of a deliberate plan by management and centered on the economic dimension of the competitive process in the market.

As regards organizations confronted with socio-environmental demands, much research has been done on the process of strategy formation. There remains, however, the little-investigated area of the political-institutional space where the rules of the game are drawn up and which is subject to the multiple pressures exerted by the various stakeholders. 'Stakeholders' refers to all those parties interested in the strategic direction of the company and which influence them or are influenced by them. In other words, according to the classical definition of Freeman (1984), the groups whose support the organization cannot fail to take into account, otherwise it would run the risk of ceasing to exist. Similarly Bensédrine (1997) notes the need to analyse the process of socio-environmental strategy formation, not only as a method for traditional planning, but also as a political exercise in the search for legitimacy in a context of debate, negotiations and conflicts where companies can intervene in the definition of rules.

A similar argument is used by Machado-da-Silva et al. (1998) in examining competitiveness. They defend the use of an integrated perspective built on the premise of an economic approach and a political-institutional approach considered as facets of the same rationale. The former supposes the use of strategy as an instrument to maximize the efficiency of the organization given certain competition, such as in the exchange of goods and services. The political-institutional dimension leads to the establishment and spread of rules of behaviour and representation of interests which are needed for organizational legitimacy. Organizations under pressure from the economic context and the political-institutional context are evaluated for both their economic efficiency and the extent to which they fulfill social demands.

Thus, the strategy of organizations dealing with socio-environmental demands can be understood as both a political-institutional process and an economic process. This is because it involves the constant construction of arrangements for negotiation among actors in conflict in a specific institutional space. The analysis and interpretation of the political-institutional dimension of the formation process for socio-environmental strategies can be enhanced by the sociological approach *logiques d'action* (Amblard et al., 1996; Bernoux and Herreros, 1996; Bernoux, 1998).

This analytical framework has its roots in the French sociology of organizations: Crozier and Friedberg (1977), Boltanski and Thévenot (1991), Callon and Latour (1991). The *logiques d'action* approach proposes the investigation of the process of strategy formation using an analytical framework which adds notions of 'power', 'conflict', 'strategic actors', 'cooperation', 'rules', 'conventions', 'translation' (see below) and 'agreements'.

Therefore, according to Amblard et al. (1996), the analyses of Crozier and Friedberg (1977) and Friedberg (1993) avoid falling into the trap of an economic interpretation of strategy formation. Organizational strategy is perceived as going further than rational choice and planning to embrace factors of a political, social and environmental nature which also intervene in its definition and implementation. This strategic analysis assumes that organizational strategies are the consequence of regularity, consistency or patterns of behaviour of strategic actors. These actors construct strategies which reflect their values and degree of perception of the situation with the aim of securing their ability to influence. Such values, degrees of perception and means of influence are, however, conditioned by the limits of individual rationality (Simon, 1957). In a given situation, the actors may not always choose the best strategy, but a satisfactory arrangement considering their limited information-processing skills and their restricted capacity for action. Power games among strategic actors are dynamic and reciprocal, established through interaction and constantly negotiated as a balance between conflict and cooperation.

By highlighting the power games played out among strategic actors, Crozier and Friedberg (1977) categorize organizations as political systems in which strategies are played out. Conflict and power games are not viewed as an impediment to competition; on the contrary, they are taken as socialization elements or means of interaction among strategic actors which result in the construction of agreements. Thus, according to Friedberg (1993), the actors enter into a power relationship to gain cooperation, as the pursuit of individual interests does not necessarily guarantee the collective interest. Crozier and Friedberg (1977) highlight the idea of organizational strategy as a socially constructed process and, at the same time, a multifaceted product of a set of interrelationships among actors in which power games can always be found.

Despite the fact that Crozier and Friedberg (1977) and Friedberg (1993) introduced the concept of a strategic actor and incorporated the dimensions of power and conflict into the analysis of the process of formation of organizational strategies, their approach fails to deal with the issue of regulation of conflict or of the conditions for reaching agreements and compromises among the actors. Boltanski and Thévenot (1991) present arguments that can fill this gap. This approach focuses on the production of legitimate and justified agreements, analyzing the ways that actors find to cooperate in conflict, despite their diverging interests. According to these authors, for there to be coordination, certain conventions need to be established by the actors involved. They can either be drawn up in written documents or remain as informal agreements.

For Boltanski and Thévenot (1991) and Livian and Herreros (1994) the identification of the principles of legitimacy or type of rationality which characterize the 'worlds' to which the actors belong, is a necessary phase in the negotiation of conflicts, the production of rules and the building of agreements. The behavior of the actors is then interpreted through these principles of legitimacy around which the individuals sustain their arguments and with which they represent themselves.

It is impossible, according to Boltanski and Thévenot (1991), to achieve coordination among actors when they remain immersed in the *logiques d'action* of their particular world. To manage conflict, bases for agreement cannot be found in social behaviour and objects in isolation. On the contrary, such bases have to be constructed from an understanding of the interplay of the varying rationalities.

To complete the *logiques d'action* framework the principle of 'translation' of Callon and Latour (1991) figures as a final element needed to decodify the different interpretive schemes of strategic actors into common elements, revealing mechanisms for agreements and zones of cooperation in the conflict. 'Translate' here means to make intelligible for the person with a '*logique d'action* A' the opinion hitherto unintelligibly presented by the person with '*logique d'action* B', in an operation creating an 'intelligibility link' among heterogenous parties.

Finally, we reach the conclusion that often management situations bring into play the objectives and interests of various strategic actors, possessing multiple rationalities which are often in conflict. In fact, most situations of conflict have a dimension of mutual dependence, characterized by the conflict–cooperation dichotomy as opposed to the classical game model of win–lose. These situations are marked by the interdetermination of equilibria (Nash, 1949) or non-zero sum cooperative games (Axelrod, 1992; Brandenburger and Nalebuff, 1996; Schelling, 1986). They are situations in which the word 'cooperation' does not necessarily refer to an amicable agreement, as friendship is not indispensable for there to be cooperation among actors in a conflict, but a situation of mutual interdependence or reciprocity (Cordonier, 1997; Lecomte, 1998).

THE GAME: ARACRUZ VERSUS TUPINIQUIM AND GUARANI INDIANS

To analyse the case of Aracruz Celulose S.A. versus Tupiniquim and Guarani Indians an approach from *logiques d'action* proposed by Amblard et al. (1996) was used. This approach helps to contextualize, analyse and understand the political strategy-building process used by the actors involved in situations of socio-environmental conflict. According to Polansky (1995), analysing how the actors deal with the situation facilitates the analysis of conflict management, which is instrinsic to the strategic process of socio-environmental management.

The Historical Perspective of the Conflict and Cooperation

The Aracruz company came into being in 1967 in the midst of land disputes between Indians and COFAVI (Vitória Iron and Steel Company), the company from which Aracruz bought the lands to plant the eucalyptus forests. In 1983, after the first process of demarcation of the land, Aracruz signed its first agreement with the Tupiniquim and Guarani Indians. In this agreement the company transferred about 1700 hectares to the Indians (Aracruz, 1988b).

In the period between 1988 and 1997, which was marked by the search for cooperation within the context of the latent conflict, the Brazilian Constitution was promulgated. It recognized the Indians as peoples who were culturally differentiated and replaced the prevailing idea, which had until then focused on the need to integrate these communities into national society (FUNAI, 1999a). After the Indians' second demand to extend their area by 4492 hectares in 1993 and FUNAI's (National Foundation for the Indian) recommendation to increase the reserves by 13 579 hectares, Aracruz stepped up its search for cooperation within the conflict by engaging itself as a technical-financial partner of NISI-ES (Interinstitutional Nucleus for Indigenous Health). NISI-ES was created in 1994 with the main objective of designing projects for the sustainable development of the indigenous peoples (NISI, 1998). The Indians themselves launched an international campaign together with the main stakeholders of Aracruz to demarcate the 13 579 hectares recommended by FUNAI. Aracruz contested the demarcation by FUNAI in the courts and reinforced its strategy through its alliance with NISI-ES, focusing discussion on sustainable projects to satisfy the socio-economic needs of the Indians.

The first months of 1998 were marked by a return to heightened conflicts within the framework of latent cooperation. Aracruz suffered a second demarcation of land. The Indians failed to accept the decision of the Justice Ministry to increase their reserves by only 2571 hectares. Aracruz negotiated two more agreements with the Indians in April 1998, mediated by FUNAI and the Federal Public Ministry (Lorentzen, 1998).

The period between 1993 and 1998 is the subject of more detailed study in the following sections. However, the historical context highlights two important aspects in the analysis of socio-environmental conflicts: the unstable balance between cooperation and conflict and the non-permanent nature of the agreements.

The Management of Socio-Environmental Conflicts

The analysis of the management of the Aracruz versus Indians conflict is carried out in Tables 9.1 to 9.7 giving emphasis to the *logiques d'action* of the actors involved in the situation. Table 9.1 presents what Aracruz and the Indians recognize to be the problem according to their appreciation of the situation.

The actors' differing perceptions of the problem lead them to different ways to regulate the conflict. Their freedom is restricted by external rules which are imposed on all the actors involved in the situation. However, the exact way in which the rules are used to control the situation is a function of the game played by the actors. The set of rules in the Aracruz

Table 9.1 The problem(s) according to the main actors

Aracruz	Indigenous associations
A lack of long-term projects decided on by the indigenous communities themselves to help them with their survival and improve their quality of life in a sustainable manner	Insufficient land in the reserves for the Indians to carry on their traditional way of life and culture based on subsistence agriculture, hunting, fishing, gathering of fruit, honey and materials for making utensils and houses

Source: Drawn up by the author from information available in: Aracruz (1996, 1997b and 1998a).

Table 9.2 The set of external rules to control the conflict

- Public hearing for the demarcation of traditionally indigenous areas required by article 19 of Act 6001/73 and established by presidential decrees 22/91 and 1775/96;
- The Brazilian Constitution of 1988, that establishes:
  - Title II, Chapter I, Article 5: the guarantee of property rights;
  - Title IV, Chapter V, Article 129: one of the institutional functions of the Federal Public Ministry is the defense of the rights and interests of Indians according to the rules of the legal system;
  - Title VIII, Chapter VIII, Articles 231 and 232: recognition of the rights of Indians to lands traditionally occupied by them and the legitimacy of indigenous organizations in the defense of their rights and interests.

Source: Author's own from information available at: Aracruz (1996, 1997a); Brasil (1988a), FUNAI (1999a , 1999b).

Table 9.3 The arguments presented by the actors

Aracruz	Indigenous associations
Aracruz considers the Indians' demands unfounded, using the following counter-arguments: 1. Legal land distribution by the King of Portugal became effectively and legally extinct through a process involving various systems of regulations between 1759 and 1853 2. The 1934 Constitution only recognizes the demarcation rights of lands to Indians if they have occupied them on a permanent basis, though it fails to define in the text the concept of permanence. The 1988 constitution, in turn, recognizes the legitimacy of the Indians' right to possess the land traditionally occupied by them; however, it establishes four simultaneous and accumulative prerequisites: that the land be occupied by Indians on a permanent basis; that the land be used for their productive activities; that the land be indispensible for the preservation of environmental resources and that the land be required for the maintenance of their welfare and physical and cultural reproduction 3. All the land in question was acquired by Aracruz through legal means from previous owners, based on documents and deeds which clearly prove the existence of a successive chain of ownership, as stipulated in the Brazilian constitution	The indigenous demands are based on two arguments: 1. That the land under dispute was donated to them in 1610 by the Portuguese Crown under the land distribution system 2. That since 1934 the Brazilian constitution(s) have recognized the demarcation rights of lands traditionally occupied by Indians

Source: Author's own using information available from: CIMI (1996) and Aracruz (1997a; 1998a, 1998b).

versus Indians conflict and the actors' arguments are presented in Tables 9.2 and 9.3.

The actors play with the law to draw up a set of autonomous rules, formalized in agreements which satisfy the objectives and interests of each side

Table 9.4 The key objects negotiated in the search for an agreement between the actors

Aracruz	Indigenous associations
• Health Project for the Indigenous Communities carried out and coordinated by NISI, aiming at self-sustainability for the communities involved • Forestry Project	International campaign for the extension and demarcation of Tupiniquim and Guarani lands carried out and coordinated by CIMI-Leste

Table 9.5 The strategies formulated by the actors

Aracruz	Indigenous associations
Aracruz works simultaneously with four strategies drawn up throughout the process: 1. to influence state authorities in the financial-economic sector in its favor; 2. to support the projects carried out by NISI as a technical and financial partner; 3. not to recognize the land considered by the Indians as being theirs or having been traditionally indigenous; 4. to extend the company's Forestry Program to the indigenous communities	The Indians make use of just one strategy: 1. To influence and mobilize public opinion in the Indigenous Associations' favor and other stakeholders of Aracruz (clients, shareholders and governmental organizations) through national and international campaigns which highlight the cause ofthe Indians and the occupation of the land in question

Source: Author's own using information available from: CIMI (1996); Lorentzen (1998); Aracruz (1998a, 1998b, 1999).

in the game. Table 9.4 shows the key objects negotiated, which enable us to understand better the strategic choices made by the actors in the socio-environmental game.

To understand the rationale behind the agreements between Aracruz and the Indians we trace the paths of the choices made by these actors. Table 9.5 throws some light on the dynamics of agreements reached between Aracruz and the Tupiniquim and Guarani Indians. These agreements are the product of strategies constructed during the course of meetings, conflicts and agreements between these actors.

Table 9.6 The agreements reached by the actors in the conflict

The agreements signed by the Indians–FUNAI–Public Ministry–Aracruz:
• The indigenous reserves are increased by a total of 2599 hectares, according to Decree from the Justice Ministry 193, 194 and 195 published 9 March 1998
• Aracruz continues with the technical and financial partnership project with NISI, with a minimum contribution of US$7000/year
• Aracruz agrees to contribute US$10 million over the next 20 years to projects in the areas of education, health, social welfare and housing carried out by the Tupiniquim and Guarani and Tupiniquim de Comboios Indigenous Associations
• Aracruz agrees to contribute US$170 000 (at most) over the following years to the payment of the electricity and water bills of the indigenous communities
• The Indians agree to maintain the cultivation of eucalyptus in the 2571 hectares transferred to their reserves, thus becoming partners in Aracruz's Forestry Program
• The indigenous association of Tupiniquim de Comboios receives, apart from the 243 hectares determined in the ministerial decree, a further 185 hectares of arable land, a tractor, a truck and farm tools to carry out sustainable farming projects

Source: Author's own using information available from: Lorentzen (1998); Aracruz (1998a, 1998b, 1999); Brasil (1998b).

The strategy adopted by the Indians takes on the form of a legitimate instrument of urgency for all those representing the interests of the indigenous cause. It is therefore able to exert greater influence because its target public are the stakeholders of Aracruz, key actors in the formation of its socio-environmental strategies.

On the other hand, the set of strategies used by Aracruz reveals two aspects:

- A defensive aspect. Aracruz keeps some room for manoeuvre and therefore protects itself against future demands from the Indians through strategies 1 and 3 in Table 9.5. Aracruz makes use of strategies of influence as an irrefutable right (Lorentzen, 1998) to convince the authorities of the economic and financial sectors of the government that the land dispute with the Indians constitutes a double threat to:
  - The survival of Aracruz as a company: the transfer of the 13 579 hectares to the Indians represents 40 percent of the cultivated area surrounding the plant. This land is essential for the

Table 9.7 The cooperation-conflict balance in the case of Aracruz and the Tupiniquim and Guarani Indians

The agreements reached demonstrate the limits which result from the overlapping of the classical limits of the dominant world views of the actors involved in the conflict. The balance between conflict and cooperation in the Aracruz versus Guarani and Tupiniquim case shows that:

- On the one hand, Aracruz fails to recognize the demands of the Indians as legitimate; on the other hand, the company learns that it is responsible for a socio-environmental asset whose origin and basis is in the traditional domestic world. In other words, the company knows that it is located on a site that has material and symbolic value for the Indians, which had hitherto not been taken into consideration by the company. This asset is the main object of the Aracruz versus Indians conflict and not the 13 579 hectares themselves
- Aracruz recognizes that to continue in the competitive world, of which it is part, it not only has to satisfy its own interests efficiently and adopt socio-environmental strategies related to the principles of the world of trade and industry, but also incorporate the interests and values inherent to the worlds of its stakeholders
- The Indians, in turn, who defend their values and perceptions inherent in their dominant world (traditional-domestic) have learned to recognize the need to give preference to a technical-economic dimension. An illustration of this overlapping of *logiques d'action* was the fact that the Indians began to cultivate eucalyptus in partnership with Aracruz's Forestry Project. The cultivation of this tree symbolizes their entry into a world marked by the incessant search for increased productivity through biotechnology
- The exchange mechanisms that result from these agreements can be described as exchanges of favor rather than exchanges of equivalence, i.e. things are exchanged between the business world and the Indians not for their commercial value, but for their worth in maintaining the relationship
- Negotiated agreements have prevailed over court decisions as the land disputes have remained within the administrative sphere through the formalization of agreements rather than through court proceedings

technical-economic viability of the company whose market edge stems from its strategy of leading in low cellulose production costs (Aracruz, 1998a).

- The Brazilian legal system as it protects private property and is therefore important for future investment in the country.

- An offensive aspect. Aracruz strives to improve its capacity for action though the creation of new relationships with the Indians using strategies 2 and 4 in Table 9.5:

- Technical-financial partnership with NISI between 1994 and 1997 including action plans in the areas of education, agriculture and health. This cooperative socio-environmental strategy reinforces the perception of Aracruz *vis-à-vis* the situation, that is, that the Indians have no long-term projects for the sustainability of the reserves.
- The extension of the Aracruz Forestry Program to include the indigenous community consists of providing saplings of eucalyptus and other native species of trees, supplies and technical support to secure continuity of forestry activities of high-productivity eucalyptus in the indigenous lands and the formalization of a sales contract for the wood between the Indians and Aracruz. This strategy has enabled Aracruz to guarantee a supply of eucalyptus with low transport costs and it has also invalidated the Indians' argument that the lands they possessed were insufficient to restore their traditional way of life (Lorentzen, 1998).

The agreements signed between Aracruz and the Indians define a set of rules that allow the actors to adjust their individual behaviour to the situation. This set of agreements, described in Table 9.6, dictates the means that Aracruz and the Indians understand and recognize as valid.

This outcome does not mean, however, that over the next decades it will not be necessary for both parties constantly to monitor and control the state of these agreements as regards the transparency and mutual trust gained and the results achieved. The coexistence and durability of this new balance between offensive and defensive aspects of socio-environmental strategies depends on follow-up to the agreements by both parties and their mediation of individual and collective interests. An analysis of the current state of affairs is presented in Table 9.7.

CONCLUSION

The starting point for this chapter was to describe and analyse the formation process of the socio-environmental strategies of Aracruz Celulose S.A. in the specific conflict situation between the company and a group of its stakeholders: the Tupiniquim and Guarani Indians. On comparing the data obtained in this research with the traditional analytical framework on company strategy, the shortcomings of the traditional literature on strategy became clear. It also revealed the limitations of traditional approaches that view circumstances of conflict as negative events, simple win–lose games, and a threat to maintaining a company's competitive edge.

This chapter has attempted to demonstrate that company strategies extend into their political-institutional space. This space is made up of stakeholders and is a place of constant debate, conflict and negotiation where companies can influence and be influenced in the definition of rules and agreements. To understand this case, the analysis made use of a perspective in which strategies are formed over time and are subject to alteration and 'comings and goings'. This strategy-building process is understood using the *logiques d'action* approach from the French sociology of organizations. It analyses the confrontation of the varying rationalities in play and the creation of circumstances that allow for there to be cooperation and the drawing up of agreements among the parties in conflict, without treating them as winners or losers, but rather as satisfied adversaries.

Socio-environmental strategies reveal that they are both the product and process of interactive games. Thus, the strategic process of the socio-environmental management of Aracruz can be better understood using the argument that companies construct a set of strategic political alliances, negotiations and conflict regulation through their interaction with stakeholders in order to influence the rules of the game.

Finally, we conclude that the socio-environmental strategies of Aracruz Celulose S.A. follow a continuum of mediation of conflict. Conflict resulting from the meeting of different rationales is neither understood as a negative phenomenon, nor an exception which proves an obstacle to strategy-building for competitive advantage. On the contrary, multiple visions are taken into account and are essential to the process of shaping corporate socio-environmental strategies to reach satisfactory agreements with stakeholders. It is exactly the mediation of conflict which maintains the equilibrium of conflict and cooperation in situations marked by mutual interdependence. Company versus stakeholder games are rarely resolved, but managed. The management of such games is a constant search for temporary and successive equilibria and for new areas of agreement. These areas overcome the restrictions of former commitments to satisfy the demands of a new phase of the conflict caused by the constant changes of competitive dynamics. Agreements are transitory and usually fail to resolve the conflict. The agreements reached between Aracruz and the Indians have not resolved, nor will they resolve the land dispute. They merely serve to open further space for cooperation between differing worlds with differing interests.

REFERENCES

Amblard, H., P. Bernovx, G. Herreros and Y.-F. Livian (1996), *Les Nouvelles Approaches Sociologiques des Organisations*, Paris: Seuil.

Andrade, J.C.S., C.C. Dias and R.H. Quintella (1998), 'Analysis of corporate socioenvironmental strategy formulation process through game approach: the case of Aracruz Celulose S.A.', *Business Strategy and the Environment*, **2** (3), 12–24.
Ansoff, I. (1977), *Estratégia Empresarial*, São Paulo: McGraw Hill.
Aracruz Celulose S.A. (1996), *Annual Report for Year Ended December 31, 2006*, Rio de Janeiro: Aracruz Celulose.
Aracruz Celulose S.A. (1997a), 'Environment: questions and answers', accessed at www.aracruz.com.br.
Aracruz Celulose S.A. (1997b), 'Forestry', accessed at www.aracruz.com.br.
Aracruz Celulose S.A. (1998a), *Aracruz e os Índios Assinam Acordo em Questão de Terras*, Rio de Janeiro: Aracruz Celulose S.A.
Aracruz Celulose S.A. (1998b), *Aracruz News*, **10** (4), 10–13.
Aracruz Celulose S.A. (1998c), *Aracruz News*, **12** (4), 12–15.
Aracruz Celulose S.A. (1998d), 'Perfil Corporativo da Aracruz', accessed at www.aracruz.com.br.
Aracruz Celulose S.A. (1999), 'Aracruz and the Guarani and Tupinikim Land Claim', accessed at www.aracruz.com.br.
Avenier, M.R. (1996), *La Stratégie Tatonnante: des Interactions Récursives entre Vision et Action Stratégiques*, Aix en Provence: GRASCE.
Axelrod, R. (1992), Donnant Donnant: théorie du comportement coopératif, Paris: Odile.
Bensédrine, J. (1997), 'Les Stratégies des Entreprises dans les Processus Institutionnels: le Cas des Producteurs de CFC et la Protection de la Couche d'Ozone', doctoral dissertation, ESSEC/IAE, Aix-en-Provence, France.
Bernoux, P. (1998), 'A quoi sert la sociologie des organisations?', *Sciences Humaines*, **10** (20), 12–15.
Bernoux, P. and G. Herreros (1996), 'Méthodologie pour l'intervention: la sociologie des logiques d'action', in H. Amblard, P. Bernoux, G. Herreros and Y.-F. Livian (eds), *Les Nouvelles Approches Sociologiques des Organisations*, Paris: Seuil.
Boltanski, L. and L. Thévenot (1991), *De la justification. Les économies de la grandeur*, Paris: Gallimard.
Brandenburger, A. and B. Nalebuff (1996), 'The right game: use game theory to shape strategy', *Harvard Business Review*, **2** (3), 20–25.
Brasil (1988a) *Constituição: República Federativa do Brasil*, Brasília: Centro Gráfico do Senado Federal.
Brasil (1988b) Portarias Ministério da Justiça 193, 194 e 195/98. *Diário Oficial da República Federativa do Brasil*, Brasília: Imprensa Federal.
Callon, M. and B. Latour (eds) (1991), *La Science telle qu'elle se fait*, Paris: La Découverte.
Carrieri, A.P. (1998), Pesquisa sobre estratégia: do discurso dominante à uma nova narrativa, XXII ENANPAD, Foz do Iguaçu, Brazil: ANPAD, pp. 50–65.
Chaffee, E. (1985), 'Three models of strategy', *Academy of Management Review*, **10** (1), 89–98.
CIMI (1996), papers from the International Campaign for the Extension and Demarcation of the Indigenous Lands of the Tupinikim and Guarani, regarding the Executive Commission of the Tupinikim and Guarani, and Aracruz Celulose, Brasília: CIMI.
Citicorp Securities Incorporation (1998), *Made in Brazil*, Sao Paulo: Aracruz Celulose.
Cordonier, L. (1997), *Coopération et reciprocité*, Paris: PUF.

Crozier, M. and E. Friedberg (1977), *L'acteur et le système*, Paris: Seuil.
Freeman, R.E. (1984), *Strategic Management: a Stakeholder Approach*, Boston, MA: Pitman; cited in R. Mitchell, B. Agle and D. Wood (1997), 'Toward a theory of stakeholder identification and salience: defining the principle of who and what really counts', *Academy of Management Review*, **22** (4), 853–86.
Friedberg, E. (1993), *Le Pouvoir et la Règle*, Paris: Seuil.
FUNAI (1999a), *A Importância da Constituição 1988*, accessed at www.funai.gov.br.
FUNAI (1999b), *Terras Indígenas*, accessed at www.funai.gov.br.
Hofer, C. and D. Schendel (1978), *Strategy Formulation: Analytical Concepts*, Boston, MA: Pitman.
Knights, D. and G. Morgan (1991), 'Corporate strategy, organizations and subjectivity: a critique', *Organization Studies*, **12** (2), 251–73.
Lecomte, J. (1998), 'Conflit et coopération: la théorie des jeux', *Sciences Humaines*, **82** (2), 10–12.
Livian, Y.F. and G. Herreros (1994), 'L'apport des economies de la grandeur: une nouvelle grille d'analyse des organisations?', *Révue Française de Géstion*, **101** (3), 43–59.
Lorentzen, E.S. (1998), 'Settlement of land question between Guarani and Tupinikin Indians and Aracruz Celulose S.A.', Rio de Janeiro: Aracruz Celulose S.A.
Machado-da-Silva, C.L., V.S. Fonseca and B.H.R. Fernandes (1998), 'Mudança estratégica nas organizações: perspectivas cognitiva e institucional', XXII ENANPAD, Foz do Iguaçu, Brazil: ANPAD, pp. 120–35.
Nash, J. (1949), 'Essays on Game Theory', reprinted in J. Lecomte (1998), 'Conflit et coopération: la théorie des jeux', *Sciences Humaines*, **82** (2), 12–14.
Núcleo Interinstitucional da Saúde Indígena (NISI) (1998), *O que é o Núcleo Interinstitucional da Saúde Indígena?*, Aracruz, Brazil: FUNAI.
Polansky, M.J. (1995), 'Incorporating the natural environment in corporate strategy: a stakeholder approach', *Journal of Business Strategy*, **12** (2), 151–68.
Schelling, T.C. (1986), *Stratégie du Conflit*, Paris: Puf.
Simon, H. (1957), *Models of Man, Social and Rational*, New York: John Wiley & Sons.
Von Neumann, J. and O. Morgenstern (1944), 'Théorie des jeux et comportement économique', reprinted in J. Lecomte (1998), 'Conflit et coopération: la théorie des jeux', *Sciences Humaines*, **82** (2), 14–16.
Whipp, R. (1996), 'Creative deconstruction: strategy and organization', in S.R. Clegg, C. Hardy and W. Nord (eds), *Handbook of Organization Studies*, London: Sage, pp. 22–45.
Yin, R.K. (1991), *Case Study Research: Design and Methods*, London: Sage.

10. Regulating business for sustainable development

Peter Utting

One of the greatest challenges in the contemporary era of globalization and economic liberalization is how to ensure that the freeing-up of markets and the increasing dominance of transnational corporations (TNCs) in global trade, value chains, foreign direct investment and consumer culture do not undermine patterns of development that are ecologically sustainable, socially inclusive and rights based. Several decades ago, many policy-makers, activists and scholars looked to the state to protect against the perverse effects of markets and corporate power. With the rise of neoliberal orthodoxy in the 1970s and 1980s, perversity was not only downplayed in certain circles but also associated more with state failure. Markets, it was assumed, could be kept in check largely by a minimalist state and what became known as corporate environmental and social responsibility (hereafter referred to as CSR).

The CSR agenda that took off internationally in the 1990s centered heavily on the promotion of voluntary initiatives to minimize malpractice or improve aspects of company performance that relate to the environment, labor standards and community welfare. Such initiatives often involved attempts to improve environmental management systems, eco-efficiency, working conditions in TNC affiliates, and relations with local communities. Non-state actors, in particular TNCs, business associations and non-governmental organizations (NGOs), played a key role not only in promoting the philosophy of voluntarism and CSR but also in setting standards, facilitating implementation, monitoring compliance and reporting progress.

It would be wrong, however, to regard this apparent transfer of regulatory authority from state to non-state actors as simply part of a broader trend of 'deregulation' associated with neoliberalism. What has occurred is a more complex process of 're-regulation', where the rolling back of the state in certain areas of the economy and the freeing-up of markets have gone hand in hand with the strengthening of governmental and inter-governmental rules to protect and promote, for example, certain types of property rights, international trade, foreign direct investment and the environment (Braithwaite and Drahos, 2000). Important differences in the trajectory and content of regulatory reform and approach are also apparent under different varieties or models of capitalism, North and South (Hall and Soskice, 2001; Huber, 2002; Whitley, 2000), as well as in specific country and industry contexts.

In the field of CSR, re-regulation is associated with the changing character of institutional forms that have characterized the rise of private authority in recent decades (Cutler et al., 1999; Haufler, 2001). Since the late 1990s, in particular, there has been a gradual scaling-up and ratcheting-up of standards and implementation procedures related to CSR, with regulatory authority being assumed to a greater extent by NGOs and multi-stakeholder institutions or public–private partnerships, practising so-called civil regulation and co-regulation (Murphy and Bendell, 1997, 1999; Hanks, 2002; Utting, 2002a; Zammit, 2003). These 'collective' or more 'socialized' forms of private authority (O'Rourke, 2003) or 'collaborative governance' (Zadek, 2005) are increasingly supported by governments and intergovernmental organizations. More recently still, some civil society organizations, activist networks and public authorities are demanding 'corporate accountability' through regulatory arrangements that go beyond conventional voluntary approaches by, inter alia, placing greater emphasis on corporate obligations, legalistic approaches and some form of punishment in cases of non-compliance (Bendell, 2004; Broad and Cavanagh, 1999; Newell, 2002).

This chapter examines the evolution of CSR and business regulation associated with environmental and social aspects with a view to understanding its potential to reassert social control over TNCs and minimize corporate malpractice related to sustainable development. I first describe the increasing role of both private and non-governmental authority in the social regulation of business, and how the CSR agenda has evolved to embrace a broader range of issues and practices. Next I examine the gradual hardening of regulatory approaches, from softer voluntary initiatives that characterized corporate self-regulation to 'co-regulation' and multi-stakeholder initiatives; and, more recently, the renewed attention to legalistic approaches and issues of compliance and enforceability within the emerging corporate accountability agenda.

The following section introduces the notion of 'articulated regulation', which refers to the coming together of different regulatory approaches in ways that are complementary and synergistic. While this is potentially an important feature of the emerging corporate accountability agenda, it has received little attention in conceptual and strategic thinking. Four forms of articulated regulation are identified. They include complementarity between different non-governmental regulatory systems, the interface between confrontational and collaborationist forms of civil society activism, linkages between voluntary and legalistic approaches or public policy, and greater policy coherence at both the micro level of the firm and the macro level of government and international policy.

As a basis for understanding the potential and limitations of the ratcheting-up and scaling-up of CSR and corporate accountability, the next section looks at the theory and dynamics of progressive institutional reform. The discussion focuses on the way in which different elements related to crisis, agency, ideas, institutions and structure intervene and interact to explain processes of institutional change; how these aspects have shaped the CSR and corporate accountability agendas; and what they tell us about the possibilities for transforming the canvas of fragmented, experimental and fledgling initiatives into a more generalized feature or variant of 'stakeholder capitalism'.[1]

The concluding section suggests that the major obstacles confronting these different agendas are structural and political. While the mainstream CSR agenda has amassed considerable political momentum, its proponents generally ignore the extent to which the scaling-up and deepening of CSR confronts a contradictory macro policy environment. The corporate accountability movement, for its part, attempts to address certain structural dimensions but confronts the major political challenge of not only overcoming powerful opposition but also building alliances and networks within and across societal actors and regions.

A RAPIDLY EVOLVING AGENDA

Private regulation related to CSR has evolved considerably over the past two decades. When the contemporary CSR agenda took off, particularly in the build-up to and aftermath of the 1992 Earth Summit in Rio de Janeiro, it centred very much on a limited range of environmental and social initiatives; a small group of global brand name corporations, often reacting defensively to activist pressures; and a few management tools, innovations and concepts. These included, for example, selected improvements in environmental management systems, eco-efficiency, and self-prescribed and self-monitored company or industry-based codes of conduct.

Today we see more companies and industries involved, more issues on the agenda, and some transnational corporations (TNCs) and organized business interests not simply reacting to pressure but being more proactive, and attempting to apply CSR principles, policies and practices more systematically throughout corporate structures. The range of CSR interventions has broadened to include stakeholder dialogues, external monitoring and verification, 'triple bottom-line' reporting and accounting,[2] certification and labelling, and public–private partnerships. Furthermore, CSR policies and practices are reaching deeper into corporate structures.

The CSR agenda has incorporated a growing number of elements associated with the international rights-based agenda, notably children's, labour and indigenous rights. Particular issues of global concern such as HIV/AIDS and violent conflict, are also being addressed. More recently still, CSR is being linked explicitly to the global poverty reduction agenda, as attention focuses on how TNCs and other companies can alleviate poverty at the so-called 'bottom of the [income] pyramid'.[3]

Also evident are new institutional arrangements involving various forms of non-governmental regulatory action where civil society organizations not only attempt to exert pressures on business through confrontational activism but work collaboratively with companies, business associations, and governmental and intergovernmental organizations through various types of partnerships and service delivery activities. Increasingly, NGOs are taking the lead in organizing, or are participating in multi-stakeholder initiatives associated with standard-setting, company reporting, monitoring, certification and learning about good practice (Utting, 2002a).

Such initiatives include:

- Certification schemes, for example, the International Organization for Standardization (ISO) 14001 (environmental management standards), the Forest Stewardship Council (sustainable forest management), Rainforest Alliance (agriculture, forestry and travel), the Fair Labor Association (FLA) and Social Accountability International's (SAI) SA8000 (labor standards).
- Global Framework Agreements, where international trade union organizations negotiate accords with TNCs that agree to apply certain standards throughout their global structure (for example, agreements between the International Union of Food and Allied Workers/IUF and Chiquita and Danone, and between the International Federation of Chemical, Energy, Mine and General Workers' Union/ICEM and Statoil, Eni and Lukoil).
- Standard-setting and monitoring schemes associated, for example, with anti-sweatshop initiatives such as the Clean Clothes Campaign (CCC), and the Worker Rights Consortium (WRC).
- Initiatives that emphasize stakeholder dialogues and learning about good practice, such as the Global Reporting Initiative (GRI, promoting sustainability or triple bottom line reporting), the Ethical Trading Initiative (ETI, promoting social standards throughout supply chains), and AccountAbility's AA1000 (promoting social and ethical accounting).

Voluntary approaches are also being actively promoted by multilateral organizations and governments, through such initiatives as the United Nations Global Compact, which encourages companies to adhere to ten principles derived from international environmental, labor, human rights and anti-corruption law. At the 2002 World Summit on Sustainable Development (WSSD) several initiatives were launched, including the World Bank's Global Gas Flaring Reduction Partnership (GGFR), which currently includes ten companies and 11 governments; and the United Kingdom (UK) government's Extractive Industries Transparency Initiative (EITI). The following year, several of the world's leading banks that finance dams, power plants, pipelines and other infrastructure projects agreed to adhere to a set of international environmental and social-impact standards developed by the World Bank and the International Finance Corporation (IFC), known as the Equator Principles.

Multi-stakeholder initiatives constitute important elements of the new institutionalism and the drive for 'good governance' and 'embedded liberalism' that are core features of the post-Washington Consensus, where it is increasingly recognized that there is a need for institutions that can minimize the perverse social, environmental and developmental effects of open markets, economic liberalization and corporate globalization (Ruggie, 2003).

Many of these initiatives have addressed some of the more obvious limitations inherent in corporate self-regulation. Certain schemes have greater legitimacy and are conducive to democratic governance by engaging a broader range of actors or stakeholders in consultative and decision-making processes, and by involving governments. They have also contributed to harmonizing standards and implementation procedures, and to imposing some order on what was becoming a confusing array of codes of conduct. And they have tried to encourage companies to internalize social and environmental standards more systematically. As a result, in some sectors, CSR initiatives are penetrating TNC supply chains as opposed to remaining at the level of parent firms and affiliates. Multi-stakeholder initiatives have also played a key role in the evolution of the CSR agenda by expanding the number of issues on the CSR table (Haufler, 2004). Procedural aspects have sometimes been improved with companies having to accept independent monitoring as opposed to relying exclusively on internal monitoring or no monitoring at all; and they are having to measure concrete changes in performance.

To some extent, therefore, multi-stakeholder initiatives involve a ratcheting-up of standards and a hardening of the soft voluntarism that characterized the early experience of CSR, which centered on corporate self-regulation. Indeed, some see company participation in such initiatives as indicative of a particular stage of an evolutionary learning and implementation curve. According to Zadek, CSR companies tend to move through various stages, described as 'defensive', in which they deny they are part of the problem; 'compliance', in which they adopt a policy which is seen as a cost; 'managerial', in which the issue is embedded in their core management processes; 'strategic', where addressing the issue is seen as good for business; and 'civil', where they encourage their peers to address the issue also. One of the ways they operationalize this latter stage is by participating in multi-stakeholder initiatives (Zadek, 2004).

In practice, certain multi-stakeholder initiatives are more effective than others in relation to different regulatory functions. Referring to non-governmental systems of labor regulation, O'Rourke has placed such initiatives on a spectrum, 'from purely "privatized" regulation . . . to more "collaborative" regulation, to more "socialized" regulation' (O'Rourke, 2003, pp. 19–20). The 'privatized' variant, for example, is likely to facilitate easy access to the factory floor and to managers in order to obtain and disseminate information. The 'collaborative' system may be more effective at supply chain monitoring and in convincing global corporations of the need to gradually raise the bar in terms of standards and compliance. And the 'socialized' system may facilitate easier access to workers and local stakeholders, be more transparent in terms of public disclosure, and be freer to expose malpractice in the public domain.

While addressing some of the limitations that characterize company self-regulation, multi-stakeholder initiatives yield, in fact, a very mixed scorecard, reflected in the following traits. First, they involve only a small fraction of the world's 70 000 TNCs, 700 000 affiliates and several million suppliers.[4] The world's largest CSR-related certification scheme, namely ISO 14001, which assesses the quality of environmental management systems, involved approximately 90 000 facilities (not all companies) by the end of 2004.[5] The most prominent international scheme promoting CSR – the United Nations Global Compact – had enlisted the support of 2323 companies by the end of 2005.

Many of the companies involved in multi-stakeholder initiatives, however, are large TNCs. Such corporations, for example, are among the 39 members of the Ethical Trading Initiative (ETI) or the 19 active members of the Fair Labour Association (FLA). The Global Compact has enlisted the support of one-fifth of the Global Fortune 500 companies. But the participation of a global player in a multi-stakeholder initiative or its engagement with the CSR agenda should not be taken to mean that CSR practices have been internalized throughout the corporate structure or, indeed, that participation signifies a major change in corporate performance related to social, environmental and human rights aspects. In reality, CSR practices often remain limited to specific ad hoc interventions. This is apparent in relation to the Global Reporting Initiative, where by December 2005, 751 companies claimed to be using one or some of the reporting guidelines but only 120 were using them more systematically. It is also apparent in relation to the reporting on CSR best practices by companies involved with the Global Compact. Indeed, a 2004 evaluation of the Global Compact carried out by McKinsey & Company found that membership of the compact stimulated only 9 percent of the participating companies to take actions that they would not otherwise had taken had they remained outside the initiative.[6] In the vast majority of cases (91 per cent), companies were doing things they would have done anyway (51 percent), albeit more efficiently or quickly, or had remained largely inactive (40 percent).

Second, the procedures adopted by certain schemes to encourage compliance with the standards they promote often remain weak. The Global Compact and the Global Reporting Initiative, for example, rely on dialogue and best practice learning rather than monitoring compliance. ISO 14001 certification indicates whether or not a company has in place elements of an environmental management system, not whether it has actually improved its environmental impacts (Krut and Gleckman, 1998). Schemes, such as the Worker Rights Consortium (WRC) and the Clean Clothes Campaign (CCC), adopt more rigorous monitoring procedures but directly engage far fewer companies.

In response to criticism and so-called learning by doing, several schemes have belatedly strengthened disclosure requirements. The United Nations Global Compact, for example, issued new guidelines in July 2005 requiring participating companies to disclose annually what actions they have taken to implement the Global Compact Principles, in order to avoid being declared 'inactive'. A mild complaints procedure was also introduced. Similarly, in February 2006, the IFC revised its social and environmental standards for private sector projects in which it participates. The new standards include provisions for greater disclosure of information to the public by IFC and client companies, and contain stronger requirements for community engagement and consultation, biodiversity protection, community and worker grievance mechanisms, use of security forces, and greenhouse gas monitoring. The Equator Principles were also revised in July 2006, taking into account the new IFC guidelines and some NGO concerns.

Third, some schemes tend to be fairly top-down, technocratic and couched in a discourse that frowns upon 'command and control' regulation, which is deemed unworkable, too slow or outmoded. In contrast, voluntary approaches tend to be portrayed as innovative, pragmatic, consensual and modern. In a similar vein, various forms of protest and confrontational activism, which have played a crucial role in improving corporate social and environmental performance, are deemed to be ideological or passé (SustainAbility, 2003).

The tendency to marginalize the role of public policy and to emphasize the role of selected actors and institutions in the promotion of socially responsible business partly explains the minimalist role often assigned to local and national institutions in developing countries in the design and implementation of CSR standards (Kemp, 2001; Ascoly and Zeldenrust, 2001). While some multi-stakeholder approaches have governance structures that are genuinely participatory, others have not. Key actors or stakeholders, notably workers or trade unions, and relevant interest groups in developing countries, are sometimes poorly represented and relatively voiceless in the Northern-centric consultation and decision-making processes that often characterize multi-stakeholder initiatives (Bendell, 2004; Utting, 2002a).

Fourth, some schemes have not seriously addressed the question of what impact CSR is having on developing countries and the possible tensions and contradictions between CSR and development (Blowfield, 2004; Kabeer, 2004; UNRISD, 2004). It is often assumed that anything that involves improved environmental and social standards in TNC supply chains or small and medium-sized enterprises must be good for development. But this 'do-gooding' or 'win–win' approach can ignore key development issues, priorities and realities in developing countries; certain stakeholders; and the fact that raising environmental and social standards implies costs that may constrain enterprise development and employment generation, and that CSR supply chain management may be a way for TNCs to pass costs on to suppliers. It also tends to ignore more fundamental structural issues associated with corporate power and certain competitive, fiscal and lobbying practices of TNCs that are implicated in the broader problem of unsustainable or maldevelopment.

CORPORATE ACCOUNTABILITY

The above discussion suggests that two of the fundamental problems confronting the CSR agenda relate to regulation and development. The former is being addressed, to some extent, by the emerging corporate accountability 'movement', made up primarily of NGOs, trade union organizations, scholars and related networks, but also certain mainstream political and business actors and institutions. Whereas the CSR movement of the 1980s and 1990s was led mainly by business organizations and professionalized NGOs, now Northern governments and multilateral organizations are more involved.

The process of ratcheting-up voluntary initiatives, or the gradual hardening of softer approaches, has recently entered a new phase. This involves an approach to regulation that emphasizes not only more effective codes of conduct, monitoring, reporting and certification systems but also recourse to public policy and law. This new approach is encapsulated in the term 'corporate accountability'. In contrast to the conventional notion of CSR, which implies self-regulation, voluntarism and ethical responsibility, corporate accountability implies answerability, or an obligation to answer to different stakeholders, and an element of enforceability, where non-compliance results in some sort of penalty (Newell, 2002; Bendell, 2004). It also implies applicability or universality, in the sense that CSR standards apply to a far broader range of companies, rather than simply to those individual companies that choose to adopt voluntary initiatives (Dwight Justice, cited in UNRISD, 2004). Some strands of the corporate accountability movement are concerned with mechanisms that not only hold corporations to account but also curb the concentration of corporate power.[7]

In recent years, there has been a wave of international agreements, proposals and campaigns associated with corporate accountability. Many of these initiatives are led by civil society organizations.

- Friends of the Earth International proposed that the 2002 World Summit on Sustainable Development (WSSD) consider a Corporate Accountability Convention that would establish and enforce minimum environmental and social standards, encourage effective reporting and provide incentives for TNCs taking steps to avoid negative impacts. The International Forum on Globalization has advocated the creation of a United Nations Organization for Corporate Accountability that would provide information on corporate practices as a basis for legal actions and consumer boycotts. Christian Aid has proposed the establishment of a Global Regulation Authority that would establish norms for TNC conduct, monitor compliance and deal with breaches.
- Several trade union and non-governmental organizations in the United States have launched the International Right to Know campaign to demand legislation that would oblige US companies or foreign companies traded on the US stock exchanges to disclose information on the operations of their overseas affiliates and major contractors.
- There have been calls, particularly in the United States, for the 're-chartering' of corporations, to revive a system whereby states granted corporations a charter. This license to operate stipulated certain responsibilities and obligations and, periodically, had to be renewed.

- In the United Kingdom, over 100 civil society, party political and other organizations have joined the Corporate Responsibility Coalition (CORE), which is calling for mandatory triple bottom line reporting, legal liability for human rights and environmental abuses committed by UK companies abroad, and extending the director's duties so that they take into account not only the impact of decisions on shareholders but also their impact on other stakeholders.
- Various NGOs and lawyers have called not only for extending international legal obligations to TNCs in the field of human rights but also for bringing corporations under the jurisdiction of the International Criminal Court.
- In 2002, a coalition of civil society organizations and the financier, George Soros, launched the Publish What You Pay Campaign, which calls for a regulatory approach to ensure that extractive companies in the oil and mining industries disclose the net amount of payments made to national governments.

Governmental, regional and multilateral institutions have promoted various initiatives, including the following, which are relevant from the perspective of environmental protection and environmental justice:

- The Voluntary Principles on Security and Human Rights were launched by the US and UK governments in 2000. Supported by several NGOs and companies in the extractive industries, as well as the governments of Norway and the Netherlands, the Principles aim to facilitate risk assessments, strengthen human rights safeguards in security arrangements, improve company relations with local communities and mitigate any potential for conflict.
- A UK law requires pension funds to report on social and environmental aspects. In early 2005, the Labour government published a draft 'corporate manslaughter' bill which, if passed, would hold companies criminally liable for deaths arising from gross negligence on the part of senior management. The French government requires all nationally listed corporations to report on a range of sustainability issues.
- The European Parliament passed a resolution in 1999 calling for a code of conduct for European TNCs operating in developing countries, and in 2002 the European Commission presented a strategy to promote CSR.
- The United Nations Sub-Commission on the Promotion and Protection of Human Rights adopted, in 2003, the United Nations Norms on the Responsibilities of Transnational Corporations and

Other Business Enterprises with Regards to Human Rights. The Norms failed to get the political backing from the Commission on Human Rights, which is required for them to become international law. The Commission did, however, pass a resolution to appoint a Special Representative of the UN Secretary-General to continue the process of dialogue on this issue, and a group of ten global corporations agreed to participate in the Business Leaders Initiative on Human Rights to explore how the Norms could be applied in practice.

- The Guidelines for Multinational Enterprises of the Organization for Economic Co-operation and Development (OECD) were revised in 2000, in part by strengthening aspects related to internal environmental management systems and greater disclosure on environmental information, and by enhancing the role of 'national contact points', which constitute a form of complaints procedure.
- The Convention on Access to Information, Public Participation in Decision-making and Access to Justice in Environmental Matters, also know as the Aarhus Convention, was adopted in 1998. A compliance procedure was adopted in 2002, and in 2004 the Complaints Committee began to hear submissions from NGOs alledging non-compliance with the Convention (Abrahams, 2004). A legally-binding Pollutant Release and Transfer Register Protocol was also adopted in 2003.
- Building upon the Food and Agriculture Organization of the United Nations (FAO) voluntary International Code of Conduct on the Distribution and Use of Pesticides, the Rotterdam Convention on Prior Informed Consent, which aims to regulate the export of hazardous chemicals, was adopted in 1998 and entered into force in 2004.

While standard-setting and other regulatory action related to CSR are often undertaken by self-appointed entities whose accountability to external agents may be quite limited, the theory and practice of corporate accountability highlights issues of legitimacy and democratic governance, including the question of who decides and who speaks for whom. It also focuses attention on complaints procedures or complaints-based systems of regulation that facilitate the task of identifying, investigating, publicizing and seeking redress for specific instances of corporate malpractice. As discussed below, this is an alternative or complementary approach to regulatory systems that involve broad but relatively superficial systems of reporting, monitoring, auditing and certification.

Corporate accountability also suggests that if CSR is to be meaningful and really work for development and democratic governance, then it is not enough for companies to improve selected aspects of environmental management systems and working conditions, and to engage in community projects and corporate giving. Structural and macro-policy issues also need to be addressed, including, for example, perverse patterns of labor market flexibilization and subcontracting that can result in the deterioration of labor standards and labour rights in developing countries (Cappellin and Giuliani, 2004; Sood and Arora, 2006); corporate taxation and transfer pricing practices that deprive developing country governments and economies of essential resources (Riesco, 2005); the concentration of economic power in large companies and their competitive advantage over small enterprises and infant industries (van Tudler, 2002; Zammit, 2003); and the political influence of TNCs and business-interest lobbies (Bhagwati, 2004; Balanyá et al., 2000).

ARTICULATED REGULATION

An important contribution of some of the analysis, activism and policy proposals associated with co-regulation and corporate accountability is that they go beyond the conventional polarized debate about the virtues and limitations of voluntary versus mandatory approaches. This debate has been useful for demystifying the somewhat utopian and feel-good discourse of win–win scenarios and 'partnerships' that embellishes CSR and fails to problematize sufficiently the role of TNCs in global governance and development. It has also been useful in highlighting the tensions and trade-offs between different regulatory approaches, and in reminding the critics of corporate globalization of the regulatory limitations – past and present – of both state and multilateral institutions. But the polarized nature of the debate has diverted attention away from the interface of so-called soft and hard, or voluntary and legalistic approaches, which is potentially a fruitful area for regulatory intervention. If co-regulation or collaborative governance refer to the coming together – through multi-stakeholder initiatives, participatory decision-making processes and partnerships – of different actors to facilitate the design and implementation of standards, what might be called 'articulated regulation' refers to the coming together of different regulatory approaches in ways that are complementary, mutually reinforcing and synergistic, or less contradictory. Some of the discussion and proposals related to corporate accountability center on more complex or pluralistic institutional arrangements that occupy this terrain.

This section discusses four forms of articulated regulation. The discussion is not meant to suggest that other regulatory approaches are inconsequential or unnecessary, or indeed that the approaches mentioned here necessarily have positive outcomes from the perspective of sustainable development. It merely suggests the need to think beyond the voluntary versus binding, soft versus hard dichotomy, and to expand, in a sense, the notion of co-regulation, which has focused primarily on the articulation of actors – for example, business interests, NGOs and multilateral organizations – usually for the purpose of designing and implementing voluntary initiatives or public–private partnerships.

Articulating Non-Governmental Systems of Regulation

The first type of articulated regulation involves complementarities between different forms of private and non-governmental authority. O'Rourke and others have examined the need and scope for building complementarity between the different emerging systems of non-governmental labor regulation (O'Rourke, 2003; see also Sabel et al., 2000). As noted above, some multi-stakeholder initiatives are more effective than others in relation to different regulatory functions. The notion of articulated regulation, then, relates partly to 'connecting these initiatives in some inter-operable way [that] might help to overcome the challenges of access, scope and credibility' (O'Rourke, 2003).

Complementarity within non-governmental systems is particularly important in relation to trade unions and NGOs. Despite some progress in terms of dialogue and collaboration via certain multi-stakeholder and other initiatives, there is still considerable tension between some trade union organizations and NGOs that are working with companies and multi-stakeholder initiatives to promote labor standards and rights. Much of this tension revolves around trade union concerns that many NGOs are largely unaccountable, are not legitimate representatives of workers, and that the CSR initiatives and processes they propose are largely detached from democratic processes and public policy, or deflect attention from fundamental issues such as the denial of labor rights in China and other countries (UNRISD, 2004; Utting, 2002a). Some NGOs, for their part, tend to regard trade union structures as ossified, corrupt and patriarchal. Certain multi-stakeholder initiatives such as the WRC and the CCC have promoted more collaborative relationships and forms of participation.

One particular area where the complementarity and interoperability of non-governmental systems needs to be strengthened relates to complaints procedures. In the debate about CSR and its capacity to regulate corporate behavior, considerable attention has focused on developing standards and systems related to monitoring, verification and reporting. While this focus has played an important role in highlighting the limits of internal monitoring and the need for hard data, more systemic approaches and independent verification, the NGOs and companies involved face the somewhat daunting task of gathering information and checking on the implementation of numerous standards contained in codes of conduct and reporting and certification guidelines throughout vast corporate structures and ever-lengthening global supply chains. They often rely on commercial auditing techniques and analytical frameworks that ignore the root causes of non-compliance and fail to obtain reliable information from workers, producers, managers and communities (Maquila Solidarity Network, 2005; O'Rourke, 2000). Both the cost and complexity of such 'extensive' approaches seriously compromise their feasibility and scaling-up (Utting, 2002a).

A complementary regulatory arrangement involves strengthening more 'intensive' approaches involving various forms of complaints procedures or complaints-based systems of regulation. Rather than trying to span a broad spectrum of TNC activities, complaints procedures enable different types of stakeholders and entities to identify specific abuses or instances of malpractice. Numerous types of institutions can and do function on the basis of complaints procedures. Trade unions, for example, often take action when a company is in breach of a specific component of a collective bargaining agreement. Watchdog NGOs, ombudsman-type institutions, the judicial process and the investigative media also function on the basis of complaints procedures. The OECD's National Contact Points constitute a complaints procedure. Some of the non-governmental regulatory institutions, such as the WRC and the CCC, function wholly or partly on the basis of complaints procedures, and other multi-stakeholder initiatives, such as the FLA, have adopted such processes.

The Confrontation–Collaboration Nexus

The notion of articulating different forms of non-governmental regulation can also be applied to the interface between formal non-governmental regulatory systems involving standard-setting and related operational activities, and the informal realm of social activism or 'street regulation'. The dynamism and effectiveness of particular CSR initiatives is often linked to this dual presence of 'collaboration' and 'confrontation' (Bendell and Murphy, 2002; Utting, 2005). Whereas collaboration can serve to construct a road map for reform and institutionalize the reform process, confrontation is often crucial for generating the political will needed to change the status quo, and keep the reform process 'honest' and dynamic. Confrontational activism, including various types of protest, campaigns, watch-dog activities and 'naming and shaming', remains a key driver of voluntary initiatives, despite the tendency of some CSR leaders and practitioners to argue that social militancy is a thing of the past and that stakeholder dialogue and partnerships are the key for advancing the CSR agenda.

It is the co-existence of these two forms of civil society regulatory action that often accounts for the ratcheting-up and scaling-up of particular multi-stakeholder initiatives. Sustained 'anti-' movements, such as the anti-sweatshop and anti-logging campaigns, are particularly important in this regard, and partly explain the dynamism and uptake of schemes associated with the FLA and the Forest Stewardship Council (Conroy, 2002).

Voluntary and Legalistic Approaches

A third form of articulated regulation refers to the arena where voluntary and legalistic approaches or public policy interact in a complementary or synergistic way (Gunningham and Sinclair, 2002; UNRISD, 2004; Utting, 2002a; Ward, 2003). Over and above the fact that CSR should imply respect for existing environmental, labor and human rights law, and involve going 'beyond compliance', articulation can manifest itself in numerous ways.

International soft law, which is the basis of many CSR standards, may be non-binding but nevertheless carries moral authority. It is applicable to a broad universe of agents (for example, all governments or corporations), and may encourage or require national governments to incorporate its provisions in legislation at the national level. This has occurred to some extent, for example, in the case of the International Code of Conduct on the Distribution and Use of Pesticides.

Hard law may demand voluntary approaches, for example, requiring companies to be more transparent and to report on their social or environmental performance but not specifying what that performance should be. If performance standards are found to be low, then it is up to such actors and entities as civil society organizations, the media and public opinion to expose, name and shame or otherwise bring pressure to bear on a company to improve its performance. Pollutant Release and Transfer Registers (PRTRs), which impose reporting obligations on companies producing toxic substances, now exist in certain countries, as well as internationally through the PRTR Protocol signed in 2003.

Other laws related, for example, to freedom of association and freedom of information, pave the way for CSR by creating an enabling institutional environment, which safeguards and facilitates the role of actors and organizations that can exert pressures on companies, such as trade unions, NGOs and the media. And laws on misrepresentation and false advertising frame voluntary reporting by companies (Ward, 2003, p. 5).

Forms of 'negotiated agreements', which are sometimes used in the field of waste management and other areas of environmental protection, establish legally grounded objectives or targets, and involve some element of sanction in cases of non-compliance, but they grant the companies involved the flexibility to decide how to comply in the most cost-effective way (Hanks, 2002).

The mere threat of mandatory regulation, at both national and international levels, has long been a crucial driver of voluntary CSR action and soft law. The voluntary guidelines for transnational corporations and international codes of conduct that were established in the 1970s emerged in a context where several developing-country governments were calling for binding regulations on TNCs. More recently, the considerable impetus behind voluntary company triple bottom line reporting and revenue transparency in the United Kingdom has occurred in a context where a broad-based coalition of actors has called for mandatory reporting.

Litigation has important implications for CSR. Cases of 'foreign direct liability', for example, where parent companies are held legally accountable in their home countries for malpractice abroad, aim 'to generate legal precedents at the boundaries of CSR' (Ward, 2003: 7).

Public policy can promote voluntary initiatives through market-based incentives associated, for example, with taxation, subsidies and credit (Welford, 2002).

Stock market regulations can require all listed companies to adopt CSR standards. The listing of certain South African companies, for example, on the New York Stock Exchange appears to have prompted some improvements in corporate social and environmental performance in South Africa. And in the country itself, the Johannesburg Stock Exchange now requires listed companies to adhere to the King Report's Code of Corporate Practice and Conduct (Fig et al., 2003; International Labour Office (ILO) Socio-Economic Security Programme, 2004).

CSR standards may be incorporated into contracts of different types, for example, agreements related to international investment and trade (UNCTAD, 2003), or contracts of chief executive officers (CEOs) which specify the use of CSR indicators in performance reviews and the calculation of bonuses.[8] The Voluntary Principles on Security and Human Rights have been incorporated into legal agreements involving host governments and oil companies (Commission on Human Rights, 2006).

Voluntary initiatives that are derived from international law or are adopted by democratically elected governments or intergovernmental processes are often considered to have greater legitimacy and carry more legal weight (Bernstein and Cashore, 2004). This point is often emphasized by those in the legal community, as well as by some trade union organizations that are concerned about the increasing role of largely unaccountable NGOs in designing labor standards (UNRISD, 2004).

While the United Nations Global Compact has been used to fend off harder regulatory initiatives, it also can be said to articulate voluntary and legalistic approaches, given the fact that it promotes principles derived from international law and reinforces the notion that international human rights law applies not only to states but also to corporations.

Articulation may be sequential, with voluntary initiatives paving the way for harder or legalistic initiatives once a particular standard which gains broader 'cultural' acceptance, is internalized by business and other actors, and when coalitions of organizations and actors backing the ratcheting-up of standards or legalistic approaches expand, sometimes with the support of certain business interests.

Articulation applies more generally to the interface between CSR and public governance, and the need to recognize that voluntary approaches often work best 'where government and the public sector is effective, predictable and clear . . . where citizens and workers are empowered and human rights are respected; and where principles and institutions of justice . . . public participation and access to information are all recognized' (Halina Ward, quoted in UNRISD, 2004).

Policy Coherence

The above forms of articulated regulation relate to approaches concerned explicitly with improving social, environmental and human rights aspects of company performance. The need to articulate regulatory systems is also apparent in another sense. Companies attempting to engage with the CSR agenda are typically enmeshed in two very different regulatory environments, one involving norms, rules and institutions that promote social and environmental protection; and another associated with a variety of incentives and pressures aimed at enhancing or securing conditions for profitability and growth through cost-reduction, deregulation and flexibilization. These two environments are in constant tension and, in some respects, are contradictory. This, of course, reflects the age-old tension between commodification, accumulation and efficiency, on the one hand, and social protection and equity, on the other hand, that has characterized development under capitalism. In certain historical contexts, however, as argued in the final section of this chapter, such contradictions have been managed through forms of articulated regulation that enable social and economic policies to be mutually reinforcing or at least less contradictory.

A fourth arena of articulated regulation, then, relates to the need for policies to work in tandem rather than against each other, or to constitute enabling rather than disabling environments for institutional reforms associated with the ratcheting-up and scaling-up of CSR and corporate accountability. Such 'policy coherence' is required both at the micro level of the firm and the macro level of government and international policies. The ratcheting-up and scaling-up of CSR and corporate accountability policies and practices currently confront two fundamental contradictions. Firstly, TNC affiliates and suppliers in global value chains are often confronted by seemingly contradictory policies of parent companies or large buyers, which insist on higher environmental and labor standards and compliance with codes of conduct, on the one hand, but simultaneously impose tough contract conditions that squeeze margins and delivery schedules, increasing the intensity of labor and overtime, on the other hand. Secondly, government and international policy often 'talk the talk' of social and sustainable development but 'walk the walk' of macroeconomic and other deregulatory policies that may inhibit growth, small enterprise development and infant industries, and result in the deterioration of the environment and labor standards, particularly in developing countries.

While such contradictions are, to some extent, features of certain patterns of capitalist development, they can be modified and managed in ways that are less contradictory. In relation to contradictions at the level of the firm it is important, for example, for companies to get CSR out of the ghetto of an individual office or unit, or even the mindset of a particular CEO, and attempt to mainstream or internalize CSR culture and policies throughout the corporate structure, to introduce CSR criteria into incentive systems, and not simply to impose tougher CSR conditions on suppliers but share responsibility for the costs involved, and ensure that CSR initiatives translate into productivity gains (Utting, 2003; Zadek, 2004).

In relation to the macro contradictions, particularly important are policies, laws and civil society campaigns related to rights-based approaches to development, environmental and social justice, tax justice, greater 'policy space' for developing countries,[9] more equitable North–South trade relations, and the democratization of international institutions. But policy coherence must also address the contradictions mentioned above between economic development and CSR and corporate accountability initiatives that aim to raise environmental and labor standards. Proponents of these approaches need to be more sensitive to the developmental implications of their proposals and initiatives, and to recognize that efforts to improve standards in developing countries need to be accompanied by – and should not contradict – efforts to enhance the capacity and competitive position of local firms, to create a more equitable playing field internationally, and to realize the principle of 'special and differential treatment' for developing countries.

From the perspective of sustainable development, policy incoherence related to CSR and corporate accountability also manifests itself in the fact that investment and consumption patterns remain largely off-limits in the CSR agenda. Instead attention still tends to focus on eco-efficiency, sometimes defined in terms of how to produce more with less (Holliday et al., 2002; Welford, 2002). Even in the current context of high oil prices and threats to supplies, as well as increasing global awareness of global warming, CSR discourse and initiatives in the oil industry often ignore the bigger picture. Companies like BP may be trying to rebrand themselves as going 'Beyond Petroleum', but reality is more complex. Some shareholders and companies are paying greater attention to investment in renewables and natural gas, but more immediate concerns with energy shortages, high oil prices and extraordinary profits appear to have stimulated greater investment not only in traditional exploration or sites, but also in so-called unconventionals (such as tar sands, shale and coal-bed methane) that have worrisome environmental implications. Shell reportedly claims that, within a decade, unconventionals could make up more than one-fifth of the company's total resource base (*The Economist*, 2005; Utting and Ives, 2006).

THE DETERMINANTS OF PROGRESSIVE INSTITUTIONAL REFORM

Why are we seeing an apparent ratcheting-up of standards, and regulatory authority being increasingly assumed by civil society organizations and multi-stakeholder entities? Are these developments likely to overcome the limitations, referred to above, that often characterize multi-stakeholder approaches and non-governmental regulatory systems? And should we expect to see any significant progress on the CSR and corporate accountability fronts, in terms of these ad hoc initiatives and fledgling approaches becoming a more generalized feature or variant of stakeholder capitalism?

To answer these questions it is necessary to say something about the theory of institutional change and to weigh up the different factors and forces that shape institutional outcomes and trajectories of change. This requires looking at the way in which multiple factors and contexts associated with injustice or crisis, and the role of 'agency' and organized interests, as well as ideas, institutions and structures, intervene and interact. This type of analysis brings us, of course, to the age-old question that has preoccupied social scientists regarding the relative weight that should be accorded to structure and agency, social constructivism and realism, ideas and interests, social learning and societal pressures, and the relationship between them (Hall, 1993; Ruggie, 1998; Bøås and McNeill, 2004). A thorough examination along these lines is obviously beyond the scope of this chapter but it is important to refer to these sets of factors and determinants for three main reasons. First, because there is a tendency within the field of CSR and corporate accountability for different actors and perspectives to overstate the relative importance of one or other determinant to the exclusion of others. Second, the analysis of CSR is often compartmentalized in particular disciplines and subdisciplines, and different schools of thought often talk past, rather than to, each other. Third, a consideration of each aspect tells us something about the substance and limits of CSR and corporate accountability, and their transformative potential.

Crisis and Agency

A useful starting point is Polanyi's notion of the need for markets to be embedded in institutions that mitigate their negative social and environmental impacts, and his analysis of the 'double movement'. This suggested that the crude liberalization and excessive reliance on the self-regulating market that characterized late nineteenth-century globalization, was responsible for generating perverse social conditions, and a social and political reaction that resulted in the re-embedding of markets through various institutional and political arrangements (Polanyi, 1957). From this perspective, voluntary initiatives, corporate self-regulation and certain forms of non-governmental regulatory action can be seen as part and parcel of broader efforts to promote 'embedded liberalism' (Ruggie, 2003), or as important elements of a new social compact adapted to contemporary globalization (Hopkins, 1999), where openness of markets is secured on the basis of a compromise involving CSR.

In the 1980s and 1990s, a series of events and conditions contributed to the reality or perception that contemporary patterns of capitalist development and economic liberalization were fuelling crises of various sorts. These included signs of environmental crisis related to deforestation, the pollution or contamination of cities and rivers, global warming and ozone depletion; the human and developmental costs of structural adjustment programs and 'the race to the bottom'; persistent mass poverty and the growing gap between rich and poor; explicit manifestations of corporate greed and conspicuous consumption; and the growing imbalance between corporate rights and obligations. Public awareness and civil society concerns were heightened as a result of a series of high-profile cases involving TNCs. These included, for example, the Union Carbide gas leak in Bhopal, India in 1984; the Exxon-Valdez oil tanker disaster in 1989; deforestation or forest degradation associated with farming and forestry systems linked to McDonalds, Mitsubishi and Aracruz; environmental and social impacts, and human rights abuses, linked to mining and oil companies like Rio

Tinto and Shell; and sweatshop conditions in supply chains of Nike and other companies.

New social movements and transnational activism focused the spotlight on corporate malpractice and demanded institutional reforms. NGOs proliferated during this period and an increasing number began to engage with CSR issues. They assumed, however, certain characteristics that shaped their strategies, demands and proposals. Compared to corporatist entities such as trade unions, which had been one of the principal change agents of previous decades, NGOs were relatively weak and fragmented. Nor were they empowered through their relations with political parties, as the labor movement had been. And the types of demands they put forward as well as their tactics were conditioned by the tendency for many NGOs to become more involved in service delivery, consultative and commodified activities. There was, in fact, a blurring of the distinction between an important strand of 'civil society' and 'business' not only in terms of service activities but also in legal form, as some 'NGOs' established themselves as limited liability companies.

Certain strands of governance theory help to explain the evolving nature of attempts to bring big business under social control. Not only the perverse effects of commodification and economic liberalization but also the perceived or real limitations of government and intergovernmental regulation fueled the search for 'third way' alternatives. Furthermore, globalization, ever-expanding value chains, increasing complexity, uncertainty and risk require institutions at multiple levels that can enhance systemic coordination and stability. Forms of multiplayered and multilayered governance, where different actors (private, civil society, governmental and intergovernmental) come together both on an organizational basis in networks, and on an ideological and ethical basis through shared values and agreed norms (Keohane and Nye, 2002), appear to offer considerable potential in this regard. The political underpinnings of this approach have to do not only with the reality or threat of pressure 'from below' but also new configurations of power involving multiple actors at different levels (Held, 2003).

The role of agency in shaping the CSR agenda relates, of course, as much to the political strategies of corporations and business organizations as it does to civil society actors. It was the large global brand name companies that were particularly susceptible to the above pressures, and they mobilized effectively to influence, if not lead, the CSR 'movement' (Utting, 2005) and to shape the agenda on their terms. This leadership role – and the shift from reactive or defensive posturing to proactive engagement, noted above – can be usefully explained in Gramscian terms (Levy and Newell, 2002). Throughout much of the history of capitalism, elites have attempted to rule through consensus or 'hegemony'. This involves not only accommodating certain oppositional demands but also exercising moral, cultural and intellectual leadership (Utting, 2002b). Such an approach is particularly obvious in the field of CSR and in relation to big business engagement with multi-stakeholder approaches and public–private partnerships. Through such arrangements big business has skillfully opened up or accessed another arena for shaping the public policy process (Richter, 2001, 2003).

French regulation theory provides further insights into the capacity of capitalist elites and relations to adapt in socially sensitive ways in order to secure conditions for ongoing and long-term accumulation (Lipietz, 1992). Crucial in this regard is the role of extra-economic factors (of the type typically associated with CSR), namely institutions, shared visions, agreed standards, networks, partnerships and new modes of calculation (Jessop, 1999). Also relevant for the analysis of CSR is the capacity of systems to adapt to a large extent on their own terms and to resist external interventions (Jessop, 1999).

Indeed, a major challenge to the corporate accountability agenda comes from certain organized business interests that have proved quite adept at mobilizing to resist certain efforts to strengthen the regulatory environment. This can be seen, for example, in the political backlash in the United States against attempts to reapply the Alien Torts Claims Act (ATCA)[10] (Taylor, 2004). Or it can take the form of attempts to reassert the model of softer voluntary approaches and corporate self-regulation, albeit with some fine-tuning and compromises.

In the realm of international policy-making related to corporate regulation, the discourse and practice of voluntary initiatives has long been used as a means of crowding out the consideration or adoption of other regulatory approaches. The use of the soft to displace the hard was seen clearly at the WSSD in Johannesburg when business interests rallied against certain proposals for 'corporate accountability', arguing that their involvement in company reporting and public–private partnerships obviated the need for harder regulatory action. And even many of the partnership proposals that were announced at the summit have not been implemented (Commission on Sustainable Development, 2004).

A similar response is playing out in relation to the UN Norms on the Responsibilities of TNCs and Other Business Enterprises with Regard to Human Rights, referred to above.[11] The Norms attempt to address some of the weaknesses that characterize the Global Compact and voluntary initiatives more generally, namely picking and choosing among standards, weak compliance with agreed standards, and free-riders. The Norms pull together a wide range of standards that are derived from international law that applies to states, but which are commonly found in multi-stakeholder initiatives. They state that all TNCs and related companies have an obligation to uphold such standards, and they propose an implementation and monitoring mechanism. They push the envelope even further by stipulating 'adequate reparation' in cases of stakeholders affected by non-compliance.

Some of these harder aspects were anathema to certain business interests and governments, and the 2004 session of the UN Commission on Human Rights, which considered the draft Norms, not only reminded the Sub-Commission on the Promotion and Protection of Human Rights that the Norms had no legal status and that it was not to perform any monitoring function, but also that it had never been asked to draft any such norms in the first place (ECOSOC, 2004). One of the reasons put forward by opponents was that they were essentially unnecessary since voluntary instruments such as the Global Compact and the OECD Guidelines on Multinational Corporations already exist. This was the position, for example, of the International Chamber of Commerce.

At the April 2005 session of the Commission on Human Rights, there was a new twist in the process of considering the Norms. A resolution, originally proposed by the United Kingdom and several other governments, was passed that omitted all reference to the Norms. These were seen as divisive and an obstacle to achieving the type of broad-based consensus needed to move forward. It was agreed, however, to continue the dialogue on business and human rights via the appointment by the United Nations Secretary-General of a Special Representative. A block of mainly developing countries, which included South Africa, Egypt and Cuba, as well as several NGOs, pushed unsuccessfully for an amended resolution that not only acknowledged the groundwork that had already been done via the Norms but also incorporated references to regulatory and developmental problems associated with TNCs and corporate power.[12] While most governments and NGOs welcomed the appointment of a Special Representative, there were concerns that an agreement to keep talking and not to build on the Norms represented a step backwards.

The interim report of the Special Representative, published in February 2006, appeared to side with the opinion of the ICC and some business leaders by dismissing the Norms as a 'distraction'. Even the wording coincided with that apparently used by one of industry's most prominent proponents of voluntary CSR approaches in a consultation organized three months earlier.[13] Instead, the way forward lay with 'principled pragmatism' (Commission on Human Rights, 2006), an approach that would essentially continue the process of scaling-up and ratcheting-up existing voluntary initiatives, and expanding forms of 'collaborative governance' involving co-regulatory or multi-stakeholder initiatives, as well as some of the regulatory initiatives referred to above that operate at the interface of voluntary and legalistic approaches. Specific reference was made to such aspects as extending the extraterritorial application of some home countries' jurisdiction for the extreme human rights abuses committed by their firms abroad; best practice learning and capacity-building in developing countries; the development of effective impact assessment tools; and extending CSR and monitoring initiatives to state-owned enterprises.

Ideas, Knowledge and Learning

Crisis, interest group contestation and political maneuvering only partly explain why particular agendas and processes of institutional reform emerge. It is also important to consider other conditions and contexts related to the role of ideas, how knowledge becomes embedded, and the ways in which pre-existing institutions and structures shape the substance, scope and pace of reform.[14]

Concerning the role of ideas, certain terms, concepts and schools of thought have been up for grabs and have been quickly assimilated and disseminated by key actors that are shaping the CSR agenda. The speed and force with which particular ideas have informed global discourse may say as much about the consolidated and globalizing nature of so-called epistemic communities (Haas, 1990), that is, the formal and informal networks through which ideas are disseminated and learning takes place, as it does about the inherent worth of the ideas themselves. The notion of epistemic communities is also useful for nuancing the idea that the uptake of new thinking and policies is essentially a function of the capacity of powerful actors and institutions to impose them on others. In the field of CSR such communities are particularly strong, involving not only experts and advocates associated with civil society, business, governmental and international organizations, but also scholars in higher education, notably the field of business administration, which has expanded massively since the 1980s. The internalization of new ideas should also be analysed in the context of changes occurring in management and technocratic culture where, to some extent, reflexivity and social learning have become more prominent features of both private and public bureaucracies in the modern era of risk and complexity (Hall, 1993; Ruggie, 1998).

What are the sets of ideas that have shaped the mainstream CSR agenda? Particularly influential have been those associated with ecological modernization, new institutional economics (NIE), and stakeholder and organizational theory. Ecological modernization highlighted the role of technological and managerial innovations in improving the efficiency of resource use; win–win, as opposed to zero-sum, scenarios; systems-based approaches, and the capacity of existing institutions to internalize care for the environment, without fundamental restructuring (Hajer, 1995). NIE emphasized the need for institutions that can minimize transaction costs (Toye, 1995). These include risks to corporate reputation and sales posed by activists and 'ethical consumers', or risks and uncertainty that derive from the rapidly changing geography and structures of production and exchange in the context of globalization. Formal and informal institutions are needed to minimize such risks and to reinforce corporate control over suppliers and other stakeholders associated with global value chains. Thinking related to the concept of social capital, which emphasizes the economic benefits derived from collaborative relations and trust, reinforced this approach. CSR, multi-stakeholder initiatives and public–private partnerships are particularly relevant in this regard (Utting, 2000, 2002b).

From the field of management studies emerged various concepts that have influenced CSR policy and practice. The type of systems-based management approaches and the notion of responsiveness to selected stakeholders (for example, customers) that underpinned the concept of total quality management[15] resonated with stakeholder theory. The latter questioned the notion that the social responsibility of an enterprise consisted solely of making money for its owners or shareholders. The critique that developed in the 1970s and 1980s emphasized the multiple responsibilities of companies beyond the purely economic, and the fact that sound or strategic management required responsiveness and accountability to a variety of stakeholders who affect or are affected by the operations of a company (Freeman, 1984). Since the notion of 'responsibility' relates to the realm of ethics and principles, attention soon turned to the nuts and bolts of how to improve the quality of CSR actions or 'corporate social performance', which includes not only motivating principles but also processes and observable outcomes (Hopkins, 1999). Engagement with stakeholders was crucial not just for ethical reasons but also for key aspects of management associated with organizational learning, knowledge management and various advantages that derive from networking (Ruggie, 2001; Zadek, 2001).

While these ideas challenged some aspects of neoliberal and management orthodoxy that had disregarded the reality of market failure and the complex determinants of successful enterprise, they did not really question fundamentals to do with labour market flexibilization, structural adjustment, free trade and investment, the downsizing of the state, and corporate-driven globalization.

The ideas taken up by the corporate accountability movement, however, were somewhat different. Two strands of thinking were particularly influential: rights-based approaches to development, and anti- or alternative globalization. The former not only emphasized the recognition of human rights as an objective of development, but also emphasized the key role of legal instruments at international, regional and national levels (Overseas Development Institute, 1999). For some, rights-based approaches also included a strong political element, namely that of empowerment, or the notion that the recognition and realization of rights depended crucially on increasing the capacity of disadvantaged groups in society to exert claims on the powerful. Other challenges were posed by activists and scholars who were highly critical of dominant patterns of globalization and adhered to the slogan of the World Social Forum that 'A Better World is Possible'. Those calling for a more fundamental reshaping or rolling-back of globalization emphasized the need to reassert social control over corporations via civil society, social movements, national policy and regulations, and international rules designed and implemented by democratic institutions; the downsizing or break-up of corporations; halting altogether certain economic activities that have perverse social and environmental impacts; redirecting state resources and creating a policy environment conducive to local development and small enterprises; subsidiarity; and collective property rights (Broad, 2002).

Structural Constraints and Spaces

Civil society pressures, corporate political strategies and the role of ideas explain to a considerable extent the content and dynamics of the CSR and corporate accountability agendas and movements. Corporate engagement with the CSR agenda was relatively easy since it posed no fundamental threat to corporate interests or the dominant neoliberal macroeconomic regime. This agenda assumes that capitalism can largely reform itself through relatively minor adjustments to existing institutions.

Indeed, the pattern of institutional reform related to CSR is very much conditioned by a range of structural factors and contexts that work for and against CSR. When assessing the potential for CSR to impact business practices and improve working conditions, it is important to recognize the reality of enterprise and labor market structures. In developing countries, in particular, the bulk of labor is associated with the informal sector and most enterprise activity is associated with small and medium-sized enterprises (SMEs) that are either disconnected from, or loosely connected to, TNC supply chains (Zammit, 2003).

The pressures on companies to prioritize 'business-as-usual' practices and shareholder interests over other stakeholder interests are intense (Cutler, 2004), and they are institutionalized in legal and incentive structures, as well as in corporate or management culture. As noted above, this often results in onerous contract conditions and pressures on suppliers. Structural conditions associated with 'cheap consumerism' *à la* Wal-Mart also restrict the scope for expanding so-called ethical consumer markets for socially and environmentally produced products, and partly explain the stubbornness of fair trade and ethical investment markets to break out of their very niche status. Such structural constraints go some way to explaining the relatively weak uptake and implementation of many CSR initiatives, as well as the litany of cases or exposés of 'greenwash', 'bluewash' and malpractice involving so-called CSR companies, leaders and organizations.[16]

The problem, however, is not just that structural conditions impose limits on CSR, or that perversity and do-gooding coexist; it is also that the scaling-up of the CSR agenda or the process of embedding liberalism seem to be dwarfed by ongoing economic liberalization or 'disembedding' of the type exposed by Joseph Stiglitz in *The Roaring Nineties* (2004), theorized by Mark Blyth in *Great Transformations* (2002) and documented empirically by the International Labour Office (ILO Socio-Economic Security Programme, 2004). Yet the scale of this disembedding is often downplayed or wished away in mainstream CSR discourse, or it is assumed that the CSR snowball, as it gathers momentum, will eventually outstrip and overtake any disembedding process.

In practice, as noted above, we do see some ratcheting-up and scaling-up of voluntary CSR standards and implementation procedures. The question that needs to be asked, however, is how does this process fare in relation to counter-trends involving ratcheting-down, that is, with policies and processes associated with economic liberalization or disembedding that can have perverse social, environmental and other developmental impacts. If one considers the pace and scale of certain policies and processes that characterize neoliberal reform, then one might be excused from concluding that any scaling-up or ratcheting-up of CSR pales in comparison. Such policies and processes include 'flexibilization' of labor markets and subcontracting that often undermine labor standards and labor rights; permissive fiscal 'reform' and tax avoidance and evasion that reduce corporate taxation and deprive developing country governments of revenues; and the so-called 'race to the bottom' or cut-and-run tactics that see companies relocate to countries where labor costs and labor rights impose fewer constraints.[17]

They also include the downsizing of state institutions and the rolling-back of state services and welfare benefits. In such a context, the question to be asked of CSR is not only whether voluntary initiatives are going beyond the minimum social and environmental standards set by law, but also whether companies are filling the gaps associated with state retrenchment.

It would be wrong to assume, however, that basic structural contexts and trends associated with capitalism and corporate globalization make a nonsense of CSR; that is, the profit motive, shareholder interests or TNC strategies are at odds with forms of do-gooding that may detract from short-term shareholder returns, contradict the tendency to externalize costs, or actually increase costs (Henderson, 2001). While possibly overstated, there is some validity to the assertion, continually emphasized by CSR exponents and business leaders, that there is a business case for CSR and scope for win–win opportunities related to improved social, labor and environmental performance, on the one hand, and competitive advantage, risk and reputation management, productivity gains related, for example, to employee motivation and reduced staff turnover, and even cost reduction through aspects such as eco-efficiency, on the other hand (Porter and van der Linde, 1995; Holliday et al., 2002).

As noted above, it is also wrong to assume crudely that labor and environmental conditions are particularly bad in TNC production facilities located in developing countries or even in Export Processing Zones. In terms of some indicators, such as health and safety standards, pay, and pollution per unit of output, they are often better than those found in other enterprises (Kabeer, 2004; UNRISD, 2005; Bhagwati, 2004). Of greater concern in some industries and countries is the tendency for TNCs to shed their core labor or expand production by relying more on subcontracting arrangements that are often associated with low pay, poor working conditions and non-existent labor rights (Razavi et al., 2004).

Just as structural factors can be invoked to explain the limits of CSR, they also explain, to some extent, the emergence and dynamism of CSR. Far from simply contradicting or constraining CSR, certain structural conditions that characterize contemporary capitalism and patterns of industrial organization actually suggest the need for institutional and management reforms of the type associated with CSR (Utting, 2000). This is apparent in relation to intangible assets, global value chains, flexibilization and the increasing number of factors and institutions that impact economic coordination systems.

Intangible assets such as brand names have increased dramatically in value. CSR is a crucial weapon to defend such brands against risks and to enhance brand value though improved company and product reputation and image (Jenkins, 2002). Global value chains have lengthened and deepened through foreign direct investment, networking and subcontracting. This expansion of relations with a broader range of enterprises is partly driven by the need for greater flexibility of production systems as companies seek to adjust quickly to rapid changes in consumer demand and new market opportunities. CSR institutions such as codes of conduct, certification and labelling can play an important role in the development of collaborative relations between the firms that make up a network or commodity chain. CSR has also become a key means of ensuring that the corporate centre in these systems controls the chain and links on the periphery of that chain, through, for example, the introduction of codes of conduct, certification and other requirements in supply chain management, or acquiring additional eyes and ears, not only through NGOs and auditing firms engaged in monitoring and certification, but also through the type of global framework agreements entered into with international trade union organizations (Utting, 2002a).

Given the scale and complexity of those systems, TNCs, as central players, and other organized business interests must preoccupy themselves not only with the more immediate aspects of production, marketing, costs of production, prices and profits, but also with a multiplicity of other institutions that facilitate the coordination and smooth functioning of economic systems (Shafaeddin, 2004; Hall and Soskice, 2001) and reduce transaction costs. Such institutions include, for example, networking, various types of alliances, partnerships, trusts, multi-stakeholder dialogue and so forth; that is, precisely the types of institutions and relations that characterize and are promoted by CSR.

While structural arguments are often used to explain or refute the possibility of CSR, the above discussion suggests that the structural context and its relationship with CSR is far more complex, and is likely to vary in different industry and societal settings, as well as under different varieties or models of capitalism. While it does not constitute the straitjacket that some critics portray, it does constrain the room for manoeuvre. But it can also facilitate some types of movement and approaches associated with CSR.

FUTURE DIRECTIONS

Let us now return to the question of what we can expect in terms of any significant advance on the CSR and corporate accountability fronts, and the institutionalization of these approaches as core components of a more generalized model of stakeholder capitalism.

As a general observation, despite some signs of a reaction to CSR,[18] we can probably expect more of the same in terms of gradual scaling-up and incremental ratcheting-up. Corporate bankruptcy scandals and more regular exposés of greenwash and bluewash have kept the perception and reality of crisis and the abuse of corporate power very much alive. This has served to sustain the pressures on global corporations to engage with the CSR agenda and for some hardening of softer approaches. Furthermore, the CSR service industry, which includes NGOs and multi-stakeholder initiatives, is expanding, and a growing body of governmental, regional and intergovernmental organizations are supporting such initiatives and approaches. The learning processes and 'path dependency' that characterize the CSR experience at the company and industry level also reinforce the tendency for incremental change, as does the fact that the ratcheting-up of CSR may be part and parcel of a political strategy to accommodate or fend off harder approaches related to corporate accountability and law. But it seems clear that any significant advance in relation to both mainstream CSR or the more transformative corporate accountability agenda would require a more conducive structural and political environment.

The challenge confronting the ratcheting-up and scaling-up of CSR is perhaps more substantive than political. Politically, the CSR movement is rather strong. Indeed, the reason CSR has been catapulted onto the world stage and become a standard feature of mainstream discourse, lies in the fact that it is being promoted by a fairly broad coalition of social forces. In fact, it has brought together the reformist wings of two of the most influential movements of modern times, namely, certain actors associated with neoliberalism and a looser melange of social forces and ideologies associated with sustainable development. Perhaps its weakest flank, politically, is that which involves the (economic) developmental constituency, comprising some Southern governments, economists and multilateral organizations. They are concerned with the protectionist, cost and employment implications of CSR, and see good government policy (social, labor market, industrial and macroeconomic) and democratic international governance – and not simply good company behavior – as the key to improving the social conditions of workers and communities (Bhagwati, 2004; DFID, 2003; Kabeer, 2004; UNCTAD, 1999; Zammit, 2003).

The major substantive weakness of the CSR agenda seems to reside in the fact that it is swimming against a strong current of neoliberal reform that promotes forms of deregulation and flexibilization – or disembedding – that often have the effect of lowering standards. Put another way, it attempts to modify relatively minor aspects of that reform project without seriously questioning its fundamentals. Whether by design or default, such fundamentals also relate to corporate power and the lobbying capacity and political influence of global corporations. In this regard, the key challenge confronting the CSR agenda appears to be its relationship to neoliberalism.

At best, CSR can contribute to raising awareness of certain social and environmental problems and serve to caution against blind faith in both market forces and state regulatory capacity. It may also reinforce some aspects of the normative culture and culture of compliance associated with rights-based approaches to development and governance (ODI, 1999), and add to the pool of institutions needed to ensure that markets behave more as the servants than the masters of humanity. Furthermore, we have seen that the CSR agenda is not static, but is constantly evolving and expanding, and is characterized by the gradual scaling-up of CSR initiatives and the incremental hardening of softer regulatory approaches, which derive from societal pressures, institutionalization and social learning.

At worst, CSR involves a transfer of regulatory authority to largely unaccountable agents and renders more stable and palatable a model of capitalism that generates or reinforces widespread social exclusion, inequality and environmental degradation. The likelihood that this worst-case scenario will materialize increases in contexts where the CSR agenda marginalizes issues of empowerment, redistribution, and the crucial role of public policy and trade unions in social protection and embedded liberalism. It will also gain ground where neoliberal reform projects are being actively pursued, and where the proponents of CSR disregard the multiple developmental implications of their own reform agenda and the concentration of economic power and political influence in TNCs.

The corporate accountability movement generally pays more attention to these aspects and is, therefore, quite different. Indeed, one way of characterizing and distinguishing the CSR and corporate accountability agendas is in terms of how they relate to three of the principal reform agendas of the contemporary era, namely neoliberalism, embedded liberalism and progressive variants of alternative globalization. The CSR agenda straddles both the neoliberal and embedded liberalism camps. To the extent that it works within the framework of economic liberalization and corporate-led globalization, the agenda is more palliative than transformative. The corporate accountability agenda also has one leg in the embedded liberalism camp, as is evident in the promotion of initiatives involving standard-setting, code implementation, monitoring and certification – or ratcheted-up variants of CSR. But it has another leg grounded in the anti- or alternative globalization camp where issues of redistribution, empowerment, participation and legalistic regulation of markets and corporations assume center stage.

As such, the corporate accountability agenda will inevitably face considerable opposition and resistance from the powers that be. In this sense, one of its main challenges is political, namely how to mobilize the social and political forces, and build the broad-based coalitions and networks required to promote progressive institutional change. This requires confronting the difficult question of alliances and compromises involving business interests, and exploring more systematically the potential for the type of complementary, synergistic and pluralistic approaches to regulation outlined above. It also requires reconnecting activism with democratic party politics and processes, and forging links between campaigns and different types of activism – notably trade unions and NGOs, as well as North and

South. Moving forward in this latter regard, however, will require greater sensitivity to development issues and the views and participation of governments and civil society actors from the global South.

NOTES

1. The term 'stakeholder capitalism' is usually employed to characterize a 'European' model where the interests of labor and social dialogue feature more prominently, as compared to an 'Anglo-Saxon' (United States and United Kingdom) model, which is thought to place more emphasis on the interests of shareholders. In the context of this chapter, the term is used more loosely as a convenient label to describe any model that in given historical contexts is noted for its social and redistributive features as in the case, for example, of early twentieth century Fordism in the United States, post-World War II social democracy in Europe, and the so-called corporate social welfare model in East Asia.
2. The term 'triple bottom line' refers not only to profitability but also to social and environmental objectives of business performance (Elkington, 1997).
3. See Prahalad (2005); United Nations Development Programme (UNDP) Commission on the Private Sector and Development (2004); World Commission on the Social Dimension of Globalization (2004); and United Nations Millennium Project (2005).
4. For data on the number of TNCs and TNC affiliates, see UNCTAD (2005).
5. While ISO 14001 certification continues to expand at a healthy rate, it is notable that the rate of expansion is far less than that achieved for quality management certification under the ISO 9000 series. Whereas 90 000 entities obtained ISO 14001 certification during the scheme's first ten years of existence, the corresponding figure for ISO 9000 certification of approximately 410 000 facilities was nearly five times greater (see ISO, 2004, 2005).
6. Of this 9 percent, two-thirds (6 percent) replied that 'change would have been difficult to implement without being a participant' while one-third (3 percent) replied that 'the change would not have happened without being a participant' (McKinsey & Company, 2004).
7. See, for example, International Forum on Globalization (2002) and Broad (2002).
8. See, for example, the commentary on the Norwegian company, Statoil, in ILO Socio-Economic Security Programme (2004, p. 357).
9. The term 'policy space' refers to the notion that developing-country governments should have more space to design policies attuned to local and national concerns, priorities, and economic, political and institutional realities, rather than be subservient to standardized policy prescriptions that emanate from international financial institutions and donor governments.
10. Through this law, passed in 1789, foreign nationals can bring a case to a US court for a civil wrong committed in violation of international law (Abrahams, 2004).
11. The Norms were drafted by a working group of experts established in 1999 by the United Nations Sub-Commission on the Promotion and Protection of Human Rights, adopted in their draft form by the sub-commission in August 2003, and submitted to the Commission on Human Rights.
12. The author participated in two of the meetings that considered the draft resolution.
13. In the consultation on Human Rights and the Extractive Industry, organized in November 2005 by the United Nations High Commissioner for Human Rights in cooperation with the Special Representative on Human Rights and TNCs, Sir Mark Moody Stuart, former Chairman of Royal Dutch/Shell and currently Chairman of Anglo American reportedly stated: 'the draft Norms . . . were a distraction in improving national legislation and building respect for human rights across the world. He said that

we did not need more high-level norms, but detailed multi-stakeholder work on how principles could be put into operating practice.' (ECOSOC, 2005, p. 6).

14. For a recent analysis of how modern capitalism has been shaped by the interplay of ideas, interests and institutions, see Blyth (2002). For a similar analysis related to corporate environmental responsibility, see the work of David Levy, including Levy and Newell (2002); Levy and Kolk (2002); and Levy and Egan (2003).
15. For a discussion on the links and parallels between total quality management and CSR or 'total responsibility management', see Waddock and Bodwell (2002).
16. 'Greenwash' is defined in the Oxford dictionary as 'Disinformation disseminated by an organization so as to present an environmentally responsible image.' The term 'bluewash' was coined to refer to the process of image enhancement that takes place when companies associate themselves with the United Nations (symbolized by its blue flag) (Bruno and Karliner, 2000; CorpWatch, 2000). In both cases, as Bruno and others point out, image enhancement often takes place against a backdrop where companies are doing little, if anything, to change their relationship to society and the environment significantly (Greer and Bruno, 1996). Various types of award schemes, such as the Greenwash Awards, organized by CorpWatch, and the Public Eye Awards in Davos, organized by Swiss-based NGOs, identify Global Compact and other companies that continue to act irresponsibly in relation to labor, environmental, human rights and fiscal practices (www.corpwatch.org and www.evb.ch, accessed in June 2005).
17. There are concerns, for example, that such practices will escalate with the phasing out of the Multi-Fibre Arrangement in January 2005. This deregulatory measure terminates the quotas on textile imports to the United States and Europe from developing countries.
18. Some suggest the need to jettison the CSR project, partly because of what are considered to be its flawed assumptions and negative impacts for individual firms in terms of cost, market access and competitiveness (Henderson, 2001; *The Economist*, 2005), as well as the fact that the privatization of regulatory authority transfers responsibility to largely undemocratic or unaccountable private and non-governmental institutions. From a developmental perspective, there are also concerns that CSR throws up barriers to trade and employment (Kabeer, 2004), and ultimately enhances the competitive advantage of big business.

REFERENCES

Abrahams, D. (2004), *Regulating Corporations: A Resource Guide*, Geneva: UNRISD.

Ascoly, N. and I. Zeldenrust (2001), *Discussing Key Elements of Monitoring and Verification*, Amsterdam: SOMO.

Balanyá, B., A. Doherty, O. Hoedeman, A. Ma'anit and E. Wesselius (2000), *Europe Inc.: Regional and Global Restructuring and the Rise of Corporate Power*, London: Pluto Press.

Bendell, J. (2004), 'Barricades and boardrooms: A contemporary history of the corporate accountability movement', United Nations Research Institute for Social Development (UNRISD) Programme on Technology, Business and Society paper no. 13, Geneva: UNRISD.

Bendell, J. and D.F. Murphy (2002), 'Towards civil regulation: NGOs and the politics of corporate environmentalism', in P. Utting (ed.), *The Greening of Business in Developing Countries: Rhetoric, Reality and Prospects*, London: Zed Books, pp. 245–67.

Bernstein, S. and B. Cashore (2004), 'The two-level logic of non-state global governance', paper prepared for the Conference on Changing Patterns of Authority in the Global Political Economy, University of Tübingen, Tübingen, Germany, 14-16 October.

Bhagwati, J. (2004), *In Defense of Globalization*, New York: Oxford University Press.

Blowfield, M. (2004), 'Implementation deficits of ethical trade systems: lessons from the Indonesian cocoa and timber industries', *Journal of Corporate Citizenship*, **13**, 77–90.

Blyth, M. (2002), *Great Transformations: Economic Ideas and Institutional Change in the Twentieth Century*, Cambridge: Cambridge University Press.

Bøås, M. and D. McNeill (2004), *Global Institutions and Development: Framing the World?* London: Routledge.

Braithwaite, J. and P. Drahos (2000), *Global Business Regulation*, Cambridge: Cambridge University Press.

Broad, R. (ed.) (2002), *Global Backlash: Citizen Initiatives for a Just World Economy*, New York: Rowman & Littlefield.

Broad, R. and J. Cavanagh (1999), 'The corporate accountability movement: lessons and opportunities', *Fletcher Forum of World Affairs*, **23** (2), 151–69.

Bruno, K. and J. Karliner (2000), *Tangled up in Blue: Corporate Partnerships at the United Nations*, San Francisco, CA: Transnational Resource and Action Center (TRAC).

Cappellin, P. and G.M. Giuliani (2004), 'The political economy of corporate responsibility in Brazil', UNRISD Programme on Technology, Business and Society paper no. 14, Geneva: UNRISD.

Commission on Human Rights (2006), *Promotion and Protection of Human Rights: Interim Report of the Special Representative of the Secretary-General on the Issue of Human Rights and Transnational Corporations and other Business Enterprises*, 62nd session, UN Doc. E/CN.4/2006/97, 22 February, New York: United Nations.

Commission on Sustainable Development (2004), *Partnerships for Sustainable Development: Report of the Secretary-General*, New York: United Nations.

Conroy, M. (2002), 'Can advocacy-led certification systems transform global corporate practices?' in R. Broad (ed.), *Global Backlash: Citizen Initiatives for a Just World Economy*, New York: Rowan & Littlefield, pp. 210–15.

Corpwatch (2000), 'Letters to Kofi Annan blasting the global compact corporations', accessed June 2005 at www.corpwatch.org/article.php?id=961#july20.

Cutler, A.C. (2004), 'Problematizing corporate social responsibility under conditions of late capitalism and postmodernity', paper prepared for the Conference on Changing Patterns of Authority in the Global Political Economy, University of Tübingen, Tübingen, Germany, 14-16 October.

Cutler, A.C., V. Haufler and T. Porter (eds), (1999), *Private Authority and International Affairs*, State University of New York (SUNY) Series in Global Politics, Albany, NY: SUNY.

Department for International Development (DFID) (2003), 'Labor standards and poverty reduction', accessed April 2005 at www.dfid.gov.uk/pubs/files/labourstandardsJune04.pdf.

The Economist (2005), 'A survey of corporate social responsibility', (special edition), 22 January, pp. 3–18.

ECOSOC (see United Nations Economic and Social Council).

Elkington, J. (1997), *Cannibals with Forks: The Triple Bottom Line of Twentieth Century Business*, Oxford: Capstone Publishing.

Fig, D., A. Bezuidenhout, R. Hamman and R. Omar (2003), 'Reflections on corporate social and environmental responsibility in South Africa: an overview', paper presented at UNRISD Conference on Corporate Social Responsibility and Development: Towards a New Agenda?, Geneva, 17-18 November.

Freeman, R.E. (1984), *Strategic Management: A Stakeholder Approach*, Boston, MA: Pitman.

Greer, J. and K. Bruno (1996), *Greenwash: The Reality Behind Corporate Environmentalism*, Penang: Third World Network.

Gunningham, N. and D. Sinclair (2002), *Leaders and Laggards: Next Generation Environmental Regulation*, Sheffield: Greenleaf Publishing.

Haas, E. (1990), *When Knowledge is Power: Three Models of Change in International Organizations*, Berkeley, CA: University of California Press.

Hajer, M. (1995), *The Politics of Environmental Discourse: Ecological Modernization and the Policy Process*, Oxford: Clarendon Press.

Hall, P. (1993), 'Policy paradigms, social learning, and the state: the case of economic policymaking in Britain', *Comparative Politics*, (April), 275–96.

Hall, P. and D. Soskice (eds) (2001), *Varieties of Capitalism: The Institutional Foundations of Comparative Advantage*, Oxford: Oxford University Press.

Hanks, J. (2002), 'Promoting corporate environmental responsibility: what role for "self-regulatory" and "co-regulatory" policy instruments in South Africa?' in P. Utting (ed.), *The Greening of Business in Developing Countries: Rhetoric, Reality and Prospects*, London: Zed Books, pp. 187–215.

Haufler, V. (2001), *A Public Role for the Private Sector: Industry Self-regulation in a Global Economy*, Washington, DC: Carnegie Endowment for International Peace.

Haufler, V. (2004), 'MNCs, intervention, and the international community: unexpected expectations?' paper prepared for the Conference on Changing Patterns of Authority in the Global Political Economy, University of Tübingen, Tübingen, Germany, 14-16 October.

Held, D. (2003), 'From executive to cosmopolitan multilateralism', in D. Held and M. Koenig-Archibugi (eds), *Taming Globalization: Frontiers of Governance*, Cambridge: Polity Press.

Henderson, D. (2001), *Misguided Virtue: False Notions of Corporate Social Responsibility*, London: Institute for Economic Affairs.

Holliday, C., S. Schmidheiny and P. Watts (2002), *Walking the Talk: The Business Case for Sustainable Development*, Sheffield: Greenleaf Publishing.

Hopkins, M. (1999), *The Planetary Bargain: Corporate Social Responsibility Comes of Age*, London: Macmillan.

Huber, E. (ed.) (2002), *Models of Capitalism: Lessons for Latin America*, University Park, PA: Pennsylvania State University Press.

International Forum on Globalization (2002), *Alternatives to Economic Globalization: A Better World is Possible*, San Francisco, CA: Berrett-Koehler.

International Labour Office (ILO) Socio-Economic Security Programme (2004), *Economic Security for a Better World*, Geneva: International Labour Organization.

International Organization for Standardization (ISO) (2004), 'The ISO survey of ISO 9001 and ISO 14001 certificates – 2003', accessed June 2005 at www.iso.org/iso/en/iso9000-14000/pdf/survey2003.pdf.

International Organization for Standardization (ISO) (2005), 'The ISO survey of ISO 9001 and ISO 14001 certificates – 2004', accessed September 2005 at www.iso.org/iso/en/prods-services/otherpubs/pdf/survey2004.pdf.

Jenkins, R. (2002), 'Corporate codes of conduct: self-regulation in a global economy', in NGLS/UNRISD (eds), *Voluntary Approaches to Corporate Responsibility: Readings and a Resource Guide*, NGLS Development Dossier, Geneva: United Nations.

Jessop, B. (1999), 'The social embeddedness of the economy and its implications for economic governance', Lancaster University Department of Sociology draft paper, Lancaster, accessed 25 February 2005 at www.comp.lancaster.ac.uk/sociology/soc016rj.html.

Kabeer, N. (2004), 'Globalization, labor standards, and women's rights: dilemmas of collective (in)action in an interdependent world', *Feminist Economics*, **10** (1), 3–35.

Kemp, M. (2001), *Corporate Social Responsibility in Indonesia: Quixotic Dream or Confident Expectation?,* UNRISD Programme on Technology, Business and Society paper no. 6, Geneva.

Keohane, R. and J. Nye Jr. (2002), 'Governance in a globalizing world', in R. Keohane, *Power and Governance in a Partially Globalized World*, London: Routledge, pp. 193–218.

Krut, R. and H. Gleckman (1998), *ISO 14001: A Missed Opportunity for Global Sustainable Industrial Development*, London: Earthscan.

Levy, D. and D. Egan (2003), 'A neo-Gramscian approach to corporate political strategy: conflict and accommodation in the climate change negotiations', *Journal of Management Studies*, **40**, 803–29.

Levy, D. and A. Kolk (2002), 'Strategic responses to global climate change: conflicting pressures on multinationals in the oil industry', *Business and Politics*, **4** (3), 275–300.

Levy, D. and P. Newell (2002), 'Business strategy and international environmental governance: toward a neo-Gramscian synthesis', *Global Environmental Politics*, **2** (4), 84–101.

Lipietz, Alain (1992), *Towards a New Economic Order: Postfordism, Ecology and Democracy*, Cambridge: Polity Press.

Maquila Solidarity Network (2005), 'Codes memo', 18, Dec 2004/Jan 2005, accessed June 2005 at www.maquilasolidarity.org/resources/codes/pdf/codesmemo18.pdf.

McKinsey & Company (2004), 'Assessing the Global Compact's impact', accessed 25 February 2005 at www.unglobalcompact.org.

Murphy, D.F. and J. Bendell (1997), *In the Company of Partners: Business, Environmental Groups and Sustainable Development Post-Rio*, Bristol: Policy Press.

Murphy, D.F. and J. Bendell (1999), *Partners in Time? Business, NGOs and Sustainable Development*, UNRISD discussion paper no. 109, Geneva.

Newell, P. (2002), 'From responsibility to citizenship: corporate accountability for development', *IDS Bulletin*, **33** (2), 91–100.

O'Rourke, D. (2000), 'Monitoring the monitors: a critique of Pricewaterhouse-Coopers (PwC) labor monitoring', accessed 25 February 2005 at http://Web.mit.edu/dorourke/www/index.html.

O'Rourke, D. (2003), 'Outsourcing regulation: analyzing nongovernmental systems of labor standards and monitoring', *Policy Studies Journal*, **31** (1), 1–29.

Overseas Development Institute (ODI) (1999), 'What can we do with a rights-based approach to development?', ODI briefing paper, London, September.

Polanyi, K. (1957), *The Great Transformation: The Political and Economic Origins of our Time*, Beacon Hill, Boston, MA: Beacon Press.

Porter, M.E. and C. Van der Linde (1995), 'Green and competitive: ending the stalemate', *Harvard Business Review*, (September–October), 120–34.

Prahalad, C.K. (2005), *The Fortune at the Bottom of the Pyramid: Eradicating Poverty Through Profits*, Upper Saddle River, NJ: Wharton School Publishing.
Razavi, S., R. Pearson and C. Danloy (2004), *Globalization, Export-Oriented Employment and Social Policy: Gendered Connection*, Geneva: UNRISD, and Houndmills: Palgrave Macmillan.
Richter, J. (2001), *Holding Corporations Accountable: Corporate Conduct, International Codes, and Citizen Action*, London: Zed Books.
Richter, J. (2003), *Building on Quicksand: The Global Compact, Democratic Governance, and Nestlé*, Geneva: CETIM and IBFAN-GIFA, and Zurich: Berne Declaration.
Riesco, M. (2005), 'Pay your taxes! Corporate social responsibility and the mining industry in Chile', in M. Riesco, G. Lagos and M. Lima, *The 'Pay your Taxes' Debate: Perspectives on Corporate Taxation and Social Responsibility in the Chilean Mining Industry*, UNRISD Programme on Technology, Business and Society, paper no. 16, Geneva, pp. 1–34.
Ruggie, J.G. (1998), 'What makes the world hang together? Neo-utilitarianism and the social constructivist challenge', *International Organization*, **52**, 855–85.
Ruggie, J.G. (2001), 'global_governance.net: The Global Compact as learning network', *Global Governance*, **7** (October–December), 371–8.
Ruggie, J.G. (2003), 'Taking embedded liberalism global: the corporate connection', in D. Held and M. Koenig-Archibugi (eds), *Taming Globalization: Frontiers of Governance*, Cambridge: Polity Press.
Sabel, C., D. O'Rourke and A. Fung (2000), *Ratcheting Labor Standards: Regulation for Continuous Improvement in the Global Workplace*, World Bank Social Protection discussion paper no. 0011, Washington, DC.
Shafaeddin, S.M. (2004), *Who is the Master? Who is the Servant? Market or Government? An Alternative Approach: Towards a Coordination System*, Geneva: UNCTAD.
Sood, A. and B. Arora (2006), 'The political economy of corporate responsibility in India', UNRISD Programme on Technology, Business and Society paper no. 18, Geneva.
Stiglitz, J.E. (2004), *The Roaring Nineties: Why We're Paying the Price for the Greediest Decade in History*, London: Penguin Books.
SustainAbility (2003), *The 21st Century NGO: In the Market for Change*, London: SustainAbility.
Taylor, M. (2004), 'Corporate fallout detectors and Fifth Amendment capitalists: corporate complicity in human rights abuse', in UN Global Compact and Office of the High Commissioner for Human Rights (ed.), *Embedding Human Rights into Business Practice*, New York: UN Global Compact Office, pp. 44–8.
Toye, J. (1995), 'The new institutional economics and its implications for development theory', in J. Harris, J. Hunter and C.M. Lewis (eds), *The New Institutional Economics and Third World Development*, London: Routledge, 49–68.
United Nations Conference on Trade and Development (UNCTAD) (1999), *World Investment Report 1999: Foreign Direct Investment and the Challenge of Development*, Geneva: UNCTAD.
United Nations Conference on Trade and Development (UNCTAD) (2003), *FDI Policies for Development: National and International Perspectives*, Geneva: UNCTAD.

United Nations Conference on Trade and Development (UNCTAD) (2005), *World Investment Report 2005: Transnationalization and the Internationalization of R&D*, Geneva: UNCTAD.
United Nations Development Programme Commission on the Private Sector and Development (2004), *Unleashing Entrepreneurship: Making Business Work for the Poor*, report to the Secretary-General of the United Nations, New York: United Nations Development Programme.
United Nations Economic and Social Council (ECOSOC) (2004), *Report to the Economic and Social Council of the Sixtieth Session of the Commission*, UN Doc. E/CN.4/2004/L.11/Add.7, April 22, New York: United Nations.
United Nations Economic and Social Council (ECOSOC) (2005), 'Promotion and protection of human rights. Report of the United Nations High Commissioner for Human Rights on the sectoral consultation entitled "Human rights and the extractive industry"', UN Doc. E/CN.4/2006/92, 19 December, New York: United Nations.
United Nations Millennium Project (2005), *Investing in Development: A Practical Plan to Achieve the Millennium Development Goals*, New York: Earthscan and Millennium Project.
United Nations Research Institute for Social Development (UNRISD) (2004), *Corporate Social Responsibility and Development: Towards a New Agenda?*, conference news report of the UNRISD Conference, 17-18 November 2003, Geneva.
United Nations Research Institute for Social Development (UNRISD) (2005), *Gender Equality: Striving for Justice in an Unequal World*, Geneva: UNRISD.
Utting, P. (2000), *Business Responsibility for Sustainable Development*, UNRISD occasional paper no. 2, Geneva.
Utting, P. (2002a), 'Regulating business through multistakeholder initiatives: a preliminary assessment', in NGLS/UNRISD (eds), *Voluntary Approaches to Corporate Responsibility: Readings and a Resource Guide*, NGLS Development Dossier, Geneva: United Nations.
Utting, P. (ed.) (2002b), *The Greening of Business in Developing Countries: Rhetoric, Reality and Prospects*, London: Zed Books.
Utting, P. (2003), 'Corporate responsibility and labour issues in China: reflections on a Beijing conference', *Journal of Corporate Citizenship*, **10** (Summer), 21–7.
Utting, P. (2005), 'Corporate responsibility and the movement of business', *Development in Practice*, **15** (3–4) (June), 375–88.
Utting, P. and K. Ives (2006), 'The politics of corporate responsibility and the oil industry', *St Antony's International Review*, University of Oxford, Oxford.
van Tudler, R. (2002), 'The power of core companies', *EBF Debate*, **10**, (Summer), accessed in June 2005 at www.ebfonline.com/debate.
Waddock, S. and C. Bodwell (2002), 'From TQM to TRM: total responsibility management approaches', *Journal of Corporate Citizenship*, **7** (Autumn), 113–26.
Ward, H. (2003), *Legal Issues in Corporate Citizenship*, Stockholm: Swedish Partnership for Global Responsibility, and London: IIED.
Welford, R. (2002), 'Disturbing development: conflicts between corporate environmentalism, the international economic order and sustainability', in P. Utting (ed.), *The Greening of Business in Developing Countries: Rhetoric, Reality and Prospects*, London: Zed Books, pp. 135–58.
Whitley, R. (2000), *Divergent Capitalisms: The Social Structuring and Change of Business Systems*, Oxford: Oxford University Press.

World Commission on the Social Dimension of Globalization (2004), *A Fair Globalization: Creating Opportunities for All*, Geneva: International Labour Organization.

Zadek, S. (2001), *The Civil Corporation: The New Economy of Corporate Citizenship*, London: Earthscan.

Zadek, S. (2004), 'The path to corporate responsibility', *Harvard Business Review*, **82** (12) (1 December), 125–32.

Zadek, S. (2005), 'The logic of collaborative governance: corporate responsibility, accountability and the social contract', John F. Kennedy School of Government Corporate Social Responsibility Initiative working paper no. 3, Harvard University Center for Business and Government, Cambridge, MA, August.

Zammit, A. (2003), *Development at Risk: Rethinking UN–Business Partnerships*, Geneva: South Centre/UNRISD.

11. The professionalization of sustainability

Deborah Rigling Gallagher

Businesses are increasingly called on to incorporate considerations of environmental and social sustainability into strategic operations, along with the economic aspects of their operations. They are asked by customers, employees and other stakeholders to move firm practices from a focus on profitability, short-term compliance and eco-efficiency to consider the long-term social and environmental impacts of operations. They respond to demands that products and services have minimal impacts on the environment and promote social equity, and showcase sustainability reports on their websites. Firms have been encouraged to develop eco-enterprise strategies (Stead and Stead, 2000), strategic management tools that enable firms to 'stand for sustainability' by incorporating a 'sustainability-centered values network'. Understandably, the development of such a sustainability-centered network necessarily depends on organizational members coming together to share and apply knowledge of sustainability grounded in their individual professional training and identification. Early research (Wilensky, 1964; Hall, 1968) focused on standard organizational forms and processes, but presaged a professionalization process in which the outcome might be a network form. This chapter considers that process in detail.

This study focuses on the process of creating a shared professional identity based on sustainability, which we term the professionalization of sustainability. It considers how firm members, working together across professional disciplines, join their knowledge and values to create a new professional identity centered on sustainability. It uses a single case-study of a multidisciplinary real estate firm to evaluate how, in the cross-disciplinary setting of brownfield redevelopment, the emergent views and underlying professional values of knowledge workers, such as planners, lawyers, financial analysts and engineers, may combine to affect sustainable redevelopment outcomes. The study considers how multidisciplinary teams of brownfield professionals develop common language, professional norms, values and identities in the context of sustainability. It asks what social institutions and processes exist to foster such development. And how professional conflicts are addressed.

This chapter first provides an overview of the theory and process of professionalization, focusing on past and current research and noting research gaps. Concepts inherent in professionalism are considered to propose a set of research questions. Next, background on the public policy framework applied to contaminated real estate, or brownfields, is provided, and the challenges faced by redevelopers and policy-makers seeking sustainable outcomes at brownfield sites are described. This is followed by an overview of the research methodology which utilized grounded theory to analyze case-study data from a private equity firm, Cherokee Investment Partners, which manages a $1 billion portfolio of brownfield sites across North America and Western Europe. Results from a questionnaire administered to employees and their network of professional associates involved in business execution are then presented. Finally, implications for business and public policy are provided, focusing on the design of systems to foster a common knowledge of sustainability principles in cross-disciplinary business settings, which could, in turn, accelerate the professionalization of sustainability.

PROFESSIONALISM

The concept of professionalism was conceived beginning in the early twentieth century as a normative value system. Those such as Durkheim (1957) and Marshall (1950) described professionalism as a communitarian process by which individual members of an occupation join forces to meet the emerging needs of their community. Under this conception professionals, generally knowledge workers, unite to solve the difficult and vexing problems of the day and are rewarded with their community's admiration and trust as well as higher status (Evetts, 2003). For example, professionals, such as lawyers, engineers and planners, are socialized through rigorous education and subsequent membership in professional associations to develop common workplace value systems and identities, and in turn are rewarded with higher salaries, and in most cases, the public's trust.

Professionalization is typically described as a process of learning and adopting the behavioral standards and normative values of a given occupation (Black, 1970). It has been defined as 'the social process whereby any occupational group may take on one or more elements of an ideal type profession', a profession that is a 'model of occupational structure characterized by certain specified elements' (Vollmer and Mills, 1965). Professionalization has been said generally to occur in a series of four steps: the creation of a specialized knowledge base, the development of skills that are transferable, the development of a career focus and, finally, the development of a shared code of ethics supported by public trust (Wilensky, 1964; Caplow, 1966). Early research also considered that professionalization would be advanced by the existence of standard organizational settings: autonomous professional settings such as law firms, heterogeneous settings such as schools or public agencies and departments of larger firms (Hall, 1968).

In a multidisciplinary work environment focused on sustainability, a straightforward four-step professionalization process is unlikely to occur. Although transferable skills such as legal and engineering analysis are beneficial, the knowledge required to confront the challenge of sustainability is less specialized, and more multidisciplinary. And, while a shared code of ethics supported by the public trust is required, a career focus is not. The end result of a process of professionalization is not likely to be a new bureaucratic form such as a single-focus sustainability law firm, but rather a network of sustainability professionals who are boundary-spanners within an existing organization.

Early work on professionalization described knowledge workers coming together from established professions with standardized training, certification and ethics. But early researchers, who considered that 'the newer professions do not seem as professionalized on the attributes' of hierarchy, division of labor, rules, procedures, impersonality and technical competence (Hall, 1968), did not envision the challenge that the creation of a sustainable world poses. In this new context of sustainability, knowledge workers come together due to a sense of calling to work with like-minded professionals. They form a new code of ethics based on minimizing environmental impacts and promoting intergenerational equity. The professionalization of sustainability is transformative. Professionals who choose to work in sustainable development must adapt existing knowledge and skills and envision a new career path. They work in network structures developing strong and loose ties with others undergoing a similar transformative professional change, adapting work practices to comport with an evolving shared ethic of social and environmental sustainability.

In light of this background on professionalization, several questions are proposed to assist in the discovery of how the process may occur in the context of sustainability-focused work. First, how do established professional identities evolve to take on the characteristics of sustainability? Second, what are the attributes of a shared professional ethic of sustainability? Third, what processes and procedures are employed to develop such a shared professional ethic? Fourth, how are conflicts between primary professional identities addressed? And finally, what do outcomes based on the professionalization of sustainability look like? Each of these questions is examined below following a discussion of the research setting and methodology.

THE BROWNFIELD CHALLENGE

This chapter takes as its research setting the engagement of multiple professionals working to address brownfield remediation and redevelopment. A brownfield is defined as 'real property, the expansion, redevelopment, or reuse of which may be complicated by the presence or potential presence of a hazardous substance, pollutant, or contaminant' [42 U.S.C. § 9601(39)]. The United Kingdom and the rest of the European Union apply a more expansive definition that includes any previously developed property, as well as contaminated sites. It has been estimated that there are as many as 500 000 brownfields in the US (Lee and Seago, 2002), 30 000 in Canada (NRTEE, 2003) and 150 000 within the EU countries (Alberini et al., 2005).

It has been suggested that the brownfield problem grew out of two concurrent issues: the failure of omnibus government clean-up programs such as the US Superfund program (Simons, 1997) and the downsizing of the developed world's manufacturing economy (Alberini et al., 2005) that resulted in tens of thousands of vacant, abandoned or underused industrial sites. The problem was amplified because environmental contamination was and continues to be perceived by investors and developers as an undefined, open-ended risk; pollution adds a level of technical complexity and liability exposure that creates further barriers to investment and entry into brownfield redevelopment efforts.

However, beginning in 1997, there have been significant changes in public policy and growing government action to promote brownfield clean-up and redevelopment. In the United States this includes the Small Business Relief and Brownfield Revitalization Act of 2001, which provides liability relief and funding to encourage reclamation of contaminated, underutilized real estate. Similarly in the United Kingdom, the Environment Agency is 'committed to bringing more land into sustainable use and concentrating development on brownfield sites' (EA, 2005). Moreover, in the face of the significant number of idle and contaminated, yet potentially valuable sites, government programs were created to encourage brownfield reclamation though public–private partnerships. These programs offer developers attractive incentives, such as simplified clean-up requirements and liability protection, limited government oversight and, in some cases, loans and grants from state-supported redevelopment funds. In addition, government authorities may trade valuable entitlements, such as a zoning change from low density to high or from industrial to residential, for a commitment by the developer to remediate. They may also provide tax increment funding and other incentives, provided the developer can demonstrate a commensurate public benefit.

Government brownfield policies were also designed to slow the pace of environmentally unsustainable suburban sprawl and development on greenfields, uncontaminated and undeveloped lands, beyond urban transportation networks (Greenberg et al., 2001). These policies also focus on social sustainability: the revitalization of poor urban neighborhoods and the creation of jobs for their inhabitants.

In the United States, brownfield redevelopment was traditionally undertaken on a project-by-project basis. Of late, however, United States government policies have influenced brownfield redevelopment projects to be less focused on parcel-by-parcel real estate renewal; instead they have become integral components of larger community redevelopment efforts, as has long been the case in Europe (DeSousa, 2004; Wernstedt et al., 2004).

Brownfields and Sustainability

The four main components of brownfield redevelopment where sustainable practices are considered and can be applied include: initiation, evaluation, transaction and implementation (ASTM, 2003). Initiation includes designation of the site as a brownfield, which can be started by a government agency interested in addressing the pollution, or by a potential investor and developer interested in the property as a business opportunity. Evaluation entails an assessment of the viability of the brownfield redevelopment and includes a review of real estate issues, as well as the site environmental conditions. Transaction is the change in ownership and will usually include a resolution of clean-up responsibilities and liability. And finally, implementation includes obtaining entitlements, implementing land-use planning, conducting remediation and beginning development of the built environment.

Essentially, sustainability means that decisions made today should not reduce the options of future generations, but pass on to them a natural, economic and social environment that provides a high quality of life. Brownfield projects are increasingly at the center of community revitalization plans, and their outcomes are being designed to meet present and future citizens' needs by focusing on longer-term financial, social and environmental sustainability.

This focus on sustainability is relatively straightforward: brownfield projects must be financially viable to attract investors and developers and be economically sustainable, contribute to environmental sustainability by remediating past contamination and ensuring they can be safely reused, and designed to increase social sustainability by transforming previously

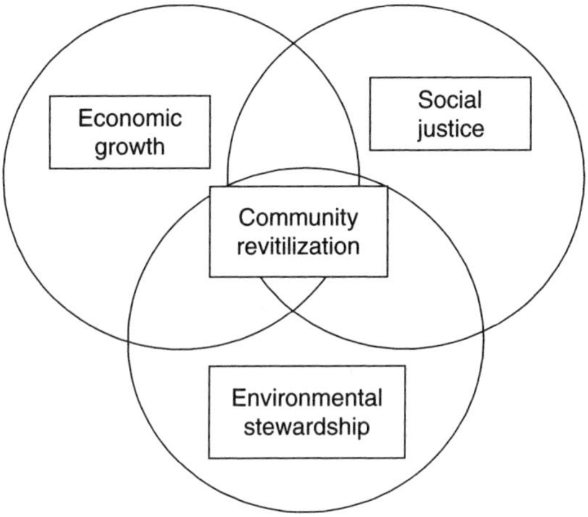

Figure 11.1 Sustainable brownfield redevelopment

blighted real estate to a more productive use, which in turn provides economic opportunities to citizens living in poverty (see Figure 11.1). For example, a brownfield project may cover many acres devoted to open space, include commercial and residential developments which incorporate 'green' architecture, provide links to transportation hubs and promote physical fitness through bike paths and nature trails. For example, buildings constructed on former brownfield sites may obtain certification under LEED, Leadership in Energy and Environmental Design, a voluntary national sustainable building standard sponsored by the US Green Building Council.

Clearly, brownfield redevelopment comprises some inherently sustainable aspects. For example, pollution may be cleaned up and an old industrial site may be brought back into productive use and returned to a city's tax roles. However, simply redeveloping a brownfield site does not ensure sustainable outcomes. Brownfield redevelopment may result in a myriad of negative impacts, including, for example, gentrification, displacement and loss of property through eminent domain, poor reuse choices driven by private gain rather than the public good, aggressive use of risk-based remediation resulting in high levels of residual pollution, traffic congestion and a lack of stakeholder involvement.

As a result, to bring more complete sustainable outcomes, experts associated with brownfield redevelopment must arrive at a common working definition of sustainability and sustainable development, a difficult task given the variety of professional identities that come together on these projects and the ongoing fundamental debate over the definition of sustainability.

The challenge of sustainably redeveloping contaminated, abandoned or underutilized property can certainly be viewed as one of the more vexing problems of the twenty-first century, requiring the essential talents and skills of a cross-section of professionals, such as financial analysts, lawyers, architects and engineers to solve. In this context engineers are called upon to remediate environmental contamination, financial analysts quantify the sites' economic risk and potential for future profit, lawyers and government agents develop voluntary clean-up contracts and partnership agreements, and architects and land planners design development plans which address social concerns, such as gentrification and displacement.

The real estate development process is inherently collaborative; however, brownfield redevelopment, especially when focused on sustainability, requires more attention to long-term financial, environmental and social viability, and must be conjointly and holistically confronted. New ways of interacting and new professional associations are necessarily required. Under this rubric, an engineer designing remediation technologies not only accounts for the clean-up, but also works with planners and government officials to address long-term economic and environmental impacts and community social concerns, such as gentrification and green space preservation. Similarly, land planners and architects work alongside engineers and financial analysts to revitalize brownfield properties by designing sustainable developments which weigh impacts on disadvantaged communities and integrate remediation with ecosystem preservation, public transportation and neighborhood economic opportunity.

To enable such cross-disciplinary work in the name of sustainability, membership organizations, professional language and training programs must be realigned and perhaps even redesigned to refocus professional norms and identities on the tenets of sustainability. Brownfield professional practice is necessarily relocated at the intersection of environmental, social and economic goals.

Policy-makers seeking to foster sustainable development in the 1990s described the need for the engagement of multiple professionals. They noted that its success would require 'long-term disciplinary, multi- and interdisciplinary study' (World Bank, 1995). Current research on the professionalization of sustainability describes that the 'process of institutionalization [of sustainable development] is quite advanced and multidimensional, ranging from the establishment of professional journals to bureaucracies, training programs, and international treaties' (Aguirre, 2002). As early as 1996, the civil engineering profession was seeking to re-educate its members to 'develop sustainable planning processes. This includes public participation, multidisciplinary teams, baseline sustainable development studies, strategic planning, life-cycle consequences, monitoring and evaluation'

(Quinn, 1996). Researchers studying professionalization processes in the context of global problems have suggested that 'the modern state needs professions both to promote occupational integration and social cohesion' (Evetts, 1998). These are arguably both requirements of the tripartite focus on economic, social and environmental aspects required of sustainable brownfields redevelopment projects.

METHODOLOGY

Case-Study Selection

This study employs a single case-study methodology, which offers an opportunity for an in-depth examination of a previously unexamined phenomenon, the professionalization of sustainability in a multidisciplinary setting. This rationale for study design is that of the revelatory case (Yin, 2003), wherein 'an investigator has an opportunity to observe and analyze a phenomenon previously inaccessible to scientific investigation'. Cherokee Investment Partners, an international brownfield redevelopment firm with headquarters in Raleigh, North Carolina and offices in Denver, Toronto, New Jersey and London, was chosen as the single case to examine.

Cherokee is the largest firm in the world specializing in the acquisition, remediation and sustainable redevelopment of brownfields, having acquired over 500 properties since 1990. The firm currently retains over $1 billion of brownfield properties throughout North America and Western Europe. To encourage transactions, Cherokee acquires assets for cash and indemnifies sellers from environmental liability through the use of insurance policies and other risk transfer methods. After acquisition, properties are remediated and repositioned for reuse.

Cherokee is an appropriate setting in which to study the professionalism of sustainability for three reasons. First, it is an international firm, with sites in the United States, Canada and Europe, so inferences about the development of sustainability-focused professional identities will have broad applicability. Second, the firm routinely assembles multidisciplinary teams of environmental and real estate professionals to work on its projects. Finally, in recent years Cherokee has increasingly concentrated its business on sustainable development, drawing upon the expertise of notable sustainability thought leaders to assist in framing its organizational mission and policies. For example, Cherokee has partnered with William McDonough, author of the Hanover Principles (McDonough and Braungart, 1992), to guide planners to sustainable development outcomes. He has been assisting the firm in developing its sustainability vision and outlining systems and procedures to ensure that principles such as recognition of interdependence, respect for consequences of design decisions and continuous improvement through knowledge-sharing are incorporated into projects. The firm has articulated a mission and vision focused on sustainability, which firm leaders believe translates into a brand image that has enabled them to obtain prime mover benefits.

Data Collection

Case-study data were collected from four sources. Primary firm documents, such as an annual sustainability report published by Cherokee, protocols and marketing materials, as well as secondary information such as media reports were analyzed. In addition, a short questionnaire was administered to Cherokee employees and their wider network of professional associates (including service providers) with various roles in redevelopment projects across the United States, Canada and Europe. The questionnaire was first pilot tested. Ninety-two questionnaires were sent to associates via email. Forty-one associates completed the questionnaires, for a response rate of 45 percent. Finally, follow-up interviews were conducted with firm leaders.

Data Analysis

A grounded theory methodology (Strauss and Corbin, 1998) was used to examine emergent constructs and build theory inductively from review of qualitative case-study data. In contrast to other modes of theory development, in which concepts and relationships between them are set out a priori, and data are used to confirm or deny their plausibility, a grounded theory approach is guided first and foremost by data. Questionnaire, primary and secondary data were entered into a qualitative database, using NVivo software. Data were first examined using an open coding approach, in which data were associated with codes such as 'professional norms and ethics', 'learning processes' and 'sustainability outcomes'. Analysis proceeded through the identification of relationships among constructs as data from subsequent documents and questionnaires were examined and no new concepts were apparent.

RESULTS

In this study, five important concepts were identified. First, the respondents indicated multiple professional identities. Second, they combined personal values with professional ethics to develop an integrated identity with regard to sustainability. Third, their perspectives on sustainability were informed and influenced by their professional environment that included common training and opportunities for working together and sharing ideas. Fourth, as the nascent professional ethic of sustainability evolved at the firm, conflicts between professional norms occasionally occurred and management intervention was necessary. And fifth, resulting outcomes reflected a growing common professionalization of sustainability.

Professional Identity

When asked to identify their profession from a list of eight professions most commonly associated with brownfield work – engineer, scientist, geologist, architect/designer, land planner, attorney, real estate development manager, government environmental or planning official – about a third of the respondents indicated multiple professional profiles or identities. For example, an engineer might also identify himself as a scientist, real estate manager or government official or, alternatively, a land planner might identify himself as a real estate development manager.

The professional profiles indicated by the 41 respondents are summarized in Table 11.1. They appear to be influenced by both their work experience and their education. A majority of the respondents held a baccalaureate degree in combination with one or more professional graduate degrees in technical disciplines, law or business.

Table 11.1 Professional profiles and number of respondents

Profile	No. of respondents	Profile	No. of respondents
Environmental engineer	5	Architect/designer	–
Environmental scientist (includes geologists)	6	Land Planner/architect/ designer	1
Environmental engineer/ scientist	3	Attorney	7
Real estate manager	8	Government official	1
Real estate manager/ engineer/scientist	2	Government official/engineer	1
Real estate manager/ land planner	2	Financial manager/other	4
Real estate manager/ land planner/architect/ designer	1	Total respondents	41

Thus, this case-study evidence suggests that in the brownfield setting professionals may not be limited to standard professional identification patterns. This result is amplified when respondents described the professionals they most often worked with on brownfield redevelopment projects. Every respondent indicated that he or she worked closely with members of other professions and close to half (45 percent) indicated that they routinely worked with all eight types of brownfield professionals identified in the questionnaire.

Of the 41 respondents, 24 focused their work solely on Cherokee's US brownfield acquisitions and real estate assets, and 17 worked on brownfield projects throughout the organization, including sites located in Canada, the United Kingdom and in other European Union member countries.

Professional Ethic of Sustainability

One of the aims of this study was to examine how professional norms and ethics affect the development of a singular professional ethic of sustainability. How, for example, would the ethical cannon held by a professional engineer to 'hold paramount the safety, health and welfare of the public' (NSPE, 2003) influence the ethic applied in the context of sustainable redevelopment of brownfields.

The data from Cherokee employees and associates indicate that in this setting their professional norms and ethics, such as transparency, responsiveness, trust and honesty, become integrated with personal values about social justice and environmental stewardship. The result is the creation of a professional sustainability ethic centered on community. The idea of a community in harmony with its environment and the professional's responsibility in both creating and maintaining its long-term viability is at the center of this nascent sustainability-based professional identity. Respondents described this sustainability ethic:

> Our work has its roots in Civil Engineering and thus shares its altruism. Much of our work, for example, is designed to ultimately benefit communities and the environment.

> We . . . produce results that we can be proud of when the communities are alive and thriving in the years to come.

An engineer and a real estate development manager provided these statements, respectively. Respondents expressing similar views indicated that Cherokee, with its articulated sustainability vision and where casual discussions about sustainability principles are encouraged, fosters the sustainability professionalization process.

It should be noted, however, that while some professionals are actively engaged in a process of combining personal values and professional ethics to develop a sustainability-focused professional ethic, others have been left behind. Some respondents indicated that maintaining their primary professional identities as lawyers, engineers and financial managers was paramount and more valuable to the brownfield redevelopment endeavor than a reconfigured ethic centered on a somewhat nebulous and evolving concept such as sustainability. Some worried about 'greenwashing' and whether their professional 'norms and ethical requirements could be in direct conflict with the financial objectives' of brownfield projects, such as short-term profitability.

Working Together, Sharing Ideas and Common Training

Research has shown that multiparty collaboration can lead to consensus, learning and problem-solving (Turcotte and Pasquero, 2001), even as difficult problems are confronted. Sustainable brownfield redevelopment is such a problem. The Cherokee case-study presents evidence that in working together, sharing ideas and engaging in common, formal training, individual personal values and primary professional norms and ethics can be combined to foster a sustainability-focused professional ethic.

Formal training was seen to play a small, albeit important role in the professionalization of sustainability in Cherokee's cross-disciplinary brownfield redevelopment setting. At many of the firm's locations groups participate in in-house seminars on sustainability issues provided by experts in the field. In addition, employees and associates are encouraged to attend training seminars. In particular, the firm's association with the Urban Land Institute (ULI) has proven influential. ULI, a US-based non-profit membership-supported research and education association, is a leading proponent of new urbanism and sustainable planning. This organization plays a vital institutional role in the socialization of sustainability professionals at Cherokee. Firm employees and associates of many professional stripes have become members of the organization, attending seminars and forums on sustainable development and, more recently, participating in ULI leadership positions.

Working together and sharing ideas play a larger role than formal training in cultivating a professional thesis of sustainability at Cherokee. These activities provide opportunities for professionals to apply their primary professional norms and share personal values about sustainability in designing and implementing brownfield redevelopment solutions. Associates describe their experiences in the following fashion:

> In working with other types of professionals, the scope of considering all matters, which might necessarily affect a development, increases the chances of sustainability. Each profession will have its opinion and advice on everything from ethical conduct, human rights, profitable growth and environmental issues. It is only by sharing the thought processes with others that hopefully the optimum outcome can be developed.

> In liaising with other professionals sharing views and information generally results in the optimization of the overall environmental sustainability of a proposal.

> The diverse professional experience, backgrounds and perspectives within our organization increase the opportunity for sustainable concepts to be shared and implemented.

While attendance at in-house seminars and brownfield-oriented conferences sponsored by normative institutions such as ULI, bar associations or engineering professional societies were important in fostering associates' professional ethics of sustainability, it was the firm's routine multidisciplinary team-oriented work that was most cited as influential in this regard. Brainstorming sessions, or 'happenstance' conversations between team members 'in the context of specific projects' were said to be invaluable tools for melding personal values with professional norms to professionalize sustainability thinking. The projects themselves provided critical settings for the dilemma of concurrently addressing multiple goals of economic efficiency, environmental restoration and community redevelopment to be confronted:

> . . . ongoing project management meetings provide the opportunity for interactions between the various professional disciplines involved to help adapt and implement sustainable development principles into the project.

Often these confrontations were catalyzed by meetings with associates more peripheral to the firm, for example Cherokee's outside environmental service providers, regulators or local redevelopment agencies. One respondent described the situations in which professional norms of sustainability were brought to bear:

> We share our ideas about sustainability with the client and authorities and try to convince them that sustainable solutions might be of advantage.

The practice of engaging external stakeholders has been shown to advance the practice of sustainability (Gallagher, 2005). The professional practice of sustainability at Cherokee attempts to incorporate such an approach, driven by planning professional norms. A general practice of planning is to engage in community-wide charrettes. These multi-day planning meetings bring designers, planners and community stakeholders together to arrive at a common vision of development outcomes. At most Cherokee sites charrettes are an integral component of the brownfield redevelopment process. The charrette experience serves as a mechanism not only to incorporate stakeholder concerns, but also to introduce and highlight a key planning professional norm to other professionals. Engineers, for example, accustomed to singularly relying on their own expertise, are asked in charrettes to seek the advice and counsel not only of others within the firm, but also of external stakeholders. In follow-up interviews Cherokee leaders expressed the view that while exposure to external stakeholder perspectives on sustainability engenders frustration on the part of some professionals, overall it enhances the development of a sustainability-focused professional ethic within the firm.

Resolving Conflicts

Gray (2004) describes a process by which parties with different frames of reference may be able to recognize those differences and go on to address intractable problems. The process involves recognizing the existence of disparate frames and then arriving at a consensus. Within the consensus power is conferred to a largely democratic group decision which may or may not reinforce each individual's original position (Gray, 1989). In the sustainable brownfields redevelopment setting the consensus-building process invoked during the development of sustainability-focused professional norms is a work in progress.

For example, some associates at Cherokee see a disparity between professional groups in terms of willingness to advance sustainability concepts. One associate explained: 'while many engineers and planners and clients have embraced sustainability and are making genuine efforts to incorporate the principles in their thinking and planning, others see sustainability as a necessary evil'. Another asserted that 'architects and planners would have the most focus on sustainability; with bankers and lawyers this is not so often a topic (but might be)'. When these disparities are unable to be reconciled, unsustainable outcomes result. A case in point is an early Cherokee site in California. The professional perspectives of financial analysts promoting economic sustainability outweighed the input of other professionals emphasizing environmental and social concerns, and a sprawling retail development anchored by a general merchandiser superstore was the outcome.

Follow-up interviews with company leaders suggested that a number of mechanisms for resolving such conflicts have been instituted. First and foremost, the company's CEO has consistently made it clear that redevelopment outcomes are to focus jointly on economic, social and environmental sustainability. Additionally, the firm has taken steps to enforce sustainable practices through management of its supply chain. An ISO 14001 certified environmental management system emphasizes sustainability throughout Cherokee operations. Contract associates are required to adopt sustainable practices. Each of these practices underscores the importance of developing a shared professional norm based on sustainability.

Sustainable Outcomes

How, then, has the development of a professional ethic of sustainability affected specific brownfield outcomes? Respondents provided examples of how professionals incorporated sustainability principles into brownfield redevelopment projects across the US, Canada and Europe. These descriptions are verified by press reports and firm documents. For example, green space is preserved and public education and outreach tools are used. Smart growth principles are applied and public transit-oriented development designs implemented. Finally, technologies such as energy-saving construction and building materials and reuse of natural resources are implemented. One project in particular, a large brownfield redevelopment project in Charleston, South Carolina, is notable for both its cross-disciplinary project team and the sustainability outcomes that result. A participant in the project describes it as:

> . . . integrated into the transportation and neighborhood fabric of the city; [it incorporates] density levels that support sound use of infrastructure (physical and social); [includes] marsh restoration; community support [and] revitalization.

While some employees and staff labor on the periphery of sustainability, describing a desire for 'the experts to explain to me the sustainability issues and alternatives on a project', most find the cross-disciplinary interaction beneficial to the design and implementation of sustainable brownfield redevelopment outcomes. These outcomes result when opportunities for formal and ad hoc discussions are provided, thus fostering a professionalization of sustainability, which for some has become 'second nature'.

IMPLICATIONS FOR BUSINESS AND POLICY

In this study, by examining a single setting in which a variety of professionals work together to address a vexing social problem, we have made the case that the professionalization of sustainability can, and moreover should, be advanced. We have shown that older conceptions of professionalization based on processes requiring standardized training and career paths, and resulting in non-network organizational forms, do not necessarily apply in the new context of sustainability. In this study we showed how individuals from multiple professions, embodying a range of norms and ethics, came together in the brownfield setting to solve a challenging social problem: the concurrent restoration of contaminated land and damaged ecosystems, and creation of long-term economic and social opportunity for host communities and investors. This challenge is by its nature an exercise in sustainability: old properties are cleaned and reused, communities are revitalized and green space is preserved, providing long-term economic, social and environmental benefits. Thus it is not surprising that the diverse professionals called upon to address the brownfield challenge find themselves integrating personal values and professional ethics into a new professional identity, that of the sustainability professional.

What can be learned from this particular setting that may be used by other businesses aspiring to focus on sustainability outcomes? First, it is important for an organization to articulate a sustainability vision. That vision should inform an operating framework, which describes how the organization will address the social and environmental impacts of its products and services. Employees and associates rely on such a framework to set goals and objectives and to resolve the inevitable conflicts that arise.

Second, it is critical to provide opportunities for both primary professional development and cross-disciplinary interaction. Professionals should be encouraged to explore sustainability from their disciplinary bases. In addition, diverse employees should be provided with opportunities to learn about and discuss sustainability principles both informally and formally with the imprimatur of institutions which exist to advance sustainability. These opportunities will lead to stronger network formations and advance the development of a firm's eco-enterprise strategy. Moreover, firms should confront the possibility of producing sustainable outcomes with external stakeholders such as neighbors, customers, suppliers and regulators. These interactions enhance sustainability thinking and often lead to improved outcomes.

Finally, and perhaps most importantly, employees should be encouraged to explore and nurture their own personal values related to sustainability and to apply them in their professional practice. In the past professionalization was considered to be supported by attitudinal attributes such as a belief in public service and in self-regulation, and a sense of calling to a particular field (Hall, 1968). This study confronts that view by examining a new work environment. It uses the setting of sustainability-based work, to show

how professionals come together not because of the call of a single field, but out of a larger sense of calling to address a set of daunting environmental and social problems. Finally, this study demonstrates that when sustainability thinking in a professional setting becomes 'second nature', based on shared values and ethics, the professionalization of sustainability is assured.

REFERENCES

Aguirre, Benigno, E. (2002), 'Sustainable development as collective surge', *Social Science Quarterly*, **83** (1), 101–18.

Alberini, Anna, Alberto Longo, Stefania Tonon, Francesco Trombetta and Margharita Turvani (2005), 'The role of liability, regulation and economic incentives in brownfield remediation and redevelopment: evidence from surveys of developers', *Regional Science and Urban Economics*, **35** (4), 327–51.

American Society for Testing and Materials (ASTM) (2003), *E1984-03 Standard Guide for Process of Sustainable Brownfields Redevelopment*, West Conshohocken, PA: ASTM International.

Black, Gordon (1970), 'A theory of professionalism in politics', *American Political Science Review*, **64** (3), 865–8.

Caplow, Theodore (1966), 'Sequential steps in professionalization', in H.L. Vollmer and D.L. Mills (eds), *Professionalism*, Englewood Cliffs, NJ: Prentice-Hall.

DeSouza, Christopher A. (2004), 'The greening of brownfields in American cities', *Journal of Environmental Planning and Management*, **47** (4), 579–600.

Durkheim, Emile (1957), *Professional Ethics and Civic Morals*, London and New York: Routledge.

Environment Agency (EA) (2005) *Brownfield Land Redevelopment: Position Statement*, London: EA.

Evetts, Julia (1998), 'Professionalism beyond the nation-state: international systems of professional regulation in Europe', *International Journal of Sociology and Social Policy*, **18** (12), 47–64.

Evetts, Julia (2003), 'The sociological analysis of professionalism: occupational change in the modern world', *International Sociology*, **18** (2), 395–415.

Gallagher, Deborah R. (2005), 'Building environmental management systems focused on sustainability: the influence of employees, company leaders and external stakeholders', in Mark Starik, Sanjay Sharma, Carolyn Egri and Rick Bunch (eds), *New Horizons in Research in Sustainable Organizations: Emerging Ideas, Approaches and Tools for Practitioners and Researchers*, Sheffield: Greenleaf Publishing.

Gray, Barbara (1989), *Collaborating: Finding Common Ground for Multi-Party Problems*, San Francisco, CA: Jossey-Bass.

Gray, Barbara (2004), 'Strong opposition: frame-based resistance to collaboration', *Journal of Community and Applied Social Psychology*, **14** (3), 166–76.

Greenburg, Michael, Karen Lowrie, Henry Mayer, K. Tyler Miller and Laura Solitare (2001), 'Brownfield redevelopment as a smart growth option in the United States', *Environmentalist*, **21**, 129–43.

Hall, Richard H. (1968), 'Professionalization and bureaucratization', *American Sociological Review*, **33** (1), 92–104.

Lee, John E. and W. Eugene Seago (2002), 'Policy entrepreneurship, public choice and symbolic reform analysis of section 198, the brownfields tax incentive, carrot or stick or just nevermind', *William and Mary Environmental Law and Policy Review*, **26**, 613–83.

Marshall, T.H. (1950), *Citizenship, Social Class and Other Essays*, Cambridge: Cambridge University Press.

McDonough, William and Michael Braungart (1992), *The Hannover Principles: Design for Sustainability*, Charlottesville, VA: William McDonough & Partners.

National Roundtable on the Environment and the Economy (NRTEE) (2003), *Cleaning up the Past, Building the Future: A National Brownfield Redevelopment Strategy for Canada*, Ottawa: Renouf.

National Society of Professional Engineers (NSPE) (2003), *Code of Ethics for Engineers*, Alexandria, VA: NSPE.

Quinn, Larry (1996), 'Sustainability: another new paradigm', *Civil Engineering*, **66** (10), 6.

Simons, R.A. (1998), *Turning Brownfields into Greenbacks*, Washington, DC: Urban Land Institute.

Stead, Jean Garner and Edward Stead (2000), 'Eco-enterprise strategy: standing for sustainability', *Journal of Business Ethics*, **24**, 313–29.

Strauss, Anselm and Juliet Corbin (1998), *Basics of Qualitative Research: The Techniques and Procedures for Developing Grounded Theory*, 2nd edn, Thousand Oaks, CA: Sage.

Turcotte, Marie-France and Jean Pasquero (2001), 'The paradox of multistakeholder collaborative roundtables', *Journal of Applied Behavioral Sciences*, **37** (3), 447–76.

Vollmer, H.M. and D.L. Mills (1965), 'Some comments on "The professionalization of everyone" ', *American Journal of Sociology*, **70** (4), 480–81.

Wernstedt, Kris, Lauren Heberle, Anna Alberini and Peter Meyer (2004), 'The brownfields phenomenon: much ado about something or the timing of the shrewd?', Resources for the Future discussion paper 04-46, Washington, DC.

Wilensky, Harold L. (1964) 'The professionalization of everyone', *American Journal of Sociology*, **52** (2), 137–58.

World Bank (1995), *Mainstreaming the Environment: The World Bank Group and the Environment since the Rio Earth Summit*, Washington, DC: World Bank.

Yin, Robert K. (2003), *Case Study Research: Design and Methods*, 3rd edn, Thousand Oaks, CA: Sage.

Index